Crystal Reports® 9 on Oracle®

D1407585

Annette Harper

McGraw-Hill/Osborne

New York   Chicago   San Francisco
Lisbon   London   Madrid   Mexico City   Milan
New Delhi   San Juan   Seoul   Singapore   Sydney   Toronto

The McGraw·Hill Companies

McGraw-Hill/Osborne
2100 Powell Street, 10th Floor
Emeryville, California 94608
U.S.A.

To arrange bulk purchase discounts for sales promotions, premiums, or fund-raisers, please contact
McGraw-Hill/Osborne at the above address. For information on translations or book distributors
outside the U.S.A., please see the International Contact Information page immediately following the
index of this book.

Crystal Reports® 9 on Oracle®

1234567890 CUS CUS 019876543

ISBN 0-07-223079-7

Publisher	Brandon A. Nordin
Vice President & Associate Publisher	Scott Rogers
Editorial Director	Wendy Rinaldi
Project Editors	Betsy Manini, Patty Mon, Jenn Tust
Acquisitions Coordinator	Athena Honore
Technical Editor	Deborah Bechtold
Copy Editor	Sally Engelfried
Proofreader	Stefany Otis
Indexer	Valerie Perry
Production Supervisor	James Kussow
Composition	Tabitha M. Cagan
Illustrators	Kathleen Edwards, Melinda Lytle, Michael Mueller, Lyssa Wald
Series Designer	Peter F. Hancik, Roberta Steele
Cover Series Designer	Pattie Lee

This book was composed with Corel VENTURA™ Publisher.

This book is dedicated to my husband, Chris.

Without his encouragement and support,
it would not exist.

He is the strength behind my commitment,
the sounding board for my ideas,
and the heart in my soul.

About the Author

Annette Harper has worked with Crystal Reports for more than eight years and with Oracle for five years. She was previously the Division Manager of Decision Support for the Investment Department of the Nationwide Insurance Company, where she led the reporting and data warehousing teams. Annette now runs her own consulting firm, Sage Link, LLC, (www.sage-link.com) doing report and database consulting. She holds the Oracle Certified Professional DBA designation (OCP) for both Oracle 8*i* and Oracle 9*i*. She is also a Crystal Reports Authorized Crystal Engineer (ACE), and a Master CNE.

Annette's e-mail address is annette@sage-link.com, and she encourages readers to contact her with any comments or questions about the book.

Contents

Acknowledgments

I would like to thank Wendy Rinaldi at Osborne/McGraw-Hill for seeing a worthwhile book in an unsolicited book proposal; Athena Honore for keeping track of everything throughout the project; Deborah Bechtold for her technical insights; and Betsy Manini and Sally Engelfried for improving the quality of my writing.

Thanks to my daughter, Katie, for putting up with no Mom for the summer, and to my mother and sisters for "not calling till after 6 PM."

Introduction

Crystal Reports 9 is a wonderful, full-featured, report-writing tool. If you are using Crystal Reports with Oracle databases, the topics in this book will make you a better report developer. All major RDBMS have many similarities, but an in-depth understanding of your particular database, in this case Oracle, will allow you to take advantage of its unique features. You will create reports that are more efficient and will do so quickly and easily; you will develop reports that run faster, use fewer server and network resources, and are easier to maintain. You will also reduce development time and be able to solve complicated reporting problems using Oracle features.

This book assumes that you have a moderate level of expertise with Crystal Reports 9. It does not cover generic report-writing topics. You should investigate one of the other available Crystal Reports books if you need to learn Crystal Reports.

There is often perceived to be a wide gulf between "report writers" and "database developers." This distinction is artificial. As a report developer, you are writing queries against the database just as any database developer would. You might even be creating views and stored procedures. A couple of significant differences are that you are probably not modifying data, and you are probably returning more information per query than the typical application query would require. Hence, this book does not cover database modification, but it does cover query optimization. To write truly efficient, powerful reports, you need to have a solid understanding of the database and how it processes your queries. This book will supply you with the Oracle information that you need as a report writer.

In addition to coverage of basic Oracle topics, such as structures, datatypes, and the SQL SELECT statement, you will find chapters dealing with creating stored procedures for use with Crystal Reports, picking the best connection methods, optimization from both within Crystal Reports and on the backend. Many sample queries and reports are given, including subreports that you can add to your own reports that display the database statistics and execution plan for the main report. A database dictionary report is developed that you can use in your own environment to document your database structures, and the Crystal repository is ported to Oracle and given Oracle security features.

In some situations, two plus two is much greater than four. When you add Oracle-specific skills to your Crystal Reports skills, you will advance to the next level of report development.

About the Source Code

All report files, SQL scripts, and other files referenced in this book are available for download from www.osborne.com. From the Osborne home page, click the Free Code link and you will be taken to the downloads page. Scroll down until you see Crystal Reports 9 on Oracle. Under the book title, there are links to three zip files.

The first link contains all required files. You should download and unzip them for use as you read the book. The files are organized by chapter number and some chapters have subfolders for lower levels of organization. Three types of files exist in the download; Crystal Reports 9 report files (rpt), Oracle SQL scripts (sql), and plain text files (txt).

The last two links contain an Oracle export or dump of the XTREME schema used in the book, one for Oracle 9.2, and one for Oracle 8.1.7. The use of these files is optional and is an alternative method for populating the XTREME schema given in Chapter 1. Download the file for your version of Oracle only if you wish to import the XTREME schema directly. See Chapter 1 for instructions.

Connectivity, Authentication, and Privileges

T his chapter covers the installation and configuration of the components required to use Crystal Reports with Oracle. The Crystal Reports Access sample database and reports are modified for use with Oracle. Different connectivity options are compared, and Oracle user IDs, authentication methods, and basic database privileges are explained. After reading this chapter, you will be able to connect to Oracle from Crystal Reports using one of seven possible methods, and you will understand the tradeoffs of those connection methods.

All connectivity discussions that follow assume Crystal Reports version 9, Oracle 9*i* (with differences for Oracle 8*i* noted), and a Windows client workstation. A direct client/server type of connection is also assumed. Connection through a middle tier or application server is not covered.

Making the Connection

Getting Crystal Reports to interface with Oracle requires two levels of drivers. At the lower level, for all connectivity options except Wire Protocol, the Oracle client (Oracle networking components) must be installed and functional. At the higher level, you can use the Crystal native Oracle OCI connection components, ODBC or OLE DB.

Database Administrator Tasks

For some of the materialized views used in the book, the database parameter Query Rewrite Enabled must be set to True:

```
ALTER SYSTEM SET QUERY_REWRITE_ENABLED=TRUE;
```

Your DBA will need to create a database role and grant it privileges as shown:

```
CREATE ROLE XTREME_REPORTER;

GRANT ALTER SYSTEM, CREATE MATERIALIZED VIEW
     TO XTREME_REPORTER;
GRANT EXECUTE ON DBMS_FLASHBACK TO XTREME_REPORTER;
GRANT SELECT ON V_$SESSION TO XTREME_REPORTER;
GRANT SELECT ON V_$SESSTAT TO XTREME_REPORTER;
GRANT SELECT ON V_$SQL TO XTREME_REPORTER;
GRANT SELECT ON V_$SQLAREA TO XTREME_REPORTER;
GRANT SELECT ON V_$SQL_CURSOR TO XTREME_REPORTER;
GRANT SELECT ON V_$SQL_PLAN TO XTREME_REPORTER;
GRANT SELECT ON V_$SQL_PLAN_STATISTICS TO XTREME_REPORTER;
GRANT SELECT ON V_$SQL_WORKAREA TO XTREME_REPORTER;
GRANT SELECT ON V_$STATNAME TO XTREME_REPORTER;
GRANT SELECT ON V_$SQLTEXT TO XTREME_REPORTER;
```

The DBA also needs to create a user named XTREME. The XTREME user must have the CONNECT and RESOURCE roles in addition to the XTREME_REPORTER role. The password for the XTREME user is assumed to be "xtreme" throughout the book, but it can be anything you desire. The XTREME schema will be used as the Oracle incarnation of the Crystal Reports Xtreme Access database:

```
CREATE USER XTREME IDENTIFIED BY XTREME;
GRANT CONNECT, RESOURCE, XTREME_REPORTER TO XTREME;
GRANT QUERY REWRITE TO XTREME;
```

Text files containing these commands are available in the download files for the book at Chapter 1\XTREME DBA Script.sql and XTREME DBA Script 8i.sql.

Installation of Oracle Components

The following instructions will install the Oracle client, the Oracle ODBC driver, and the Oracle OLE DB provider.

Oracle Client

The Oracle client software or networking components are usually installed either by the DBA or systems administrator or as part of an Oracle-based application. An installation will be described here, but other installation methods are possible. In addition to the networking components, the following discussion will explain the installation of the Oracle OLE DB provider and the Oracle ODBC driver. Neither of these drivers is recommended for use with Crystal. Their installation is included if you wish to compare them to other drivers.

The Oracle tool SQL*Plus is used in some sections of the book and will be installed along with the networking components. SQL*Plus or some other tool that enables the user to execute SQL and PL/SQL is required for testing of queries and creating backend objects to optimize report writing. No serious Oracle report writer should consider development without access to such a tool.

For installation and verification of the Oracle client, you will create an Oracle service name, also called the TNS name. You will need to know the host name and port number of the Oracle database that you will connect to, along with the user ID and password you should use for the Xtreme user in order to create the TNSnames.ORA file.

The installation described in this chapter uses the Oracle 9*i* Database, release 2 for Microsoft Windows NT/2000/XP, set of three CDs. Alternatively, the client files can be downloaded from technet.oracle.com or may be supplied on a separate client-only CD.

Insert CD 1 of 3 and run setup.exe if it does not launch automatically. From the Welcome screen, select Next and you will see Figure 1-1. Choose Next.

You will then see the product options shown in Figure 1-2. The options may differ if you are not using the Database CD. Choose the Client option and click Next. Choose Runtime and click Next.

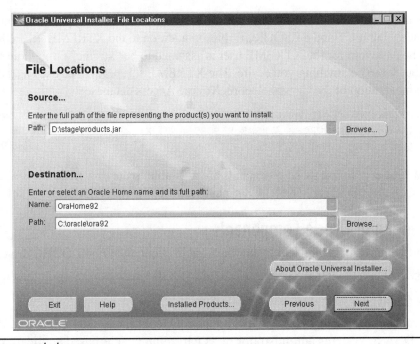

Figure 1-1   *File locations*

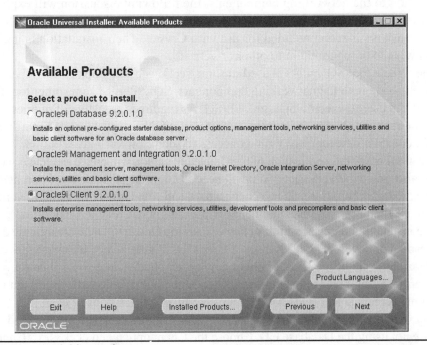

Figure 1-2   *Available products*

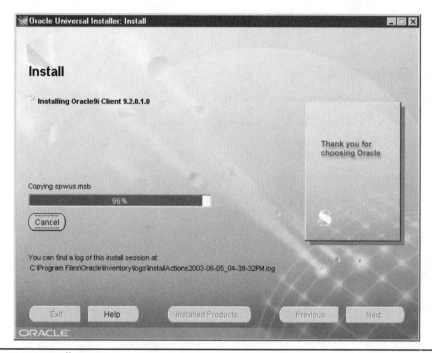

Figure 1-3   *Install screen*

You will see a Summary screen listing the components that will be installed. Click Install, and the screen in Figure 1-3 will appear.

During this stage, you may be asked to insert another disk. When the install completes, the Net Configuration Assistant will start, as shown in Figure 1-4.

On the Oracle Net Configuration Welcome screen, choose No and then Next to create the Oracle service name. See Figure 1-5. If your environment uses a directory service, consult your DBA for setup instructions.

On the Database Version screen, choose 8*i* or Later Database or Service and click Next. Enter the service name of the Oracle database that you want to use for the sample database for the book. This should be the global database name including the Oracle domain, such as Ora92.StageLink. Click Next. Choose TCP as the network protocol and click Next. Enter the host name of the database server, verify the port number (the default of 1521 is provided), and click Next.

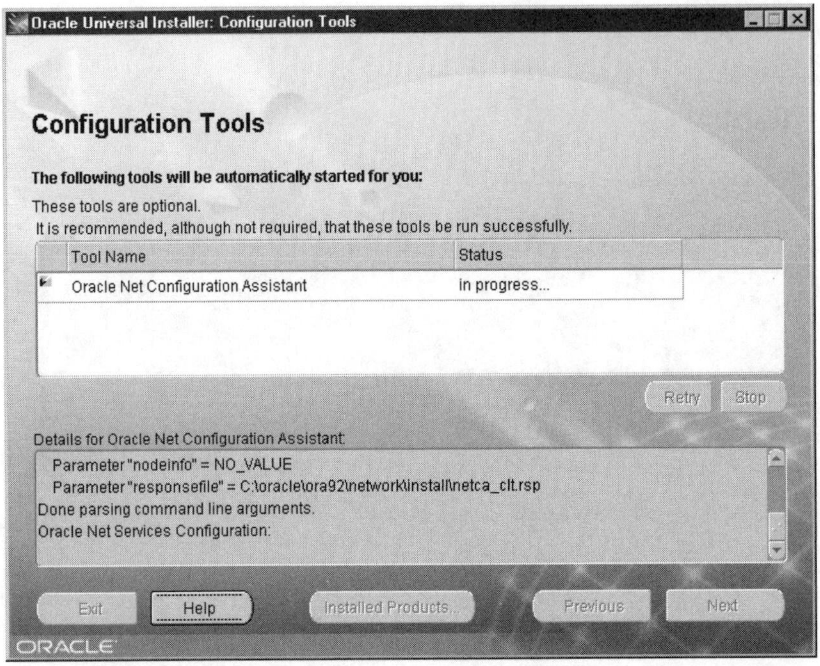

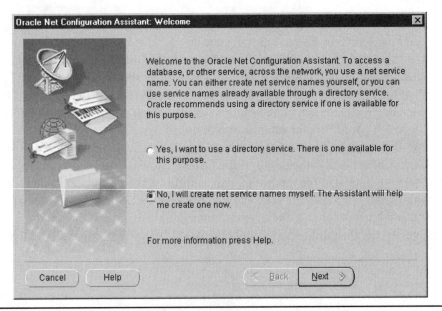

Figure 1-4 *Configuration Tools screen*

Figure 1-5 *Net Configuration Welcome screen*

On the Test screen, select Yes to perform a test. If the test does not succeed and you see a screen like Figure 1-6, choose Change Login, and enter Xtreme for the username and password.

Select OK, and you should see the successful login screen as shown in Figure 1-7. If the test is still unsuccessful, click Back to verify the selections you have made in each of the screens.

Choose Next and set the Net Service Name to ORA. ORA is used throughout the book and in the supplied Crystal Reports. Creating your TNS Name as ORA will allow you to use the supplied reports without needing to change the data source location.

Choose Yes to configure a second Net Service Name. This second name is used in some reports in the book. Complete the dialogs exactly as you did for ORA, but set the Net Service Name to ORA2. Then choose No when you're asked if you need to configure another Net Service Name. Continue choosing Next until you reach the screen with the Finished button. Click Finished. Back in the Universal Installer, choose Next. When you see the screen in Figure 1-8, choose Exit.

You have completed the Oracle client installation. You should now verify that you can log in to ORA as the user Xtreme from SQL*Plus.

Installation of the client for Oracle 8*i* is very similar, although some screens may differ slightly.

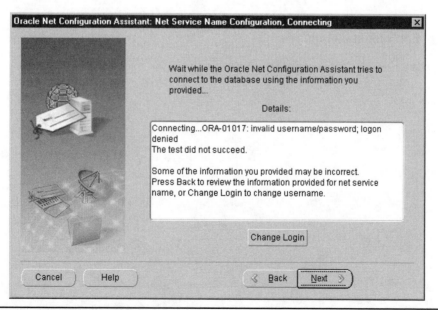

Figure 1-6   *Connecting failed*

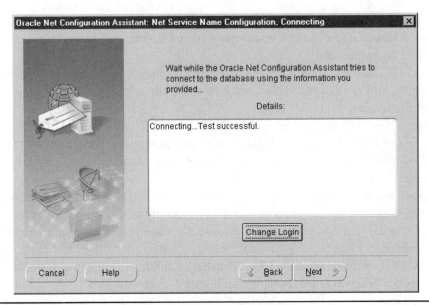

Figure 1-7 Connecting successful

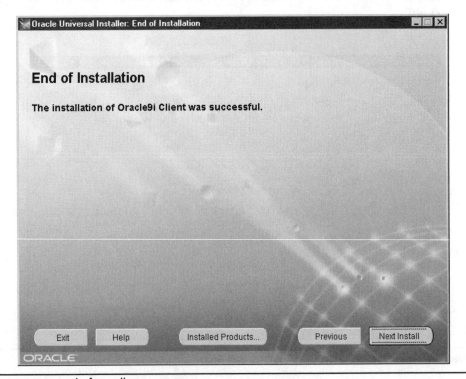

Figure 1-8 End of Installation screen

Oracle ODBC

To install the Oracle ODBC driver, download the most recent version of the Oracle ODBC drivers for your database version from technet.oracle.com. The book uses ora9204.exe for Oracle 9*i* and ora8178b.exe for Oracle 8*i*. Unzip the file to a temporary folder. Go to Start | Programs | Oracle Installation Products | Universal Installer. From the Welcome screen, choose Next. Browse to the location where you unzipped the files. Continue browsing down the path to \stage\Disk1\stage\products.jar, as shown in Figure 1-9. Choose Next.

The summary screen will be displayed. Choose Install. The Install screen will appear and when the install is finished, you will see the End of Installation window. Choose Exit.

Installation steps for the 8*i* ODBC driver are identical.

Oracle OLE DB

To install the Oracle OLE DB drivers, download the most recent version of the Oracle OLE DB Provider for your database version from technet.oracle.com. OraOLEDB_81730.zip and OraOLEDB_92020.exe are used in this book.

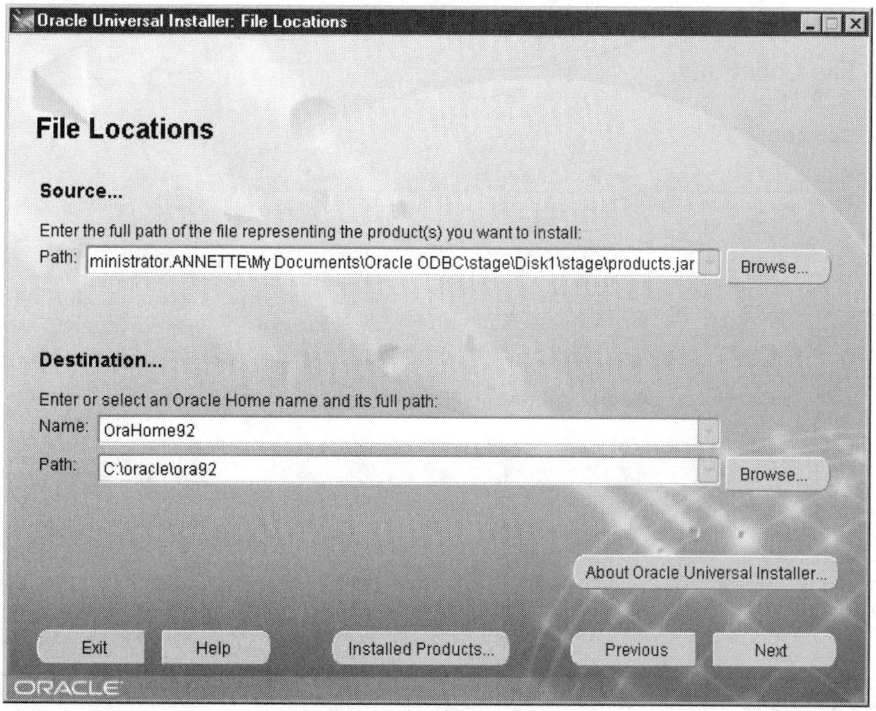

Figure 1-9   *File locations for ODBC installation*

Uninstalling older versions of the OLE DB provided is recommended before installation of the new versions.

For Oracle 9*i,* unzip the download file. It will unzip into the same directory where the zip file resides. Under that directory, run \Disk1\Install\Win32\setup.exe. The Universal Installer will run with the correct path already listed in the box, as shown in Figure 1-10. Choose Next. On the Summary screen, choose Install. The progress bar will be displayed, and finally, the End of Installation screen will appear. Choose Exit, and the installation will be complete.

For Oracle 8*i,* unzip the download file into a temporary directory. From the temporary directory, run \install\win32\setup.exe. The rest of the installation is similar to the 9*i* installation just discussed.

Installation of the Crystal XTREME Sample Data

Crystal Decisions distributes an Access database and sample reports with the Crystal Reports application. The database contains data for a fictional company called Xtreme Mountain Bikes, Inc., which will be used as the data source for the sample reports.

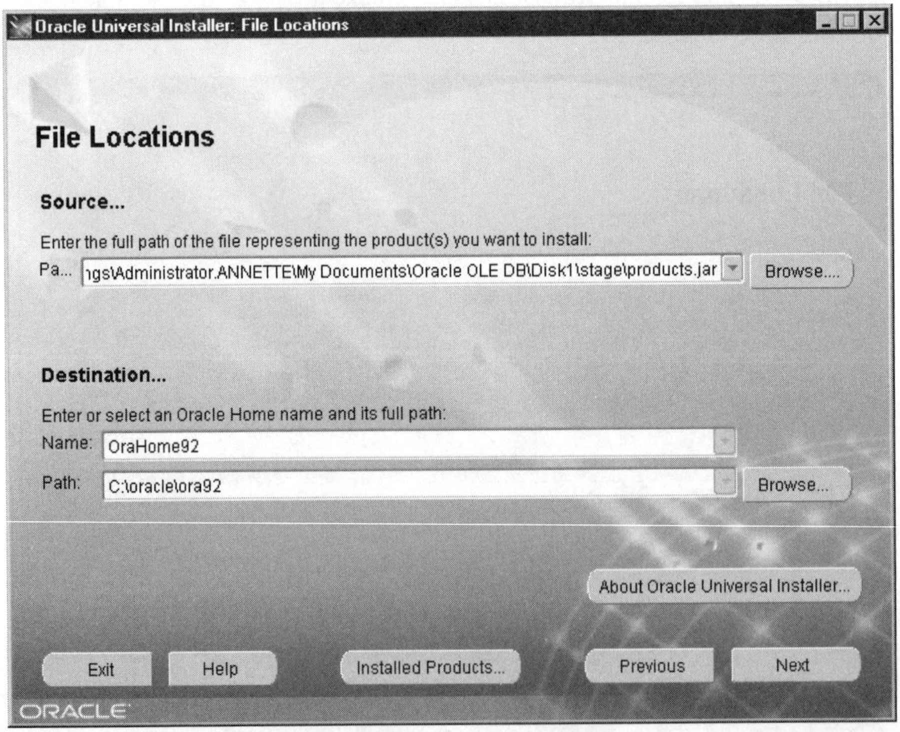

Figure 1-10   *OLE DB file locations*

For use with this text, the sample data has been uploaded to Oracle, and the sample reports have been revised to point to the XTREME schema. Two methods for uploading the data from Access to Oracle are described in this section.

Dump File Method

Dump files containing the Xtreme database can be found in the download files. The filename is XTREME92.DMP for the Oracle 9*i* version and XTREME817.DMP for the Oracle 8*i* version. To import the Xtreme data to your Oracle database, you will need to execute the following statement at a system command prompt or from Start | Run:

```
IMP xtreme/xtreme@ora FILE=xtreme92.dmp
```

This statement assumes that the Xtreme user's password is xtreme, your database service name is ORA, and the XTREME92.dmp file is located in your root directory. You should modify the password, TNS name, and file path and name as needed for your environment.

Upload Method

The dump files are large, so an alternative method for obtaining the sample data is provided here. The alternative involves uploading the sample data from the Crystal-supplied Access database. This method will upload only the data originally supplied with Crystal Reports.

Create Schema Objects   The first step is to create the schema objects, which you will populate with data from the sample Access database. Log in as the Xtreme user and run either Chapter 1\XTREME Objects for Oracle 9i.sql, or XTREME Objects 8i.sql for Oracle 8*i* databases. The schema objects will be created.

Populate Schema Objects   Open the sample Access database that is installed with Crystal Reports at C:\Program Files\Crystal Decisions\Crystal Reports 9\Samples\ En\Databases\xtreme.mdb. To create database links to the Oracle tables, choose File | Get External Data | Link Tables. In the Files of Type box, choose ODBC. Choose the Oracle ODBC connection. Note that even if you have already installed the Crystal ODBC drivers for Oracle, they will not work for this task (they are licensed for use only from Crystal Reports). Log in as Xtreme. Choose the Credit, Customer, Employee, Employee_Addresses, Financials, Orders, Orders_Detail, Product, Product_Type, Purchases, Supplier, and Xtreme_Info tables, and links will be created.

Once the links are created, choose New Query. Select Simple Query Wizard, and pick the Employee table in the Tables/Queries drop-down box. Move all fields from Available Fields to Selected Fields as shown here:

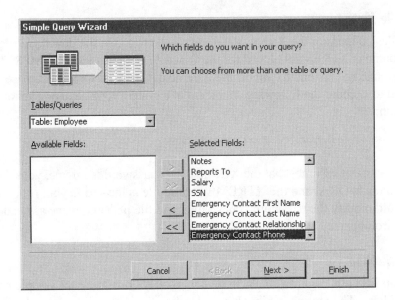

Click Next, leave the Detail radio button selected, and choose Next. Name the query Employee Upload Query and select the Modify Query Design radio button. Click Finish. When the query design appears, choose Query | Append Query and select XTREME_EMPLOYEE in the drop-down (XTREME_EMPLOYEE is the name that has been given to the linked Employee table in the Oracle XTREME schema). Click OK. On the Employee Upload: Append Query screen, you may notice that some Append To fields are missing. These fields are not shown when the Oracle field name does not match the Access field name due to embedded spaces. For each missing Append To field, select the proper Oracle field from the cell's drop-down box as shown in the following illustration:

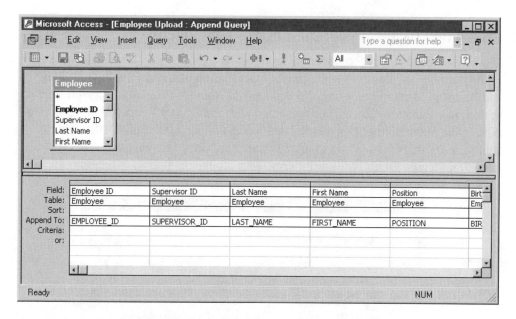

Run the query to upload the Employee records from Access to Oracle.

Repeat this process for each linked table in this order: Employee, Employee_Addresses, Product_Type, Product, Supplier, Customer, Credit, Financials, Purchases, Orders, and Orders_Detail.

The Orders and Purchases tables have fields defined as Booleans, which are uploaded to Oracle as 0 for False and -1 for True. The convention used in the book is 0 for False and 1 for True. To modify the fields, run the following update queries:

```
UPDATE ORDERS SET Shipped=1 WHERE Shipped=-1;
UPDATE ORDERS SET Payment_Received=1 WHERE Payment_Received =-1;
UPDATE PURCHASES SET Received=1 WHERE Received =-1;
UPDATE PURCHASES SET Paid=1 WHERE Paid =-1;
```

Populate Book-Only Objects

A few of the objects in the XTREME schema were added to demonstrate various capabilities for this book. To populate them, run the Chapter 1\Populate Book Objects.sql script.

Sample Xtreme Reports

The sample reports provided with Crystal Reports were converted to use the native Oracle driver and the Oracle TNSname, ORA, and are available with the download files for the book at Chapter 1\Crystal Sample Reports.

Installation of the Crystal Data Access Components

The Crystal Data Access components required for using Oracle as a data source for reports can be installed during the original installation of Crystal Reports, or they can be installed later via the Control Panel | Add/Remove Programs | Crystal Reports option. In either case, you will be presented with the Crystal Reports 9 Setup dialog box. In the Setup dialog, expand the Data Access folder. Under the ODBCDrivers folder, verify that Oracle is set to install to the hard drive (shown next). This will install the Crystal ODBC drivers for Oracle.

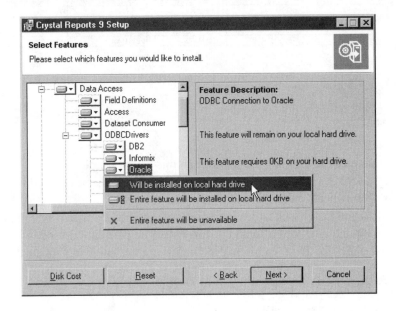

In addition, verify that Oracle and OLE DB Data are also set to install to the hard drive. (See the following illustration.) This will ensure that the DLLs required for native access and access via OLE DB from Crystal Reports are installed.

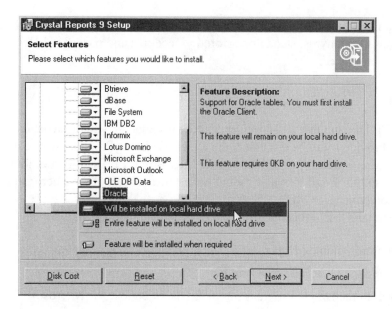

Continue clicking Next until the install completes.

Configuration of the Native Oracle OCI

Crystal Reports supports what it calls "native" Oracle connections via its Native Oracle OCI Connectivity driver. This type of connection from Crystal makes calls directly to the Oracle Call Interface or OCI.DLL, bypassing the extra layers imposed by ODBC or even OLE DB connections. The native connection has many benefits over OLE DB or ODBC connections and should be used where possible, unless there is a specific reason to prefer one of the other connection types. A comparison of the benefits of each connection type is shown later in this chapter in Table 1-1. For Crystal Reports version 9, the Oracle client must be version 8.0.6 or later to support the native connection type.

To create a native connection, execute the following steps:

1. From Crystal Reports, open the Database Expert.
2. Expand the Create New Connection folder.
3. Open the Oracle Server folder.
4. Fill in the TNS name of your database in the Service field, enter your user ID and password, and then click the Finish button.
5. Your connection will open and a list of the database schemas that your user ID can access will appear as folders.

Expanding a schema folder will display the object type folders under which the tables, views, synonyms, standalone stored procedures and packages belonging to the schema are listed.

OLE DB

To use OLE DB, an OLE DB Provider must be installed on your system. Two possible OLE DB Providers will be discussed, the Oracle OLE DB Provider, whose installation was covered in a preceding section, and the Microsoft OLE DB Provider for Oracle. The Microsoft OLE DB Provider should be installed as part of the Microsoft Data Access Components or MDAC.

To create an OLE DB connection, execute the following steps:

1. Open the Database Expert.
2. Expand the OLE DB (ADO) folder.
3. Scroll to the Oracle Provider for OLE DB, or choose the Microsoft OLE DB Provider for Oracle and click Next.
4. Enter the necessary connection information and click Finish. The Data Source textbox should be filled in with the TNS name of the Oracle database you wish to connect to.
5. The connection will be made and schemas that you have access to will be displayed.

ODBC Connection Setup

To use ODBC connectivity from Crystal Reports, two configuration steps are required. First, an ODBC Data Source Name (DSN) must be created using the ODBC Administrator. Second, a Crystal data source that uses the ODBC DSN must be created.

DSN Creation

DSN creation for several different Oracle ODBC drivers will be covered. Note that each is an ODBC driver for Oracle; they are simply supplied by different vendors.

Crystal ODBC for Oracle   The Crystal Reports ODBC driver was installed with the Crystal Reports product as discussed previously. This driver is owned and developed by DataDirect and is licensed for use with Crystal Reports. It is not usable outside of Crystal Reports.

To configure an ODBC Data Source Name for the Crystal ODBC driver, execute the following steps:

1. Open the ODBC Data Source Administrator, which may be accessed from the Control Panel or Control Panel | Administrative Tools, depending on your version of Windows.

2. You may configure a User DSN, a System DSN, or a File DSN. A User DSN will be available only to you. A System DSN will be available to anyone logged on to the system where it is defined. A File DSN stores the connection information in a text file that may be copied readily from computer to computer. For the example, you will set up a System DSN. Choose the System DSN tab. Choose Add.

3. Scroll to the CR Oracle ODBC Driver 4.10. This is the Crystal Reports ODBC driver for Oracle.

4. Click Finish and enter your choice of a Data Source Name and Description, and the TNS name for the database you wish to connect to in the Server Name box. See Figure 1-11.

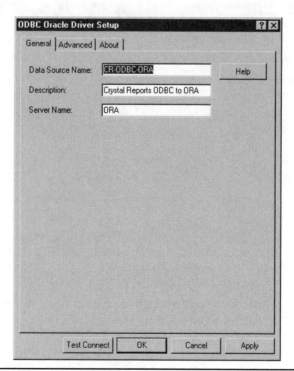

Figure 1-11   *Crystal Reports ODBC DSN*

5. Click Test Connect. A logon box will appear.

6. Enter your username and password and click OK to test the connection.

7. Click OK to return to the ODBC configuration. Choose OK again and your DSN will be created.

Oracle ODBC   To set up an Oracle ODBC DSN, execute the following steps:

1. From the ODBC Administrator, choose the System DSN tab. Then choose Add.

2. Scroll to the Oracle in [OracleHome] driver name, where [OracleHome] is your Oracle Home directory. Click Finish. The Oracle ODBC Driver Configuration dialog box will appear.

3. Enter your desired Data Source Name and Description. From the TNS Service Name drop-down box, choose the service that you wish to connect to. Enter your User ID. Your screen should be similar to the following illustration. Click Test Connection.

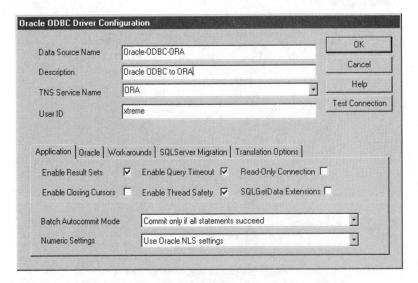

4. A logon box will appear. Enter your password and click OK.

5. The connection will be tested. Click OK to return to the ODBC Administrator, and click OK again. Your DSN will be created.

Microsoft ODBC   To set up a Microsoft Oracle ODBC DSN, execute the following steps:

1. From the ODBC Administrator, choose the System DSN tab. Then choose Add.

2. Scroll to the Microsoft ODBC for Oracle driver name. Click Finish. The Microsoft ODBC for Oracle Setup dialog box will appear.

3. Enter your desired Data Source Name and Description, your User ID in the User Name box, and the service that you wish to connect to in the Server box. Click OK, and your DSN will be created. There is no Test Connection capability. See the following illustration for an example:

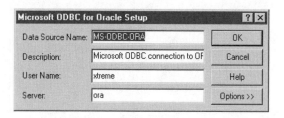

Crystal Wire Protocol ODBC for Oracle   To set up a Crystal Wire Protocol ODBC DSN, execute the following steps. Note that installation of the Oracle client is not required when using the Wire Protocol driver.

1. From the ODBC Administrator, choose the System DSN tab. Then choose Add.

2. Scroll to CR Oracle Wire Protocol ODBC Driver. Click Finish. The ODBC Oracle Wire Protocol Driver Setup dialog will appear.

3. Enter your desired Data Source Name and Description and the IP address or host alias for the machine where the database resides in the Host box. If the port differs from the default of 1521, enter the correct value. Enter the database name in the SID field, as shown in Figure 1-12.

4. Click Test Connect.

5. Enter your username and password and click OK. Your connection will be tested.

6. Click OK, and your DSN will be created.

Crystal Connection Setup

Once the ODBC DSNs are created, Crystal connections can be configured. The Crystal-side configuration is the same for all ODBC drivers.

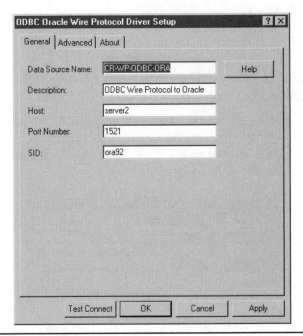

Figure 1-12   *Wire Protocol DSN*

To connect to Oracle from Crystal Reports using ODBC, execute the following steps:

1. From the Database Expert, under Create New Connection, choose ODBC (RDO).

2. Select the Select Data Source radio button and find the DSN that you created in the previous section.

3. Enter your user ID and password and click Finish.

4. The connection will be opened, and the list of schemas to which you have access will be displayed.

Choosing a Connection Method

As just described, there are several ways to connect to Oracle from Crystal Reports. Table 1-1 lists different capabilities and requirements for seven different connection types; note that results may differ depending on your environment. In addition, the table is specific to the stated versions of each piece of software or middleware, and the capabilities can be dependent upon driver settings. These settings are noted where known.

If you need to make a decision about which type of access to use, you should determine the required capabilities and test the various connection methods in your own particular environment. You should also measure response time, which varies dramatically across the various connection types.

Before doing extensive tests, you should be aware that the most recent service packs or hot fixes for Crystal Reports are available from www.crystaldecisions.com. You will be warned that the hot fixes have not been through a full QA regression test and must decide for yourself whether to take the risk in using them. Updates for the Oracle components can be downloaded from technet.oracle.com.

Other notes concerning various drivers are

▶ For the Crystal ODBC drivers, both regular and Wire Protocol, stored procedures owned by other users will be displayed in the Database Expert only if the ODBC Advanced option Use Current Schema for SQL Procedures is unchecked. The downside to unchecking this option is the increase in time required to open the Database Expert. I have seen it take 40 minutes in my test environment.

▶ When using the Crystal-supplied ODBC drivers, you must verify that the Advanced option Procedure Returns Results is checked if you plan to use stored procedures.

▶ For the Oracle ODBC driver and OLE DB Provider, stored procedures can be called from SQL Commands using the {Call ...} syntax with the Oracle 9*i* provider, but not using the BEGIN ... END, anonymous block syntax.

▶ When using the Microsoft OLE DB provider with stored procedures, it is vital that you give each column an alias in the SELECT query that defines the REF Cursor.

▶ You may receive an error stating that the table does not exist when refreshing reports that use stored procedures and an OLE DB provider. Answer No when asked if you want to delete the table, and the report will run as expected.

▶ When writing stored procedures, never return datatypes that the particular connection method you are using does not support.

▶ To access stored procedures owned by other users, you must have the EXECUTE privilege for the stored procedure.

▶ Crystal will truncate some of the Oracle string types. CLOBs and NCLOBs will be truncated at 64K bytes and Longs will be truncated at 4000 bytes.

▶ Object columns, nested tables, and varrays cannot be used directly with Crystal Reports, but workarounds exist and are discussed in subsequent chapters.

The Crystal Data Access Component drivers installed with Crystal Reports or via a hot fix or service pack for Crystal Reports and used in Table 1-1 are

▶ Native: crdb_oracle.dll, version 9.2.1.116

▶ OLE DB: crdb_ado.dll, version 9.2.0.517

▶ ODBC: crdb_odbc.dll, version 9.2.1.593

The other required OLE DB or ODBC drivers used in Table 1-1 are

▶ MS OLE DB: MDAC 2.7

▶ Oracle OLE DB: oraoledb.dll, version 9.2.0.2 (8.1.7.3 for Oracle 8*i*)

▶ Crystal ODBC: cror818.dll, version 4.10.0.4

▶ Oracle ODBC: sqora32.dll, version 9.2.0.4.0 (8.1.7.8.0b for Oracle 8*i*)

▶ MS ODBC: msorcl32.dll, version 2.573.9030

▶ Crystal Wire Protocol ODBC: crora18.dll, version 4.10.0.4

Note that table values shown in parentheses are the Oracle 8*i* values where they differ from the 9*i* values.

Note that for the Oracle ODBC driver, other combinations of software versions have fewer problems. With the particular combination listed in Table 1-1, an error is generated as soon as Crystal Reports attempts to list the field names. Older Crystal Reports hot fix versions such as 9.2.3.666 do not have this problem.

Crystal Reports Developer Version 9.2.3.687	**Oracle Client 9.2.0.1.0 (8.1.7.0.0)**						**No Client**
		OLE DB		**ODBC**			
	Native	**MS**	**Oracle**	**Crystal**	**Oracle**	**MS**	**Wire Protocol**
Installation and Configuration Requirements							
Requires installation of Oracle networking components (client)	Yes	Yes	Yes	Yes	Yes	Yes	No
Requires installation of OLE DB provider	No	Yes	Yes	No	No	No	No
Requires installation of ODBC driver and DSN creation	No	No	No	Yes	Yes	Yes	Yes
Driver Properties							
Thread safe	Yes	Yes	Yes	Yes	Yes	No	Yes

Table 1-1   *Connectivity Comparison*

| Crystal Reports Developer Version 9.2.3.687 | Oracle Client 9.2.0.1.0 (8.1.7.0.0) | | | | | | No Client |
| | Native | OLE DB | | ODBC | | | |
	Native	MS	Oracle	Crystal	Oracle	MS	Wire Protocol
Using Stored Procedures Directly (SPs appear as tables in the Crystal Reports Database Expert)							
Can use stored procedures (strongly typed)	Yes	Yes	No	Yes	No	No	Yes
Can use stored procedures (weakly typed)	Yes	Yes (No)	No	Yes	No	No	Yes
Can use packaged stored procedures	Yes	Yes	No	Yes	No	No	Yes
Can access stored procedures in other schemas	Yes	Yes (No)	No	Yes	No	No	Yes
Calling Stored Procedures from SQL Commands							
Can call stored procedures	No	Yes	Yes	Yes	Yes	No	Yes
Can use stored procedures inside packaged stored procedures	No	Yes	Yes	Yes	Yes	No	Yes
Can access stored procedures in other schemas	No	Yes	Yes	Yes	Yes	No	Yes
Can execute multiple statements in SQL Command	No	Yes	No	Yes	No	No	Yes
Crystal Environment							
Indexes color coded in Database Expert	No	Yes	Yes	Yes	Yes	Yes	Yes
BLOBs OK	Yes	No	Yes	Yes	No*	No	Yes
CLOBs OK	Yes	No	Yes	Yes	No*	No	Yes
ROWIDs OK	Yes	No	No*	Yes	No*	No	Yes
NCLOBs OK	Yes	No	Yes	No (Yes)	No*	No	No (Yes)
LONGs OK	Yes	Yes	Yes	Yes	No	Yes	Yes
NCHARs OK	Yes	Yes	Yes	Yes	No*	Yes	No (Yes)
NVARCHAR2s OK	Yes	Yes	Yes	Yes	No*	Yes	No (Yes)
Synonyms for database links usable as tables from Database Expert	No	No	No	No	No	No	No
Database links or synonyms usable in SQL Commands	Yes	Yes	Yes (No)	No (Yes)	No (Yes)	Yes	Yes

* These field types are usable if referenced in a SQL Command rather than picked in the Database Expert.

Table 1-1   *Connectivity Comparison* (continued)

Crystal Database Options

Crystal Reports maintains a set of database options. To see the options, right-click any data source in the Database Expert and choose Options. A window similar to Figure 1-13 will be displayed.

The Database Options settings apply to every data source, but the effect of the settings may differ between connectivity types. For instance, leaving System Tables unchecked for the Crystal ODBC driver will result in the SYS and SYSTEM schema being excluded from the Database Explorer lists, but it has no impact on the native driver, which shows the SYS and SYSTEM schemas regardless of this setting. You should set the Explorer Options section according to your preferences.

Advanced Options

The settings in the Advanced Options section can be used to fine-tune some performance characteristics. These settings are global settings that may be overridden for individual reports using the File | Report Options dialog.

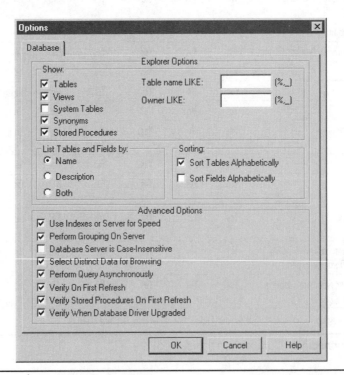

Figure 1-13   *Database Options*

Use Indexes or Server for Speed

This option is checked by default. Unchecking it will cause a reduction in performance because appropriate indexes will not be used, so make sure that this option is checked. The following illustration shows a SQL execution plan if you check Use Indexes or Server for Speed.

```
Execution Plan
                                          Cost   Rows  Optimizer
Child Cursor   0
  SELECT STATEMENT                          1            CHOOSE
    TABLE ACCESS BY INDEX ROWID SUPPLIER    1       1  ANALYZED
      INDEX UNIQUE SCAN SUPPLIER_PK                 7  ANALYZED
        Access Condition: "SUPPLIER_ID"=:SYS_B_1
```

The next illustration shows the execution plan for the same SQL statement if Use Indexes or Server for Speed is not checked for the report.

```
Execution Plan
                                  Cost   Rows  Optimizer
Child Cursor   0
  SELECT STATEMENT                  2            CHOOSE
    TABLE ACCESS FULL SUPPLIER              2       7  ANALYZED
```

Perform Grouping on Server

The Perform Grouping on Server option is not checked by default and cannot be checked unless Use Indexes or Server for Speed is also checked. This setting corresponds to the Database | Perform Grouping on the Server menu option, but the menu option is at the individual report level and overrides the setting at the Database Options level. Checking this option controls whether or not Crystal will create an aggregate query when all detail sections are suppressed. You should check this option for Oracle databases.

Database Server Is Case-Insensitive

This setting has no affect on Oracle databases.

Select Distinct Data for Browsing

The Select Distinct Data for Browsing option controls the creation of the queries used to return field-browsing lists, such as in the Select Expert. The queries are always written to return 500 records. If this option is checked, the query will be a distinct query, and up to 500 distinct values will be listed. If this option is not checked, the first 500 records will be returned and the browse list will contain the distinct values contained in those records.

This setting has no impact on actual report performance because it applies only during the development of reports.

Perform Query Asynchronously

Perform Query Asynchronously is not checked by default. Checking it allows Crystal Reports to halt query execution if requested by the user.

Verify on First Refresh

Verify on First Refresh should be checked so that Crystal will verify the record structure the first time a report is run.

Verify Stored Procedures on First Refresh

Verify Stored Procedures on First Refresh should be checked so that Crystal will verify the record structure of the REF Cursor for stored procedures when a report is first run.

Verify When Database Driver Upgraded

This option should also be checked so that the database is verified if the driver is changed.

User IDs and Schemas

New Oracle users are sometimes confused by the concepts of User_IDs versus Schemas. Every Oracle User_ID that is a Database User_ID has a corresponding schema. The schema is a logical storage place for the user's objects, and its name is the same as the User_ID. Therefore, for user MARY, there is a MARY schema. If MARY has the RESOURCE privilege, she can create a table in her schema. If MARY creates a table called TAB1 in her schema and grants user JOE the SELECT privilege on it, JOE would access it as MARY.TAB1.

In most report-writing environments, users will not be reporting on objects in their own schemas. They may not even be allowed to create objects in their own schemas. They will most likely be reporting on objects in various schemas that were created specifically to hold an application's objects.

Of course, there are exceptions. An application may be written to create a set of objects for each user in each user's schema. The difficulties in reporting in such an environment are discussed in Appendix A. In the newer versions of Oracle, there can also be lightweight or proxy User_IDs. Such User_IDs do not have their own schemas; they share a schema or schemas.

Authentication Methods

Oracle allows several types of authentication. The most straightforward is when the user has an ID with a password created in the Oracle database. If your database uses this type of authentication, you will be given both a user ID and password to use for Oracle access. The other methods of authentication allow Oracle to rely on an external provider for authentication. This could be the operating system, an LDAP directory, or some other method. If any of these authentication methods are being used, check with your DBA for logon instructions. In the case of OS authentication, you would log on with either a slash (/) or a null for the username, depending on the driver, and a null password. Your credentials will then be verified with the operating system and you will be logged on.

Oracle logons are case insensitive. If your user name is XTREME, you may successfully log on as xtreme, Xtreme, or XTREME. Passwords are also case insensitive.

Database Privileges

There are two main types of privileges in Oracle: system privileges and object privileges. For reporting, you will be most concerned with object privileges that govern which tables, views, and stored procedures you can see. To access a table or view from Crystal Reports, you must have the SELECT privilege for the table or view. You do not need the UPDATE, INSERT, or DELETE privilege. To access stored procedures, you will need the EXECUTE privilege for the stored procedure.

To simplify the maintenance of privileges, Oracle uses roles. A role can be created and then granted a set of privileges. A user ID can then be granted the role. For instance, there may be a role called Reporters, and each report developer will be granted the Reporter role rather than privileges on individual objects.

In addition, you will have all privileges for any objects in your own schema—that is, the schema that matches your user ID.

Connection Options Used in Book

All examples in the rest of the book use a native connection to Oracle 9*i* except where noted. All examples have been tested for Oracle 9*i* (9.2) and Oracle 8*i* (8.1.7), with both native and Crystal Oracle ODBC connectivity using the driver versions listed in Table 1-1. Issues with any of the four combinations are noted.

CHAPTER
2

Oracle Structures

T his chapter provides an overview of the Oracle database environment with an emphasis on the concerns of a report writer. It covers the concept of schemas and describes each type of object that can be created in an Oracle database including tables, views, materialized views, dimensions, sequence generators, synonyms, indexes, and primary keys. Table relationships and their definitions are also covered. Oracle datatypes are described, including both built-in types and possible user-defined types, and the behavior of null values is explained. Oracle's built-in data dictionary views are described.

Schemas

Unlike desktop databases such as Microsoft Access, Oracle uses the concept of schemas to add a level of organization and security to the database objects. Each database user has a corresponding schema. For example, user Xtreme owned the sample data that was imported in Chapter 1. When those objects were imported, they were imported into the XTREME schema. A user's own schema is analogous to a local scope. To access objects within your schema, you may use just the name of the object. To access objects in another user's schema, you must prefix the object name with the schema name using a dot notation. Therefore, if user Joe wanted to select data from the Supplier table owned by Xtreme, he would use the syntax `SELECT ... FROM XTREME.SUPPLIER`.

   Report writing usually involves selecting from objects in schemas not owned by the report writer. Most production databases will have schemas that reflect a desired organizational concept rather than real individuals.

Objects

Oracle contains many different object types, both built-in and user defined. Report writers are most concerned with tables, views, and a certain type of stored procedure, but all object types will be covered briefly.

Tables

Tables are the basic Oracle database objects that contain data. Tables are organized in columns and rows: they are defined with certain columns or fields and data is entered in rows. When a row is added to a table, each column may be required to be populated. If a column is defined as NOT NULL, it must have a value. A column may also have a default value defined. If a column has a default value defined, the default value will be stored in the column if no value is specifically inserted for that column. If a column does not have a NOT NULL constraint, or if it has a NOT NULL constraint and a default value, it may be left out of any insert statement.

The column or field type is usually scalar and is one of the Oracle built-in datatypes that are discussed in the "Built-In" section later in this chapter, but it may also be a complex user-defined type such as a record, varray, or nested table. Object tables are tables whose rows are of a user-defined object type. Nested tables are tables that have a column that is a user-defined table type. Nested tables are problematic for report writers as none of the access methods available from Crystal Reports directly support nested tables. See the workaround for reporting on nested tables in the "Nested Tables" section later in this chapter.

Temporary tables are a special kind of table that can be created to store data that is only needed for the duration of a session or a transaction. Temporary tables can be used for reporting just like permanent tables as long as you are aware of their special characteristics. Temporary tables can be defined such that the data they contain persists for the duration of either a single transaction or a single session. The data in a temporary table is private to the session or transaction that inserts the data. This means that a given session can see only the rows that it has inserted into the temporary table. It cannot see any other session's rows. Temporary tables are emptied when the session terminates or the transaction completes, depending on its definition. Reporting from temporary tables might be useful when the reports are embedded in an application and could be used when reporting from a stored procedure, but this would have little meaning in an independent reporting environment where Crystal controls the session. Temporary tables used in stored procedures are discussed further in Chapter 5.

External tables are another special kind of table that can be included in reports. External tables are tables whose data resides outside of the Oracle database tablespaces, usually in a flat file. External tables are read-only. Reporting from external tables would be useful in situations where some portion of the report must be based on data in a comma-delimited file. If that file is defined as an external table in Oracle, it can be reported from in the same manner as any regular Oracle table. See Chapter 9 for an example of using an external table.

NOTE

External tables are not available in Oracle 8i or earlier versions.

Another option for including flat file data in a Crystal Report would be to use the text driver for ODBC. In that case, all joining, filtering, and so on would occur on the client machine where Crystal resides, whereas using an Oracle external table will push that processing to the server.

Table Types

Oracle tables can be organized and stored on disk in different ways. The type of table organization is transparent to the report writer, but that organization can be helpful to understand when trying to optimize the query upon which a report is based. The most common table type is a heap table. In a heap table, rows are not stored in any particular order. This reflects the traditional relational concept of unordered sets. Any ordering is accomplished by separate indexes on the tables. Index organized tables are tables that are stored in a particular order based on an index. Clustered tables are useful for tables whose data is often joined. In clustered tables, the related data from each table is stored together and can be accessed quickly using cluster keys.

Views

Views are stored queries. In many ways, a view can be treated as if it was a table, but thinking of views as virtual tables can be detrimental in some respects. There is no stored data associated with a view; a view is simply a query. When a view is referenced in a SELECT statement, its definition is merged with the other components of the SELECT statement and the resulting statement is parsed and executed.

For example, the XTREME schema contains the TOP_CUSTOMERS view, which is defined by the following statement:

```
CREATE OR REPLACE VIEW "XTREME"."TOP_CUSTOMERS"
    AS
SELECT XTREME.CUSTOMER.ADDRESS1,
       XTREME.CUSTOMER.ADDRESS2,
       XTREME.CUSTOMER.CITY,
       XTREME.CUSTOMER.CONTACT_FIRST_NAME,
       XTREME.CUSTOMER.CONTACT_LAST_NAME,
       XTREME.CUSTOMER.CONTACT_POSITION,
       XTREME.CUSTOMER.CONTACT_TITLE,
       XTREME.CUSTOMER.COUNTRY,
       XTREME.CUSTOMER.CUSTOMER_CREDIT_ID,
       XTREME.CUSTOMER.CUSTOMER_ID,
       XTREME.CUSTOMER.CUSTOMER_NAME,
       XTREME.CUSTOMER.FAX,
       XTREME.CUSTOMER.LAST_YEARS_SALES,
       XTREME.CUSTOMER.PHONE,
       XTREME.CUSTOMER.POSTAL_CODE,
       XTREME.CUSTOMER.REGION
```

```
FROM XTREME.CUSTOMER
WHERE ( XTREME.CUSTOMER.LAST_YEARS_SALES > '50000' );
```

If you create a Crystal Report using this view, showing Customer_ID, Customer_Name, Last_Years_Sales, and Country and specifying that the country must be 'USA', Crystal would construct the following query to send to the Oracle server:

```
SELECT "TOP_CUSTOMERS"."CUSTOMER_ID", "TOP_CUSTOMERS"."CUSTOMER_NAME",
       "TOP_CUSTOMERS"."LAST_YEARS_SALES", "TOP_CUSTOMERS"."COUNTRY"
  FROM "XTREME"."TOP_CUSTOMERS" "TOP_CUSTOMERS"
WHERE "TOP_CUSTOMERS"."COUNTRY"='USA'
```

The example report is available as Chapter 2\View Rewrite Example Report.rpt in the accompanying download file. The report will work only in an Oracle 9*i* environment because the embedded subreport uses tables that do not exist in Oracle 8*i*.

However, Oracle would merge the view definition with the query and actually parse and execute something like the following:

```
SELECT "CUSTOMER"."CUSTOMER_ID", "CUSTOMER"."CUSTOMER_NAME",
       "CUSTOMER"."LAST_YEARS_SALES", "CUSTOMER"."COUNTRY"
  FROM "XTREME"."CUSTOMER" "CUSTOMER"
WHERE ( XTREME.CUSTOMER.LAST_YEARS_SALES > '50000' )
   AND "CUSTOMER"."COUNTRY"='USA'
```

Figure 2-1 displays the report and contains a subreport showing the execution plan. As expected, the execution plan indicates that the Customer table will be accessed, not the view, Top_Customers.

Views are very useful constructs. They can be used to hide complex join logic or otherwise simplify data for the users. However, they are not tables, and the report writer needs to understand what will happen on the Oracle server when views are used.

Materialized Views

Oracle materialized views are views whose contents are stored on disk, as they do contain data. Materialized views are often created to store summaries or other complex operations where using a normal view, which would need to be re-executed each time it was called, would be inefficient. Materialized views are also used to replicate data in a distributed environment. They are refreshed as defined by the DBA, and they might be refreshed on demand, on a time schedule, or when the underlying data changes. Materialized views can be reported on just like ordinary tables and show up in Crystal Reports under the table folder.

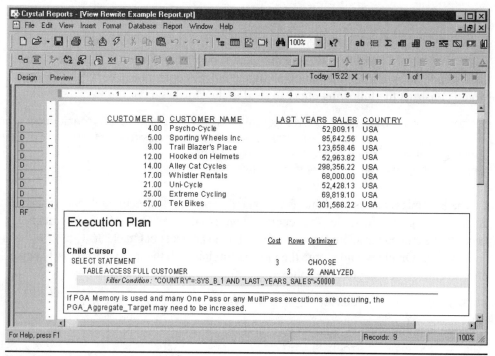

Figure 2-1 *View rewrite example*

Materialized views can also be used for transparent query rewrite. If query rewrite is enabled and a user submits a query that would execute faster against a materialized view, the query is rewritten by Oracle to use the materialized view. The user does not know that the query has been rewritten; the user just gets the results faster. See Chapter 9 for an example using materialized views.

Dimensions

Dimensions are Oracle objects that define hierarchical relationships between columns. Dimensions cannot be reported on directly. Dimensions are used in data warehousing environments.

Sequence Generators

Oracle sequence generators generate and return sequential numbers. They are often used to generate unique keys for inserted rows and are of little, if any, use in a report. However, they can be called using a Crystal SQL Expression field or in a SQL Command or stored procedure. The syntax to generate sequence numbers is `[sequence name]` `.NEXTVAL`.

Synonyms

Synonyms allow the creation of aliases for tables, views, materialized views, sequences, procedures, functions, and packages. They can be used to hide the location of, or simplify the names of, objects. There can be private synonyms that are available only to the user who created them and public synonyms which can be used by anyone connected to the database. Synonyms are often created by the DBA for tables, views, and packages that are used frequently.

For example, without synonyms, if a user other than Xtreme needed to query the table XTREME.CUSTOMER, that user would have to use the entire qualified name of the table:

```
SELECT * FROM XTREME.CUSTOMER;
```

However, if a public synonym has been created such as the following:

```
CREATE  PUBLIC SYNONYM "CUST" FOR "XTREME"."CUSTOMER";
```

the user can type a simpler statement:

```
SELECT * FROM CUST;
```

In Crystal Reports, the display of synonyms is dependent on the options set for the database. In the Database Expert, right-click a database name and choose Options. If you want to see synonyms, check the Synonyms box, as shown in Figure 2-2.

Private synonyms will show up under the schema folder of the logged-in user, as shown in Figure 2-3. Public synonyms will be listed under the public folder.

There are many predefined public synonyms in any Oracle database. Expect to see a long list of objects under the public folder, if you choose to see synonyms. The majority of the pre-existing public synonyms are for the static data dictionary views or for the dynamic performance views. These special views are discussed in the section "Data Dictionary Views" later in this chapter.

Indexes

Indexes are Oracle objects that help to decrease the time required to return data to the user. An index is associated with a table, including materialized view tables, but they can be created and dropped independently of the table. Indexes use storage

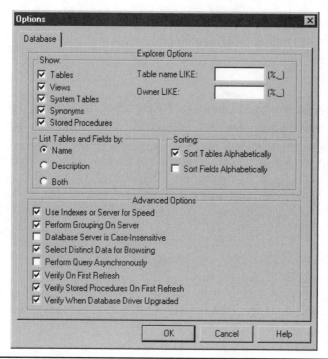

Figure 2-2   *Database options*

space but cannot be reported on directly. An index is based on one or more columns in a table and speeds access to the rows of the table in the defined sort order of the indexed columns. Proper table indexing is of primary importance to the report developer concerned with optimizing report display.

Oracle supports several different types of indexes including B-tree, reverse key, bitmap, bitmap join, cluster, domain, and function-based indexes. An index can be defined as unique, which guarantees that no two rows in the table will have the same value for the indexed column(s). If an index is not defined as unique, identical values can exist. An index can be defined on a single column or on multiple columns. A multiple column index is called a compound or concatenated index.

A B-tree is the default index type, and a B-tree index is a hierarchy. The leaf nodes contain pointers to the actual row data. The higher-level branches contain a path that becomes more refined the closer it gets to the leaf nodes. The number of levels of a B-tree index is an indication of its efficiency; the fewer the levels, the faster the access. If you imagine a tree where a leaf on one twig is the record that you need, to get to that leaf, you would start at the trunk and at each fork you would take the branch that leads to the leaf you need.

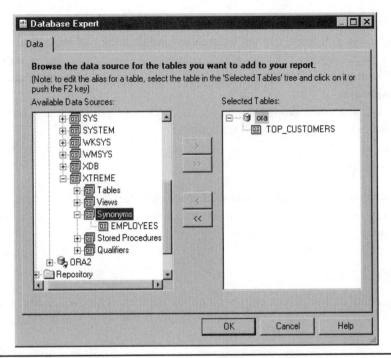

Figure 2-3 *Synonyms folders*

A reverse key index is also a B-tree, but the column values are reversed during storage. Therefore, a column that contains "ABCD" would be indexed as "DCBA." Reverse key indexes are used to spread key values out across the B-tree and help balance the index. This is useful in cases where the indexed column is populated by a sequence.

A bitmap index is useful for columns of low cardinality that are used frequently in select queries. They are used extensively in data warehouse environments. The cardinality of a column refers to the number of different values stored in that column for the table. For example, if the country column contains only the values "USA" or "CAN" in a table with 10,000 rows, that would be low cardinality. The cardinality is computed as the number of distinct values over the number of rows. The suggested cardinality for using a bitmap index is 1 percent. In this case, our cardinality is 2/10,000 or 0.02 percent, and a bitmap index would be advantageous.

Bitmap join indexes are indexes that precalculate a join. They are also used in a data warehouse environment.

NOTE

Bitmap join indexes are not available in Oracle 8i or previous versions.

Indexing for query optimization is discussed in detail in Chapter 7.

Though Crystal Reports can tag the indexed fields in the Database Expert for some data access types, it does not make any distinction for other types. For example, Figure 2-4 shows the linking dialog for a native connection. The native connection shows no indexes.

Figure 2-5 shows the linking dialog for an ODBC or OLE DB connection. The indexed fields are tagged with different colors.

Primary Keys

Primary keys are maintained via non-null unique indexes. A table can have only one primary key, which can contain one or more columns. The fields of the primary key uniquely identify the rows in a table.

Database Links

A database link defines a connection to another database. Once a database link is created, it can be used to query data in the remote database to which it links, as if

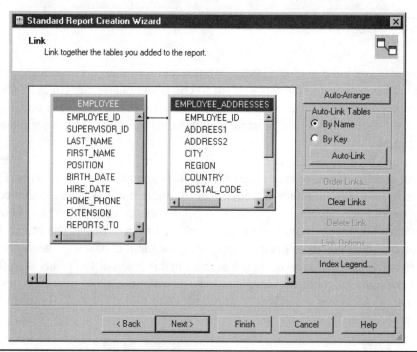

Figure 2-4   *Native connection linking dialog*

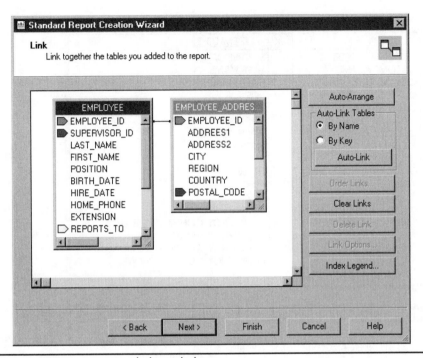

Figure 2-5   *ODBC connection linking dialog*

that data was in the original database. Database links are not displayed in Crystal's Database Expert, so they cannot be selected like tables. To use a database link, you can use a SQL Command, view, or stored procedure. To access a table in a linked database, you must append the link name to the table reference as shown:

```
SELECT * FROM scott.emp@link_name
```

Relationships

It is vital for report writers to understand the proper relationships between tables for the data structures on which they need to report. Linking tables inappropriately can lead to erroneous results. In Oracle databases, relationships between tables are maintained via referential integrity constraints. Foreign key constraints are created that link the foreign key field in the child table to the primary key field in the parent table. For example, Figure 2-6 shows the relationships in the XTREME sample

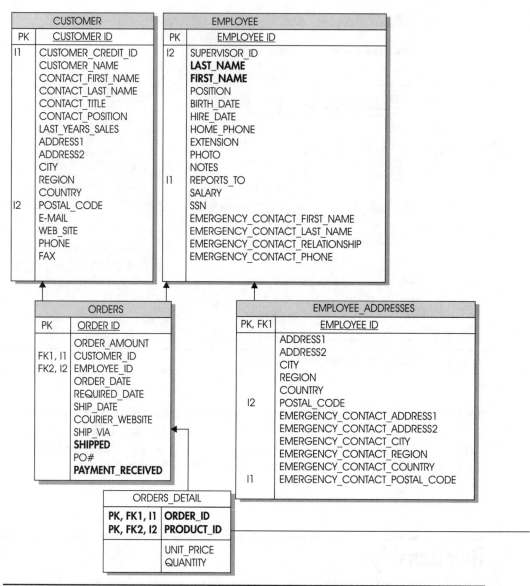

Figure 2-6 *XTREME data model*

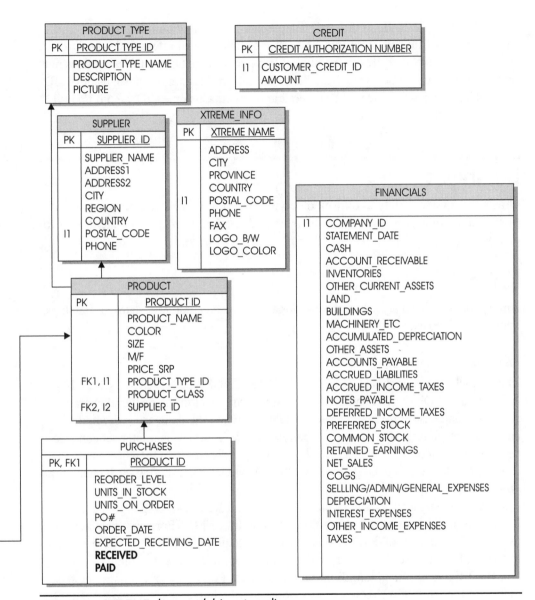

Figure 2-6   *XTREME data model* (continued)

tables. The Customer_ID in the Orders table is a foreign key pointing to the Customer_ID in the Customer table. Because of this defined referential integrity constraint, no Customer_ID can be entered into a row in the Orders table if it does not first exist in the Customer table. Note, however, that in this case, Orders.Customer_ID is nullable, so a null value could be entered into Orders.Customer_ID even if no null Customer.Customer_ID existed.

Datatypes

Oracle has a wide variety of built-in datatypes. Crystal Reports recognizes some of them and not others. In addition to the built-in datatypes, users may create their own datatypes.

Built-In

Among the built-in datatypes are the categories of character, numeric, dates, timestamps, intervals, and binary.

Character

The character types include CHAR, VARCHAR2, NCHAR, NVARCHAR2, CLOB, NCLOB, and LONG. All character types store string data in the declared character set for the database. The character set is declared when the database is created and can be a foreign language as well as the typical ASCII set. A character set can also be single byte or multibyte. The ASCII character set is single byte, where each character is defined by a single byte. Multibyte character sets define each character with multiple bytes.

All Oracle character datatypes map to the Crystal Reports String type. Crystal Reports seems to truncate all string fields at 64K for display. For some data access methods, CLOBs, NCLOBs, LONGs, NCHARs, and NVARCHAR2s cause errors in Crystal Reports. See Table 1-1, at the end of the first chapter, for details.

CHAR fields are fixed length up to 2,000 bytes. For single-byte character sets, that would mean 2,000 characters. If a double-byte character set was used, 1,000 characters would be the maximum. They are padded with trailing blanks up to the defined size of the field. However, Crystal Reports treats CHAR fields like any other String field and ignores the trailing blanks.

VARCHAR2 fields are variable length, where the maximum size is declared at creation. They can hold up to 4,000 bytes. The number of characters that can be stored is dependent on the character set, as with CHAR fields. Note that the VARCHAR datatype is still supported but not recommended for use.

NCHAR fields are fixed-length Unicode character fields. The size for NCHAR fields is declared in number of characters rather than number of bytes, but the maximum size is 2,000 bytes. Therefore, for a double-byte character set, the maximum length would be 1,000 characters.

NVARCHAR2 fields are similar to VARCHAR2 fields but are for Unicode characters. The size is declared in characters as with the NCHAR type, and the maximum size is 4,000 bytes.

LONG fields are similar to Access Memo fields, and they can hold up to 2GB of characters. The LONG datatype is being phased out and should not be used. Oracle allows only one LONG column per table.

CLOBs (Character Large Objects) are intended to replace the LONG type and can contain up to 4GB of characters. Multiple CLOB fields are allowed in a table.

NCLOBs are the Unicode version of CLOBs.

Numeric

The numeric category contains the types NUMBER and FLOAT.

NUMBER fields contain variable length signed values between 1.0×10^{-130} and $9.9...9 \times 10^{125}$ with 38 degrees of precision. A number field can be declared with a precision and a scale. The precision is the total number of digits, and the scale is the number of digits to the right of the decimal point. If no precision or scale is provided, the maximum is assumed.

FLOAT fields are a subtype of NUMBER. FLOAT fields contain floating-point values with up to 30 degrees of precision.

Dates

The date category contains only one type, DATE.

The Oracle DATE datatype contains both a date component and a time component. Oracle DATE fields will be mapped to Crystal Reports Date and Time fields. The range of dates that Oracle can store is from January 1, 4712 BCE through December 31, 4712 CE. The time component of an Oracle DATE field is stored in 24-hour format as HH:MM:SS. The time component cannot store fractions of seconds. Unless a time is specifically inserted, the time portion will be 00:00:00. Both Oracle and Crystal Reports interpret this empty time of 00:00:00 as 12:00:00 AM.

If most of your Oracle DATE fields do not contain a time component, it will save you formatting time if you set the default format for Crystal Reports Date and Time fields to exclude the time portion. Go to File | Options and choose the Fields tab as shown in Figure 2-7. Click the Date and Time button and choose the Date and Time tab.

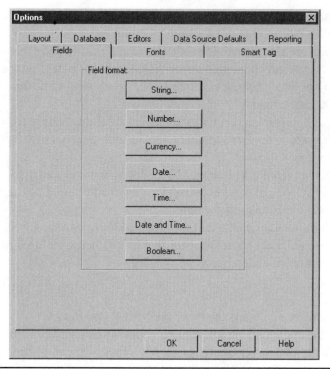

Figure 2-7   *Crystal field options*

Set the Style to a choice that excludes time components (see Figure 2-8) and click OK. Hereafter, your Oracle date fields will be displayed by default with no time component. If you need to display the time component for a particular Oracle date field, just format that individual field.

Timestamps

The timestamp category contains TIMESTAMP, TIMESTAMP WITH TIME ZONE, and TIMESTAMP WITH LOCAL TIME ZONE. TIMESTAMP fields contain a date and time, including fractional seconds. The precision of the fractional seconds can be declared between zero and nine, but defaults to six. TIMESTAMP WITH TIME ZONE fields are TIMESTAMP fields plus a time zone indicator. The time zone indicator can be either a region name or an offset from UTC (Universal Time Coordinate, or Greenwich Meantime). TIMESTAMP WITH LOCAL TIME ZONE fields are identical to TIMESTAMP WITH TIME ZONE fields except that the time zone is normalized

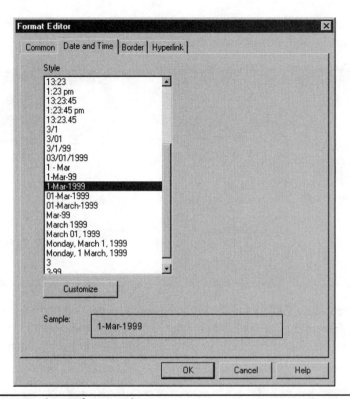

Figure 2-8   *Date and Time format editor*

to the database time zone when data is stored. When a field of type TIMESTAMP
WITH LOCAL TIME ZONE is queried, the value and time zone returned are adjusted
to the client's time zone.

NOTE

The timestamp datatypes are new to Oracle 9i.

None of the time zone datatypes is supported by any of the currently available
Crystal Reports access methods. The workarounds for accessing this type of Oracle
data from Crystal Reports involves converting these datatypes to the DATE datatype
or a string datatype. This can be done internally via a SQL Expression field. If you

only need to display the field values, you can use the TO_CHAR function. Create a new SQL Expression field and enter the formula shown here:

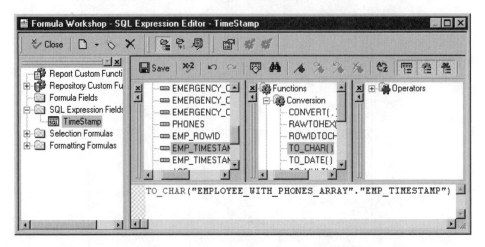

This will return a TIMESTAMP field formatted with the default timestamp format. In this case, something like 04-FEB-03 06.20.55.981000 PM will be returned. If you want to format the field differently, you can append a format string such as the one shown here:

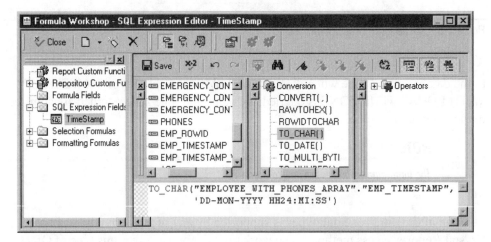

This will return something like 04-FEB-2003 18:20:55. See Oracle documentation for possible formatting strings.

If you need to use the timestamp as a date, you can create a SQL Expression like the one shown here:

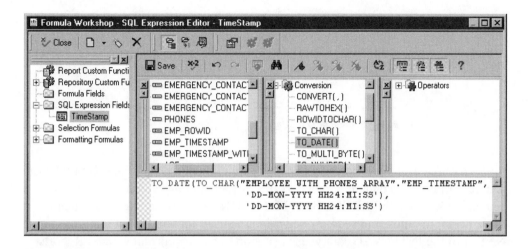

TIMESTAMP Conversion Function   If you need to report often on TIMESTAMP types, you should create a conversion function in Oracle. Because SQL Expressions cannot be stored in the Repository for reuse, creating an Oracle function will minimize the effort involved.

Here is the DDL for a timestamp to date conversion function:

```
CREATE OR REPLACE  FUNCTION "XTREME"."TIMESTAMP_TO_DATE"
      (TimestampVar IN TIMESTAMP)
  RETURN DATE AS
BEGIN
  RETURN TO_DATE(TO_CHAR(TimestampVar,'DD-MON-YYYY HH24:MI:SS'),
                                     'DD-MON-YYYY HH24:MI:SS');
END;
```

To use this function from Crystal Reports, you still must create a SQL Expression field as shown in the following illustration, but the complexity of the operation is hidden.

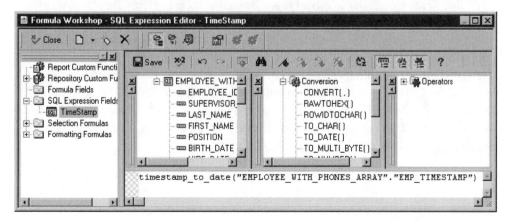

Intervals

The interval category contains the types INTERVAL YEAR TO MONTH and INTERVAL DAY TO SECOND.

NOTE

The interval datatypes are new to Oracle 9i.

INTERVAL datatypes represent periods of time. INTERVAL YEAR TO MONTH is used for intervals containing numbers of years and months and might be used for something like age. INTERVAL DAY TO SECOND is used for intervals containing days, hours, minutes, and seconds and might be used for something like runtime. Neither of the INTERVAL datatypes is supported by any current Crystal Reports access method. Workarounds involve converting the INTERVAL fields to NUMBER. The Oracle function EXTRACT can be used to pull out the individual year, month, day, hour, minutes, and seconds from the INTERVAL types. Here is a formula that will convert an INTERVAL YEAR TO MONTH to a NUMBER of months:

```
EXTRACT(YEAR FROM "EMPLOYEE_WITH_PHONES_ARRAY"." AGE")*12
+EXTRACT(MONTH FROM "EMPLOYEE_WITH_PHONES_ARRAY"."AGE");
```

Binary

The binary category contains the types BLOB, BFILE, RAW, LONG RAW, and ROWID.

BLOB fields contain unstructured binary data up to 4GB. They can be used to store graphics, video, and sound files. Some of the Crystal Reports access methods do not support BLOBs. BLOBs do not support some graphics formats. See Table 1-1 for details.

BFILE fields are similar to other binary fields, but their contents are stored outside the database in files and are read-only. The BFILE field contains a locator for the file.

RAW and LONG RAW types are being phased out by Oracle and should no longer be used.

ROWID fields are binary fields used for the storage of Oracle row addresses. Some of the Crystal Reports access methods do not support ROWIDs. See Table 1-1 for details. Oracle has built-in functions to convert ROWIDs to character if you need to report on ROWIDs and your access method will not allow it. The Oracle function ROWID_TO_CHAR can be used in a SQL Expression.

User-Defined

Oracle allows the creation of user-defined types. There are four kinds of user-defined types; object types, REFs, varrays, and nested tables.

Object types have a name and attributes and may have methods. The attributes of an object type can be Oracle built-in datatypes or other user-defined types. Object types are similar to object types in programming languages such as C. REFs are pointers to objects. Varrays and nested tables are collection types and are discussed in the "Collections" section later in this chapter. Any of these user-defined types can be used as column types in Oracle tables. However, object type columns cannot be used directly in Crystal Reports. An example of a workaround for simple object type columns follows. See the "Collections" section for workarounds for varrays and nested tables.

Though object types may contain other object types, here we will discuss a simple case where the object column is defined by a record type that in turn consists of two columns of Oracle built-in datatypes. The object type description for the phone_rec type follows:

```
SQL> DESC phone_rec
Name                                      Null?     Type
----------------------------------------- --------  ------------
PHONE_TYPE                                          VARCHAR2(20)
PHONE_NO                                            VARCHAR2(20)
```

The pertinent fields from the table using the phone_rec type are described next:

```
SQL> DESC employee_with_phones_array
Name                                      Null?     Type
----------------------------------------- --------  ------------
EMPLOYEE_ID                               NOT NULL  NUMBER(10)
....
PHONE_RECORD                                        PHONE_REC
```

To report on object columns like these using native Oracle SQL, the object field names are concatenated to the object column name, and a table alias is required. For example, the following command fails with an invalid identifier error:

```
SQL> SELECT employee_id, phone_record.phone_type,
  2          phone_record.phone_no
  3  FROM employee_with_phones_array;
SELECT employee_id, phone_record.phone_type, phone_record.phone_no
                    *
```

```
ERROR at line 1:
ORA-00904: "PHONE_RECORD"."PHONE_NO": invalid identifier
```

However, the following command succeeds:

```
SQL> SELECT e.employee_id, e.phone_record.phone_type,
  2   e.phone_record.phone_no
  3   FROM employee_with_phones_array e;

EMPLOYEE_ID PHONE_RECORD.PHONE_T PHONE_RECORD.PHONE_N
----------- -------------------- --------------------
          4 HOME                 (555)123-4567
          7 HOME                 (555)123-4567
         12 HOME                 (555)123-4567
```

To report from object types in Crystal Reports, you must use pass-through SQL. You can use a Crystal Reports SQL Command but, surprisingly, not a Crystal Reports SQL Expression. Of course, an Oracle view or stored procedure that pulls out the attributes of the object can also be used.

It is not clear why a SQL Expression field cannot be used for reporting on simple object columns. Crystal Reports always constructs its queries using table aliases where the table alias is the entire table name minus the schema name. Using the preceding example, if a SQL Expression field is created whose definition is "EMPLOYEE_WITH_PHONES_ARRAY"."PHONE_RECORD"."PHONE_NO", and that SQL Expression field is placed on the report along with the Employee_ID field, you would expect Crystal to generate a query such as the following:

```
SELECT "EMPLOYEE_WITH_PHONES_ARRAY"."EMPLOYEE_ID",
       "EMPLOYEE_WITH_PHONES_ARRAY"."PHONE_RECORD"."PHONE_NO"
  FROM "XTREME"."EMPLOYEE_WITH_PHONES_ARRAY"
           "EMPLOYEE_WITH_PHONES_ARRAY"
```

This query works when executed from SQL*Plus. However, attempting this in the report developer returns an invalid identifier error from the SQL Expression Editor. Therefore, you must use a SQL Command, Oracle view, or stored procedure.

An object table is a special kind of table defined completely by an object type. Two object tables have been added to the XTREME schema. The first is called Phone_Object_Table and is a table of the user-defined type Xtreme.Phone_Rec. This table can be reported on from Crystal Reports. It is a table of a simple object type and Oracle will automatically translate the fields in the object type into regular table fields for querying. The second object table is the Contact_Object_Table. It is defined by a more complex object type where one type is nested inside another. In this case, Crystal can directly access fields from the parent object type but not from the nested object type.

Collections

There are two types of collection objects in Oracle, varrays and nested tables. Both collection types can be used to define columns in Oracle tables.

Varrays

Varrays are one kind of user-defined collection type. Varray is short for variable array and is an ordered list of some variable type. The type can be a scalar type, such as number or varchar2, or a complex type, such as a record. Varrays differ from nested tables in several ways. Varrays have an inherent order and an upper limit put on their size, whereas nested tables are unordered and their size is not limited. They also differ in the manner in which they are stored in Oracle. However, from the report writer's perspective, they can be treated identically.

Varrays can appear as columns in tables, be returned from procedures, or used to create a more complex type. The table XTREME.EMPLOYEE_WITH_PHONES_ARRAY is a sample table containing a varray. It is not one of the original Crystal Decisions sample tables but one that has been created by duplicating the XTREME.EMPLOYEE table and moving the two phone numbers into an array. The Oracle types involved are shown next:

```
SQL> DESC xtreme.phone_array_type;
 xtreme.phone_array_type VARRAY(5) OF XTREME.PHONE_REC
 Name                            Null?    Type
 ------------------------------  -------- -----------------------
 PHONE_TYPE                               VARCHAR2(20)
 PHONE_NO                                 VARCHAR2(20)


SQL> DESC xtreme.employee_with_phones_array;
 Name                            Null?    Type
 ------------------------------  -------- -----------------------
 EMPLOYEE_ID                     NOT NULL NUMBER(10)
 SUPERVISOR_ID                            NUMBER(10)
 LAST_NAME                       NOT NULL VARCHAR2(20)
 FIRST_NAME                      NOT NULL VARCHAR2(10)
 POSITION                                 VARCHAR2(30)
 BIRTH_DATE                               DATE
 HIRE_DATE                                DATE
 EXTENSION                                VARCHAR2(4)
 PHOTO                                    BLOB
 NOTES                                    CLOB
 REPORTS_TO                               NUMBER(10)
 SALARY                                   NUMBER(19,4)
 SSN                                      VARCHAR2(12)
```

```
EMERGENCY_CONTACT_FIRST_NAME           VARCHAR2(20)
EMERGENCY_CONTACT_LAST_NAME            VARCHAR2(20)
EMERGENCY_CONTACT_RELATIONSHIP         VARCHAR2(20)
PHONES                                 XTREME.PHONE_ARRAY_TYPE
```

Attempting to report on a varray field directly from Crystal Reports fails for every connection type. If the varray is listed as a normal field in a select query executed from an Oracle tool, Oracle returns the contents of the varray in a single formatted field as shown in this SQL*Plus query. The field wraps to two lines, but it is just one field.

```
SQL> SELECT employee_id, phones
  2  FROM xtreme.employee_with_phones_array;


EMPLOYEE_ID
-----------
PHONES(PHONE_TYPE, PHONE_NO)
------------------------------------------------------------
          1
PHONE_ARRAY_TYPE(PHONE_REC('Home', '(206)555-9857'),
 PHONE_REC('Emergency', '2065555321'))

          2
PHONE_ARRAY_TYPE(PHONE_REC('Home', '(206)555-9482'),
 PHONE_REC('Emergency', '2065553656'))
```

The phone field is returned as a LOB. This causes an inconsistent datatypes error when used in Crystal Reports.

Oracle SQL has the capability to unnest the varray, so reporting workarounds will need to use pass-through SQL, as in a Crystal Reports SQL Command object, an Oracle view, or an Oracle stored procedure. The Oracle TABLE command must be used, and the result is as if the varray were a child table joined to the parent table, returning a row for every element of each original row's varray, as shown next. The number of elements in the varray can differ from row to row.

```
SQL> SELECT employee_id, p.*
  2  FROM xtreme.employee_with_phones_array e,
  3        table(e.phones) p;

EMPLOYEE_ID PHONE_TYPE           PHONE_NO
----------- -------------------- --------------------
          1 Home                 (206)555-9857
          1 Emergency            2065555321
          2 Home                 (206)555-9482
          2 Emergency            2065553656
```

The Crystal Reports example solution is a very simple report of employee phone numbers. The main report uses XTREME.EMPLOYEE_WITH_PHONES_ARRAY and shows only the first and last names of the employees. To get the phone numbers for each employee, you create a subreport. In the subreport, you use a SQL Command defined as shown here:

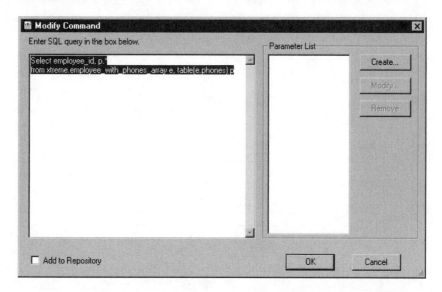

Linking the subreport to the main report on employee_id will then result in the report shown in Figure 2-9.

This report is saved as Chapter 2\Varray Example Report.rpt in the download file. This workaround is usable for all connections types.

Attempts to link the SQL Command directly into the main report will result in an error. If you need to do this, the solution is to create an Oracle view containing the same query as the SQL Command and then use that to link to the main table in the main report. This works for all connection types.

Nested Tables

Nested tables can be treated the same as varrays for reporting purposes. You must use the TABLE command to unnest the table.

NOTE
Varrays and nested tables can be multidimensional in Oracle 9i. For example, you can create a varray of a varray type.

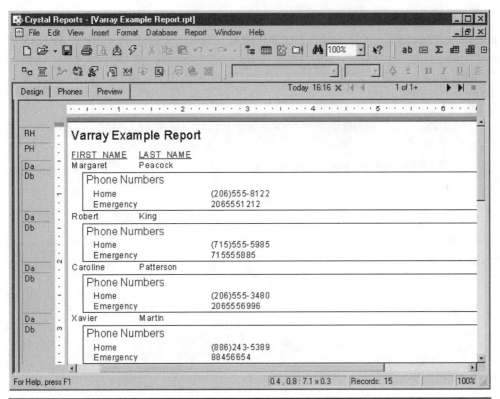

Figure 2-9 *Varray example report*

Nulls

The Oracle null value is an important concept for report writers to understand. A null indicates the lack of a value. Any column of any datatype may contain nulls if the NOT NULL constraint has not been implemented for that column. Null is not equivalent to zero nor to an empty string. In addition, while Oracle currently treats a zero-length string as equivalent to a null, that may not continue in the future.

Any null appearing in an expression, except concatenation, will cause that expression to return null. All Oracle built-in scalar functions will return null if one of their arguments is null except NVL, REPLACE, and CONCAT. Most Oracle built-in aggregate functions ignore nulls. This may or may not be the behavior you desire. For example, if you use the AVERAGE function on ten values where two of those values are null, the numerator will be the sum of the eight non-null values and the denominator will be eight, not ten. If you need to treat the null values as zero for aggregation purposes, use the NVL function to convert nulls to zero before applying the aggregation function.

You must also be cautious when doing comparisons involving columns that may contain null values. Comparing a null value to anything (even another null value) will return UNKNOWN. If you do such a comparison in a WHERE clause, no records will be returned when the condition evaluates to UNKNOWN, but there will be no indication that it is because of nulls or that the condition returns no rows. You should always use the NVL function on any columns that might contain nulls in comparison operations.

The IS NULL condition can be used in the WHERE clause to filter rows out of result sets where a specific column, or an expression, is null. If you want to specifically check for and filter null values, use IS NULL. If you want to compare two fields where one or both of them may contain null values, use NVL. IS NOT NULL is the negation of IS NULL.

Linking on Nulls

Understand the fields that you use for linking in Crystal Reports. If you link from a child table column that allows nulls, unless there is a null value in the corresponding parent table column, none of the rows with null foreign key values will be in the result set.

Data Dictionary Views

Oracle maintains certain system tables and views that describe the database itself. The tables are not directly accessible, but the system creates views that users can query to explore the database structure. These views are the data dictionary views. They are sometimes called "System" tables or "Catalog" tables. For the report writer, these views are a vital source of information about existing tables, views, columns, and referential integrity constraints.

Data dictionary views are customized for three user types. The views prefixed with USER_ show all objects in the logged in user's schema. The views prefixed with ALL_ show all objects that the logged in user has access to. The ALL_ views will show all objects in the logged-in user's schema as well as any other for which objects the user has been granted privileges. The DBA_ views show all objects in the database, but a user must have the SELECT_ANY_TABLE privilege or the SELECT_CATALOG_ROLE role to select from the DBA_ views.

Table 2-1 lists a subset of the available data dictionary views along with a short description of the view content. The ALL_ views are shown, but DBA_ or USER_ can be substituted if desired. Consider that "for all objects that the user has privileges to" is appended to each description. For a full listing of the data dictionary views and an expanded description, see Oracle documentation.

Table Name	Description
ALL_ALL_TABLES	Lists table level information for all object and relational tables
ALL_ARGUMENTS	Describes the arguments of procedures and functions
ALL_CATALOG	Lists all indexes, tables, clusters, views, synonyms, and sequences
ALL_COL_COMMENTS	Shows the comments on table and view columns
ALL_COL_PRIVS	Shows the privileges on columns where the current user is the owner, grantor, or grantee, including columns in objects owned by PUBLIC
ALL_COL_PRIVS_MADE	Shows the privileges on columns where the current user is the owner or grantor
ALL_COL_PRIVS_RECD	Shows the privileges on columns where the current user or PUBLIC is the grantee
ALL_COLL_TYPES	Describes all varrays and nested tables
ALL_CONS_COLUMNS	Shows all columns used in constraints
ALL_CONS_OBJ_COLUMNS	Shows all object columns used in constraints
ALL_CONSTRAINTS	Describes constraint definitions
ALL_DB_LINKS	Shows all DB links
ALL_DEPENDENCIES	Shows all object dependencies
ALL_DIMENSIONS	Lists all dimension objects
ALL_DIRECTORIES	Lists all directories
ALL_EXTERNAL_LOCATIONS	Describes the locations of external tables
ALL_EXTERNAL_TABLES	Lists all external tables
ALL_IND_COLUMNS	Lists all columns in indexes
ALL_IND_EXPRESSIONS	Lists all function-based index expressions
ALL_INDEXES	Lists all indexes
ALL_JOIN_IND_COLUMNS	Shows the join conditions of bitmap join indexes
ALL_MVIEWS	Lists all materialized views
ALL_NESTED_TABLES	Lists all nested tables
ALL_OBJ_COLATTRS	Shows all object columns and attributes

Table 2-1   *Description of Selected Data Dictionary Views*

Table Name	Description
ALL_OBJECT_TABLES	Lists all object tables
ALL_OBJECTS	Lists all database objects
ALL_PROCEDURES	Lists all procedures
ALL_SEQUENCES	Lists all sequences
ALL_SOURCE	Shows the source text for all objects
ALL_SYNONYMS	Lists all synonyms
ALL_TAB_COLUMNS	Describes the columns of all tables, views, and clusters
ALL_TAB_COMMENTS	Shows the comments on all tables and views
ALL_TAB_PRIVS	Lists the grants on objects where the user or PUBLIC is the grantee
ALL_TAB_PRIVS_MADE	Lists the object grants made by the current user or made on objects the current user owns
ALL_TAB_PRIVS_RECD	Lists the object grants where the user is the grantee
ALL_TABLES	Lists all relational tables
ALL_TRIGGER_COLS	Describes the use of columns in triggers
ALL_TRIGGERS	Lists all triggers owned by the user or on objects owned by the user
ALL_TYPES	Lists all object types
ALL_USERS	Lists all user IDs
ALL_VARRAYS	Lists all varrays
ALL_VIEWS	Lists all views

Table 2-1   *Description of Selected Data Dictionary Views* (continued)

This chapter presented a high-level overview of Oracle structures and described how they are seen or used in Crystal Reports. The next chapter will cover basic Oracle SELECT statements.

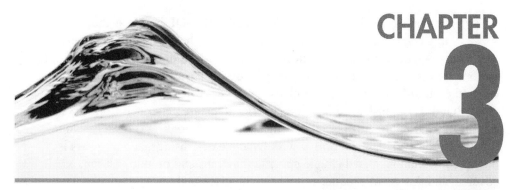

CHAPTER
3

Oracle SQL

he purpose of this chapter is to cover Oracle SQL basics as they relate
to Crystal Reports. A generic knowledge of the SQL SELECT statement
is assumed and only Oracle-specific, new to 9*i*, or otherwise uncommon
options are discussed in any detail. New join options available in Oracle 9*i* are also
covered. The SELECT list, FROM clause, WHERE clause, ORDER BY clause,
and GROUP BY clause are explained, and how they are generated from Crystal
Reports is shown. Oracle operators, comparison conditions, and aggregation
functions are covered, and working with Oracle dates, strings, and numbers is
described. Commonly used Oracle-specific functions and pseudo columns are
covered, and the use of subqueries will also be discussed.

Basic SELECT Statement

The basic SELECT statement can take one of the following two forms. Refer to
Oracle documentation for a full list of possible clauses and options. Various clauses
of the SELECT statement are discussed in more detail in following sections.

The first form uses the WHERE clause to create the table joins:

```
SELECT [list of columns or expressions separated by commas]
  FROM [list of tables separated by commas]
 WHERE [join conditions and filtering conditions]
 GROUP BY [optional list of columns to group by]
 ORDER BY [optional list of columns to order by]
HAVING [optional group filtering conditions]
```

The second form uses the new Oracle 9*i* join syntax:

NOTE

The second form is not available in Oracle 8i or previous versions.

```
SELECT [list of columns or expressions separated by commas]
  FROM [tables with join expressions]
 WHERE [filtering conditions]
 GROUP BY [optional list of columns to group by]
 ORDER BY [optional list of columns to order by]
HAVING [optional group filtering conditions]
```

Aliases can be created for columns, expressions, or tables simply by inserting the desired alias immediately following the column name, expression, or table name. The keyword AS may be used for clarity preceding the alias. Column or expression aliases are returned as the column name and table aliases are used as shortcuts for the full schema qualified table name, within the query for linking, or when it is otherwise necessary to distinguish which table a field belongs to.

It is rare for Oracle table, view, or column names to be defined with mixed-case characters. They are usually defined in uppercase only. If the objects are defined in Oracle using uppercase, they can be listed in the query in upper, lower, or mixed case and the query will succeed. If an object name is defined with mixed case in Oracle, then the object name must be enclosed in double quotes in the SELECT statement; otherwise, Oracle will return an error saying that the object cannot be found.

The keyword DISTINCT can be added before the SELECT list to return only one row if there are multiple rows with the same column values. The DISTINCT keyword applies to the entire SELECT list and can cause increases in processing time due to the comparing and filtering that must be done. Avoid using DISTINCT if it is not required.

Except for omission of the HAVING clause, Crystal Reports constructs SELECT statements of the first form when you use the Crystal experts to create a report. Crystal always creates aliases for tables where the alias is the table name without the schema name and will always prefix column names with the alias it defined for the table. Crystal also always encloses object names with double quotes. If you want to return distinct records, choose the Database menu item and then the Select Distinct Records option, and DISTINCT will be added to the query.

SELECT List

The SELECT list is simply a list of columns or expressions that the user wishes to return. Columns are specified by using the column name as defined in the table. A table and/or schema qualifier or alias should be added to the column name with dot notation if it is needed to distinguish the correct column from other like-named columns from other tables in the query. Expressions are valid computations resulting in a single value. Expressions can be single row or summary level if the corresponding GROUP BY clause is included and can include functions, but not procedures. An expression can even be an entire SELECT statement as long as it returns only one value.

The asterisk can be used as a shorthand symbol that means all columns. For example, if you have a command like the following, all columns from the Employee table will be selected.

```
SELECT * FROM Employee
```

The asterisk can be prefixed with a table name or table alias to indicate all columns from a particular table.

```
SELECT Product.*, d.Order_ID
  FROM Product JOIN Orders_Detail d
      ON (Product.Product_Id=d.Product_Id)
```

FROM Clause

The tables listed in the FROM clause can be database tables or views or entire SELECT statements. If a SELECT statement is used it is called an in-line view.

Join Types

One of the most basic and valuable features of a relational database is the ability to join two tables together. Crystal Reports uses the Links tab of the Database Expert to enable the user to establish links via a GUI interface. In a simple linking example such as that shown in Figure 3-1, Crystal will generate an equal inner join.

The join that Crystal generates can be seen by selecting the Database menu item, then the Show SQL Query option. The SQL is shown here:

```
Show SQL Query                                              [X]

SELECT "EMPLOYEE"."EMPLOYEE_ID", "EMPLOYEE"."SUPERVISOR_ID",
"EMPLOYEE"."LAST_NAME", "EMPLOYEE"."FIRST_NAME",
"EMPLOYEE_ADDRESSES"."ADDRESS1", "EMPLOYEE_ADDRESSES"."CITY",
"EMPLOYEE_ADDRESSES"."COUNTRY", "EMPLOYEE_ADDRESSES"."POSTAL_CODE"
FROM  "XTREME"."EMPLOYEE" "EMPLOYEE", "XTREME"."EMPLOYEE_ADDRESSES"
"EMPLOYEE_ADDRESSES"
WHERE ("EMPLOYEE"."EMPLOYEE_ID"="EMPLOYEE_ADDRESSES"."EMPLOYEE_ID")

                                                          OK
```

It is the (`"EMPLOYEE"."EMPLOYEE_ID"` = `"EMPLOYEE_ADDRESSES"`
. `"EMPLOYEE_ID"`) part that implements the join.

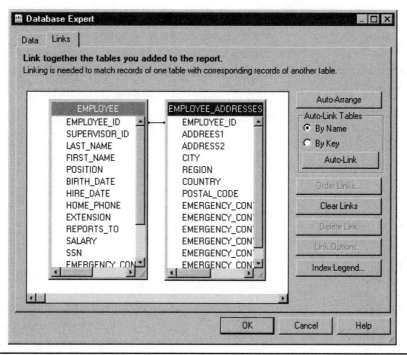

Figure 3-1   *Database Expert simple join*

Joins have several possible types. A join might be an inner join, a left outer join, a right outer join, or a full outer join. The link type might be equal, greater than, greater than or equal, less than, less than or equal, or not equal. The most common joins are equal inner joins and equal left outer joins. In an equal inner join, records from each table are returned if the values in the join columns are equal. Any records from either table that do not have exact matches in the other table are ignored. In an equal left outer join, all records from the left-hand table are returned and any records from the right-hand table whose join columns match are merged into the matching row. For left-hand rows with no match, null column values are appended to the row. Equal right outer joins are identical to equal left outer joins except that all rows from the right-hand table are returned and matching left-hand table rows are merged. In equal full outer joins, rows with identical values in the join columns from each table are merged, rows from either table that did not have matches are also returned, and the missing columns are populated with null values. It is common to assume an equal join and omit the word equal when describing joins.

Nonequal joins are similar to equal joins except that more than one row from the left-hand table may be joined to more than one row from the right-hand table. For example, say that you want to know, for Product_ID 4103 for the month of May for each ship_date the quantity to ship on that date and the total quantity shipped up to and including that date. You need to display the sum of the quantity shipped on that date, which is straightforward, but you also need to sum the quantities shipped before that date. Breaking down the process, first you need the quantities by date for the product for May:

```
SQL> SELECT ship_date, SUM(quantity) quantity
  2    FROM Orders JOIN Orders_Detail USING (Order_Id)
  3   WHERE product_id=4103
  4     AND ship_date BETWEEN TO_DATE('01-MAY-02','DD-MON-YY')
  5                       AND TO_DATE('31-MAY-02','DD-MON-YY')
  6   GROUP BY ship_date;


SHIP_DATE   QUANTITY
---------  ----------
02-MAY-02          2
04-MAY-02          5
09-MAY-02          3
```

Then you need to join each record to every record that shipped earlier or on the same date:

```
SQL> SELECT a.ship_date, a.quantity, b.ship_date, b.quantity
  2  FROM (SELECT ship_date, SUM(quantity) quantity
  3          FROM Orders JOIN Orders_Detail USING (Order_Id)
  4         WHERE product_id=4103
  5           AND ship_date BETWEEN TO_DATE('01-MAY-02','DD-MON-YY')
  6                             AND TO_DATE('31-MAY-02','DD-MON-YY')
  7         GROUP BY ship_date) a,
  8       (SELECT ship_date, SUM(quantity) quantity
  9         FROM Orders JOIN Orders_Detail USING (Order_Id)
 10        WHERE product_id=4103
 11          AND ship_date BETWEEN TO_DATE('01-MAY-02','DD-MON-YY')
 12                            AND TO_DATE('31-MAY-02','DD-MON-YY')
 13        GROUP BY ship_date) b
 14 WHERE a.ship_date >= b.ship_date;


SHIP_DATE   QUANTITY SHIP_DATE   QUANTITY
---------  ---------- ---------  ----------
09-MAY-02          3 09-MAY-02          3
09-MAY-02          3 04-MAY-02          5
09-MAY-02          3 02-MAY-02          2
04-MAY-02          5 04-MAY-02          5
```

```
04-MAY-02              5 02-MAY-02              2
02-MAY-02              2 02-MAY-02              2
```

This result shows the May 9 record joined to the May 2, May 4, and May 9 records, the May 4 record joined to the May 2 and May 4 records, and the May 2 record joined to itself.

Finally, you need to sum the "b" values to get the month to date quantities:

```
SQL> SELECT a.ship_date, MIN(a.quantity) "Shipped on Ship Date",
  2          SUM(b.quantity) "Shipped up to Ship Date"
  3  FROM (SELECT ship_date, SUM(quantity) quantity
  4        FROM Orders JOIN Orders_Detail USING (Order_Id)
  5        WHERE product_id=4103
  6          AND ship_date BETWEEN TO_DATE('01-MAY-02','DD-MON-YY')
  7                            AND TO_DATE('31-MAY-02','DD-MON-YY')
  8        GROUP BY ship_date) a,
  9       (SELECT ship_date, SUM(quantity) quantity
 10        FROM Orders JOIN Orders_Detail USING (Order_Id)
 11        WHERE product_id=4103
 12          AND ship_date BETWEEN TO_DATE('01-MAY-02','DD-MON-YY')
 13                            AND TO_DATE('31-MAY-02','DD-MON-YY')
 14        GROUP BY ship_date) b
 15  WHERE a.ship_date>=b.ship_date
 16  GROUP BY a.ship_date
 17  ORDER BY a.ship_date;

SHIP_DATE Shipped on Ship Date Shipped up to Ship Date
--------- -------------------- -----------------------
02-MAY-02                    2                       2
04-MAY-02                    5                       7
09-MAY-02                    3                      10
```

Note that this result can be obtained in a simpler manner by using the Oracle SQL for Analysis functions. See the "Analysis" section in Chapter 4 for more details.

Pre-Oracle 9*i* Joining

Prior to Oracle version 9*i*, all linking was done in the WHERE clause. A clause would be written in the form `Table1.LinkField [operator] Table2.LinkField`, where the operator could be =, <=, <, >, >=, <>, !=, and so on. To accomplish a left outer or right outer join, the (+) symbol was added to the appropriate side of the condition. A full outer join could not be done without using a UNION operation.

In Crystal Reports, to change the link type, go to the Database Expert, Links tab, select the link and click Link Options, or right-click the link and select Link Options. The Link Options dialog will be displayed, as shown here:

The next illustration shows the SQL for a left outer join using pre-9*i* syntax as it is generated in Crystal Reports.

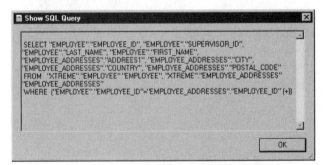

The next illustration shows a right outer join using pre-9*i* syntax as it is generated in Crystal Reports.

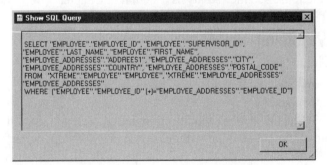

Choosing Full Outer Join with an Oracle 9*i* database results in the error shown here:

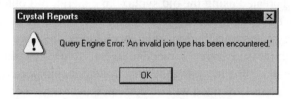

The Full Outer Join radio button is available when using the native driver even though choosing it causes an error. It is not available with the ODBC drivers or the OLE DB drivers.

Link types can be changed from the Link Options dialog as well. The less than, greater than, not equal, and so on, types work as expected. Join types other than equal are rarely used, but they can be the proper answer for some problems, as shown in the preceding example. Note that nonequal joins are not the same as one-to-many joins, as a one-to-many join only joins if the condition field is equal in both tables. The following illustration shows a not equal join.

In this case, each Employee record would be joined to each Employee_Addresses record where Employee.Employee_ID is not equal to Employee_Addresses .Employee_ID. This is not a sensible join.

9*i* Joining

Oracle 9*i* implements SQL 1999 compliant join operations. You can use this new join terminology in Crystal Reports SQL Commands, Oracle views, and Oracle Stored Procedures, but the Crystal Report designer still uses Oracle 8 syntax.

The execution plan that is generated using the new join syntax may differ from the plan that would be created using the old syntax. In general, full outer joins appear to be optimized with the new syntax, right and left outer joins seem to be equivalent, and inner joins may sometimes be less efficient. If large tables are being joined, a comparison of both methods is recommended to determine the optimal execution plan. Since Oracle recommends using the new syntax, it is expected that any deficiencies in the plans generated will be corrected over time. For now, it may be possible to use optimizer hints to cause the plan created by the new syntax to match the plan created by the old syntax.

Cross Join

A cross join produces a Cartesian product of the tables if no conditions are added to the WHERE clause:

```
SELECT "EMPLOYEE"."EMPLOYEE_ID", "EMPLOYEE"."FIRST_NAME",
       "EMPLOYEE"."LAST_NAME", "EMPLOYEE_ADDRESSES"."CITY",
       "EMPLOYEE_ADDRESSES"."COUNTRY"
  FROM "XTREME"."EMPLOYEE" "EMPLOYEE"
       CROSS JOIN
       "XTREME"."EMPLOYEE_ADDRESSES" "EMPLOYEE_ADDRESSES"
```

This statement results in every row from Employees being joined to every row in Employee_Addresses. Cross joins are rarely useful and are usually the result of forgetting to add the join criteria to the statement.

Natural Join

A natural join automatically joins the two tables on all fields with the same name and type:

```
SELECT "EMPLOYEE_ID", "EMPLOYEE"."FIRST_NAME",
       "EMPLOYEE"."LAST_NAME", "EMPLOYEE_ADDRESSES"."CITY",
       "EMPLOYEE_ADDRESSES"."COUNTRY"
  FROM "XTREME"."EMPLOYEE" "EMPLOYEE"
       NATURAL JOIN
       "XTREME"."EMPLOYEE_ADDRESSES" "EMPLOYEE_ADDRESSES"
```

This statement will join Employee to Employee_Addresses on the Employee_ID field from each table using an equal inner join, since that is the only column in both tables of the same name.

Note that for a natural join or a JOIN USING, you cannot use a schema name in the SELECT list for the join field. Here you can use just "EMPLOYEE_ID" with no schema qualifier.

JOIN USING

The JOIN USING syntax lets you pick which columns to use to implement the join. The columns must have the same name, as in a natural join, but you can list only those fields that you want to join on and exclude any other fields that might be named the same. A JOIN USING clause results in an equal inner join:

```
SELECT "EMPLOYEE_ID", "EMPLOYEE"."FIRST_NAME",
       "EMPLOYEE"."LAST_NAME", "EMPLOYEE_ADDRESSES"."CITY",
       "EMPLOYEE_ADDRESSES"."COUNTRY"
  FROM "XTREME"."EMPLOYEE" "EMPLOYEE"
       JOIN
       "XTREME"."EMPLOYEE_ADDRESSES" "EMPLOYEE_ADDRESSES"
       USING ("EMPLOYEE_ID")
```

JOIN ON

The JOIN ON syntax allows you to specify join fields from the two tables where the column names may not match:

```
SELECT "EMPLOYEE"."EMPLOYEE_ID", "EMPLOYEE"."FIRST_NAME",
       "EMPLOYEE"."LAST_NAME", "EMPLOYEE_ADDRESSES"."CITY",
       "EMPLOYEE_ADDRESSES"."COUNTRY"
  FROM "XTREME"."EMPLOYEE" "EMPLOYEE"
       JOIN
       "XTREME"."EMPLOYEE_ADDRESSES" "EMPLOYEE_ADDRESSES"
       ON ("EMPLOYEE"."EMPLOYEE_ID"=
           "EMPLOYEE_ADDRESSES"."EMPLOYEE_ID")
```

In this case, you must qualify the joined field name with a table name or alias when using it in the SELECT list. You can include anything in the ON clause that you would have previously used in a WHERE clause. However, it is beneficial to keep filtering clauses in the WHERE clause and joining clauses in the ON clause for clarity.

OUTER

OUTER JOINS can be specified in Oracle 9*i* using the OUTER keyword. You no longer need to use the (+) operator:

```
SELECT "EMPLOYEE"."EMPLOYEE_ID", "EMPLOYEE"."FIRST_NAME",
       "EMPLOYEE"."LAST_NAME", "EMPLOYEE_ADDRESSES"."CITY",
       "EMPLOYEE_ADDRESSES"."COUNTRY"
  FROM "XTREME"."EMPLOYEE" "EMPLOYEE"
       LEFT OUTER JOIN
       "XTREME"."EMPLOYEE_ADDRESSES" "EMPLOYEE_ADDRESSES"
       ON ("EMPLOYEE"."EMPLOYEE_ID"=
           "EMPLOYEE_ADDRESSES"."EMPLOYEE_ID")
```

The preceding statement results in a left outer join. The OUTER keyword can be omitted if desired.

```
SELECT "EMPLOYEE"."EMPLOYEE_ID", "EMPLOYEE"."FIRST_NAME",
       "EMPLOYEE"."LAST_NAME", "EMPLOYEE_ADDRESSES"."CITY",
       "EMPLOYEE_ADDRESSES"."COUNTRY"
  FROM "XTREME"."EMPLOYEE" "EMPLOYEE"
       RIGHT OUTER JOIN
       "XTREME"."EMPLOYEE_ADDRESSES" "EMPLOYEE_ADDRESSES"
       ON ("EMPLOYEE"."EMPLOYEE_ID"=
           "EMPLOYEE_ADDRESSES"."EMPLOYEE_ID")
```

The preceding statement results in a right outer join.

```
SELECT "EMPLOYEE"."EMPLOYEE_ID", "EMPLOYEE"."FIRST_NAME",
       "EMPLOYEE"."LAST_NAME", "EMPLOYEE_ADDRESSES"."CITY",
       "EMPLOYEE_ADDRESSES"."COUNTRY"
  FROM "XTREME"."EMPLOYEE" "EMPLOYEE"
       FULL OUTER JOIN
       "XTREME"."EMPLOYEE_ADDRESSES" "EMPLOYEE_ADDRESSES"
       ON ("EMPLOYEE"."EMPLOYEE_ID"=
           "EMPLOYEE_ADDRESSES"."EMPLOYEE_ID")
```

The preceding statement results in a full outer join. Full outer joins were not possible prior to Oracle 9*i* without using a UNION operation.

Filtering

Restricting the records returned based on some selection criteria is done in the WHERE clause. The Crystal Reports Select Expert translates the user's choices into expressions in the WHERE clause. For complex filtering, the selection formula can be modified manually.

Ordering

Ordering the records returned is implemented using the ORDER BY clause. Each field is sorted in the order specified (by default, the sort order is ascending, but a descending sort order can be specified).

Crystal Reports will generate the ORDER BY clause depending on any existing group's Insert Group Options and the Record Sort Order options, as shown in Figure 3-2 and Figure 3-3. However, choosing the group option to sort in original order will have no impact because Oracle will sort the GROUP BY fields in ascending order by default. If the Sort In Specified Order is selected, then the sort cannot be done on the server and will be done locally.

Grouping

Grouping is accomplished using the GROUP BY clause, which also performs a sort on the grouped fields. You must use a GROUP BY clause if you wish to use any aggregation functions such as SUM. Adding a group in Crystal Reports will not necessarily add a GROUP BY clause to the SQL query. An Oracle SELECT statement containing a GROUP BY clause will return data only at the grouped level; it will not return any detail rows. If a Crystal Report has a group and the detail rows are suppressed, Crystal will add a GROUP BY clause to the SQL query. If multiple

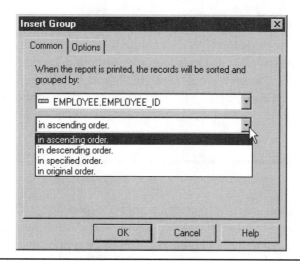

Figure 3-2   *Insert Group Common Options*

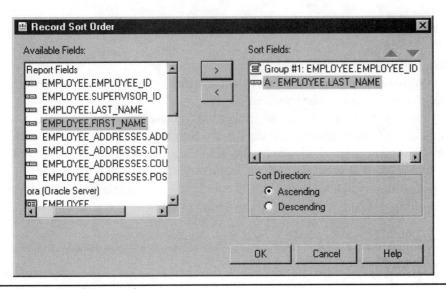

Figure 3-3   *Record Sort Order*

groups exist and detail rows are suppressed, Crystal will add a GROUP BY clause for the innermost not suppressed group.

Group Filtering

Oracle SQL supports using the HAVING clause to specify filtering at the group level. The HAVING clause is discussed in more detail in Chapter 4. Crystal Reports allows group selection formulas, but these are not translated into the SQL query and passed to the server. Group filtering that is done with Crystal options will be done locally.

Operators

Oracle SQL operators are used to create complex expressions. The available arithmetic operators are + (addition), – (subtraction), * (multiplication), and / (division). The concatenation operator is ||. Crystal Reports shows the Oracle operators in the SQL Expression Editor in the Operators box, as shown here:

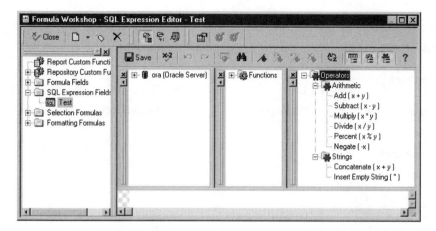

There are some errors in the Crystal listing. The % operator is shown, but it is not a valid Oracle operator and any SQL Command containing it will fail. Also, the + is shown as the concatenation operator, but it will only work for numeric addition, not for string concatenation; you must use the double pipes (||) for concatenation. The * is listed as the multiplication operator. This is not correct, but Crystal converts it to × in the SQL query, so it is not a problem.

Oracle Comparison Conditions

Comparison conditions are used in the WHERE clause or HAVING clause to compare one expression to another. In addition to the usual =, <>, <, >, <=, >=, you can also use IS NULL, IS NOT NULL, LIKE, BETWEEN, NOT BETWEEN, IN, NOT IN, and EXISTS. Comparison conditions can be joined with AND or OR and negated with NOT.

Table 3-1 shows how the Crystal condition is translated into an Oracle WHERE clause when using the Crystal Reports Select Expert to create selection formulas. The strings used in the LIKE and NOT LIKE conditions can contain the Crystal wildcard characters ? and *, which are translated to the corresponding Oracle wildcard characters _ and %.

To use Oracle's IN, BETWEEN, or EXISTS comparison conditions in the WHERE clause, you must use a SQL Command, view, or stored procedure.

Aggregation

If a GROUP BY clause is specified in the query, then aggregation functions can be used. Table 3-2 shows Crystal's summary functions and how they are translated into

Select Expert Wording	Select Formula	Crystal Generated WHERE Clause
Is equal to	=	=
Is not equal to	<>	<>
Is one of	In [ ]	Series of (field=value1 or field=value2 or …)
Is not one of	Not (field in [ ])	Series of Not (field=value1 or field=value2 or …)
Is less than	<	<
Is less than or equal to	<=	<=
Is greater than	>	>
Is greater than or equal to	>=	>=
Is between	Field in value1 to value2	(field>=value1 and field<=value2)
Is not between	Not (field in value1 to value2)	NOT (field>=value1 and field<=value2)
Starts with	Field starts with string	Field like string%
Does not start with	NOT (Field starts with string)	Field not like string%
Is like	Field like string	Field like string
Is not like	NOT (field like string)	Field not like string
Is null	IsNull()	Field IS NULL
Is not null	Not IsNull()	Field IS NOT NULL

Table 3-1   *Comparison Conditions*

the database query. It also shows an alternative Oracle aggregation function that can be used in pass-through SQL.

The Crystal SQL column assumes that lower-level detail is suppressed or hidden and that grouping on the server is turned on. Otherwise, Crystal will not do any aggregation in the SQL query. If this column contains "Local", it means that the aggregation is done locally and not pushed to the server. The Oracle Aggregation column displays an Oracle function that could be used in a SQL Command, view, or stored procedure, which is equivalent to the Crystal summary function. See Chapter 6 for detailed examples of Oracle substitutes for the Crystal summary functions.

NOTE

The percentile functions are new to Oracle 9i.

In cases where the Crystal summary would be evaluated locally, performance gains can be made by substituting an Oracle function.

Crystal Summary	Available for Field Type			Crystal SQL	Oracle Aggregation
	Character	**Numeric**	**Date**		
Sum	No	Yes	No	SUM	SUM
Average	No	Yes	No	Local	AVG
Sample Variance	No	Yes	No	Local	VAR_SAMP
Sample Standard Deviation	No	Yes	No	Local	STDDEV_SAMP
Maximum	Yes	Yes	Yes	MAX	MAX
Minimum	Yes	Yes	Yes	MIN	MIN
Count	Yes	Yes	Yes	COUNT	COUNT
Distinct Count	Yes	Yes	Yes	Local	COUNT(DISTINCT())
Correlation with	No	Yes	No	Local	CORR
Covariance with	No	Yes	No	Local	COVAR_SAMP
Median	No	Yes	No	Local	PERCENTILE_CONT(0.5) PERCENTILE_DISC (0.5)
Mode	Yes	Yes	Yes	Local	See Chapter 6
Nth largest	Yes	Yes	Yes	Local	See Chapter 6
Nth smallest	Yes	Yes	Yes	Local	See Chapter 6
Nth most frequent	Yes	Yes	Yes	Local	See Chapter 6
Pth percentile	No	Yes	No	Local	PERCENT_RANK
Population Variance	No	Yes	No	Local	VAR_POP
Population Standard Deviation	No	Yes	No	Local	STDDEV_POP
Weighted Average With	No	Yes	No	Local	See Chapter 6

Table 3-2   *Summary Functions*

Other available Oracle 8*i* functions include CUME_DIST, DENSE_RANK, FIRST_VALUE, LAG, LAST_VALUE, LEAD, NTILE, RANK, RATIO_TO_REPORT, and linear regression functions. FIRST and LAST are additional functions available in Oracle 9*i*.

Working with Dates

As discussed in Chapter 2, Oracle has one datatype called DATE, which includes the date and the time down to the second. Oracle SQL accepts date literals in expressions as well as numerous date functions. A date literal is a string representation of a date, such as '12-FEB-2002'. In Oracle tools, the format of the date literal must match the instance or session setting for the NLS_DATE_FORMAT parameter.

Dates in the Selection Formula

Any selection criteria containing dates that is built using the Crystal Reports Select Expert will automatically create a selection formula that wraps the Crystal DateTime function around the date. This in turn will be translated into the SQL Query using the Oracle To_Date function, as in the following example:

```
WHERE   "EMPLOYEE"."BIRTH_DATE" <
        TO_DATE ('08-12-1972 00:00:00', 'DD-MM-YYYY HH24:MI:SS')
```

If you create the selection formula yourself, you should also use the Crystal DateTime function or the Crystal Date function. Using date literals will not be accepted in selection formulas.

Date Literals in SQL Expressions

Date literals are allowed in Crystal Reports SQL Expressions. The Crystal Reports help states that when logging on to Oracle, the date format is changed to match the default Crystal Reports date format. This would seem to mean that Crystal is setting the session's NLS_DATE_FORMAT to match its own default DateTime format. However, testing shows that, no matter what the default Crystal DateTime format is set to, date literals of only a specific format are accepted. The accepted format is Year/Month/Day, where the year must be 4-digit; the month can be 2-digit, the 3-character abbreviation, or the whole month name; and the delimiter can be "/" or "–". This may be a bug. It is always safer to use the TO_DATE Oracle function with a specific format string instead of date literals.

DateTime Functions

Crystal Reports contains many date functions that can be used in formulas, but none of the Crystal Report date functions is translated to equivalent Oracle date functions in the SQL Query. If numerous or complex date manipulations are required, this could cause a slowdown in processing. To move this processing to the server, use SQL Expressions containing Oracle date functions.

The Oracle function TO_DATE is used to convert a string to a date. This function is normally used with two parameters, the string that needs to be converted, and the string that contains the date format:

```
TO_DATE ('08-12-1972', 'DD-MM-YYYY')
```

If the format string is omitted, the date string must be in the same format as the NLS_DATE_FORMAT Oracle initialization parameter. A third parameter can be used to support globalization. See Oracle documentation for valid format strings.

Oracle has many DateTime functions:

TO_CHAR	NUMTOYMINTERVAL
ADD_MONTHS	ROUND
CURRENT_DATE	SESSIONTIMEZONE
CURRENT_TIMESTAMP	SYS_EXTRACT_UTC
DBTIMEZONE	SYSDATE
EXTRACT	SYSTIMESTAMP
FROM_TZ	TO_DSINTERVAL
LAST_DAY	TO_TIMESTAMP
LOCALTIMESTAMP	TO_TIMESTAMP_TZ
MONTHS_BETWEEN	TO_YMINTERVAL
NEW_TIME	TRUNC
NEXT_DAY	TZ_OFFSET
NUMTODSINTERVAL	

Some of these functions use, or return, datatypes of timestamp or interval. Note that timestamp and interval types cannot be used directly by Crystal Reports. You can use any of the Oracle DateTime functions in Crystal SQL Expressions even though some of them do not appear in the SQL Expression Editor lists.

NOTE

The functions listed in the preceding paragraph that use timestamp or interval datatypes are not available in Oracle 8i or previous versions.

Working with Strings

Crystal Reports contains many string functions that can be used in formulas, but none of the Crystal Report string functions is translated to equivalent Oracle character functions in the SQL Query. As with date and time data, if numerous or complex string manipulations are required, this could cause a slowdown in processing. To move this processing to the server, use SQL Expressions containing Oracle string functions.

Oracle character functions include the following:

TO_NUMBER	RPAD
CHR	RTRIM
CONCAT	SOUNDEX
INITCAP	SUBSTR
LOWER	TRANSLATE
LPAD	TRIM
LTRIM	UPPER
NLS_INITCAP	ASCII
NLS_LOWER	INSTR
NLSSORT	TRANSLATE
NLS_UPPER	LENGTH
REPLACE	

Most of these functions can be used with all Oracle character types, including CLOBs and LONGs. You can use any of the Oracle character functions in Crystal SQL Expressions even though some of them do not appear in the SQL Expression Editor.

Working with Numbers

Crystal Reports contains many mathematical functions that can be used in formulas, but none of the Crystal Report math functions is translated to equivalent Oracle numeric functions in the SQL Query. Again, numerous or complex arithmetic manipulations could cause a slowdown in processing. Use SQL Expressions containing Oracle numeric functions to move this processing to the server.

Oracle numeric functions include the following:

TO_CHAR	LN
ABS	LOG
ACOS	MOD
ASIN	POWER
ATAN	ROUND
ATAN2	SIGN
BITAND	SIN
CEIL	SINH
COS	SQRT
COSH	TAN
EXP	TANH
FLOOR	TRUNC

You can use any of the Oracle numeric functions in Crystal SQL Expressions even though some of them do not appear in the SQL Expression Editor.

Other Common Functions

Several Oracle built-in functions are commonly used in queries. Probably the two that are used most often are NVL and DECODE. You can use any of these functions in Crystal SQL Expressions even though some of them do not appear in the SQL Expression Editor.

NVL

NVL is an extremely useful function that allows you to replace a null value with an appropriate substitute when needed. The following example will return 'Not Shipped' if the Ship_Via field is null. NVL can also be used for numbers where a common replacement for null would be zero.

```
NVL("ORDERS"."SHIP_VIA", 'Not Shipped')
```

NVL2

NVL2 is a variation of NVL that allows you to return one value if the test value is null and a different value if the test value is not null:

```
NVL2("ORDERS"."SHIP_VIA", 'Ship Via is not null',
                          'Ship Via is null')
```

COALESCE

COALESCE is another variant of NVL. It takes a list of expressions and returns the first one that evaluates to a non-null value. The following example returns the Ship_Date if it is not null. If the Ship_Date is null and the Required_Date is not null, it returns the Required_Date. If both the Ship_Date and Required_Date are null, it returns the Order_Date. If all three are null, it returns null.

```
COALESCE("ORDERS"."SHIP_DATE","ORDERS"."REQUIRED_DATE",
         "ORDERS"."ORDER_DATE")
```

NOTE

The COALESCE function is new to Oracle 9i.

DECODE

The DECODE function takes a test value and a list of pairs of values. It returns the second value in the pair where the test value matches the first value in the pair. In the example that follows, if Employee_ID=1, then 'Joe' will be returned; if Employee_ID=2, then 'Jane' will be returned; if Employee_ID is not 1 or 2, then 'Everyone else' will be returned:

```
DECODE("ORDERS"."EMPLOYEE_ID", 1, 'Joe', 2, 'Jane',
                              'Everyone else')
```

CASE

The Oracle CASE keyword is not really a function but an expression that can be used in a SQL query. In its simple format, it is similar to the DECODE function:

```
CASE "ORDERS"."EMPLOYEE_ID"
  WHEN 1 THEN 'Joe'
  WHEN 2 THEN 'Jane'
  ELSE 'Everybody else'
END
```

It can also be used in a more complex manner where each condition is not relative to the same field, but completely independent. This called a searched case statement.

```
CASE
  WHEN "ORDERS"."ORDER_AMOUNT">10000 THEN 'Big Order'
  WHEN "ORDERS"."CUSTOMER_ID"=5 THEN 'Big Customer'
  ELSE 'Normal Order'
END
```

NOTE

Simple case expressions were available in Oracle 8i, but searched case expressions are new to Oracle 9i.

GREATEST

The GREATEST function returns the largest value from a list of values. If items in the list are not of the same type, they are converted to the type of the first value. In the following example, whichever date is the latest will be returned. GREATEST is not the same as MAX. MAX is an aggregation function that returns the greatest value in a column over the entire group, whereas GREATEST is a single row function.

```
GREATEST("ORDERS"."ORDER_DATE","ORDERS"."REQUIRED_DATE",
        "ORDERS"."SHIP_DATE")
```

LEAST

The LEAST function returns the smallest value from a list of values. As with GREATEST, if items in the list are not of the same type, they are converted to the type of the first value. In the example that follows, whichever date is the earliest will be returned. LEAST is not equivalent to MIN:

```
LEAST("ORDERS"."ORDER_DATE","ORDERS"."REQUIRED_DATE",
"ORDERS"."SHIP_DATE")
```

Pseudo Columns

Pseudo columns are values that Oracle maintains. You can select them as if they were regular columns.

ROWNUM

The rownum pseudo column is a number showing in what order Oracle selected the rows in the result set. The rownum value can vary depending on ORDER BY clauses and other conditions. It does not represent a constant value for each row in a table. The rownum pseudo column is often used to limit the result set for sampling purposes or to create Top-N type queries.

To limit the number of rows returned, create a SQL Expression whose value is rownum and then use that SQL Expression in the select formula. Be aware that the rownum determination is happening before the sort so this will not return the top 15 Employee_IDs, just the first 14 rows retrieved from Orders sorted by Employee_ID. The sort happens after the retrieval:

```
SELECT "ORDERS"."EMPLOYEE_ID", "ORDERS"."ORDER_AMOUNT",
       "ORDERS"."ORDER_ID", (rownum)
  FROM "XTREME"."ORDERS" "ORDERS"
  WHERE (ROWNUM)<15
  ORDER BY "ORDERS"."EMPLOYEE_ID"
```

To create a Top-N query using rownum, you must use a SQL Command. For instance, if your SQL Command contained the following statement, you would get the smallest 14 orders by Order_amount:

```
SELECT * FROM
   (SELECT "ORDERS"."EMPLOYEE_ID",
           "ORDERS"."ORDER_AMOUNT", "ORDERS"."ORDER_ID"
      FROM   "XTREME"."ORDERS" "ORDERS"
     ORDER BY "ORDERS"."ORDER_AMOUNT")
WHERE ROWNUM<15
```

ROWID

The ROWID pseudo column is the physical row address. Even this value should not be considered constant for a row. It can change in cases of row migration or table restructuring.

Subqueries

Subqueries are queries that are nested inside another query. Subqueries can appear in two places in SELECT statements. A subquery in the FROM clause is also called an inline view. This example shows an inline view:

```
SELECT "EMPLOYEE_ID",
       "ORDERS"."ORDER_AMOUNT",
       "ORDERS"."ORDER_ID",
       "ORDERS3"."AVG_ORDER"
  FROM "XTREME"."ORDERS" "ORDERS"
       JOIN
       (SELECT "ORDERS2"."EMPLOYEE_ID",
               AVG("ORDERS2"."ORDER_AMOUNT") AVG_ORDER
          FROM "XTREME"."ORDERS" "ORDERS2"
          GROUP BY "ORDERS2"."EMPLOYEE_ID") "ORDERS3"
       USING ("EMPLOYEE_ID")
  ORDER BY "ORDERS"."ORDER_AMOUNT"
```

A subquery in the WHERE clause is called a nested subquery. Subqueries can be nested inside other subqueries. This example shows an uncorrelated nested subquery:

```
SELECT "ORDERS"."EMPLOYEE_ID",
       "ORDERS"."ORDER_AMOUNT", "ORDERS"."ORDER_ID"
```

```
      FROM "XTREME"."ORDERS" "ORDERS"
  WHERE "ORDERS"."ORDER_AMOUNT">
                    (SELECT AVG("ORDERS2"."ORDER_AMOUNT")
                      FROM "XTREME"."ORDERS" "ORDERS2")
  ORDER BY "ORDERS"."ORDER_AMOUNT"
```

If a nested subquery contains a reference to a field in the main query in its WHERE clause, it is called a correlated nested subquery. This example shows a correlated nested subquery:

```
SELECT "ORDERS"."EMPLOYEE_ID", "ORDERS"."ORDER_AMOUNT",
       "ORDERS"."ORDER_ID"
  FROM "XTREME"."ORDERS" "ORDERS"
  WHERE "ORDERS"."ORDER_AMOUNT">
          (SELECT AVG("ORDERS2"."ORDER_AMOUNT")
            FROM "XTREME"."ORDERS" "ORDERS2"
            WHERE "ORDERS2"."EMPLOYEE_ID"="ORDERS"."EMPLOYEE_ID")
  ORDER BY "ORDERS"."ORDER_AMOUNT"
```

This chapter covered basic Oracle SELECT statement construction. How Crystal Reports constructs SQL statements to send to Oracle was demonstrated, as were statement options beyond the simple syntax used by Crystal. The next chapter will describe more complex SELECT statement options.

Oracle Advanced SELECT Options

IN THIS CHAPTER:
HAVING Clause
Set Operations
Hierarchical Queries
WITH Clause
Aggregation
Analysis

There are many SQL Select options available in Oracle that are not commonly used or generated by Crystal Reports but that are very useful in certain reporting situations. In this chapter, many of these options will be covered. The HAVING clause allows filtering at the group level. Set operations let you do set manipulations such as unions and intersections. Hierarchical queries, similar to the Crystal Reports hierarchical grouping feature, are also described, and the WITH clause, which enables a simplified use of temporary tables, will be explained. Finally, the very powerful aggregation and analysis functions available will be covered. These functions let you easily do summarizing, ranking, and other analysis, not possible from a simple SELECT statement before Oracle 9*i*.

HAVING Clause

Crystal Reports allows you to create selection criteria on grouped data. For a simple example, create a report using the Orders table with the Order_Amount totals grouped by Employee_ID. To do this, put Employee_ID and Order_Amount fields on the report. Group by Employee_ID, subtotal Order_Amount by Employee_ID, and suppress the detail section. Check the SQL query that is generated—you can see this query in Figure 4-1.

Next, specify that you want only those employees whose total Order_Amount exceeds $700,000. Using the Select Expert, create the filter shown in Figure 4-2.

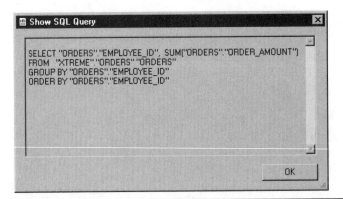

Figure 4-1   *SQL for group summary query*

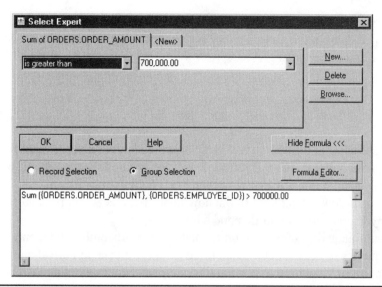

Figure 4-2   *Select Expert group selection*

Then check the SQL that Crystal generates as shown in Figure 4-3.

You will observe from viewing both screens that the SQL statement has not changed. The number of records returned is 6, one for each Employee_ID. The group filter has not been passed through to Oracle. In the download file, this report is available as \Chapter 4\Order Amount by Employee with detail hidden with group selection.rpt.

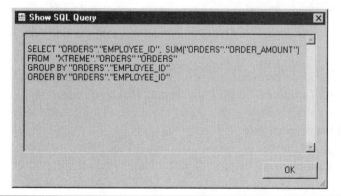

Figure 4-3   *SQL for Crystal group selection*

Oracle SQL SELECT statement syntax includes a HAVING clause that is used to filter grouped data. In this case, a query such as the following could be used to do the group filtering on the server:

```
SELECT "ORDERS"."EMPLOYEE_ID",  SUM("ORDERS"."ORDER_AMOUNT")
FROM    "XTREME"."ORDERS" "ORDERS" GROUP BY "ORDERS"."EMPLOYEE_ID"
HAVING SUM("ORDERS"."ORDER_AMOUNT")>700000;
```

You could use this formula in a SQL Command and the filtering would happen on the server with only two records returned, but you would lose the capability to drill down to the detail automatically. However, you could use on-demand subreports to mimic the drill-down capability. In the download file, this is report Chapter 4\Order Amount by Employee with on-demand subreport.rpt.

Since automatic drill down and on-demand subreports both issue identical database queries to get the detail data, there is no difference in performance from the database point of view for that portion of the report. However, using the HAVING clause for the main report is optimized for returning only the groups that are needed. The report writer must determine if the trade-off between increased performance and added complexity is worthwhile for any given report.

Set Operations

Using Oracle set operations is not possible if Crystal creates the report query. In order to take advantage of a set operation such as UNION, you must write the query yourself using SQL Commands, stored procedures, views, or Crystal Query files.

UNION

The UNION operation takes the result set of one SELECT statement and appends it to the result set of another SELECT statement. This operation adds rows. Joins, on the other hand, merge rows together so that you get a larger row. UNION creates more rows of the original size.

For example, a phone list is needed that contains the phone numbers for customers, employees, and suppliers in the same report. Phone numbers for each of these entities is stored in a separate corresponding table. A UNION operation allows you to treat them as if they were all in the same table.

```
SELECT 'Customer' Type,
       Customer_Name Organization,
       Contact_Last_Name Last_Name,
```

```
        Contact_First_Name First_Name,
        Phone
   FROM Customer
UNION
SELECT 'Employee', Null,
       Last_Name, First_Name, Home_Phone
  FROM Employee
UNION
SELECT 'Supplier', Supplier_Name,
        Null, Null, Phone
  FROM Supplier
ORDER BY 3, 4
```

Note that the column names or aliases from the first SELECT statement are the ones used for the entire result set. The number and types of columns in the second and third SELECT statements must match the number and types in the first SELECT statement, though column size can vary. If any duplicate rows are returned, UNION will eliminate them.

An ORDER BY clause is added at the end; this means that the resulting rows from all SELECT statements are sorted as one group. Only one ORDER BY clause is allowed, so individual SELECT statements cannot have their own ORDER BY clause.

UNION ALL

UNION ALL differs from UNION in one respect: UNION ALL will not remove duplicate rows. Because of this, UNION ALL is more efficient than UNION because it does not have to find and eliminate the duplicate rows, but it should be used only if you do not want duplicates eliminated, or if you are certain that there are no duplicates. No sort operation is required.

INTERSECT

INTERSECT returns rows only if they exist in both result sets. For example, the following query would return any phone numbers that show up in any two of the three tables:

```
SELECT Phone FROM Customer
  INTERSECT
  SELECT Home_Phone FROM Employee
UNION
  SELECT Home_Phone FROM Employee
    INTERSECT
```

```
  SELECT Phone FROM Supplier
 UNION
  SELECT Phone FROM Customer
   INTERSECT
 SELECT Phone FROM Supplier
```

Joining this result to the full phone list will return the complete row data for the rows with duplicate phone numbers:

```
SELECT a.Type, a.Organization, a.Last_Name, a.First_Name,
       Phone
from (SELECT 'Customer' Type,
              Customer_Name Organization,
              Contact_Last_Name Last_Name,
              Contact_First_Name First_Name,
              Phone
         FROM Customer
       UNION ALL
       SELECT 'Employee', Null,
              Last_Name, First_Name, Home_Phone
         FROM Employee
       UNION ALL
       SELECT 'Supplier', Supplier_Name,
              Null, Null, Phone
         FROM Supplier) a
JOIN
     (SELECT Phone FROM Customer
       INTERSECT
      SELECT Home_Phone FROM Employee
     UNION
      SELECT Home_Phone FROM Employee
       INTERSECT
      SELECT Phone FROM Supplier
     UNION
      SELECT Phone FROM Customer
       INTERSECT
      SELECT Phone FROM Supplier) b
USING (Phone)
```

The preceding query uses the 9*i* join syntax; the 8*i* version of this query is located in the download files as Chapter 4\Intersect Query for 8i.SQL.

MINUS

The MINUS set operation will return all rows that exist in the first query that do not exist in the second query. It subtracts any rows from the first query that match rows in the second query. Rows that exist in the second query but not the first are not returned.

For example, to find the product_ids for any products that have never been ordered, use the following query.

```
SELECT product_id FROM product
MINUS
SELECT distinct product_id FROM orders_detail
```

Hierarchical Queries

Just as Crystal Reports can do hierarchical grouping locally, Oracle can do hierarchical queries on the back end. To create a hierarchical query, you must use the CONNECT BY PRIOR clause. This clause defines the hierarchical relationship similar to the way the WHERE clause defines a join relationship. Though the PRIOR keyword can go on either side of the equality statement, it needs to be associated with the child field. The optional START WITH clause defines the root of the tree. In this case, the SUPERVISOR_ID is null if an employee has no supervisor. The optional ORDER SIBLINGS BY clause is used to sort the rows that are at the same level in the hierarchy:

```
SELECT employee_id, first_name||' '||last_name Name,
       SYS_CONNECT_BY_PATH(level||' '||First_Name||
                    ' '||Last_Name,'\') path
FROM employee
START WITH supervisor_id IS NULL
CONNECT BY PRIOR employee_id=supervisor_id
ORDER SIBLINGS BY employee_id
```

NOTE

The ORDER SIBLINGS BY and SYS_CONNECT_BY_PATH options are new to Oracle 9i.

The pseudo column Level displays the level of the row in the tree. The rows at the top of the tree are level 1, children of level 1 are level 2, children of level 2 are level 3, and so on. The function SYS_CONNECT_BY_PATH is only valid in a hierarchical query; it is used to create a string containing the path from the top of the tree down to the current row, with a user-defined delimiter separating the levels.

Using Crystal Reports hierarchical grouping features, you can summarize at the tree levels. No such built-in capability exists in Oracle. To duplicate that capability, the SYS_CONNECT_BY_PATH can be parsed to create fields to group by:

```
SELECT employee_id, Name, salary, position,
       NVL(SUBSTR(path, INSTR(path,'\',1,1)+3,
           INSTR(path,'\',1,2)-INSTR(path,'\',1,1)-3),
           Name) Level_1_Supervisor,
       NVL(SUBSTR(path, INSTR(path,'\',1,2)+3,
           INSTR(path,'\',1,3)-INSTR(path,'\',1,2)-3),
           Name) Level_2_Supervisor,
   FROM (SELECT employee_id,
         first_name||' '||last_name Name, salary,
         SYS_CONNECT_BY_PATH(LEVEL||' '||First_Name||'
              '||Last_Name,'\') path, position
          FROM employee
         START WITH supervisor_id IS NULL
        CONNECT BY PRIOR employee_id=supervisor_id) p
```

The Chapter 4\Oracle Hierarchy.rpt report shows the result of using the preceding query as a SQL Command for Oracle 9*i*.

Whether you use Crystal hierarchical grouping or Oracle hierarchical grouping will depend on your needs. Each grouping will result in slightly different displays with their own pros and cons.

WITH Clause

The WITH clause is also known as the subquery factoring clause. The WITH clause precedes the SELECT list and allows you to create temporary tables to use in the SELECT statement. The temporary tables are created in the logged in user's temporary tablespace automatically. The WITH clause can improve the clarity of statements as well as make them more efficient by storing intermediate results.

NOTE

The subquery factoring clause is new to Oracle 9i.

The following example computes the minimum modal salary for employees by position:

```
WITH Counts as
     (SELECT Position, Salary, COUNT(Salary) M
        FROM Employee
       GROUP BY Position, Salary),
    MaxCounts AS
     (SELECT Position, MAX(M) MaxM
        FROM Counts
       GROUP BY Position)
SELECT Counts.Position, MIN(Counts.Salary) Min_Modal_Salary
  FROM Counts, MaxCounts
 WHERE Counts.Position=MaxCounts.Position
   AND Counts.M=MaxCounts.MaxM
 GROUP BY Counts.Position
```

The preceding example will create two temporary tables, Counts and MaxCounts, from which it will return the final results based on the subsequent SELECT statement.

Aggregation

Oracle 8*i* and Oracle 9*i* SQL have some aggregation capabilities that do not exist in standard SQL. These summary operations can be used in SQL Commands, stored procedures, and views.

ROLLUP

ROLLUP and CUBE are extensions to the GROUP BY clause that create additional rows in the result set that contain summary values that would not ordinarily be returned. For instance, the following query containing a ROLLUP command will return records containing the sums at the (country), (country and region), (country, region, and city), and (country, region, city, and customer) grouping levels:

```
SELECT "CUSTOMER"."COUNTRY", "CUSTOMER"."REGION",
       "CUSTOMER"."CITY", "CUSTOMER"."CUSTOMER_NAME",
       SUM("CUSTOMER"."LAST_YEARS_SALES") SALES,
       DECODE(GROUPING_ID("CUSTOMER"."COUNTRY",
                          "CUSTOMER"."REGION",
```

```
                    "CUSTOMER"."CITY",
                    "CUSTOMER"."CUSTOMER_NAME"),
              0,'CUSTOMER',1,'CITY',3,'REGION',
              7,'COUNTRY',15,'GRAND','ERROR') GROUPLEVEL
  FROM    "XTREME"."CUSTOMER" "CUSTOMER"
  WHERE   ("CUSTOMER"."COUNTRY"='England'
          OR "CUSTOMER"."COUNTRY"='USA')
  GROUP BY ROLLUP ("CUSTOMER"."COUNTRY", "CUSTOMER"."REGION",
                    "CUSTOMER"."CITY", "CUSTOMER"."CUSTOMER_NAME")
```

This query returns the following result:

COUNTRYREGIONCITY			CUSTOMER_NAME	SALES	GROUPLEVEL
USA	AL	Huntsville	Psycho-Cycle	52809.105	CUSTOMER
USA	AL	Huntsville		52809.105	CITY
USA	AL			52809.105	REGION
USA	CA	Irvine	Changing Gears	26705.65	CUSTOMER
USA	CA	Irvine		26705.65	CITY
USA	CA	San Diego	Sporting Wheels Inc.	85642.56	CUSTOMER
USA	CA	San Diego		85642.56	CITY
USA	CA	Newbury Park	Rowdy Rims Company	30131.455	CUSTOMER
USA	CA	Newbury Park		30131.455	CITY
USA	CA			142479.665	REGION
USA	FL	Clearwater	Extreme Cycling	69819.1	CUSTOMER
USA	FL	Clearwater	Wheels and Stuff	25556.105	CUSTOMER
USA	FL	Clearwater		95375.205	CITY

NOTE

The SUPERVISOR_ID function is new to Oracle 9i.

A query of this type can be used in a Crystal Reports SQL Command to precompute summary values. The rows could be formatted to highlight the summary rows using conditional formatting based on the GROUPING_ID.

The advantage of performing a rollup on the server is minimal in most cases, but it does push all summarization to the server. Even in cases where grouping on the server is taking place in Crystal Reports, only the lowest-level summaries are computed on the server. Higher-level summaries are computed locally. Using ROLLUP, all summaries can be precomputed.

CUBE

The CUBE keyword creates a summary for every possible combination of the GROUP BY fields as in a cross tab. Imagine that you want to know how many employees report to their supervisor. (Crystal's XTREME data has both a Reports_To and a Supervisor field in its EMPLOYEE table.) The following query will show you where SUPERVISOR_ID is the same as REPORTS_TO, as well as where the fields are not the same, with employee counts for each condition:

```
SELECT NVL(supervisor_id,0) Supervisor,
       NVL(reports_to,0) Reports_To,
       COUNT(employee_id) NumEmps,
       DECODE(GROUPING_ID(NVL(supervisor_id,0),
           NVL(reports_to,0)),
           0,'Detail',1,'Total for Supervisor_ID',
           2,'Total for Reports_To',
           3,'Grand Total','?') GROUPLEVEL
FROM   employee
GROUP BY CUBE (NVL(supervisor_id,0), NVL(reports_to,0))
```

The preceding query returns the following rows:

NOTE

The SUPERVISOR_ID function is new to Oracle 9i.

SUPERVISOR	REPORTS_TO	NUMEMPS	GROUPLEVEL
		15	Grand Total
	0	2	Total for Reports_To
	2	7	Total for Reports_To
	3	2	Total for Reports_To
	5	3	Total for Reports_To
	13	1	Total for Reports_To
0		1	Total for Supervisor_ID
0	0	1	Detail
2		3	Total for Supervisor_ID
2	2	3	Detail
5		7	Total for Supervisor_ID
5	2	4	Detail
5	5	3	Detail
10		2	Total for Supervisor_ID

```
10            3            2 Detail
13                         2 Total for Supervisor_ID
13            0            1 Detail
13           13            1 Detail
```

However, the rows returned are not organized in the same way as is generally expected of a cross tab, limiting its usefulness in Crystal Reports.

Analysis

Oracle's SQL for Analysis is a complex feature. A general overview will be given here, but for a complete description see the Oracle documentation.

The SQL for Analysis functions allow you to do computations that require knowledge of preceding or subsequent rows. Using these functions, you can compute values that would require a stored procedure or complex programming in Crystal Reports.

The analysis functions use the concept of a partition, where a partition is a grouping of rows that the user defines, similar to a GROUP BY in the SELECT statement. Note that this use of the term "partition" is not related to table partitioning and applies only to the statement being processed.

Within a partition, a window may be defined with a starting and an ending point. Either or both the starting point and ending point may move, depending on their definitions. The window may be of any size, from every row in the partition to only one row, and can be based on a number of rows or a time period. If the window is defined to move, it will not move past the partition boundary but will truncate as it approaches the boundary. Therefore, if a moving window from the current row to the next five rows is defined, but the current row is three rows from the end of the partition, only three rows will be included in the computation for the current row. The ending points for a moving window are always defined relative to the current row.

The analysis functions can be broken into several categories covering different capabilities.

Ranking Functions

The ranking functions allow you to compute ranks, percentiles, and other n-tiles. The ranking functions take the following general form:

```
FUNCTION () OVER ([query_partition_clause] order_by_clause)
```

The query_partition_clause defines the groups within which the function will be calculated, and the order_by_clause defines the ordering that will be used. The function is reset between partitions. If no partition is defined, the entire result set is assumed. The order_by_clause is similar to a regular ORDER BY for a SELECT statement and has the same defaults. Options for the order_by_clause include ASC/DESC and NULLS FIRST/NULLS LAST. In general, nulls are treated the same as other values and are included in rankings. One null is considered equivalent to another null, and null will be last in an ASC order and first in a DESC order, by default.

RANK

To obtain the ranking of employee_ids by amount ordered, a RANK query such as the following may be used. Note that DESC is used so that the top sellers will be first in the ranking:

```
SQL> SELECT employee_id, SUM(order_amount) Amount,
  2         Rank () OVER (ORDER BY SUM(order_amount) DESC) Rank
  3     FROM orders
  4     GROUP BY employee_id;

EMPLOYEE_ID     AMOUNT       RANK
----------- ----------- ----------
          7  748755.94          1
          6  710401.48          2
          9  682849.21          3
          1  660756.95          4
          3  649101.99          5
          4  631799.77          6
```

To determine the same ranking by order month, modify the query as shown:

```
SQL> SELECT EXTRACT(MONTH FROM order_date) Month, employee_id,
  2         SUM(order_amount) Amount,
  3         RANK () OVER (PARTITION BY EXTRACT(MONTH FROM order_date)
  4                       ORDER BY SUM(order_amount) DESC) Rank
  5     FROM orders
  6     GROUP BY EXTRACT(MONTH FROM order_date), employee_id;

    MONTH EMPLOYEE_ID     AMOUNT       RANK
---------- ----------- ---------- ----------
        1           6   99979.24          1
        1           9   80512.61          2
```

```
1       7   80182.47      3
1       1   79581.86      4
1       4   62453.02      5
1       3   62129.83      6
2       9  135328.98      1
2       6  115022.25      2
2       3   113115.3      3
2       7  113057.19      4
2       4  105110.59      5
2       1   68762.92      6
```

More than one ranking function with different partitioning or ordering can be used simultaneously.

Top N rankings can be done as shown to get the top two employees per month:

```
SQL> SELECT *
  2  FROM (SELECT EXTRACT(MONTH FROM order_date) Month, employee_id,
  3               SUM(order_amount) Amount,
  4         RANK () OVER (PARTITION BY EXTRACT(MONTH FROM order_date)
  5                          ORDER BY SUM(order_amount) DESC) Rank
  6           FROM orders
  7          GROUP BY EXTRACT(MONTH FROM order_date), employee_id)
  8  WHERE Rank<3;

    MONTH EMPLOYEE_ID     AMOUNT        RANK
---------- ----------- ---------- ----------
        1           6   99979.24           1
        1           9   80512.61           2
        2           9  135328.98           1
        2           6  115022.25           2
```

To get the bottom two employees per month, remove the DESC option:

```
SQL> SELECT *
  2  FROM (SELECT EXTRACT(MONTH FROM order_date) Month, employee_id,
  3               SUM(order_amount) Amount,
  4         RANK () OVER (PARTITION BY EXTRACT(MONTH FROM order_date)
  5                          ORDER BY SUM(order_amount)) Rank
  6           FROM orders
  7          GROUP BY EXTRACT(MONTH FROM order_date), employee_id)
  8   WHERE Rank<3;
```

```
    MONTH EMPLOYEE_ID       AMOUNT       RANK
---------- ----------- ----------- ----------
         1           3    62129.83          1
         1           4    62453.02          2
         2           1    68762.92          1
         2           4   105110.59          2
```

DENSE_RANK

DENSE_RANK is similar to RANK. Both allow ties, and it is possible that more than one row will have the same rank. The difference between RANK and DENSE_RANK is how the next value after a tie is treated. Imagine that two rows are tied for rank five. When using RANK, the next row's rank will be seven. When using DENSE_RANK, the next row's rank will be six.

To demonstrate, the following rounds the order amount to force a tie:

```
SQL> SELECT employee_id, SUM(order_amount) Amount,
  2          ROUND(SUM(order_amount),-5) Rounded_Amount,
  3          RANK () OVER (ORDER BY SUM(order_amount) DESC) Rank,
  4          RANK () OVER (ORDER BY ROUND(SUM(order_amount),-5) DESC)
  5                       Rounded_Rank
  6    FROM orders
  7   GROUP BY employee_id;
```

```
EMPLOYEE_ID      AMOUNT ROUNDED_AMOUNT       RANK ROUNDED_RANK
----------- ----------- -------------- ---------- ------------
          7   748755.94         700000          1            1
          6   710401.48         700000          2            1
          9   682849.21         700000          3            1
          1   660756.95         700000          4            1
          3   649101.99         600000          5            5
          4   631799.77         600000          6            5
```

Now the Rounded_Rank column has four ties for first place, and the next rank shown is five. Note also that this query shows two different rankings being created simultaneously.

Switching to DENSE_RANK does not affect the Rank columns because it had no ties, but it does affect the Rounded_Rank column, which now shows the next rank as being two rather than five:

```
SQL> SELECT employee_id, SUM(order_amount) Amount,
  2      ROUND(SUM(order_amount),-5) Rounded_Amount,
```

```
  3   DENSE_RANK () OVER (ORDER BY SUM(order_amount) DESC) Rank,
  4   DENSE_RANK () OVER (ORDER BY ROUND(SUM(order_amount),-5) DESC)
  5                   Rounded_Rank
  6    FROM orders
  7    GROUP BY employee_id;
```

EMPLOYEE_ID	AMOUNT	ROUNDED_AMOUNT	RANK	ROUNDED_RANK
7	748755.94	700000	1	1
6	710401.48	700000	2	1
9	682849.21	700000	3	1
1	660756.95	700000	4	1
3	649101.99	600000	5	2
4	631799.77	600000	6	2

CUME_DIST

The cumulative distribution function, CUME_DIST, shows the ratio of the rank of the current row to the rank of the largest row in the set:

```
SQL> SELECT employee_id, SUM(order_amount) Amount,
  2        RANK () OVER (ORDER BY SUM(order_amount)) Rank,
  3        CUME_DIST () OVER (ORDER BY SUM(order_amount)) Cume_Dist
  4    FROM orders
  5    GROUP BY employee_id;
```

EMPLOYEE_ID	AMOUNT	RANK	CUME_DIST
4	631799.77	1	.166666667
3	649101.99	2	.333333333
1	660756.95	3	.5
9	682849.21	4	.666666667
6	710401.48	5	.833333333
7	748755.94	6	1

PERCENT_RANK

The PERCENT_RANK function computes the relative position of the rank within the group. It is computed as the current row's Rank-1 over the group's largest Rank-1:

```
SQL> SELECT employee_id, SUM(order_amount) Amount,
  2    RANK () OVER (ORDER BY SUM(order_amount)) Rank,
  3    PERCENT_RANK () OVER (ORDER BY SUM(order_amount)) Percent_Rank
  4    FROM orders
  5    GROUP BY employee_id;
```

```
EMPLOYEE_ID     AMOUNT        RANK PERCENT_RANK
----------- ----------  ---------- ------------
          4  631799.77           1            0
          3  649101.99           2           .2
          1  660756.95           3           .4
          9  682849.21           4           .6
          6  710401.48           5           .8
          7  748755.94           6            1
```

NTILE

The NTILE function assigns rows to buckets. The following example divides the employees into thirds using their total order amounts:

```
SQL> SELECT NTILE (3) OVER (ORDER BY SUM(order_amount)) Bucket,
  2          SUM(order_amount) Amount, employee_id
  3    FROM orders
  4   GROUP BY employee_id;

    BUCKET     AMOUNT EMPLOYEE_ID
---------- ---------- -----------
         1  631799.77           4
         1  649101.99           3
         2  660756.95           1
         2  682849.21           9
         3  710401.48           6
         3  748755.94           7
```

Note that the number of rows per bucket can vary if the NTILE number does not divide evenly into the total number of rows. In addition, if the order by expression results in ties, the row could shift buckets depending on the total number of rows, and a tied value could show up in two adjacent buckets.

ROW_NUMBER

The ROW_NUMBER function is similar to RANK, except in its treatment of ties. RANK gives the same value to every row with the same rank, while ROW_NUMBER gives sequential values as shown in the example. The order that the values are assigned within the rank is arbitrary:

```
SQL> SELECT EXTRACT(MONTH FROM order_date) Month, employee_id,
  2   ROUND(SUM(order_amount),-4) Amount,
  3   RANK () OVER (PARTITION BY EXTRACT(MONTH FROM order_date)
  4             ORDER BY ROUND(SUM(order_amount),-4) DESC) Rank,
```

```
5    ROW_NUMBER () OVER (PARTITION BY EXTRACT(MONTH FROM order_date)
6                    ORDER BY ROUND(SUM(order_amount),-4) DESC) RowN
7      FROM orders
8    GROUP BY EXTRACT(MONTH FROM order_date), employee_id;
```

MONTH	EMPLOYEE_ID	AMOUNT	RANK	ROWNO
1	6	100000	1	1
1	1	80000	2	2
1	7	80000	2	3
1	9	80000	2	4
1	3	60000	5	5
1	4	60000	5	6
2	9	140000	1	1
2	6	120000	2	2
2	3	110000	3	3
2	4	110000	3	4
2	7	110000	3	5
2	1	70000	6	6

Reporting Aggregate Functions

Reporting aggregate functions are similar to regular SQL aggregates, except that they make the aggregate value available to every detail row and do not cause detail suppression. The reporting aggregates differ from ordinary aggregates such as the simple SUM function. Using a simple SUM returns a sum at the group level of the SELECT statement. Using a reporting aggregate, SUM returns a summary value for every detail row of the SELECT statement at the level defined by the partition clause, independent of the grouping in the SELECT statement.

The syntax for reporting aggregate functions is as follows:

```
FUNCTION() OVER (partition_by_clause)
```

The reporting aggregate functions are SUM, AVG, MIN, MAX, COUNT, STDDEV, and VARIANCE. ALL, DISTINCT, and * can be used as they would normally be used with these functions. The partition_by_clause defines the grouping for the aggregation similar to a SQL GROUP BY clause. If no partition_by_clause is given, the aggregate is computed across the entire result set.

Simple Partition Summary

The following example shows a simple sum across a partition. The order amount is summed by employee_id and by month, and the month total is displayed on every row.

```
SQL> SELECT employee_id, EXTRACT(MONTH FROM order_date) Month,
  2         SUM(order_amount) Amount,
  3         SUM(SUM(order_amount))
  4  OVER (partition by extract(month from order_date)) Month_Total
  5    FROM orders
  6  GROUP BY employee_id, EXTRACT(MONTH FROM order_date);

EMPLOYEE_ID      MONTH      AMOUNT  MONTH_TOTAL
----------- ---------- ----------  -----------
          1          1    79581.86    464839.03
          3          1    62129.83    464839.03
          4          1    62453.02    464839.03
          6          1    99979.24    464839.03
          7          1    80182.47    464839.03
          9          1    80512.61    464839.03
          1          2    68762.92    650397.23
          3          2   113115.3     650397.23
```

RATIO_TO_REPORT

The RATIO_TO_REPORT function creates ratios of the current record's value to
the partition aggregate value. In the example, you can see that the Percent_of_Total
column equals the Amount/Month_Total:

```
SQL> SELECT employee_id, EXTRACT(MONTH FROM order_date) Month,
  2  SUM(order_amount) Amount,
  3  SUM(sum(order_amount))
  4  OVER (PARTITION BY EXTRACT(MONTH FROM order_date)) Month_Total,
  5       RATIO_TO_REPORT(SUM(order_amount))
  6          OVER (PARTITION BY EXTRACT(MONTH FROM order_date))
  7          Percent_of_Total
  8    FROM orders
  9  GROUP BY employee_id, EXTRACT(MONTH FROM order_date);

EMPLOYEE_ID      MONTH      AMOUNT  MONTH_TOTAL  PERCENT_OF_TOTAL
----------- ---------- ----------  -----------  ----------------
          1          1    79581.86    464839.03          .171203051
          3          1    62129.83    464839.03          .133658807
          4          1    62453.02    464839.03           .13435408
          6          1    99979.24    464839.03          .215083574
          7          1    80182.47    464839.03          .172495132
          9          1    80512.61    464839.03          .173205357
          1          2    68762.92    650397.23          .105724497
          3          2   113115.3     650397.23          .173917254
```

Windowing Aggregate Functions

The windowing functions are an extension of the reporting aggregate functions. They allow you to compute aggregates over a window within a partition. The window is a set of rows where the first row may be fixed or moving and the last row may be fixed or moving, allowing the computation of cumulative aggregates or moving aggregates. The window is always bounded by the partition boundaries.

The windowing aggregate functions are SUM, AVG, MIN, MAX, COUNT, STDDEV, VARIANCE, FIRST_VALUE, and LAST_VALUE. The syntax for a windowing aggregate function is as follows:

```
FUNCTION(expression) OVER ([query_partition_clause] order_by_clause
  [ROWS or RANGE]
  [[UNBOUNDED PRECEDING or CURRENT ROW
          or expression PRECEDING]
   or
  [BETWEEN [UNBOUNDED PRECEDING or CURRENT ROW
          or expression [PRECEDING or FOLLOWING]]
       AND [UNBOUNDED FOLLOWING or CURRENT ROW
          or expression [PRECEDING or FOLLOWING]]]])
```

The order_by_clause is not required and not important when using reporting aggregate functions because the summary is computed for the entire group so the order of the rows within the group is irrelevant. When using the windowing aggregate functions, however, the order_by_clause *is* important because the window will slide across the partition and produce different values if the rows are in a different order.

Cumulative Summary

To display a cumulative aggregation for a partition, you must specify the ROWS UNBOUNDED PRECEDING clause. This will result in all rows from the beginning of the partition up to the current row being aggregated. The following example shows the cumulative order amount, which is identical to a running total in Crystal:

```
SQL> SELECT employee_id, EXTRACT(MONTH FROM order_date) Month,
  2         SUM(order_amount) Amount,
  3         SUM(SUM(order_amount))
  4           OVER (PARTITION BY EXTRACT(MONTH FROM order_date)
  5                 ORDER BY employee_id
  6                 ROWS UNBOUNDED PRECEDING) Cum_Month_Total
  7     FROM orders
  8    GROUP BY employee_id, EXTRACT(MONTH FROM order_date);
```

EMPLOYEE_ID	MONTH	AMOUNT	CUM_MONTH_TOTAL
1	1	79581.86	79581.86
3	1	62129.83	141711.69
4	1	62453.02	204164.71
6	1	99979.24	304143.95
7	1	80182.47	384326.42
9	1	80512.61	464839.03
1	2	68762.92	68762.92
3	2	113115.3	181878.22

If a descending directive is added to the order_by_clause, a different cumulative total will result, illustrating the importance of sort order:

```
SQL> SELECT employee_id, EXTRACT(MONTH FROM order_date) Month,
  2         SUM(order_amount) Amount,
  3         SUM(SUM(order_amount))
  4           OVER (PARTITION BY EXTRACT(MONTH FROM order_date)
  5                 ORDER BY employee_id DESC
  6                 ROWS UNBOUNDED PRECEDING) Cum_Month_Total
  7    FROM orders
  8   GROUP BY employee_id, EXTRACT(MONTH FROM order_date);
```

EMPLOYEE_ID	MONTH	AMOUNT	CUM_MONTH_TOTAL
9	1	80512.61	80512.61
7	1	80182.47	160695.08
6	1	99979.24	260674.32
4	1	62453.02	323127.34
3	1	62129.83	385257.17
1	1	79581.86	464839.03
9	2	135328.98	135328.98
7	2	113057.19	248386.17

Modifying the previous query to partition by employee_id and order_by_month will result in the following SQL, which shows the cumulative order total by employee_id across the months:

```
SQL> SELECT employee_id, EXTRACT(MONTH FROM order_date) Month,
  2         SUM(order_amount) Amount,
  3         SUM(SUM(order_amount))
  4           OVER (PARTITION BY employee_id
  5                 ORDER BY EXTRACT(MONTH FROM order_date)
```

```
6                   ROWS UNBOUNDED PRECEDING) Cum_Month_Total
7     FROM orders
8     GROUP BY employee_id, EXTRACT(MONTH FROM order_date);
```

```
EMPLOYEE_ID      MONTH      AMOUNT CUM_MONTH_TOTAL
----------- ---------- ---------- ---------------
          1          1   79581.86        79581.86
          1          2   68762.92       148344.78
          1          3   58676.28       207021.06
          1          4   72431.48       279452.54
          1          5   31344.59       310797.13
          1          6      84149       394946.13
          1          7   17991.33       412937.46
          1          8   59291.32       472228.78
          1          9   24894.67       497123.45
          1         10   27652.89       524776.34
          1         11   35127.71       559904.05
          1         12   100852.9       660756.95
          3          1   62129.83        62129.83
          3          2   113115.3       175245.13
```

Now say that your boss wishes to see how the employee's monthly average changes through the year:

```
SQL> SELECT employee_id, EXTRACT(MONTH FROM order_date) Month,
  2         SUM(order_amount) Amount,
  3         AVG(SUM(order_amount))
  4          OVER (PARTITION BY employee_id
  5              ORDER BY EXTRACT(MONTH FROM order_date)
  6              ROWS UNBOUNDED PRECEDING) Running_Average
  7     FROM orders
  8     GROUP BY employee_id, EXTRACT(MONTH FROM order_date);
```

```
EMPLOYEE_ID      MONTH      AMOUNT RUNNING_AVERAGE
----------- ---------- ---------- ---------------
          1          1   79581.86        79581.86
          1          2   68762.92        74172.39
          1          3   58676.28        69007.02
          1          4   72431.48       69863.135
          1          5   31344.59       62159.426
          1          6      84149       65824.355
          1          7   17991.33      58991.0657
          1          8   59291.32      59028.5975
          1          9   24894.67      55235.9389
          1         10   27652.89       52477.634
```

```
            1        11   35127.71       50900.3682
            1        12   100852.9       55063.0792
            3         1   62129.83         62129.83
            3         2   113115.3        87622.565
```

Moving Summary

Then the boss says that only the most recent three months matter. Now you need a moving average over the last three months only. All you need to do is change the UNBOUNDED keyword to two (not three, because the current row is always included):

```
SQL> SELECT employee_id, EXTRACT(MONTH FROM order_date) Month,
  2         SUM(order_amount) Amount,
  3         AVG(SUM(order_amount))
  4          OVER (PARTITION BY employee_id
  5                ORDER BY EXTRACT(MONTH FROM order_date)
  6                ROWS 2 PRECEDING) Three_Month_Average
  7      FROM orders
  8      GROUP BY employee_id, EXTRACT(MONTH FROM order_date);
```

EMPLOYEE_ID	MONTH	AMOUNT	THREE_MONTH_AVERAGE
1	1	79581.86	79581.86
1	2	68762.92	74172.39
1	3	58676.28	69007.02
1	4	72431.48	66623.56
1	5	31344.59	54150.7833
1	6	84149	62641.69
1	7	17991.33	44494.9733
1	8	59291.32	53810.55
1	9	24894.67	34059.1067
1	10	27652.89	37279.6267
1	11	35127.71	29225.09
1	12	100852.9	54544.5
3	1	62129.83	62129.83
3	2	113115.3	87622.565

Centered Moving Summary

In retrospect, the boss would also like to see the three-month moving average calculated using the current month, previous month, and the next month. Of course, you must be careful with such computations because presumably next month's value is only known when the current row is in the past.

```
SQL> SELECT employee_id, EXTRACT(MONTH FROM order_date) Month,
  2          SUM(order_amount) Amount,
  3          AVG(SUM(order_amount))
  4           OVER (PARTITION BY employee_id
  5                 ORDER BY EXTRACT(MONTH FROM order_date)
  6                 ROWS BETWEEN 1 PRECEDING AND 1 FOLLOWING)
  7                      Three_Month_Centered
  8     FROM orders
  9     GROUP BY employee_id, EXTRACT(MONTH FROM order_date);
```

EMPLOYEE_ID	MONTH	AMOUNT	THREE_MONTH_CENTERED
1	1	79581.86	74172.39
1	2	68762.92	69007.02
1	3	58676.28	66623.56
1	4	72431.48	54150.7833
1	5	31344.59	62641.69
1	6	84149	44494.9733
1	7	17991.33	53810.55
1	8	59291.32	34059.1067
1	9	24894.67	37279.6267
1	10	27652.89	29225.09
1	11	35127.71	54544.5
1	12	100852.9	67990.305
3	1	62129.83	87622.565
3	2	113115.3	72252.99

Using RANGE

The keyword RANGE can be used with date windows. Windows created with RANGE
may have a varying number of rows in them but will have a fixed number of dates.
The example query shows a three-day average where the number of detail records
per date varies:

```
SQL> SELECT order_date, order_amount Amount,
  2          SUM(order_amount)
  3           OVER (ORDER BY order_date
  4                 RANGE BETWEEN INTERVAL '2' DAY PRECEDING
  5                     AND CURRENT ROW) Three_Day_Avg
  6     FROM orders
  7     WHERE order_date BETWEEN TO_DATE('04-01-2002','mm-dd-yyyy')
  8                     AND TO_DATE('04-30-2002','mm-dd-yyyy')
  9     ORDER BY order_date;
```

```
ORDER_DAT     AMOUNT    THREE_DAY_AVG
---------  ----------  ----------------
01-APR-02       13.5                57
01-APR-02       43.5                57
02-APR-02         29                86
03-APR-02       55.8           7812.36
03-APR-02       43.5           7812.36
03-APR-02    7534.06           7812.36
03-APR-02       43.5           7812.36
03-APR-02       49.5           7812.36
04-APR-02     9649.2          17404.56
05-APR-02       49.5          17425.06
06-APR-02    1028.55          10854.16
06-APR-02       15.5          10854.16
06-APR-02      45.68          10854.16
06-APR-02         33          10854.16
06-APR-02      32.73          10854.16
```

Note that a day interval is assumed when the window is based on a date, so the following query has the same result:

```
SELECT order_date, order_amount Amount,
       SUM(order_amount)
        OVER (ORDER BY order_date
            RANGE BETWEEN 2 PRECEDING AND CURRENT ROW) Three_Day_Avg
  FROM orders
 WHERE order_date BETWEEN TO_DATE('04-01-2002','mm-dd-yyyy')
                     AND TO_DATE('04-30-2002','mm-dd-yyyy')
 ORDER BY order_date;
```

Using an Expression for Number of Rows

An expression can be used for the number of rows in either the PRECEDING or FOLLOWING clauses. A contrived example is shown where the number of days is two if the month is April and three otherwise. A common use for this feature might be to skip holidays by using a function to return the desired number of days.

```
SQL> SELECT order_date, order_amount Amount,
  2          SUM(order_amount)
  3           OVER (ORDER BY order_date
  4      RANGE BETWEEN DECODE(EXTRACT(MONTH FROM order_date),4,2,3)
  5        PRECEDING AND CURRENT ROW) Day_Avg
```

```
  6    FROM orders
  7   WHERE order_date BETWEEN TO_DATE('04-01-2002','mm-dd-yyyy')
  8          AND TO_DATE('04-30-2002','mm-dd-yyyy')
  9   ORDER BY order_date;
```

```
ORDER_DAT     AMOUNT     DAY_AVG
---------  ----------  ----------
01-APR-02       13.5          57
01-APR-02       43.5          57
02-APR-02         29          86
03-APR-02       55.8     7812.36
03-APR-02       43.5     7812.36
03-APR-02    7534.06     7812.36
03-APR-02       43.5     7812.36
03-APR-02       49.5     7812.36
04-APR-02     9649.2    17404.56
05-APR-02       49.5    17425.06
06-APR-02    1028.55    10854.16
06-APR-02       15.5    10854.16
06-APR-02      45.68    10854.16
06-APR-02         33    10854.16
06-APR-02      32.73    10854.16
```

FIRST_VALUE and LAST_VALUE

The FIRST_VALUE and LAST_VALUE functions return the first or last value in a window, respectively. The example computes the percentage that each employee's orders were of the largest employee's orders. Note that this result could have been obtained using the RATIO_TO_REPORT function as well.

```
SQL> SELECT employee_id, EXTRACT(MONTH FROM order_date) Month,
  2          SUM(order_amount) Amount,
  3          FIRST_VALUE(SUM(order_amount))
  4           OVER (PARTITION BY EXTRACT(MONTH FROM order_date)
  5               ORDER BY SUM(order_amount) DESC) Last,
  6          100*SUM(order_amount)/
  7           FIRST_VALUE(SUM(order_amount))
  8            OVER (PARTITION BY EXTRACT(MONTH FROM order_date)
  9                ORDER BY SUM(order_amount) DESC) Percent_of_Last
 10    FROM orders
 11   GROUP BY employee_id, EXTRACT(MONTH FROM order_date);
```

EMPLOYEE_ID	MONTH	AMOUNT	LAST	PERCENT_OF_LAST
6	1	99979.24	99979.24	100
9	1	80512.61	99979.24	80.5293279
7	1	80182.47	99979.24	80.1991193
1	1	79581.86	99979.24	79.5983846
4	1	62453.02	99979.24	62.4659879
3	1	62129.83	99979.24	62.1427308
9	2	135328.98	135328.98	100
6	2	115022.25	135328.98	84.9945444

LAG/LEAD

The LAG and LEAD functions allow you to reference a value in a row that is a number of rows above or below the current row. The syntax for LAG and LEAD is as follows:

```
LAG|LEAD (expression [, offset] [, default])
    OVER ([query_partition_clause] order_by_clause)
```

LAG references rows before the current row, and LEAD references rows after the current row. Null will be returned if the reference row is outside of the partition. The expression is the column or computation to be returned, and the offset is the number of rows to reference forward or back. The offset must be a value and defaults to one. A default can be used to return a user-defined value instead of null when the reference is outside of the partition. The query_partition_clause is optional; if none is supplied, the entire result set will be assumed. The order_by_clause is required.

```
SQL> SELECT employee_id, EXTRACT(MONTH FROM order_date) Month,
  2         SUM(order_amount) Amount,
  3         LAG(SUM(order_amount),2)
  4          OVER (PARTITION BY EXTRACT(MONTH FROM order_date)
  5                ORDER BY SUM(order_amount) DESC) LAG_2,
  6         LEAD(SUM(order_amount),1,0)
  7          OVER (PARTITION BY EXTRACT(MONTH FROM order_date)
  8                ORDER BY SUM(order_amount) DESC) LEAD_1
  9    FROM orders
 10   GROUP BY employee_id, EXTRACT(MONTH FROM order_date);
```

EMPLOYEE_ID	MONTH	AMOUNT	LAG_2	LEAD_1
6	1	99979.24		80512.61
9	1	80512.61		80182.47
7	1	80182.47	99979.24	79581.86
1	1	79581.86	80512.61	62453.02
4	1	62453.02	80182.47	62129.83
3	1	62129.83	79581.86	0
9	2	135328.98		115022.25
6	2	115022.25		113115.3

FIRST/LAST

NOTE

The FIRST and LAST functions are new in Oracle 9i.

The FIRST and LAST functions allow you to return any column value or any expression computed from the row that is the first or last row returned, given a specified order. This differs from the FIRST_VALUE and LAST_VALUE functions that return the first or last column or expression defined, given the sort order. For example, say that you need the salary, employee_id, and supervisor_id of the employee with the lowest salary. Without the FIRST or LAST function, this would require a subquery as shown:

```
SQL> SELECT salary Lowest_Salary, employee_id Employee,
  2          supervisor_id Supervisor
  3     FROM employee
  4    WHERE salary=(SELECT MIN(salary) FROM employee);
```

```
LOWEST_SALARY   EMPLOYEE SUPERVISOR
------------- ---------- ----------
        18000         11         10
```

The equivalent result can be obtained using the FIRST function as shown.

```
SQL> Select MIN(salary)
  2      KEEP (DENSE_RANK FIRST ORDER BY salary) Lowest_Salary,
  3          MIN(employee_id)
  4          KEEP (DENSE_RANK FIRST ORDER BY salary) Employee,
  5          MIN(supervisor_id)
  6          KEEP (DENSE_RANK FIRST ORDER BY salary) Supervisor
  7     FROM employee;
```

```
LOWEST_SALARY    EMPLOYEE SUPERVISOR
-------------  ---------- ----------
        18000          11         10
```

However, what if there were two employees with a salary of $18,000? The first query using a subquery would return both records. The second query that uses the FIRST function would return only one row, but it might contain a mixture of data from each of the employee's rows. This is probably not desirable but can be cured in either situation by the creation of a tiebreaker condition.

Suppose there is more than one employee with the lowest salary and the employee with the earliest hire_date is desired. There are multiple methods to solve this without using the FIRST function. The example shows a solution using the subquery factoring clause (WITH):

```
SQL> WITH Poor_Emps AS
  2  (SELECT salary Lowest_Salary, employee_id Employee,
  3          supervisor_id Supervisor, hire_date
  4     FROM employee
  5    WHERE salary=(SELECT MIN(salary) FROM employee))
  6  SELECT Lowest_Salary, Employee, Supervisor
  7    FROM Poor_Emps
  8   WHERE hire_date=(SELECT MIN(hire_date) FROM Poor_Emps);

LOWEST_SALARY    EMPLOYEE SUPERVISOR
-------------  ---------- ----------
        18000          11         10
```

Using the FIRST function, the solution requires only adding the tiebreaker field to the sort:

```
SQL> SELECT MIN(salary)
  2         KEEP (DENSE_RANK FIRST ORDER BY salary,
  3               hire_date) Lowest_Salary,
  4         MIN(employee_id)
  5         KEEP (DENSE_RANK FIRST ORDER BY salary,
  6               hire_date) Employee,
  7         MIN(supervisor_id)
  8         KEEP (DENSE_RANK FIRST ORDER BY salary,
  9               hire_date) Supervisor
 10    FROM employee;

LOWEST_SALARY    EMPLOYEE SUPERVISOR
-------------  ---------- ----------
        18000          11         10
```

The FIRST and LAST functions can be used with a partition similar to previous functions that have been covered.

Linear Regression

The linear regression category of functions covers the linear regression statistics that are available. I will show a simple example, but it is beyond the scope of this book to define or discuss in detail the uses of these statistics. Further detail should be sought from Oracle documentation.

Each regression function takes two parameters that can be thought of as (y, x) coordinate pairs, where x is the independent variable and y is the dependent variable.

NOTE

Oracle documentation uses (y, x) NOT (x, y), so that is replicated here.

REGR_COUNT

REGR_COUNT returns the number of non-null pairs.

REGR_AVGX

REGR_AVGX returns the average of the x values.

REGR_AVGY

REGR_AVGY returns the average of the y values.

REGR_SLOPE

REGR_SLOPE returns the slope of the computed regression line.

REGR_INTERCEPT

REGR_INTERCEPT returns the y intercept of the computed regression line.

REGR_R2

REGR_R2 returns the R-squared or coefficient of determination of the computed regression line.

Other

There are other regression functions, and other measures can be obtained from combinations of functions.

Regression Example

Assume that you are interested in the relationship between salary and length of employment. The example computes several regression statistics, including the REGR_R2, which is not close to one, indicating a weak correlation between salary and length of employment:

```
SQL> SELECT REGR_SLOPE(Salary, SYSDATE-hire_date) slope,
  2         REGR_INTERCEPT(Salary, SYSDATE-hire_date) Intercept,
  3         REGR_R2(Salary, SYSDATE-hire_date) R_Squared,
  4         REGR_COUNT(Salary, SYSDATE-hire_date) Count,
  5         REGR_AVGX(Salary, SYSDATE-hire_date) Avg_Days,
  6         REGR_AVGY(Salary, SYSDATE-hire_date) Avg_Salary
  7    FROM employee;

    SLOPE  INTERCEPT  R_SQUARED       COUNT   AVG_DAYS AVG_SALARY
---------- ---------- ---------- ---------- ---------- ----------
.74882077 41682.4804 .000198374         15 3807.12317 44533.3333
```

However, if you group by position to produce the individual statistics for each position, you see that the correlation improves for Sales Representatives, although it does not exist for the other positions because they each have only one data point.

```
SQL> SELECT position,
  2         REGR_SLOPE(Salary, SYSDATE-hire_date) slope,
  3         REGR_INTERCEPT(Salary, SYSDATE-hire_date) Intercept,
  4         REGR_R2(Salary, SYSDATE-hire_date) R_2,
  5         REGR_COUNT(Salary, SYSDATE-hire_date) Count,
  6         REGR_AVGX(Salary, SYSDATE-hire_date) Avg_Days,
  7         REGR_AVGY(Salary, SYSDATE-hire_date) Avg_Salary
  8    FROM employee
  9    GROUP BY position;
```

POSITION	SLOPE	INTERCEPT	R_2	COUNT	AVG_DAYS	AVG_SALARY
Advertising Specialist				1	3363	45000
Business Manager				1	3700	60000
Inside Sales Coordinator				1	3730	45000
Mail Clerk				1	3745	18000
Marketing Associate				1	3380	50000
Marketing Director				1	3394	75000
Receptionist				1	3625	25000
Sales Manager				1	3869	50000
Sales Representative	2.02	26919.23	.05	6	4001	35000
Vice President, Sales				1	4298	90000

The regression functions can be used as report aggregates, windowing aggregates, or as shown, regular SQL aggregates.

Inverse Percentile

The inverse percentile functions will return the value that corresponds to a particular percentile. This is the opposite of the NTILE functions that return the percentile for a value.

NOTE

The inverse percentile functions are new in Oracle 9i.

Say that you want to know the median salary. From the following query, you can see that there are 15 salaries, so the median, or middle salary, is the eighth value, or 40,000.

```
SQL> SELECT ROW_NUMBER() OVER (ORDER BY salary) RowNo, salary
  2     FROM employee
  3   ORDER BY salary;

    ROWNO      SALARY
---------- ----------
         1       18000
         2       25000
         3       30000
         4       33000
         5       35000
         6       35000
         7       37000
         8       40000
         9       45000
        10       45000
        11       50000
        12       50000
        13       60000
        14       75000
        15       90000
```

The median is the value at the .5 percentile, so you can use the inverse percentile functions to obtain it.

```
SQL> SELECT PERCENTILE_CONT(0.5)
  2          WITHIN GROUP (ORDER BY salary) Median_Continuous,
  3          PERCENTILE_DISC(0.5)
  4          WITHIN GROUP (ORDER BY salary) Median_Discontinuous
  5     FROM employee
  6     ORDER BY salary;


MEDIAN_CONTINUOUS MEDIAN_DISCONTINUOUS
----------------- --------------------
            40000                40000
```

The PERCENTILE_CONT function will use linear interpolation between the two middle values if the number of values in the set is even. The PERCENTILE_DISC function will pick the lower value.

If you exclude employee_id 1, you will have the following values in an even numbered set:

```
SQL> SELECT ROW_NUMBER() OVER (ORDER BY salary) RowNo, salary
  2     FROM employee
  3     WHERE employee_id<> 1
  4     ORDER BY salary;

     ROWNO     SALARY
---------- ----------
         1      18000
         2      25000
         3      30000
         4      33000
         5      35000
         6      35000
         7      37000
         8      45000
         9      45000
        10      50000
        11      50000
        12      60000
        13      75000
        14      90000
```

The continuous median of this set will be between 37,000 and 45,000, and the discontinuous median will be 37,000.

```
SQL> SELECT PERCENTILE_CONT(0.5)
  2          WITHIN GROUP (ORDER BY salary) Median_Continuous,
  3          PERCENTILE_DISC(0.5)
  4          WITHIN GROUP (ORDER BY salary) Median_Discontinuous
  5     FROM employee
  6    WHERE employee_id<>1
  7    ORDER BY salary;


MEDIAN_CONTINUOUS MEDIAN_DISCONTINUOUS
----------------- --------------------
            41000                37000
```

The inverse percentile functions can be used for any value, not just the median, and they can be used as regular aggregates or reporting or windowing aggregates. See Oracle documentation for more information.

Hypothetical Rank and Distribution

The hypothetical rank function will return the rank that a row would have if it were inserted into a particular group. RANK, DENSE_RANK, PERCENT_RANK, and CUME_DIST can be used to return the corresponding hypothetical value for a supplied value.

NOTE

The hypothetical rank and distribution functions are new in Oracle 9i.

Look back at the ranked salary listing in the previous examples. Suppose that you want to know what rank a salary of 36,000 would have if it were inserted into the group. From observation, you can see that it would rank at seventh place, which the query confirms:

```
SQL> SELECT RANK(36000) WITHIN GROUP (ORDER BY salary) Test_Rank
  2     FROM employee;

 TEST_RANK
----------
         7
```

The hypothetical rank and distribution functions cannot be used as reporting or windowing functions, only as regular SQL aggregates. See Oracle documentation for more information.

WIDTH_BUCKET

The WIDTH_BUCKET function assigns a bucket number to a value. The user supplies the starting value, ending value, and number of buckets desired. Any values that fall below the starting value are assigned bucket number 0. Any values that are above the ending value are assigned to a bucket numbered one larger than the requested number of buckets.

NOTE

The WIDTH_BUCKET function is new in Oracle 9i.

Suppose that you want to create a histogram of salaries in $10,000 increments. The following query will assign salaries between $10,000 and $20,000 to bucket 1, salaries between $20,000 and $30,000 to bucket 2, and so on:

```
SQL> SELECT employee_id, salary,
  2         WIDTH_BUCKET(salary, 10000, 100000, 9) Bucket
  3    FROM employee
  4   ORDER BY 3,2,1;

EMPLOYEE_ID     SALARY     BUCKET
----------- ---------- ----------
         11      18000          1
         12      25000          2
          6      30000          3
          3      33000          3
          4      35000          3
          9      35000          3
          7      37000          3
          1      40000          4
          8      45000          4
         15      45000          4
          5      50000          5
         14      50000          5
         10      60000          6
         13      75000          7
          2      90000          9
```

If you need to perform statistical analysis in your reports, refer to more detailed documentation that specifically discusses the practical application of the useful, though often complex, statistical functions available with Oracle 9i.

This chapter covered many obscure and advanced SELECT statement options that can help solve complex reporting needs. In order to implement any of these options using Crystal Reports, the developer must use SQL Commands, views, stored procedures, or Crystal Query files. Though the options listed in this chapter are powerful, some problems require the use of stored procedures. The next chapter will describe the use of Oracle stored procedures in Crystal Reports.

CHAPTER
5

PL/SQL

The goal of this chapter is to introduce PL/SQL to those unfamiliar with it and to highlight how PL/SQL may be used in a Crystal Reports environment. This chapter contains an overview of PL/SQL, which is the Oracle embedded programming language. It describes PL/SQL code blocks and their structure as well as the creation of functions and procedures, with an emphasis on stored procedures that return reference cursors. These stored procedures can be used as data sources in Crystal Reports. This chapter should be considered an introduction only; further information about developing in PL/SQL to optimize Crystal Reports should be sought in Oracle documentation and other third-party books.

Overview

PL/SQL is a fourth-generation programming language embedded in the Oracle database. Whereas SQL is set oriented, PL/SQL has procedural elements like any modern programming language. A major difference between PL/SQL and a language such as C is that PL/SQL contains few graphical user interface capabilities. The other major difference is that PL/SQL has tight integration with the database, and SQL commands can be executed and manipulated very easily with it. Though PL/SQL can be used for the client tier of an application, this chapter concerns only PL/SQL running on the database server.

PL/SQL fully supports the Oracle SQL implementation, including all datatypes, functions, operators, and pseudo columns. PL/SQL code can be run dynamically or stored in client-side libraries, but I will be discussing PL/SQL functions, stored procedures, and triggers that are compiled and stored in the database. These executables are cached and shared among users. PL/SQL supports object-oriented programming, though that topic is not covered in depth in this book. Oracle supplies numerous prewritten PL/SQL packages which provide many different capabilities that may be used by the programmer if the DBA loads and compiles them.

Prior to Oracle 9*i,* the parser that was used to parse SQL statements sent directly to the database differed from the parser used to parse SQL statements that were embedded in PL/SQL blocks. Because of these differences, some SQL statements that executed perfectly in a native form failed when called from PL/SQL. The following are some SQL elements that are not supported from PL/SQL in Oracle 8*i* and earlier. If the desired statement can be rewritten to use dynamic SQL, it should succeed.

- ▶ ORDER BY in a subquery
- ▶ A SELECT statement as an expression in another SELECT statement field list

► Any analytical functions

► ROLLUP or CUBE

► Cursors in a SELECT statement

Report writers can benefit from using PL/SQL to create stored procedures. Crystal Reports can use the result set of a particular type of stored procedure as a report dataset. In addition, PL/SQL can be used to create functions that can be referenced in Crystal SQL Expressions or SQL Commands.

PL/SQL Structures

PL/SQL code is structured in blocks. There are two types of blocks: anonymous blocks are run interactively from an Oracle tool, and Stored Program units are named and stored in the database. There are three types of Stored Program units: procedures, functions, and packages. Procedures and functions are similar to their like-named counterparts in other languages. Packages are collections of procedures and/or functions that allow modularization of code. Triggers are special PL/SQL blocks that fire based on system, table, or view events. Stored Program units belong to specific schemas, just like table objects.

Blocks

PL/SQL blocks have three sections: a declaration section, an executable section, and an exception handling section. The declaration section is where variables are declared and is not required. The executable section contains the statements that will be executed when the block is run; this section is required. The exception section gives the developer a place to handle errors that occur during execution, and is not required. Blocks may be nested in the execution section or exception section, and entire subprograms may be defined in the declaration section.

A PL/SQL block looks like this:

```
[DECLARE ...]
BEGIN ...
[EXCEPTION ...]
END;
```

An anonymous block would look just like the preceding and could be run dynamically from an Oracle tool such as SQL*Plus. Extremely limited anonymous blocks can be run from Crystal SQL Commands, as demonstrated in the next chapter. A Stored Program unit would have additional syntax for naming purposes and be stored in the database.

Types

Built-in Oracle SQL types were discussed in previous chapters. PL/SQL has additional types and allows the user to create new types using the TYPE keyword. A type declaration must precede its use in any variable declarations.

Variables

Variables and constants must be declared before they are used in the execution section. Any SQL datatype may be used, as well as additional datatypes that are only available for use with PL/SQL, such as the Boolean type. Complex datatypes such as records and collections are also allowed. PL/SQL variables are declared with the following syntax:

```
DECLARE
  VariableName1 datatype [[NOT NULL] DEFAULT expression];
  VariableName2 datatype [[NOT NULL] := expression];
  ...
```

Variables may be declared with a default value using either the DEFAULT keyword or the assignment operator as just illustrated. Any variables declared with a default value may also be declared as NOT NULL. A variable cannot be declared as NOT NULL if no default value is supplied.

Entire subprograms may also be defined in the declaration section for use in the execution or exception sections. Subprograms defined in the declaration section of a block are considered local to the block and cannot be called from other blocks.

%TYPE   Two special attributes exist that can be used to define PL/SQL variable datatypes. When creating PL/SQL programs, it is often necessary to create variable types that correspond to existing database column types. The %TYPE attribute can be used to create a variable that has the same type as a database column:

```
VariableName Table.Column%TYPE
```

If the type of Table.Column changes, the PL/SQL block will need to be revalidated and may possibly need modifications to account for the changed type. However, the use of %TYPE is recommended because it ensures matching types and can help insulate the PL/SQL code from changes in the database.

%ROWTYPE   %ROWTYPE is similar to %TYPE, but defines an entire row:

```
VariableName Table%ROWTYPE
```

%ROWTYPE is often used when declaring the return type for cursors.

Statements

All PL/SQL statements must end with a semicolon. There are two categories of statements: simple assignment statements and more complex control structures.

Assignment   Assignment statements assign a value to a variable. Assignment is done with the assignment operator (:=) via an INTO statement, or with a subprogram parameter. Here is an example using the assignment operator:

```
VariableName2 := VariableName1+10;
```

Here is an example using a SELECT INTO statement:

```
SELECT salary INTO VariableName1
  FROM employee
 WHERE employee_id = VariableName2;
```

Control Structures   There are several statement types that control program flow within PL/SQL blocks, such as IF-THEN-ELSE, CASE, LOOP, WHILE-LOOP, and FOR-LOOP. The syntax for each control structure is shown.

IF-THEN-ELSE

```
IF condition THEN
  statement(s)
[ELSIF condition THEN
  statement(s)]
[ELSE
  statement(s)]
END IF;
```

The ELSE and ELSIF clauses are optional and multiple ELSIF clauses are allowed. IF statements may be nested.

CASE

```
CASE selector
  WHEN expression1 THEN statement(s)
```

```
  WHEN expression2 THEN statement(s)
  ...
  WHEN expressionN THEN statement(s)
[ELSE statement(s)]
END CASE;
```

Searched CASE

```
CASE
  WHEN condition1 THEN statement(s)
  WHEN condition2 THEN statement(s)
  ...
  WHEN conditionN THEN statement(s)
[ELSE statement(s)]
END CASE;
```

NOTE

The CASE statement is new in PL/SQL as of Oracle 9i.

LOOP

```
LOOP
  Statement(s)
END LOOP;
```

A LOOP statement must contain an EXIT or RETURN statement somewhere in its statement block or it will execute indefinitely. EXIT can be unconditional or contain a condition as in an EXIT WHEN statement.

WHILE-LOOP

```
WHILE condition LOOP
  Statement(s)
END LOOP;
```

FOR-LOOP

```
FOR counter IN [REVERSE] start_number ... end_number LOOP
Statement(s)
END LOOP;
```

Cursors

When any data manipulation statement is executed within PL/SQL (SELECT, INSERT, DELETE, UPDATE), a construct called a cursor is created. The cursor allows the PL/SQL code to interact with the results of the SQL statement. Cursors can be implicitly or explicitly declared. A cursor will be created implicitly for any SQL statement except those statements that return more than one row of data. For multirow result sets, a cursor must be explicitly declared.

Declaring Cursors

Cursors are defined in the declaration section like other PL/SQL variables, but they cannot be used in assignment statements or other expressions like normal variables. The syntax for declaring a cursor is as follows:

```
CURSOR cursor_name [(cursor_parameter1[, cursor_parameter2, ...])]
[RETURN return_type] IS select_statement;
```

All cursor parameters are considered IN parameters and must state the datatype. Cursor parameters can be given default values.

Opening Cursors

Opening a cursor executes the SELECT statement but does not return the result set. Any parameters that do not have default values must be specified in the open statement:

```
OPEN cursor_name [(param1_val[, param2_val, ...])]
```

Fetching from Cursors

Each call to FETCH returns one row from the cursor result set. The cursor attribute %NOTFOUND will return TRUE when no more rows are available. Fetching is commonly done in a LOOP, as shown here:

```
LOOP
  FETCH cursor_name INTO variable
  EXIT WHEN cursor_name%NOTFOUND
  -Do stuff
END LOOP;
```

The cursor attribute %FOUND will return TRUE as long as there are still unprocessed rows. A cursor can be closed before the end of the result set is reached if desired. If fetching is done past the end of the result set, no exception will be raised.

The cursor attribute %ISOPEN will return TRUE if the cursor is open. The cursor attribute %ROWCOUNT returns the number of rows successfully fetched at the time of the call.

Bulk fetching rather than row-by-row fetching can be done using the BULK COLLECT clause. To fetch using BULK COLLECT, one or more collection variables must be defined to contain the data returned. BULK COLLECT is useful to limit the number of network trips required to return the entire dataset; see Oracle documentation for more information.

Closing Cursors

Once a cursor is closed, it can be reopened with different parameter values. Rows cannot be fetched from a closed cursor. A cursor is closed using the following syntax:

```
CLOSE Cursor_Name;
```

Cursor FOR LOOPs

A cursor FOR LOOP is a shortened method of opening, fetching, and closing a cursor. The cursor_rec variable is not declared in the declaration section of the PL/SQL block, but is used only by the cursor loop and is only accessible inside the cursor loop. The syntax is shown next:

```
FOR cursor_rec IN cursor_name LOOP
  -do stuff
  -reference fields as cursor_rec.field_name
END LOOP;
```

To use this syntax, the cursor_name must have been declared previously. Another version of the cursor FOR LOOP that does not require that a cursor be declared explicitly is shown next. In this case, the SELECT statement is defined directly in the FOR LOOP.

```
FOR cursor_rec IN (select_statement) LOOP
  -do stuff
  -reference fields as cursor_rec.field_name
END LOOP;
```

REF CURSORs (Cursor Variables)

A cursor corresponds to the work area that Oracle creates to process the particular SELECT statement defined by the cursor declaration. A cursor variable is a pointer that points to or references a work area. A cursor variable contains the memory location of a cursor work area, much like pointers in other languages. A cursor cannot be passed as a parameter, but a cursor variable or REF CURSOR can.

To use cursor variables, you first create a type of REF CURSOR and then create variables or parameters of that type:

```
TYPE ref_cursor_type_name REF CURSOR [RETURN return_type];
```

Cursor variables declared without a RETURN clause are called weakly typed reference cursors; cursor variables declared with a RETURN clause are strongly typed reference cursors. The compiler will return an error if a strongly typed reference cursor is used and the return types do not match.

Opening REF CURSORs

When opening a reference cursor, the SELECT statement to be executed must be supplied.

```
OPEN cursor_var FOR select_statement;
```

No parameters can be passed when opening a reference cursor, but the SELECT statement can contain references to PL/SQL variables. A cursor variable can be reopened without first closing it.

Cursor variables can be declared as formal parameters for procedures in a package specification and/or package body, or they can be declared in standalone procedures using reference cursor types declared in other package specifications. They cannot be declared in packages directly.

Transaction Control

Transaction control statements such as COMMIT and ROLLBACK can be executed within a PL/SQL block. COMMIT ends a transaction and commits any database changes. ROLLBACK will undo any changes made since the previous COMMIT. Details about transaction control are outside the scope of this book and are typically not required for creating datasets for use by Crystal Reports. If a stored procedure needs to modify the database in any way, transaction control statements may be needed.

Subprograms

Subprograms are PL/SQL blocks that have been given names and stored in the database as database objects. They can take parameters and be executed if the user has the EXECUTE privilege for them. Subprograms may be declared as standalone routines or as a part of other packages. Subprograms must be the last objects declared in the declaration section of a block; they can be declared with definer rights or invoker rights. There are two types of subprograms: functions, and procedures.

Procedures

A procedure typically performs some action. The syntax for creating a standalone procedure is as follows:

```
CREATE [OR REPLACE] PROCEDURE procedure_name
  [(parameter[, parameter]...)]
  [AUTHID {DEFINER | CURRENT_USER}]
{IS | AS}
  [PRAGMA AUTONOMOUS_TRANSACTION;]
  [local declarations]
BEGIN
  executable statements
[EXCEPTION
  exception handlers]
END [name];
```

The parameter definition section has the following syntax:

```
parameter_name [IN | OUT [NOCOPY] | IN OUT [NOCOPY]] datatype
[{:= | DEFAULT} expression]
```

The CREATE PROCEDURE syntax is similar to the syntax for any PL/SQL block. The OR REPLACE clause is used to update a procedure of the same name that already exists. The AUTHID clause defines whether the procedure should execute with the privileges of the owner (or definer) or the user who is calling it. The DECLARE keyword is not used, but declarations are placed between the IS or AS and the BEGIN keyword. Exception handling is done in the EXCEPTION section.

A procedure is called by listing its name, along with any supplied parameter values enclosed in parentheses, followed by a semicolon. If there are no parameters, the parentheses are not used.

Crystal Reports can use a particular type of PL/SQL procedure (one that returns a reference cursor) directly. Additionally, other types of procedures can be called from REF CURSOR stored procedures or by functions that can be used in SQL Expressions, SQL Commands, or stored procedures.

Functions

A function is similar to a procedure and can have parameters. However, a function returns only one value and can be used in expressions similar to variables. Some functions can be used in SQL statements.

Syntax for function creation includes declaring the datatype of the return value:

```
CREATE [OR REPLACE ] FUNCTION function_name
  [( parameter [ , parameter ]... ) ] RETURN datatype
...
```

The RETURN statement must be used somewhere within the body of the function to indicate the value that will be returned from the function. RETURN can be used more than once within the body of the function, but the first RETURN that is encountered during execution will cause the function to end processing and return the value.

For a function to be callable from a Crystal SQL command or SQL Expression, several conditions must be met. Two of the basic conditions are that the function must be callable from a SELECT statement, and it must not modify the database or use any transaction control statements. For other restrictions refer to Oracle documentation.

An Oracle function to convert a timestamp to a date is demonstrated in Chapter 2.

Subprogram Parameters

Declared subprogram parameters cannot have a size constraint. For example, Param1 VARCHAR2 is allowed, but Param1 VARCHAR2(32) is not. If a size constraint is needed, a datatype of the desired size should be created and then used as the type for the parameter instead of using a built-in datatype.

Procedure parameters can be passed using positional notation or named notation, or a mixture of the two. Positional notation assumes that the first value in the call to the procedure should be matched to the first declared parameter for the procedure, and the second to the second, and so forth. Parameters can only be omitted from the call if they are IN parameters, have default values, and are the last parameters in the procedure declaration. Named notation uses the following syntax, where the parameters can be passed in any order. Using named notation, any IN parameters with default values can be omitted from the call.

```
Procedure_name(parameter_name_a=>parameter_value_a,
               parameter_name_b=>parameter_value_b,
               ...)
```

To use mixed notation, all parameters for which you want to use positional must come first, followed by any named notation parameters.

Functions referenced in Crystal SQL Expressions or SQL Commands must use positional notation. Stored procedure calls can use named notation in situations using pass-through SQL, if the returning REF CURSOR is defined first in the parameter list or before any parameters that will be called with named notation.

When a stored procedure dataset is chosen from the Database Expert, Crystal will generate report parameters and associated prompts for each parameter that exists, in the order they are defined, and it will include a host variable for the REF CURSOR. See the following illustration to see the Show SQL Query dialog box to call the stored procedure using the native driver.

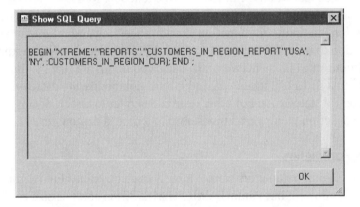

In situations where the developer wishes to hide certain parameter prompts from the user, SQL Command can be used to call the procedure, embedding default values where appropriate. The user will be prompted only for the parameters that the developer specifically defines in the SQL Command.

Suppose you want to develop a report that displays customers in a particular U.S. state and you know that you have a stored procedure that will return customer data based on the country and region. Create a report based on the stored procedure XTREME.REPORTS.CUSTOMERS_IN_REGION_REPORT. You will be prompted to enter two parameters, one for the country and one for the region (see Figure 5-1). For this particular report, the country will always be USA. You could write another procedure specifically for this report that would only have the Region parameter, but that would be a lot of work simply to avoid being prompted for the Country parameter. Another solution, at least with the Crystal Reports ODBC driver, is to put the procedure call in a SQL Command. Either of the following commands will accomplish the goal of eliminating the parameter prompt for Country:

```
{Call "XTREME"."REPORTS"."CUSTOMERS_IN_REGION_REPORT"
   ('{?State}',  'USA' )}
```

The second call demonstrates the use of named notation and would not be possible if the REF CURSOR were not listed as the first parameter for the procedure:

```
{Call
  "XTREME"."REPORTS"."CUSTOMERS_IN_REGION_REPORT"
   ("IN_COUNTRY" => 'USA', "IN_REGION" => '{?State}') }
```

NOTE

Neither these calls, nor their BEGIN ... END counterparts, work using the native driver.

Parameters have a mode defined for them. The default mode is IN, meaning that the value is passed into the procedure and inside the procedure the parameter is treated like a constant. The OUT mode is used to pass values back to the calling routine. The value passed into an OUT parameter must be a variable. It cannot be a constant or an expression. If the OUT parameter variable had a value before the subprogram

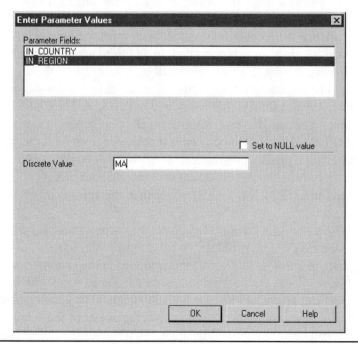

Figure 5-1   *Parameter prompts for stored procedure*

call, it will be overwritten by the subprogram. An OUT parameter is treated like a variable within the subprogram. The third available mode is IN OUT. It is similar to an OUT parameter, but its initial value inside the subprogram is whatever value was passed in the subprogram call.

Subprogram Privileges

To call a standalone subprogram, the current user must either own the subprogram, or have the EXECUTE privilege for that specific subprogram. In addition, the user may require privileges on any objects that are selected from or modified by the subprogram. The AUTHID clause of the subprogram specification determines whether the subprogram runs under the privileges of the owner or the privileges of the current user.

The default value for AUTHID is DEFINER. If a procedure is using definer rights, the schema owner's privileges are used, no matter which user is calling the subprogram. In this situation, granting the EXECUTE privilege on the subprogram is sufficient to allow the subprogram to execute, assuming a couple of things: first, the owner of the subprogram must have the necessary rights required by the statements in the subprogram granted to him directly (that is, not via any role). Therefore, if the subprogram selects from a table, the owner must have the SELECT privilege on that table granted to his user ID and not given him via a role. Secondly, the owner's rights must be in effect when the procedure is called. They must not have been revoked at any time since the subprogram was compiled. In addition, under definer rights, any object references that are not fully qualified will be resolved as if the owner of the subprogram was making the references rather than the caller of the subprogram.

The other possible value for AUTHID is CURRENT_USER. The CURRENT_USER is usually the session owner. However, if the user calls a subprogram that uses definer rights, the CURRENT_USER is the owner of that subprogram until that subprogram is finished. Therefore, if that subprogram called another subprogram that used invoker rights, the invoker rights subprogram would consider that the owner of the calling subprogram was the CURRENT_USER, rather than the session owner. It can be very confusing.

When AUTHID is set to CURRENT_USER, the current user, as just defined, needs not only the EXECUTE privilege on the subprogram, but also any other privileges required to execute the statements contained in the subprogram. In this case, the required privileges can be granted via roles and need not be granted directly. In addition, any object references that are not fully qualified will be resolved as if CURRENT_USER was making the reference, not the owner of the subprogram.

Invoker rights can be very powerful in situations where each schema has copies of the application objects. Using subprograms declared with invoker rights enables the use of one set of code for all schemas, doing away with the need to copy code as well as tables to each schema. The choice for AUTHID should be made depending on the desired security scheme for the database and the application structure.

Packages

A PL/SQL package is a collection of variable and type declarations and subprogram definitions. A package has a specification and a body. The specification is the public part of a package and contains declarations of objects that can be shared with other packages, standalone subprograms, or SQL statements. The package body contains declarations for any objects that are private to the package, along with the bodies of all cursors and subprograms, and an initialization section.

You create a package specification using the following syntax:

```
CREATE [OR REPLACE] PACKAGE package_name
  [AUTHID {CURRENT_USER | DEFINER}]
  {IS | AS}
[type declarations]
[variable declarations]
[cursor or subprogram specifications]
END;
```

A package body is created using this syntax.

```
CREATE [OR REPLACE] PACKAGE BODY package_name
  {IS | AS}
[type declarations]
[variable declarations]
[cursor or subprogram bodies]
BEGIN
[initialization statements]
END;
```

To call a subprogram that is stored in a package, you must prefix the subprogram name with the package name and possibly the schema name.

Cursors, procedures, and functions are the only object types that require any code in the package body. If no cursors, procedures, or functions are declared in the package specification, and no initialization is required, no package body needs to be created. Cursors and subprograms that need to be public must have their specifications in the package specification and their bodies in the package body. Cursors and subprograms that can be private to the package do not need a specification in the package specification.

Cursor Specifications

Cursors are declared in the specification part of a package without their defining SELECT statement. The entire cursor declaration, including the SELECT statement, must be given in the package body. This allows for changes to the SELECT statement without requiring any changes to the package specification. However, the return types must match between the package specification and the package body. Another advantage of declaring cursors in a package specification is that they can be used by other program units.

Subprogram Specifications

Subprograms are declared in the package specification by stating their name and giving the parameters and return datatypes. The subprogram specification will be identical to the subprogram body except that it is truncated before the IS or AS. The specification gives the information necessary to call the subprogram, but none of the actual implementation steps. If a subprogram does not need to be public, it does not need a specification in the package specification. It can just be defined in the declaration section of the package body.

SQL in PL/SQL

Most SQL data manipulation statements can be used with little or no modification in PL/SQL. INSERT, UPDATE, and DELETE statements can be executed directly in PL/SQL blocks. To use SELECT statements in PL/SQL, a provision must be made to store or process the returned rows. The use of cursors and cursor variables for this purpose is discussed in the preceding sections. Another method is to use the INTO clause of the SELECT statement to store the returned values in another structure.

Other types of statements cannot be executed directly in PL/SQL blocks. These statements include data definition statements such as CREATE, data control statements such as GRANT, and session control statements such as ALTER SESSION.

Native Dynamic SQL

PL/SQL has two methods for allowing dynamic execution of SQL statements. The older method relies on a built-in PL/SQL package called DBMS_SQL, and we will not be discussing it. The newer method is called Native Dynamic SQL and will be covered briefly. There are two general situations where Native Dynamic SQL is useful, for execution of data definition, data control, session control statements and programmatically created SQL statements.

PL/SQL lets you execute data manipulation SQL statements, such as SELECT, INSERT, UPDATE, and DELETE, but you cannot execute data definition statements such as CREATE or DROP, grant privileges, or execute session control statements. Native Dynamic SQL is the solution. In some situations, it is desirable to construct a SQL statement at runtime. EXECUTE IMMEDIATE can be used to run any SQL string, whether given as a constant, or constructed programmatically.

A call to the Native Dynamic SQL command EXECUTE IMMEDIATE uses the following syntax:

```
EXECUTE IMMEDIATE dynamic_string
[INTO {define_variable[, define_variable]... | record}]
[USING [IN | OUT | IN OUT] bind_argument
[, [IN | OUT | IN OUT] bind_argument]...]
[{RETURNING | RETURN} INTO bind_argument[, bind_argument]...];
```

Dynamic_string must be a valid SQL statement or PL/SQL block. If it is a SQL statement, omit the ending semicolon. If it is a PL/SQL block, include the ending semicolon. The INTO clause is optional and allows you to output results of the query into variables or PL/SQL records. Dynamic_string can be written to include bind variables. To populate the bind variable, use the USING clause. The RETURNING INTO clause is used when the SQL statement contains a RETURNING clause.

EXECUTE IMMEDIATE cannot return more than one row. If you need to execute dynamic SQL that has a multirow result set, you must use the dynamic form of the OPEN-FOR statement.

Native Dynamic SQL statements can be used in stored procedures that return datasets to Crystal Reports.

REF CURSOR Stored Procedures

PL/SQL cursors are objects that are used to process the rows returned by a query. A REF CURSOR is a pointer to a cursor. When a cursor is opened, the associated query is executed. Subsequent fetch commands will retrieve each of the individual rows of the query result set. Closing a cursor disables it and frees the associated resources. Stored procedures that return cursor variables or REF CURSORs can be used as Crystal Reports datasets and will appear in the Database Expert when the Stored Procedures database option is checked for a database.

NOTE

Stored procedures that do not return REF CURSORs will also appear in the Database Expert, but an error will be generated if they are chosen for reporting. Using some drivers, even functions will appear in the Database Expert if Stored Procedures is checked. However, only stored procedures meeting all the necessary conditions will work as datasets.

When using Oracle stored procedures as Crystal Reports datasets, several conditions must be met. The following list was compiled using the Crystal Decisions paper entitled "Oracle Stored Procedures and Crystal Reports" as a starting point. Additional conditions and other clarifications have been added.

NOTE

The following discussions consider only the native and Crystal ODBC (both regular and Wire Protocol) drivers for Oracle 8i and 9i. For other connectivity options, refer back to Chapter 1 and review Table 1-1 for tested capabilities.

Stored Procedure Requirements

1. The REF CURSOR type to be used in the stored procedure must be declared in a package prior to the declaration of the stored procedure. For Crystal Reports 9, this can be in the same package where the stored procedure is declared or in a separate package and can be either a weakly or a strongly typed REF CURSOR. Stored procedures declared inside of packages will appear under the "Qualifiers" folder of the Database Expert for the native driver and under the "Stored Procedures" folder for the ODBC drivers.

2. The stored procedure must contain a parameter of type REF CURSOR.

3. The REF CURSOR must be defined as an IN OUT parameter.

4. Any other parameters must be defined as IN only.

5. The body of the stored procedure must open the REF CURSOR. The REF CURSOR must open successfully. Crystal Reports can then fetch the records.

6. The stored procedure can have only one REF CURSOR parameter. The structure of the cursor record cannot change based on an IN parameter, even if the REF CURSOR is weakly typed.

7. The REF CURSOR must not be fetched from or closed after it is opened in the body of the stored procedure.

8. If using ODBC or OLE DB, only some drivers will work under certain conditions. Refer to Table 1-1 for details.

9. When using an ODBC driver, you must check the Procedure Returns Results checkbox on the ODBC Advanced tab for the driver.

10. Avoid using variable names or parameter names that are identical to database objects. Oracle 9*i* handles the distinction better than Oracle 8*i*, but it is best to avoid any possibility of confusion.

11. Use simple parameter types such as strings, numbers, or dates. Crystal cannot understand complex types and will not pass them properly.

A REF CURSOR type must be created before it can be used in a stored procedure. A REF CURSOR can be weakly typed or strongly typed. A weakly typed REF CURSOR is one that does not declare the record type of the cursor it references and hence can be used to reference cursors of different types at different times. A strongly typed REF CURSOR declares the record type of the cursor it references, and exceptions will be raised if it is used with an inconsistent cursor type.

When using the Crystal ODBC or Crystal ODBC WP driver, the Procedure Returns Results checkbox on the Advanced tab must be checked to enable the fetching of the dataset rows (see Figure 5-2).

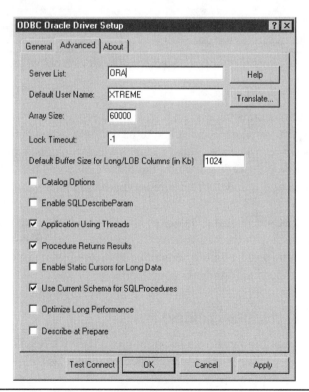

Figure 5-2   *ODBC Advanced tab for Crystal Oracle ODBC*

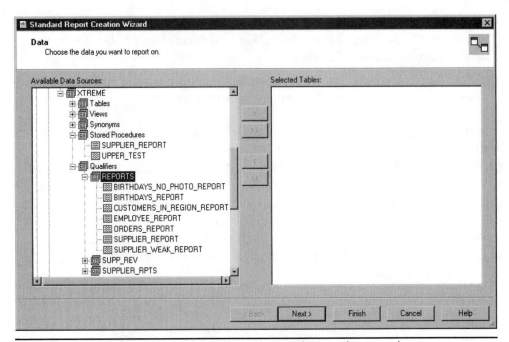

Figure 5-3 *Database Expert list for packaged procedures with native driver*

Crystal Reports 9 supports access to Oracle stored procedures inside of packages. In earlier versions, the stored procedures had to be declared outside of Oracle packages as standalone procedures. When using the native driver, standalone stored procedures appear under the Stored Procedures folder, but packaged stored procedures appear under the Qualifiers folder under a folder representing the package name, as shown in Figure 5-3.

When using ODBC drivers, the Database Expert lists the stored procedures differently than it does with the native driver. There is no Qualifiers folder. Stored procedures defined in packages are listed under the Stored Procedures folder with the package name appended to the procedure name (see Figure 5-4).

Simple Stored Procedure Example

The demonstration that follows uses a strongly typed REF CURSOR and places the stored procedure in a package. The package specification is as follows:

```
CREATE OR REPLACE   PACKAGE XTREME.SUPPLIER_RPTS   AS

TYPE Supp_Rpt_Rec_Type IS RECORD
  (Supplier_ID    Supplier.Supplier_ID%TYPE,
   Supplier_Name Supplier.Supplier_Name%Type,
   Country        Supplier.Country%Type,
   Phone          Supplier.Phone%Type,
   AUSID          number);

TYPE Supp_Rpt_Type IS REF CURSOR RETURN Supp_Rpt_Rec_Type;

PROCEDURE Supplier_Report
  (Supp_Rpt_Cur IN OUT Supp_Rpt_Type,
   Supplier_Par IN     Supplier.Supplier_Id%TYPE);

END SUPPLIER_RPTS;
```

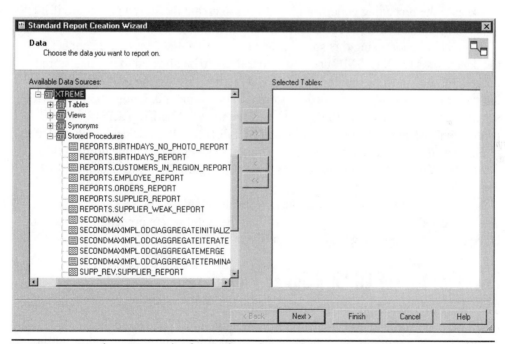

Figure 5-4   *Database Expert list for packaged procedures with ODBC driver*

The package body is as follows:

```
CREATE OR REPLACE  PACKAGE BODY XTREME.SUPPLIER_RPTS  AS
PROCEDURE Supplier_Report
  (Supp_Rpt_Cur IN OUT Supp_Rpt_Type,
   Supplier_Par IN    Supplier.Supplier_Id%TYPE)
IS
  BEGIN
    OPEN Supp_Rpt_Cur for
      SELECT Supplier_ID, Supplier_Name,
             Country, Phone, userenv('sessionid') AUSID
        FROM Supplier
       WHERE Supplier_ID=Supplier_Par;
  END Supplier_Report;

END SUPPLIER_RPTS;
```

Execute the preceding code from SQL*Plus to create the stored procedure if it is not already created in the XTREME schema.

To create a report using this stored procedure, start a new report and connect to the database as the XTREME user. For other users to be allowed to use this stored procedure, they must be granted the EXECUTE privilege for the procedure and use the native driver or call the procedure from a SQL Command. Under the XTREME schema, open the Qualifiers folder. You will see the SUPPLIER_REPORT stored procedure listed under Qualifiers, then under SUPPLIER_RPTS. Select Supplier_Report.

Because this stored procedure has an input parameter, you will be prompted for a discrete value for the Supplier_Par, as shown in Figure 5-5. Enter 2 and click OK. Finish the report as usual.

Much more complex stored procedures, capable of almost any processing need, can also be created. Stored procedures are particularly useful where procedural processing is required or where parsing must be kept to a minimum.

Privileges for REF CURSOR Stored Procedures

The owner of a stored procedure automatically has EXECUTE privileges on it. Any other user who needs to execute the stored procedure must be granted the EXECUTE privilege for it, assuming that the procedure uses definer rights. See "Subprogram Privileges" earlier in this chapter for more information about required privileges and definer versus invoker rights. The ODBC drivers do not currently display stored procedures defined in schemas other than the schema of the logged in user, so they are not directly accessible as datasets. However, stored procedures owned by other users can be called using a SQL Command.

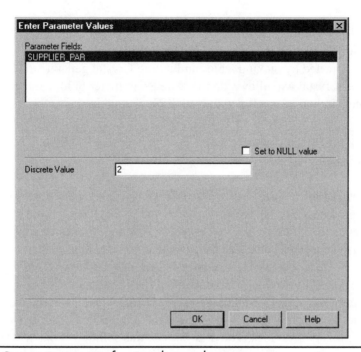

Figure 5-5   *Parameter prompts for stored procedure parameters*

NOTE

The ODBC drivers have an advanced setting called Use Current Schema for SQL Procedures that is checked by default. Unchecking this option allows the viewing of stored procedures in other users' schemas. Unchecking this option allows the viewing of stored procedures in other user's schemas. However, in my testing, it could take thirty to forty minutes to redraw the Database Expert dialog when this option is not checked, so you may find it to be an unusable option.

Stored Procedure Parameters and Crystal

Stored procedures that are intended to be used with Crystal Reports should contain only simple parameter types as Crystal will not properly interpret any complex types. String, number, and date types work well. If you choose a stored procedure as a data source for a report, Crystal will create parameters matching the procedure parameters. In the report designer, you can select those parameters and fine-tune their properties in simple ways: you can add a prompting string and set a default value, but you cannot make the parameter be a range or allow multiple values. You have similar options if you are calling the stored procedure from a SQL Command and creating your own parameters.

Multivalued Parameters

It is often desirable to allow the user to choose multiple values for a parameter. In a Crystal Report created by picking tables and letting Crystal generate the SQL query, this is possible. Crystal will allow you to create a parameter field that can accept multiple values. It then adds a list to the WHERE clause similar to the following:

```
WHERE datafield = parameter value 1 OR
      datafield = parameter value 2 OR
      datafield = parameter value 3 ...
```

When using stored procedures, multivalued Crystal parameter fields cannot be used.

If you programmatically call reports, you may be able to work around this problem using your development language. You could, for instance, populate a table with the values and base your report on a join between that table and the actual data tables. In this situation, you would have to maintain the parameter table via your application, and the report would be useless if run outside of the application.

Another option is to pass a comma-delimited string as one parameter and parse it for use in the stored procedure. The following examples demonstrate two different methods using this general idea. The drawback to this solution is that a very long string may be required, and the report user must input a comma-delimited list of values.

The first option uses a temporary table. This table is in the XTREME schema and is defined as shown:

```
CREATE GLOBAL TEMPORARY TABLE NUMBER_PARAM_TEMP
  (NUMBER_PARAM  NUMBER(10) NOT NULL,
   CONSTRAINT NUMBER_PARAM_TEMP_PK
              PRIMARY KEY(NUMBER_PARAM) USING INDEX)
ON COMMIT PRESERVE ROWS;
```

This table will hold the parameter values. A function has been created in the TOOLS package that will parse a comma-delimited string and insert the values into the temporary table. The function is called PARAM_TO_NUMBER_PARAM_TEMP. A stored procedure using this approach has been created called REPORTS.SUPPLIER_MULTI_REPORT_1. The body of the procedure is as shown:

```
PROCEDURE Supplier_Multi_Report_1
  (Supp_Rpt_Cur IN OUT Supp_Rpt_Type,
   SupplierVar  IN     VARCHAR2)
IS
  BEGIN
    TOOLS.PARAM_TO_NUMBER_PARAM_TEMP(SupplierVar);
```

```
OPEN Supp_Rpt_Cur FOR
   SELECT Supplier_ID, Supplier_Name,
          Country, Phone, userenv('sessionid') AUSID
     FROM Supplier, Number_Param_Temp
    WHERE Supplier.Supplier_id=Number_Param_Temp.Number_Param;
END Supplier_Multi_Report_1;
```

NOTE

For the native driver, the temporary table does not need to be defined with the ON COMMIT PRESERVE ROWS clause. The ODBC drivers treat transactions differently.

Create a report using this procedure and enter a comma-delimited string of values, such as "1, 2, 4" at the parameter prompt. You should see rows in the report for the Supplier_IDs of 1, 2, and 4.

The second option uses a table type. The table type has been defined in the XTREME schema as follows:

```
CREATE TYPE "XTREME"."NUMBER_PARAM_TABLE_TYPE" AS
    TABLE OF NUMBER;
```

A function has been created in the TOOLS package called PARAM_TO_NUM_ PARAM_TABLE_TYPE that will accept a comma-delimited string and return a variable of the Number_Param_Table_Type type. A stored procedure using this approach has been created called REPORTS.SUPPLIER_MULTI_REPORT_2. The body of the procedure for Oracle 9*i* is as shown:

```
PROCEDURE Supplier_Multi_Report_2
  (Supp_Rpt_Cur IN OUT Supp_Rpt_Type,
   SupplierVar   IN     VARCHAR2)
IS
  BEGIN
    OPEN Supp_Rpt_Cur for
      SELECT Supplier_ID, Supplier_Name,
             Country, Phone, userenv('sessionid') AUSID
        FROM Supplier
       WHERE Supplier_id IN
       (Select * FROM
        TABLE(TOOLS.PARAM_TO_NUM_PARAM_TABLE_TYPE(SupplierVar)));
  END Supplier_Multi_Report_2;
```

For Oracle 8*i*, the WHERE clause should be changed to

```
WHERE Supplier_id IN
(SELECT * from THE
(SELECT CAST(TOOLS.PARAM_TO_NUM_PARAM_TABLE_TYPE(SupplierVar)
          AS NUMBER_PARAM_TABLE_TYPE) FROM DUAL));
```

Create a report using Supplier_Multi_Report_2 and enter a comma-delimited string at the parameter prompt. The results should be identical to option 1.

Using Temporary Tables

Temporary tables are often used in stored procedures to store intermediate results, or even the final result of complex processing. Temporary tables are created much like regular tables, except that the keywords GLOBAL TEMPORARY are inserted between CREATE and TABLE in the data definition statement, as shown:

```
CREATE GLOBAL TEMPORARY TABLE table_name
...
  [ON COMMIT {PRESERVE|DELETE} ROWS]
```

Once a temporary table is created, its definition persists until it is dropped, just as with an ordinary table. A temporary table is different from an ordinary table in the treatment of its data. Rows in a temporary table are visible only to the session that inserted them and only until the end of the current transaction or session depending on the ON COMMIT clause. If the temporary table is defined with the ON COMMIT PRESERVE directive, the data will persist for the session. Otherwise, the data will persist for the duration of the current transaction. Multiple users can use the same temporary table and will not see each other's data.

The example in the previous section for multivalued parameters also demonstrates the use of a temporary table.

Calling Stored Procedures from SQL Commands

Stored procedures may be called from Crystal Reports SQL Commands, except when using the native driver. For some of the database drivers, stored procedures do not show up in the Database Expert or cannot be used successfully when picked from the Database Expert, but they do succeed when called from a SQL Command. Refer back to Table 1-1 (in Chapter 1) for details. Enter a statement similar to one of the following to call a procedure from a SQL Command:

```
{CALL ProcSchema.ProcPackage.ProcName(Param1, Param2,...)}
```

or

```
BEGIN
  ProcSchema.ProcPagckage.ProcName(Param1, Param2, ...);
END;
```

The REF CURSOR parameter should not be listed. For procedures, which have parameters other than the REF CURSOR parameter, create the parameters using the Create button. Positional or named notation can be used for the parameter calls. If using named notation, the REF CURSOR parameter must be listed before any parameters using named notation.

For your stored procedure, connect to XTREME using the Crystal Oracle ODBC driver or the Crystal WP Oracle ODBC driver and choose the Add Command option. You need a number parameter for the SUPPLIER_ID. Click Create, enter Supplier as the parameter name, and choose Number for the value type, as shown next.

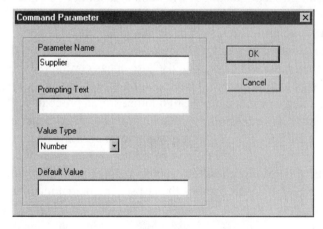

Enter the following call as the SQL Command:

```
{Call Supplier_Rpts.Supplier_Report({?Supplier})}
```

To embed the parameter name, put the cursor where the parameter needs to be inserted and double-click the parameter name. It will be inserted for you; click OK. You will be prompted to input a value for the parameter and then you will be returned to the Database Expert with the Command added as a data source to your report.

Procedures called by using an anonymous block (BEGIN ... END) can execute multiple PL/SQL statements. This functionality is not documented and hence not necessarily reliable. Experimentation shows that statements can be added after the call to the REF CURSOR stored procedure, but not before. For example, if you wanted to insert a record into an audit table when the report is run, you could add an INSERT statement after the stored procedure call, as shown:

```
BEGIN
 Reports.Supplier_Report({?Supplier});
 INSERT INTO RPT_AUDIT Values('Supplier_Report', SYSDATE);
END;
```

Because the stored procedure merely opens a cursor, any statements inserted here will happen after the cursor is opened but before any records are fetched from the cursor.

It's advisable to add any necessary processing to the stored procedure itself and not rely on this feature, especially because this type of call is not allowed when using the native driver and report users may not have the necessary privileges.

Stored Procedure Myths

There are many misconceptions about what can and cannot be done in a stored procedure that will be used by Crystal Reports. Many conditions can affect the capabilities of a stored procedure, such as driver and executable versions, so what may work in one situation may not work in another. This section clarifies some of those issues for the native and Crystal ODBC drivers as configured in Chapter 1.

The Crystal Decisions document, "Oracle Stored Procedures and Crystal Reports," states that the stored procedure cannot call another stored procedure. However, this restriction is not strictly true. Another procedure can be called either before or after the opening of the REF CURSOR, but any statements after the opening of the REF CURSOR, whether they call other stored procedures or not, must not access the records in the REF CURSOR, unless they reopen the REF CURSOR later. An OPEN statement for the REF CURSOR must be the last statement that manipulates the REF CURSOR so that Crystal Reports can start fetching the first record.

Anything can be done in the stored procedure, including any data manipulation, even updating and deleting, as long as the REF CURSOR is treated as just discussed.

The position of the REF CURSOR parameter in the parameter list does not matter. It does not need to be the first parameter or the last parameter; it can be anywhere in the list. There is an exception to this, however, when calling stored procedures from SQL Commands using named notation. If you use named notation, the REF CURSOR parameter is still referenced with positional notation and so must come before the parameters using named notation.

The EXECUTE IMMEDIATE PL/SQL directive can be used in stored procedures for Crystal Reports. EXECUTE IMMEDIATE is used to accomplish actions that are otherwise not allowed from PL/SQL, such as Data Definition Language statements (DDL), or to run a statement that is created programmatically.

Temporary tables can be created in stored procedures. They can be manipulated in stored procedures whether or not they are created in the procedure. If you are reporting from a REF CURSOR stored procedure, you must still create a REF CURSOR, even if it does nothing but SELECT * from the temporary table. Note that regular tables can also be created and/or dropped in stored procedures, but using true temporary tables is more efficient, and there is no need to drop them.

Both weakly and strongly bound REF CURSORS are usable with the native or Crystal Oracle ODBC drivers, both regular and Wire Protocol. There may be problems with other drivers (see Table 1-1 in Chapter 1) or with earlier versions of Crystal (check version numbers in Table 1-1), but if you are using Crystal 9 and are up-to-date with hot fixes and/or service packs, you should have no problems.

Issues with Stored Procedures

Database Driver Behavior

Access to stored procedures varies depending on the database driver you are using. See Table 1-1 in Chapter 1 for details. Direct access to stored procedures (defined as picking a stored procedure as a data source in the Database Expert) whether in packages or standalone, currently works for the native driver, the Crystal Reports ODBC driver, and the Crystal Reports Wire Protocol ODBC driver. However, stored procedures defined in schemas other than the schema of the logged-in user are only accessible using the native driver and the Microsoft OLE DB driver for Oracle.

Access to stored procedures via SQL Commands currently works for the Crystal Reports ODBC driver, the Crystal Reports Wire Protocol ODBC driver, the Oracle ODBC driver, and the Microsoft OLE DB driver. This access is available regardless of who owns the stored procedure, as long as the proper EXECUTE privileges have been assigned.

Columns Without Aliases

Some drivers (MS OLE DB) require that any expressions in the SELECT list of the REF CURSOR have aliases. This is good coding practice anyway, so make sure that every column in the SELECT list either is a simple database field or has an alias defined for it.

REF CURSOR Not Opened

If the REF CURSOR is not opened in the stored procedure, or if it is closed after it has been opened, an ORA-24338 statement handle not executed will result.

Linking

When using stored procedures, it is advisable to return all required fields, rather than attempting to link the REF CURSOR stored procedure to another table, view, or stored procedure. Oracle does not directly support linking stored procedure results to other objects, and Crystal Reports' behavior in this situation could be problematic. If you link the results of a stored procedure to another table or view, all JOIN processing will occur locally, and you will receive the warning shown here.

When using REF CURSOR stored procedures as datasets, you should return everything that the report needs in the stored procedure, exclusive of data required by any subreports.

Stored Procedures in Subreports

Be wary of basing subreports on stored procedures, particularly if the subreport will be placed in the detail section. If the subreport is standalone, meaning it is not linked to the main report, there should be no issue. If the subreport will be linked to the main report, be sure that each field used in the linking is also a parameter for the stored procedure. This will ensure that each execution of the subreport returns only the data needed for that instance and is not relying on the linking to do the record filtering.

For example, assume that a stored procedure exists that returns all employee IDs and their photos and has no input parameters. You have a main report that lists employees, and you use this stored procedure to create a subreport to display their photos, placing it in the detail section and linking it on the employee ID. In this case, for each employee, the stored procedure will execute, return ALL employee photos, and Crystal will filter the subreport dataset to only the current employee. This will result in much repetitive data being returned and discarded for each employee.

The solution is to modify the stored procedure to accept the employee ID as a parameter. When you define the links for the subreport, be sure to select the actual stored procedure parameter in the Subreport Parameter Field to Use box, not a Crystal generated parameter starting with "?PM."

Moving Procedures

Stored procedures are often developed in one schema and then moved to a different schema for production use. If a report has been created that references a stored procedure and that stored procedure is subsequently moved, it is simple to modify the report. Verify that the report users have been granted EXECUTE privileges on the new procedure and use the Crystal Database/Set Datasource Location to point to the new location.

Procedure/Package Invalidation

Be aware that Oracle procedures, functions, and packages can become invalid. This can happen because of changes in database structure or changes to the PL/SQL code. In many cases, the objects just need to be recompiled and will then be usable. If you have a procedure that remains invalid after recompilation, it may indicate a true syntax error in the code or a significant change to another database object used in the procedure.

Stored procedures can be extremely powerful tools in the report writer's toolbox. This chapter has served as an overview of PL/SQL and REF CURSOR stored procedures and their use in Crystal Reports. Chapter 6 will demonstrate further optimization techniques that can be employed using combinations of Crystal Reports functionality and Oracle features.

CHAPTER 6

Optimizing: The Crystal Reports Side

This chapter describes methods that can be used to optimize report performance with Oracle using Crystal Reports' internal features. Reducing the number of records returned from the database server is emphasized, both by using grouping on the server and by using SQL Expressions in the selection formula. Reducing the number of queries sent to the server by eliminating subreports is described, and moving processing to the server by replacing Crystal Reports formulas with SQL Expressions is covered in detail. An Oracle SQL Expression equivalent for almost every available Crystal Reports operator or function is listed, and methods of calculating running totals on the server are explained. The use of SQL Commands to implement queries that would otherwise be overly complex or impossible is also covered.

Reducing the Number of Records

Reducing the number of records returned to Crystal Reports is the single most important method for optimizing report processing because fewer records means less network travel time and less report processing time.

Grouping on the Server

Crystal Reports has an option called Perform Grouping On Server. If this option is turned on and only group level data is displayed in the report, Crystal will request only summary level data from the server, thereby reducing the number of rows that are returned. Perform Grouping On Server can be set individually for a report or as a default for the environment. To set it for a report, choose File | Report Options and check Perform Grouping On Server, as shown in Figure 6-1; another method is to go to the Database menu item and check Perform Grouping On Server.

To set the default value for the environment, which will affect all new reports, choose File | Options, go to the Database tab, and check Perform Grouping On Server, as shown in Figure 6-2.

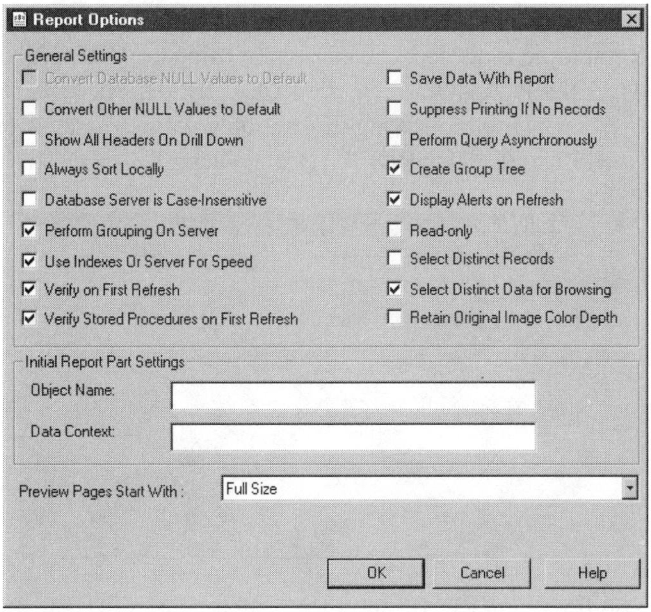

Figure 6-1 *Report options*

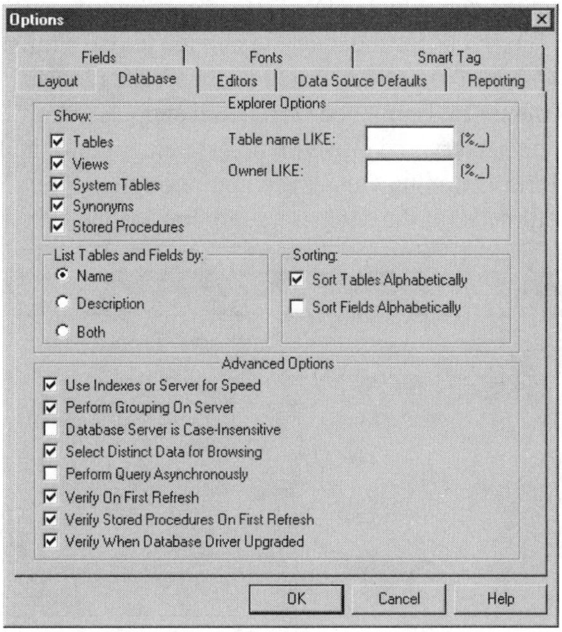

Figure 6-2 *Database options*

To demonstrate grouping on the server, say that a report showing the total order amount for each employee is needed. Create a report using the ORDERS table, and put EMPLOYEE_ID, ORDER_AMOUNT, and ORDER_ID in the detail section. A query similar to the one shown in the following illustration will be generated, and the report will display the EMPLOYEE_ID, ORDER_ID, and ORDER_AMOUNT for each order.

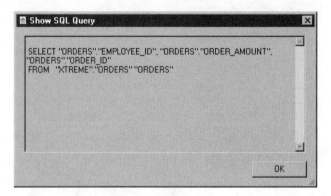

Add a group on EMPLOYEE_ID and then a subtotal on ORDER_AMOUNT by EMPLOYEE_ID to get the total for each employee. Running this report will cause 2192 records to be returned from the server. This is report Chapter 6\Order Amount by Employee with Detail.rpt.

Now suppose that the detail by ORDER_ID is not needed, so the detail section can be suppressed, which causes the query to change to one similar to the following illustration. The number of records returned is now reduced to six. This is report Chapter 6\Order Amount by Employee with detail suppressed.rpt. To see the difference between this query and one with no grouping, go to the Database menu item, uncheck Perform Grouping On Server, and rerun the report. You will see that 2192 records are returned and the database query has lost its GROUP BY clause.

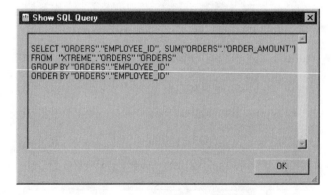

To continue, recheck Database | Perform Grouping On Server which is necessary for future report runs.

The user will be thrilled that the report runs so much faster now but might want the option to see the detail for each employee by order via drill-down. To implement drill-down, the section must be hidden rather than suppressed. Hiding the detail produces the summary query, and returns only six records as before, but drilling down on an EMPLOYEE_ID generates another query that returns the detail records for that employee. For example, drilling down on EMPLOYEE_ID 1 will return 360 records. This is report Chapter 6\Order Amount by Employee with detail hidden.rpt. In total, with one drill-down, 366 records are returned, instead of 2192.

Grouping on the Server versus Returning All Detail

When to use grouping on the server rather than returning all detail rows will depend on the specific environment. When grouping on the server, drilling down on only a few of the grouped values is more efficient than returning all of the detail records, but creating a report that uses grouping on the server when users are likely to drill down on a large portion of the summary records is not as speedy or resource efficient as returning all of the detail records in one query. Using drill-down with a server-grouped report generates many queries that return few records. Each network trip and each query parsed on the server involves overhead. If users are likely to drill-down on a large number of the summary records, you should turn off grouping on the server and let all of the detail records be returned in the main report query.

Using SQL Expressions in Selection Formulas

Reducing the number of records returned is accomplished primarily through the use of a selection formula. The selection formula determines the criteria that a row must meet in order to be returned by the query. Some record selection criteria defined in Crystal Reports selection formulas are passed through to Oracle, resulting in few records being returned; some are not. Any record selection criteria defined using the Select Expert is passed through, but *group* selection criteria defined using the Select Expert is not. Manually created criteria may be passed through, depending on their content. Any selection formula that contains references to Crystal Reports formulas, uses Crystal Reports functions other than IsNull (and a few others), or otherwise performs computations, cannot be passed through.

Appropriate use of SQL Expression fields can force record selection to occur on the server. Using a selection formula that contains functions that are not converted to their native Oracle equivalents causes all records to be returned (not excluded by other portions of the selection formula) and local filtering to be performed. For example, say you have a selection formula that returns employee records only if the employee's birthday is in January:

```
Month ({EMPLOYEE.BIRTH_DATE})=1
```

Open the report named Chapter 6\Employee Birthdays with Crystal function.rpt and preview it. Look at the SQL query, shown in the next illustration, and notice that nothing was added to the query to accomplish the birth date filtering. Therefore, all detail records will be returned from the server, and the filtering will be done locally.

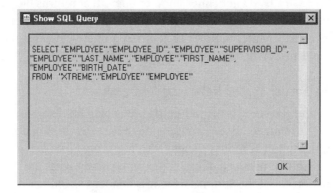

Look at the Report | Performance Information, then at the Processing section. You will see that Record Selection Done on the Database Server is listed as Partial, as shown in Figure 6-3.

If you modify the selection formula to use a SQL Expression, you can force the record selection to take place on the server. Create a SQL Expression named BirthMonth for computing the birth month using the following formula:

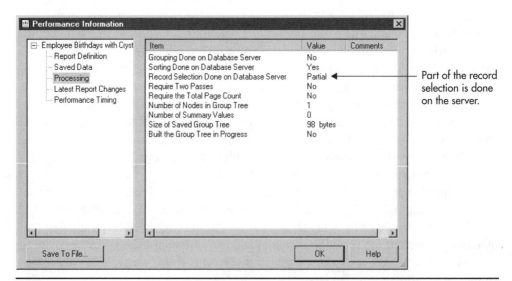

Figure 6-3   *Employee birthdays with Crystal function, performance information*

```
EXTRACT (MONTH FROM "EMPLOYEE"."BIRTH_DATE")
```

Modify the record selection formula to be as follows:

```
{%BirthMonth} = 1.00
```

Rerun the report and examine the SQL query.

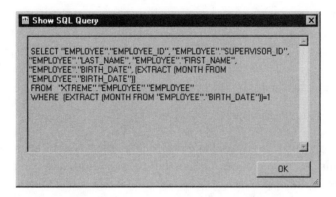

It now shows that the selection is being performed on the server. This is confirmed by the Report | Performance Information, as shown in Figure 6-4.

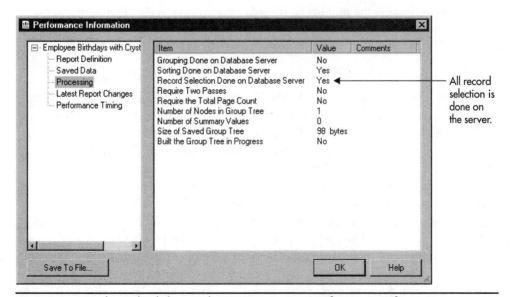

Figure 6-4   *Employee birthdays with SQL Expression, performance information*

Using SQL Expressions as replacements for Crystal Reports functions is discussed in more detail in the "SQL Expressions" section later in this chapter. Modifying your selection formulas to remove Crystal functions and replace them with SQL Expressions is a simple and highly effective method to ensure that record selection occurs on the server.

Parameters

Parameters can be used in the selection formula to limit the number of records returned. This is a commonly used method because it is effective and intuitive. To specify a parameter value so that only the data the user is concerned with is returned, insert a parameter field into the selection formula as shown:

```
{Orders.SHIPPED}= {?Shipped}
```

The use of parameters is covered in more detail in the Crystal Reports User' Guide and in other third-party references. Optimizing how Oracle parses parameterized report queries is covered in Chapter 8.

Miscellaneous Hints

In addition to limiting the number of records returned to Crystal, there are other methods to help optimize reporting.

Limiting Subreport Usage

The use of subreports can be very costly. If a subreport is placed in a detail section, it will be executed once for every detail row, that is, the subreport query will be sent to the database once for every detail row in the main report. A subreport placed in a group section will execute once for each different group value. A subreport placed in the report header or footer will execute only once for the entire report.

Many reports with subreports can be modified easily to eliminate the subreports and hence the multiple queries. Open Chapter 6\Order Detail with subreport.rpt. Run the report and scroll to the last page. You will notice that it takes a very long time to scroll to the end of the report. The lengthy time is due to the subreport being executed once for each detail record in the main report. For the sample order data, that means one query was run for the main report, and 2192 queries were run for the subreport; as shown in Figure 6-5, the subreport's Performance Timing has a large value for Time to Format All Subreport Instances. (Your actual values may differ from the figure due to differences in your environment.)

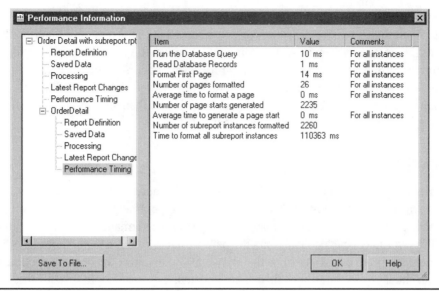

Figure 6-5   *Order detail with subreport, performance information*

Open Chapter 6\Order Detail without subreport.rpt. Run the report and scroll to the last page. Notice that the data displayed is the same as in the Order Detail with subreport report, but that there was a substantial decrease in the time required to scroll to the last record. This is achieved because the Order Detail without subreport report joins the ORDERS table to the ORDERS_DETAIL table so that the detail information is available in the main report, cutting the number of queries required to one and resulting in a substantial improvement in performance. However, the join results in a record set with multiple copies of a master row where there are multiple detail rows for that particular ORDER_ID. For example, ORDER_ID 1002 appears twice in the dataset, along with its ORDER_AMOUNT of $5,060.28. Special care must be taken when summarizing the master-level detail because of the effect of the join.

There are several options for proper handling of the duplicate master level data, depending on your needs. In the report shown, the master level fields have been moved into the group header. When a detail field is placed into a group header, Crystal Reports displays the value from the first record in the group. This option is adequate in this case because you are only displaying the master level data and not using it in computations. To use the master level data in computations, however, you would need to create a formula field that returned the maximum or minimum of the master level field and use that in any other aggregations. Because the values of the master table fields will be the same for every record in the group, any function that returns the unique value will work. You could also use the Oracle equivalent for maximum or minimum to ensure that the processing occurs on the server. A final option is to re-create the summary level data from the detail data. In this case, multiplying the UNIT_PRICE by the QUANTITY and then summing across the group will return the group's ORDER_AMOUNT.

Connection Type

The available connection types are discussed in the Chapter 1. In most situations, the native driver will be the fastest possible connection type. If an ODBC connection is required, the Wire Protocol driver may deliver the best performance. The Wire Protocol ODBC driver may be even faster than the native driver. You must experiment in your environment, given any restrictions that may exist, to discover the best connection type for your situation. As the various drivers are updated, they may leapfrog each other in performance, so it is important to stay current.

Use Union All Instead of Union

Use Union All instead of Union where possible. Union requires extra processing to filter out duplicate rows. If you know that there will never be duplicate rows, using Union All will speed up query processing.

Avoid Sort in Specified Order

Avoid use of the Crystal option to sort in a specified order because it causes the sort to occur locally, and it cannot be done on the server.

Indexed Fields

Using fields that are indexed is important in two cases. Any fields that are used for linking tables should be indexed. The Database Expert will link By Key if you so choose, as shown in Figure 6-6. Note that the By Key option does not work in the originally released version of Crystal Reports 9. You must apply the most recent hot fix to correct this problem.

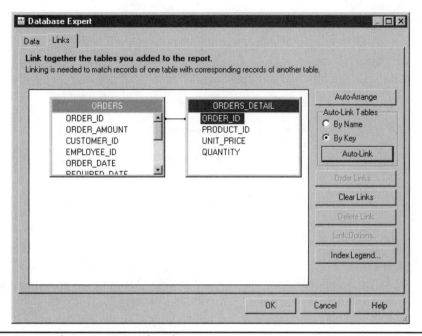

Figure 6-6   *Database Expert, Links tab*

The other case where indexing is important is in the selection formula. Fields used often for filtering should be indexed to prevent full table scans and speed up the query. See Chapter 7 for more information about appropriate database indexing.

Avoid Linking Stored Procedure Datasets to Other Objects

When using stored procedures as Crystal datasets, avoid linking those datasets to other tables, views, or stored procedures. This type of operation cannot be done on the backend and forces the linking operation to occur locally. Instead, return all required fields from the stored procedure itself.

Large Character Fields

Oracle supports several string field datatypes: CHAR, VARCHAR2, NCHAR, NVARCHAR2, CLOB, NCLOB, and LONG. However, LONG will be phased out in the future and should be replaced with CLOB or another appropriate type. Crystal treats each field as either a String or a Memo. The Oracle character types CHAR, VARCHAR2, NCHAR, and NVARCHAR2 are treated as Strings of the defined length. The Oracle LOB types, CLOB, NCLOB, and LONG, are treated as Memo fields.

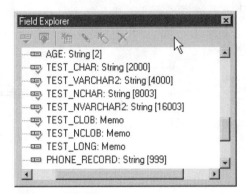

Field types that Crystal considers to be String (CHAR, VARCHAR2, NCHAR, NVARCHAR2) can be used for grouping and sorting. All of the Oracle character types can be used in formulas, although Crystal reads only the first 64K of any LOB field. Some field types are not usable by some drivers; see Table 1-1 in Chapter 1 for details.

Because some of these field types can hold a very large amount of data, it is important to reduce traffic by returning only what is truly required for any given report. Though computations can now be done on most of these field types, you should make an effort to perform any required computations with SQL Expression fields rather than formulas, especially if the computations reduce the size of the string that is returned. Likewise, although sorting and grouping on large string fields is supported, it should be avoided. If necessary, a substring of the total should be created and then grouped or sorted on, instead of the entire field.

NOTE

To see the field's datatype in the Field Explorer, right-click and check Show Field Type.

SQL Expressions

Moving processing from the Crystal Reports side to the server side can have a minimal to substantial impact on report processing time, depending on the particular type of processing involved. In some instances, it could actually adversely affect total processing time, so each environment should be individually evaluated. If, for instance, in a client/server environment, the database server is slow and has little memory, the client machines are fast, and the network is speedy, then allowing a large amount of processing to happen on the client side is advantageous. In the more common situation of a powerful server, so-so network, and mediocre clients, forcing processing to take place on the server would clearly be advantageous. In a web environment, the comparison must be between the power of the database server, the power of the report/web server, and the capabilities of the network.

Crystal Reports allows you to create selection formulas. Selection formulas are equivalent to the WHERE clause in a SELECT query. Crystal selection formulas have no SQL counterpart, as SQL Expressions are the Crystal regular formula counterparts. Selection formulas are always written in Crystal or VB syntax like regular formulas. Crystal Reports converts some operators and functions to their Oracle equivalent when they are used in selection formulas, but it does not convert all, or even most, operators or functions. Whether an operator or function is automatically converted when used in a selection formula is documented in the "Operators" and "Functions" sections, later in this chapter. Replacing expressions in a selection formula with SQL Expressions when Crystal does not perform the conversion automatically guarantees that the filtering is done on the server.

NOTE

A SQL Expression must be created and then referenced in the selection formula. SQL Expression-type code cannot be used directly in selection formulas.

Using native Oracle functionality rather than Crystal Reports formula functionality can affect the speed of report processing even when not used in the selection formula. The tables in the "Operators" and "Functions" sections list an alternative Oracle method that can be implemented in a SQL Expression for each type of Crystal Reports formula function and operator. Substitutions in a selection formula always have a positive impact, but other substitutions should be used with care, after comparing processing times. SQL Expressions created in Crystal Reports become expressions in the Select list of the resulting database query. They are usually similar to Crystal formulas and compute some value. However, an entire SELECT statement can be entered as a SQL Expression if it returns a single value and is not correlated to any field in the main query.

Within Crystal Reports formulas, the user can create straightforward formulas or entire blocks of code. Blocks of code cannot be directly translated into valid Oracle equivalents that can be passed in the SELECT clause of a query. Whenever block- type processing is required, you must create an Oracle function or procedure; you cannot create a PL/SQL block within a Crystal Reports SQL Expression. The Oracle equivalents listed in the tables in the next section assume that you are creating a SQL Expression.

Converting a Crystal formula to a SQL Expression changes the time at which the computation is evaluated as well as where it is evaluated. When using a Crystal formula, the earliest the computation is performed is while Crystal is reading the records, and the computation is performed on the client (or web server). When using a SQL Expression, the computation is evaluated on the Oracle server before Crystal begins to read any records.

Included with the XTREME Oracle sample database, as modified for this book, are PL/SQL functions that can be used to duplicate Crystal Reports functions in Oracle that cannot be duplicated easily in a SQL Expression. The code listing is shown in Appendix B, along with instructions for running it.

Operators

The possible Crystal Reports operators are listed in the Operators box of the Formula Editor, which is docked in the upper-right of the Formula Editor by default, as is the Operators box for the SQL Expression Editor. Each Crystal operator is listed in the tables in this section in the order that it appears in the Operators box as shown in the next illustration.

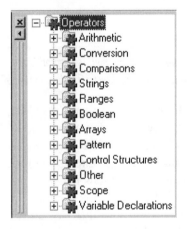

Arithmetic

Note that arithmetic operators, when used in a Selection formula, will never be converted to their Oracle equivalents. For example, if your Selection formula was the following:

```
({fieldA}+{fieldB})>100
```

the Oracle equivalent would be as shown:

```
WHERE (fieldA+fieldB)>100
```

Nevertheless, using the selection formula shown, Crystal Reports will not add this to the WHERE clause, and the record selection for this condition would be performed locally. If an equivalent SQL Expression field is built and used in the Selection formula, then the condition (and the processing) will be passed to the server.

Table 6-1 lists all available Crystal arithmetic operators as shown in the illustration and their SQL Expression equivalents.

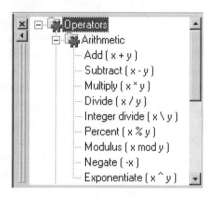

Operator	Formula	SQL Expression
Add (x + y)	{EMPLOYEE.SALARY} + 100	"EMPLOYEE"."SALARY" + 100
Subtract (x − y)	{EMPLOYEE.SALARY} − 100	"EMPLOYEE"."SALARY" − 100
Multiply (x * y)	{EMPLOYEE.SALARY} * 1.10	"EMPLOYEE"."SALARY" * 1.10
Divide (x/y)	{EMPLOYEE.SALARY}/1000	"EMPLOYEE"."SALARY"/1000
Integer divide (x\y)	{EMPLOYEE.SALARY}\25	FLOOR (ROUND ("EMPLOYEE"."SALARY")/ROUND(25)) or (XTREME function) INT_DIV ("EMPLOYEE"."SALARY", 25)
Percent (x % y)	1000 % {EMPLOYEE.SALARY}	(1000 /"EMPLOYEE"."SALARY") * 100 or (XTREME function) PERCENT (1000, "EMPLOYEE"."SALARY")
Modulus (x mod y)	{EMPLOYEE.SALARY} mod 3	MOD (ROUND ("EMPLOYEE"."SALARY"), ROUND (3)) or (XTREME function) CRMOD ("EMPLOYEE"."SALARY", 3)
Negate (−x)	−{EMPLOYEE.SALARY}	− "EMPLOYEE"."SALARY"
Exponentiate (x ^ y)	{EMPLOYEE.SALARY} ^ (1/3)	POWER ("EMPLOYEE"."SALARY", 1/3)

Table 6-1   *Arithmetic Operators*

Conversion

The currency conversion function applies Crystal Currency Formatting, so no Oracle equivalent is possible.

Comparisons

Note that Crystal Reports Comparison functions return the Boolean value of True or False when used independently of an IF statement or other programming construct. Oracle does not have a native datatype equivalent to Boolean, so the example functions return the string 'True' or 'False'. They could easily be modified to return 1 or 0, if a numeric result was desired, or any other reasonable values. Also, note that all of the Crystal Comparison functions are automatically converted to their Oracle equivalents when used in selection formulas, unlike most other Crystal operators and functions.

The Crystal comparison operators are equal (x=y), not equal (x<>y), less than (x<y), greater than (x>y), less or equal (x<=y), and greater or equal (x>=y). For each operator used in a Crystal formula or selection formula, an Oracle CASE statement can be substituted. For example, a Crystal formula such as the one shown here

```
{EMPLOYEE.SUPERVISOR_ID} = {EMPLOYEE.REPORTS_TO}
```

could be converted to the following SQL Expression:

```
CASE
  WHEN "EMPLOYEE"."REPORTS_TO" IS NULL
    THEN NULL
  WHEN "EMPLOYEE"."REPORTS_TO" = "EMPLOYEE"."SUPERVISOR_ID"
    THEN 'True'
ELSE
  'False'
END
```

The = operator can be replaced with any of the other operators. Note that the complexity in the Oracle solutions is due to the differing default treatment of nulls between Crystal Reports and Oracle, and that other possible solutions exist. For instance, for the equality operator, here is an alternative SQL Expression:

```
NVL2("EMPLOYEE"."REPORTS_TO",
      DECODE("EMPLOYEE"."SUPERVISOR_ID", NULL, NULL,
      "EMPLOYEE"."REPORTS_TO", 'True', 'False'), NULL)
```

If you are using comparisons in other programming constructs where a Boolean is expected, such as an IF statement, the Oracle comparison operators you can use are the same as the Crystal Comparison operators.

Strings

Note that using any of the Crystal Reports String operators in a selection formula will cause that portion of the formula to be evaluated locally.

Table 6-2 lists all available Crystal string operators, as illustrated next, and their SQL Expression equivalents.

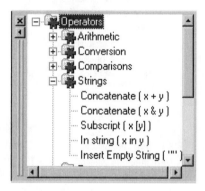

Operator	Formula	SQL Expression
Concatenate ($x + y$)	{EMPLOYEE.FIRST_NAME} + " " + {EMPLOYEE.LAST_NAME}	"EMPLOYEE"."FIRST_NAME" || ' ' || "EMPLOYEE"."LAST_NAME" (a space must follow the double pipes)
Concatenate (x & y)	{EMPLOYEE.FIRST_NAME} & " " & {EMPLOYEE.LAST_NAME}	CONCAT (CONCAT ("EMPLOYEE"."FIRST_NAME", ' '), "EMPLOYEE"."LAST_NAME")
Subscript ($x[y]$)	{EMPLOYEE.LAST_NAME} [1]	SUBSTR ("EMPLOYEE"."LAST_NAME", 1, 1)
In string (x in y)	'A' in {EMPLOYEE.FIRST_NAME}	CASE WHEN INSTR ("EMPLOYEE"."FIRST_NAME", 'A') > 0 THEN 'True' ELSE 'False' END
Insert Empty String ("")	""	''

Table 6-2   *String Operators*

Ranges

Range expressions used in selection formulas are converted to Oracle equivalents.

Table 6-3 lists all available Crystal range operators, as shown in the illustration, and their SQL Expression equivalents.

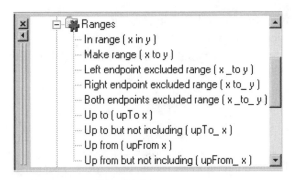

Operator	Formula	SQL Expression
In range (*x* in *y*)	{EMPLOYEE.BIRTH_DATE} in DateAdd ('yyyy', −60, CurrentDate) to DateAdd ('yyyy', −30, CurrentDate)	CASE WHEN ("EMPLOYEE"."BIRTH_DATE" > = TO_DATE ('10-03-1943', 'DD-MM-YYYY') AND "EMPLOYEE"."BIRTH_DATE" <= TO_DATE ('10-03-1973', 'DD-MM-YYYY')) THEN 'True' ELSE 'False' END or CASE WHEN "EMPLOYEE"."BIRTH_DATE" BETWEEN ADD_MONTHS (SYSDATE, −60*12) AND ADD_MONTHS (SYSDATE, −30*12) THEN 'True' ELSE 'False' END
Make range (*x* to *y*)	A range cannot be a result of a Crystal Reports formula or SQL Expression. Ranges must be used in an expression to return some other datatype. See the preceding In range examples for the creation of ranges in both Crystal formulas and SQL Expressions.	
Left endpoint excluded range (*x* _to *y*)	{EMPLOYEE.BIRTH_DATE} in DateAdd ('yyyy', −60, CurrentDate) _to DateAdd ('yyyy', −30, CurrentDate)	CASE WHEN "EMPLOYEE"."BIRTH_DATE" > ADD_MONTHS (SYSDATE, −60*12) AND "EMPLOYEE"."BIRTH_DATE" <= ADD_MONTHS (SYSDATE, −30*12) THEN 'True' ELSE 'False' END
Right endpoint excluded range (*x* to_ *y*)	{EMPLOYEE.BIRTH_DATE} in DateAdd ('yyyy', −60, CurrentDate) to_ DateAdd ('yyyy', −30, CurrentDate)	CASE WHEN "EMPLOYEE"."BIRTH_DATE" >= ADD_MONTHS (SYSDATE, −60*12) AND "EMPLOYEE"."BIRTH_DATE" < ADD_MONTHS (SYSDATE, −30*12) THEN 'True' ELSE 'False' END

Table 6-3   *Range Operators*

Operator	Formula	SQL Expression
Both endpoints excluded range (x _to_ y)	{EMPLOYEE.BIRTH_DATE} in DateAdd ('yyyy', –60, CurrentDate) _to_ DateAdd ('yyyy', –30, CurrentDate)	CASE WHEN "EMPLOYEE"."BIRTH_DATE" > ADD_MONTHS (SYSDATE, –60*12) AND "EMPLOYEE"."BIRTH_DATE" < ADD_MONTHS (SYSDATE, –30*12) THEN 'True' ELSE 'False' END
Up to (upTo x)	{EMPLOYEE.BIRTH_DATE} in upTo DateAdd('yyyy', –30, CurrentDate)	CASE WHEN "EMPLOYEE"."BIRTH_DATE" <= ADD_MONTHS (SYSDATE, –30*12) THEN 'True' ELSE 'False' END
Up to but not including (upTo_ x)	{EMPLOYEE.BIRTH_DATE} in upTo_ DateAdd('yyyy', –30, CurrentDate)	CASE WHEN "EMPLOYEE"."BIRTH_DATE" < ADD_MONTHS (SYSDATE, –30*12) THEN 'True' ELSE 'False' END
Up From (upFrom x)	{EMPLOYEE.BIRTH_DATE} in upFrom DateAdd ('yyyy', –30, CurrentDate)	CASE WHEN "EMPLOYEE"."BIRTH_DATE" >= ADD_MONTHS (SYSDATE, –30*12) THEN 'True' ELSE 'False' END
Up From but not including (upFrom_ x)	{EMPLOYEE.BIRTH_DATE} in upFrom_ DateAdd ('yyyy', –30, CurrentDate)	CASE WHEN "EMPLOYEE"."BIRTH_DATE" > ADD_MONTHS (SYSDATE, –30*12) THEN 'True' ELSE 'False' END

Table 6-3   *Range Operators* (continued)

Boolean

Note that, as previously discussed, Crystal Reports Boolean operators return the Boolean value of True or False, but Oracle does not have a native datatype equivalent to Boolean. Additionally, null conditions are not explicitly checked in these examples, so results can vary from the Crystal formula result if either operand is null.

Of the Crystal Reports Boolean operators, NOT, AND, and OR are converted to their Oracle equivalents when used in selection formulas.

Table 6-4 lists all available Crystal Boolean operators, as shown in the next illustration, and their SQL Expression equivalents.

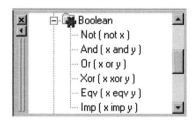

Operator	Formula	SQL Expression
Not (not x)	not ({EMPLOYEE.SUPERVISOR_ID}={EMPLOYEE.REPORTS_TO})	CASE WHEN NOT ("EMPLOYEE"."SUPERVISOR_ID" = "EMPLOYEE"."REPORTS_TO") THEN 'True' ELSE 'False' END
And (x and y)	({EMPLOYEE.SUPERVISOR_ID}={EMPLOYEE.REPORTS_TO}) and IsNull({EMPLOYEE.POSITION})	CASE WHEN ("EMPLOYEE"."SUPERVISOR_ID" = "EMPLOYEE"."REPORTS_TO") AND ("EMPLOYEE"."POSITION" IS NULL) THEN 'True' ELSE 'False' END
Or (x or y)	({EMPLOYEE.SUPERVISOR_ID}={EMPLOYEE.REPORTS_TO}) or IsNull({EMPLOYEE.POSITION})	CASE WHEN ("EMPLOYEE"."SUPERVISOR_ID" = "EMPLOYEE"."REPORTS_TO") or ("EMPLOYEE"."POSITION" IS NULL) THEN 'True' ELSE 'False' END
Xor (x xor y)	({EMPLOYEE.SUPERVISOR_ID}={EMPLOYEE.REPORTS_TO}) Xor IsNull({EMPLOYEE.POSITION})	CASE WHEN ("EMPLOYEE"."SUPERVISOR_ID" = "EMPLOYEE"."REPORTS_TO") THEN CASE WHEN NOT ("EMPLOYEE"."POSITION" IS NULL) THEN 'True' ELSE 'False' END ELSE CASE WHEN ("EMPLOYEE"."POSITION" IS NULL) THEN 'True' ELSE 'False' END END
Eqv (x eqv y)	({EMPLOYEE.SUPERVISOR_ID} = {EMPLOYEE.REPORTS_TO}) Eqv IsNull ({EMPLOYEE.POSITION})	CASE WHEN ("EMPLOYEE"."SUPERVISOR_ID" = "EMPLOYEE"."REPORTS_TO") THEN CASE WHEN ("EMPLOYEE"."POSITION" IS NULL) THEN 'True' ELSE 'False' END ELSE CASE WHEN NOT ("EMPLOYEE"."POSITION" IS NULL) THEN 'True' ELSE 'False' END END
Imp (x imp y)	({EMPLOYEE.SUPERVISOR_ID} = {EMPLOYEE.REPORTS_TO}) Imp IsNull({EMPLOYEE.POSITION})	CASE WHEN ("EMPLOYEE"."SUPERVISOR_ID" = "EMPLOYEE"."REPORTS_TO") THEN CASE WHEN ("EMPLOYEE"."POSITION" IS NULL) THEN 'True' ELSE 'False' END ELSE 'True' END

Table 6-4   *Boolean Operators*

Arrays

Array manipulation using native Oracle functionality is not possible inside a Crystal Reports SQL Expression.

Patterns

Note that both of the Crystal Reports Pattern operators convert to their Oracle equivalent automatically when used in selection formulas. The Crystal wildcard characters ? and * are equivalent to the Oracle wildcard characters _ and %.

Table 6-5 lists all available Crystal string pattern operators, as shown in the illustration, and their SQL Expression equivalents.

Control Structures

Null conditions are not specifically checked in the following examples, so differences between the results could exist if any of the operands are null.

Table 6-6 lists two of the available Crystal control structures shown in the illustration and their SQL Expression equivalents.

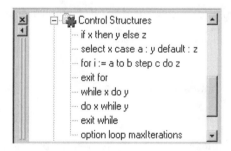

Operator	Formula	SQL Expression
Starts with (x startsWith y)	{EMPLOYEE.FIRST_NAME} startswith 'An'	CASE WHEN "EMPLOYEE"."FIRST_NAME" LIKE 'An%' THEN 'True' ELSE 'False' END
Like pattern (x like y)	{EMPLOYEE.FIRST_NAME} like '?a*n*'	CASE WHEN "EMPLOYEE"."FIRST_NAME" LIKE '_a%n%' THEN 'True' ELSE 'False' END

Table 6-5   *Pattern Operators*

Operator	Formula	SQL Expression
If *x* then *y* else *z*	if {EMPLOYEE.SUPERVISOR_ID} = {EMPLOYEE.REPORTS_TO} then 'Reports to Supervisor' else 'Does not report to Supervisor'	CASE WHEN "EMPLOYEE"."SUPERVISOR_ID" = "EMPLOYEE"."REPORTS_TO" THEN 'Reports to Supervisor' ELSE 'Does not report to Supervisor' END
Select *x* case *a: y* default: *z*	select {EMPLOYEE.BIRTH_DATE} case Is > DateAdd ('yyyy', −18, CurrentDate) : "Under 18" case Is > DateAdd ('yyyy', −21, CurrentDate) : "Under 21" default: "Over 21"	CASE WHEN "EMPLOYEE"."BIRTH_DATE" > Add_Months (SYSDATE, −18*12) THEN 'Under 18' WHEN "EMPLOYEE"."BIRTH_DATE" > Add_Months (SYSDATE, −21*12) THEN 'Under 21' ELSE 'Over 21' END

Table 6-6   *Control Structure Operators*

The remaining Control Structure operators are related to looping. It is not possible to use a looping structure in an Oracle SQL Expression.

Other

Parentheses can be used as expected inside SQL Expressions. The remaining Other operators are not usable inside an Oracle SQL Expression.

Scope

The Scope operators are not usable inside an Oracle SQL Expression.

Variable Declarations

You cannot declare variables inside an Oracle SQL Expression.

Functions

Available Crystal Reports functions are listed in the Functions box of the Formula Editor as shown in the illustation. The Functions box is docked in the upper middle of the Formula Editor by default.

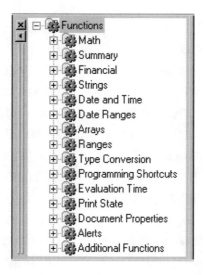

Math

Note that none of the Crystal Reports Math functions convert to its Oracle equivalent automatically when used in selection formulas.

Table 6-7 lists all available Crystal math functions, shown in the following illustration, plus the exponentiation operator, and gives SQL Expression substitutes.

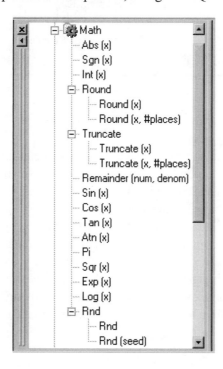

Function	Formula	SQL Expression
Abs	Abs ({ORDERS.ORDER_AMOUNT})	ABS ("ORDERS"."ORDER_AMOUNT")
Sgn	Sgn ({ORDERS.ORDER_AMOUNT})	SIGN ("ORDERS"."ORDER_AMOUNT")
Int	Int ({ORDERS.ORDER_AMOUNT})	FLOOR ("ORDERS"."ORDER_AMOUNT")
Round	Round ({ORDERS.ORDER_AMOUNT})	ROUND ("ORDERS"."ORDER_AMOUNT")
Round (x,n)	Round ({ORDERS.ORDER_AMOUNT}, 1)	ROUND ("ORDERS"."ORDER_AMOUNT", 1)
Truncate	Truncate ({ORDERS.ORDER_AMOUNT})	TRUNC ("ORDERS"."ORDER_AMOUNT")
Truncate (x,n)	Truncate ({ORDERS.ORDER_AMOUNT}, 1)	TRUNC ("ORDERS"."ORDER_AMOUNT", 1)
Remainder	Remainder ({ORDERS.ORDER_AMOUNT}, 2)	MOD ("ORDERS"."ORDER_AMOUNT", 2)
Sin	Sin ({ORDERS.ORDER_AMOUNT})	SIN ("ORDERS"."ORDER_AMOUNT")
Cos	Cos ({ORDERS.ORDER_AMOUNT})	COS ("ORDERS"."ORDER_AMOUNT")
Tan	Tan ({ORDERS.ORDER_AMOUNT})	TAN ("ORDERS"."ORDER_AMOUNT")
Atn	Atn ({ORDERS.ORDER_AMOUNT})	ATAN ("ORDERS"."ORDER_AMOUNT")
Pi	crPi	No Equivalent
Sqr	Sqr ({ORDERS.ORDER_AMOUNT})	SQRT ("ORDERS"."ORDER_AMOUNT")
Exp	Exp ({ORDERS.CUSTOMER_ID})	EXP ("ORDERS"."CUSTOMER_ID")
Log	Log ({ORDERS.CUSTOMER_ID})	LN ("ORDERS"."CUSTOMER_ID")
Rnd	Rnd	No Equivalent
Rnd(Seed)	Rnd (5)	No Equivalent
^	{ORDERS.EMPLOYEE_ID} ^ 3	POWER ("ORDERS"."EMPLOYEE_ID", 3)

Table 6-7   *Math Functions*

Summary

Note that for each Crystal summary function that has a conditional (group by) field in it, there must be a corresponding group in the report. No such restriction exists for the Oracle equivalents. The required grouping is done transparently on the server, and summaries are returned for each detail row.

The Crystal Reports summary functions are used when an aggregate value is needed in a detail row for some computation. The Oracle implementation of this type of function is called Reporting Aggregate Functions and it returns the same value for each row in a given partition or group. Oracle also defines Windowing Aggregate Functions that can be used to create moving aggregates, such as moving averages; cumulative aggregates, such as running totals; Ranking Functions that can be used to create rankings; cumulative distributions and percentiles; and Linear Regression Functions that can be used to compute regression statistics. See the "Analysis" section in Chapter 4 for details on the Oracle Analysis functions.

Note that the Oracle equivalents for the Crystal Summary functions cannot be used in Group Selection formulas. They return values for each row in the result set, even though the value may be the same for a particular set of rows. Because they are per row, they can be used in SQL Expressions, although they cannot be used in Record Selection formulas. Oracle will not allow analytical functions to be used in the WHERE clause. To enable group selection on the server, see the "HAVING Clause" section in Chapter 4.

Each summary function is shown with two forms: the most basic form, which is a summary over the entire report, and the more complex form, where the summary is for a particular group. Summary functions using the additional DateTime condition options are shown at the end of the table for the SUM summary function only.

Table 6-8 lists all available Crystal summary functions, shown in the illustration, and gives SQL Expression substitutes.

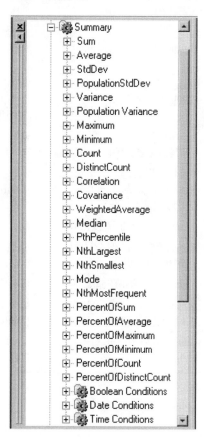

Function	Formula	SQL Expression
Sum (fld)	Sum ({EMPLOYEE.SALARY})	SUM ("EMPLOYEE"."SALARY") OVER ()
Sum (fld, condFld)	Sum ({EMPLOYEE.SALARY}, {EMPLOYEE.POSITION})	SUM ("EMPLOYEE"."SALARY") OVER (PARTITION BY "EMPLOYEE"."POSITION")
Average (fld)	Average ({EMPLOYEE.SALARY})	AVG ("EMPLOYEE"."SALARY") OVER ()
Average (fld, condFld)	Average ({EMPLOYEE.SALARY}, {EMPLOYEE.POSITION})	AVG ("EMPLOYEE"."SALARY") OVER (PARTITION BY "EMPLOYEE"."POSITION")
StdDev (fld)	StdDev ({EMPLOYEE.SALARY})	STDDEV ("EMPLOYEE"."SALARY") OVER ()
StdDev (fld, condFld)	StdDev ({EMPLOYEE.SALARY}, {EMPLOYEE.POSITION})	STDDEV ("EMPLOYEE"."SALARY") OVER (PARTITION BY "EMPLOYEE"."POSITION")
PopulationStdDev (fld)	PopulationStdDev ({EMPLOYEE.SALARY})	STDDEV_POP ("EMPLOYEE"."SALARY") OVER ()
PopulationStdDev (fld, condFld)	PopulationStdDev ({EMPLOYEE.SALARY}, {EMPLOYEE.POSITION})	STDDEV_POP ("EMPLOYEE"."SALARY") OVER (PARTITION BY "EMPLOYEE"."POSITION")
Variance (fld)	Variance ({EMPLOYEE.SALARY})	VARIANCE ("EMPLOYEE"."SALARY") OVER ()
Variance (fld, condFld)	Variance ({EMPLOYEE.SALARY}, {EMPLOYEE.POSITION})	VARIANCE ("EMPLOYEE"."SALARY") OVER (PARTITION BY "EMPLOYEE"."POSITION")
PopulationVariance (fld)	PopulationVariance ({EMPLOYEE.SALARY})	VAR_POP ("EMPLOYEE"."SALARY") OVER ()
PopulationVariance (fld, condFld)	PopulationVariance ({EMPLOYEE.SALARY}, {EMPLOYEE.POSITION})	VAR_POP ("EMPLOYEE"."SALARY") OVER (PARTITION BY "EMPLOYEE"."POSITION")
Maximum (fld)	Maximum ({EMPLOYEE.SALARY})	MAX ("EMPLOYEE"."SALARY") OVER ()
Maximum (fld, condFld)	Maximum ({EMPLOYEE.SALARY}, {EMPLOYEE.POSITION})	MAX ("EMPLOYEE"."SALARY") OVER (PARTITION BY "EMPLOYEE"."POSITION")
Minimum (fld)	Minimum ({EMPLOYEE.SALARY})	MIN ("EMPLOYEE"."SALARY") OVER ()
Minimum (fld, condFld)	Minimum ({EMPLOYEE.SALARY}, {EMPLOYEE.POSITION})	MIN ("EMPLOYEE"."SALARY") OVER (PARTITION BY "EMPLOYEE"."POSITION")
Count (fld)	Count ({EMPLOYEE.SALARY})	COUNT ("EMPLOYEE"."SALARY") OVER ()

Table 6-8   *Summary Functions*

Function	Formula	SQL Expression
Count (fld, condFld)	Count ({EMPLOYEE.SALARY}, {EMPLOYEE.POSITION})	COUNT ("EMPLOYEE"."SALARY") OVER (PARTITION BY "EMPLOYEE"."POSITION")
DistinctCount (fld)	DistinctCount ({EMPLOYEE.SALARY})	COUNT DISTINCT ("EMPLOYEE"."SALARY") OVER ()
DistinctCount (fld, condFld)	DistinctCount ({EMPLOYEE.SALARY}, {EMPLOYEE.POSITION})	COUNT DISTINCT ("EMPLOYEE"."SALARY") OVER (PARTITION BY "EMPLOYEE"."POSITION")
Correlation (fld, fld)	Correlation ({EMPLOYEE.SALARY}, {EMPLOYEE.EMPLOYEE_ID})	CORR ("EMPLOYEE"."SALARY", "EMPLOYEE"."EMPLOYEE_ID") OVER ()
Correlation (fld, fld, condFld)	Correlation ({EMPLOYEE.SALARY}, {EMPLOYEE.EMPLOYEE_ID}, {EMPLOYEE.POSITION})	CORR ("EMPLOYEE"."SALARY", "EMPLOYEE"."EMPLOYEE_ID") OVER (PARTITION BY "EMPLOYEE"."POSITION")
Covariance (fld, fld)	Covariance ({EMPLOYEE.SALARY}, {EMPLOYEE.EMPLOYEE_ID})	COVAR_SAMP ("EMPLOYEE"."SALARY", "EMPLOYEE"."EMPLOYEE_ID") OVER ()
Covariance (fld, fld, condFld)	Covariance ({EMPLOYEE.SALARY}, {EMPLOYEE.EMPLOYEE_ID}, {EMPLOYEE.POSITION})	COVAR_SAMP ("EMPLOYEE"."SALARY", "EMPLOYEE"."EMPLOYEE_ID") OVER (PARTITION BY "EMPLOYEE"."POSITION")
WeightedAverage (fld, fld)	WeightedAverage ({EMPLOYEE.SALARY}, {EMPLOYEE.EMPLOYEE_ID})	SUM ("EMPLOYEE"."SALARY" * "EMPLOYEE"."EMPLOYEE_ID") OVER () / SUM ("EMPLOYEE"."EMPLOYEE_ID") OVER ()
WeightedAverage (fld, fld, condFld)	WeightedAverage ({EMPLOYEE.SALARY}, {EMPLOYEE.EMPLOYEE_ID}, {EMPLOYEE.POSITION})	SUM ("EMPLOYEE"."SALARY" * "EMPLOYEE"."EMPLOYEE_ID") OVER (PARTITION BY "EMPLOYEE"."POSITION") / SUM ("EMPLOYEE"."EMPLOYEE_ID") OVER (PARTITION BY "EMPLOYEE"."POSITION")
Median (fld)	Median ({EMPLOYEE.SALARY})	PERCENTILE_CONT (0.5) WITHIN GROUP (ORDER BY "EMPLOYEE"."SALARY") OVER () (9i only)
Median (fld, condFld)	Median ({EMPLOYEE.SALARY}, {EMPLOYEE.POSITION})	PERCENTILE_CONT (0.5) WITHIN GROUP (ORDER BY "EMPLOYEE"."SALARY") OVER (PARTITION BY "EMPLOYEE"."POSITION") (9i only)

Table 6-8   *Summary Functions* (continued)

Function	Formula	SQL Expression
PthPercentile (fld)	PthPercentile (33,{EMPLOYEE.SALARY})	PERCENTILE_CONT (0.33) WITHIN GROUP (ORDER BY "EMPLOYEE"."SALARY") OVER () (9*i* only)
PthPercentile (fld, condFld)	PthPercentile (33, {EMPLOYEE.SALARY}, {EMPLOYEE.POSITION})	PERCENTILE_CONT (0.33) WITHIN GROUP (ORDER BY "EMPLOYEE"."SALARY") OVER (PARTITION BY "EMPLOYEE"."POSITION") (9*i* only)
NthLargest (N, fld)	NthLargest (5, {EMPLOYEE.SALARY})	See the "Nth Largest" section following this table for a solution.
NthLargest (N, fld, condFld)	NthLargest (5, {EMPLOYEE.SALARY}, {EMPLOYEE.POSITION})	See the "Nth Largest" section following this table for a solution.
NthSmallest (N, fld)	NthSmallest (5, {EMPLOYEE.SALARY})	See the "Nth Smallest" section following this table for a solution.
NthSmallest (N, fld, condFld)	NthSmallest (5, {EMPLOYEE.SALARY}, {EMPLOYEE.POSITION})	See the "Nth Smallest" section following this table for a solution.
Mode (fld)	Mode ({EMPLOYEE.SALARY})	See the "Mode" section following this table for a solution.
Mode (fld, condFld)	Mode ({EMPLOYEE.SALARY}, {EMPLOYEE.POSITION})	See the "Mode" section following this table for a solution.
NthMostFrequent (N, fld)	NthMostFrequent (2, {EMPLOYEE.SALARY})	See the "Nth Most Frequent" section following this table for a solution.
NthMostFrequent (N, fld, condFld)	NthMostFrequent (2, {EMPLOYEE.SALARY}, {EMPLOYEE.POSITION})	See the "Nth Most Frequent" section following this table for a solution.
PercentOfSum (fld, CondFld)	PercentOfSum ({EMPLOYEE.SALARY}, {EMPLOYEE.POSITION})	100 * (SUM("EMPLOYEE"."SALARY") OVER (PARTITION BY "EMPLOYEE"."POSITION")) / (SUM ("EMPLOYEE"."SALARY") OVER ())
PercentOfSum (fld, innerCondFld, outerCondFld)	PercentOfSum ({EMPLOYEE.SALARY}, {EMPLOYEE.REPORTS_TO}, {EMPLOYEE.POSITION})	100 * (SUM("EMPLOYEE"."SALARY") OVER (PARTITION BY "EMPLOYEE"."REPORTS_TO", "EMPLOYEE"."POSITION")) / (SUM ("EMPLOYEE"."SALARY") OVER (PARTITION BY "EMPLOYEE"."POSITION"))

Table 6-8 *Summary Functions* (continued)

Function	Formula	SQL Expression
PercentOfAverage (fld, CondFld)	PercentOfAverage ({EMPLOYEE.SALARY}, {EMPLOYEE.POSITION})	100 * (AVG ("EMPLOYEE"."SALARY") OVER (PARTITION BY "EMPLOYEE"."POSITION")) / (AVG ("EMPLOYEE"."SALARY") OVER ())
PercentOfAverage (fld, innerCondFld, outerCondFld)	PercentOfAverage ({EMPLOYEE.SALARY}, {EMPLOYEE.REPORTS_TO}, {EMPLOYEE.POSITION})	100 * (AVG ("EMPLOYEE"."SALARY") OVER (PARTITION BY "EMPLOYEE"."REPORTS_TO", "EMPLOYEE"."POSITION")) / (AVG ("EMPLOYEE"."SALARY") OVER (PARTITION BY "EMPLOYEE"."POSITION"))
PercentOfMaximum(fld, CondFld)	PercentOfMaximum ({EMPLOYEE.SALARY}, {EMPLOYEE.POSITION})	100 * (MAX ("EMPLOYEE"."SALARY") OVER (PARTITION BY "EMPLOYEE"."POSITION")) / (MAX ("EMPLOYEE"."SALARY") OVER ())
PercentOfMaximum (fld, innerCondFld, outerCondFld)	PercentOfMaximum ({EMPLOYEE.SALARY}, {EMPLOYEE.REPORTS_TO}, {EMPLOYEE.POSITION})	100 * (MAX ("EMPLOYEE"."SALARY") OVER (PARTITION BY "EMPLOYEE"."REPORTS_TO", "EMPLOYEE"."POSITION")) / (MAX ("EMPLOYEE"."SALARY") OVER (PARTITION BY "EMPLOYEE"."POSITION"))
PercentOfMinimum (fld, CondFld)	PercentOfMinimum ({EMPLOYEE.SALARY}, {EMPLOYEE.POSITION})	100 * (MIN ("EMPLOYEE"."SALARY") OVER (PARTITION BY "EMPLOYEE"."POSITION")) / (MIN ("EMPLOYEE"."SALARY") OVER ())
PercentOfMinimum (fld, innerCondFld, outerCondFld)	PercentOfMinimum ({EMPLOYEE.SALARY}, {EMPLOYEE.REPORTS_TO}, {EMPLOYEE.POSITION})	100 * (MIN ("EMPLOYEE"."SALARY") OVER (PARTITION BY "EMPLOYEE"."REPORTS_TO", "EMPLOYEE"."POSITION")) / (MIN ("EMPLOYEE"."SALARY") OVER (PARTITION BY "EMPLOYEE"."POSITION"))
PercentOfCount (fld, CondFld)	PercentOfCount ({EMPLOYEE.SALARY}, {EMPLOYEE.POSITION})	100 * (COUNT ("EMPLOYEE"."SALARY") OVER (PARTITION BY "EMPLOYEE"."POSITION")) / (COUNT ("EMPLOYEE"."SALARY") OVER ())

Table 6-8   *Summary Functions* (continued)

Function	Formula	SQL Expression
PercentOfCount (fld, innerCondFld, outerCondFld)	PercentOfCount ({EMPLOYEE.SALARY}, {EMPLOYEE.REPORTS_TO}, {EMPLOYEE.POSITION})	100 * (COUNT ("EMPLOYEE"."SALARY") OVER (PARTITION BY "EMPLOYEE"."REPORTS_TO", "EMPLOYEE"."POSITION")) / (COUNT ("EMPLOYEE"."SALARY") OVER (PARTITION BY "EMPLOYEE"."POSITION"))
PercentOfDistinctCount (fld, CondFld)	PercentOfDistinctCount ({EMPLOYEE.SALARY}, {EMPLOYEE.POSITION})	100 * (COUNT (DISTINCT "EMPLOYEE"."SALARY") OVER (PARTITION BY "EMPLOYEE"."POSITION")) / (COUNT (DISTINCT "EMPLOYEE"."SALARY") OVER ())
PercentOfDistinctCount (fld, innerCondFld, outerCondFld)	PercentOfDistinctCount ({EMPLOYEE.SALARY}, {EMPLOYEE.REPORTS_TO}, {EMPLOYEE.POSITION})	100 * (COUNT (DISTINCT "EMPLOYEE"."SALARY") OVER (PARTITION BY "EMPLOYEE"."REPORTS_TO", "EMPLOYEE"."POSITION")) / (COUNT (DISTINCT "EMPLOYEE"."SALARY") OVER (PARTITION BY "EMPLOYEE"."POSITION"))
Boolean Conditions	Oracle SQL Expressions cannot use Boolean fields, so there are no Oracle equivalents for these conditions	
Date For each day	SUM ({ORDERS.ORDER_AMOUNT}, {ORDERS.ORDER_DATE}, "daily")	SUM ("ORDERS"."ORDER_AMOUNT") OVER (PARTITION BY "ORDERS"."ORDER_DATE")
Date For each week	SUM ({ORDERS.ORDER_AMOUNT}, {ORDERS.ORDER_DATE}, "weekly")	SUM ("ORDERS"."ORDER_AMOUNT") OVER (PARTITION BY TO_CHAR ("ORDERS"."ORDER_DATE" + 1, 'IYYY') * 100 + TO_CHAR ("ORDERS"."ORDER_DATE" + 1, 'IW'))
Date For each two weeks	SUM ({ORDERS.ORDER_AMOUNT}, {ORDERS.ORDER_DATE}, "biweekly")	SUM ("ORDERS"."ORDER_AMOUNT") OVER (PARTITION BY TO_CHAR ("ORDERS"."ORDER_DATE" + 1, 'IYYY') || FLOOR(TO_CHAR ("ORDERS"."ORDER_DATE" + 1, 'IW')/2))

Table 6-8   *Summary Functions* (continued)

Function	Formula	SQL Expression
Date For each half month	SUM ({ORDERS.ORDER_AMOUNT}, {ORDERS.ORDER_DATE}, "semimonthly")	SUM ("ORDERS"."ORDER_AMOUNT") OVER (PARTITION BY TO_CHAR ("ORDERS"."ORDER_DATE", 'YYYY/MM/') || LEAST (CEIL (TO_CHAR ("ORDERS"."ORDER_DATE", 'DD') / 15), 2))
Date For each month	SUM ({ORDERS.ORDER_AMOUNT}, {ORDERS.ORDER_DATE}, "monthly")	SUM ("ORDERS"."ORDER_AMOUNT") OVER (PARTITION BY TO_CHAR ("ORDERS"."ORDER_DATE", 'YYYY/MM'))
Date For each quarter	SUM ({ORDERS.ORDER_AMOUNT}, {ORDERS.ORDER_DATE}, "quarterly")	SUM ("ORDERS"."ORDER_AMOUNT") OVER (PARTITION BY TO_CHAR ("ORDERS"."ORDER_DATE", 'YYYY/Q'))
Date For each half year	SUM ({ORDERS.ORDER_AMOUNT}, {ORDERS.ORDER_DATE}, "semiannually")	SUM ("ORDERS"."ORDER_AMOUNT") OVER (PARTITION BY TO_CHAR ("ORDERS"."ORDER_DATE", 'YYYY/') || CEIL (TO_CHAR ("ORDERS"."ORDER_DATE",'Q')/2))
Date For each year	SUM ({ORDERS.ORDER_AMOUNT}, {ORDERS.ORDER_DATE}, "annually")	SUM ("ORDERS"."ORDER_AMOUNT") OVER (PARTITION BY TO_CHAR ("ORDERS"."ORDER_DATE", 'YYYY'))
Time For each second	SUM ({ORDERS.ORDER_AMOUNT}, {ORDERS.ORDER_DATE}, "by second")	SUM ("ORDERS"."ORDER_AMOUNT") OVER (PARTITION BY TO_CHAR ("ORDERS"."ORDER_DATE", 'YYYY/MM/DD HH24:MI:SS'))
Time For each minute	SUM ({ORDERS.ORDER_AMOUNT}, {ORDERS.ORDER_DATE}, "by minute")	SUM ("ORDERS"."ORDER_AMOUNT") OVER (PARTITION BY TO_CHAR ("ORDERS"."ORDER_DATE", 'YYYY/MM/DD HH24:MI'))
Time For each hour	SUM ({ORDERS.ORDER_AMOUNT}, {ORDERS.ORDER_DATE}, "by hour")	SUM ("ORDERS"."ORDER_AMOUNT") OVER (PARTITION BY TO_CHAR ("ORDERS"."ORDER_DATE", 'YYYY/MM/DD HH24'))
Time For AM/PM	SUM ({ORDERS.ORDER_AMOUNT}, {ORDERS.ORDER_DATE}, "by AMPM")	SUM ("ORDERS"."ORDER_AMOUNT") OVER (PARTITION BY TO_CHAR ("ORDERS"."ORDER_DATE", 'YYYY/MM/DD PM'))

Table 6-8   *Summary Functions* (continued)

Nth Largest To compute the Nth largest value and return it in every detail row, you can use a SQL Command with a query similar to the following. Note that this case shows a rank by a grouping. Because ties are possible and only one Nth value per grouping is needed, you must add a tiebreaker field to the Rank() function. In the following example, EMPLOYEE_ID was used. The choice for N could be converted to a parameter to allow the user to select N at runtime. Note that this query returns the second largest salary for a position. If a position has only one employee, null is returned.

```
SELECT e.EMPLOYEE_ID, e.FIRST_NAME, e.SALARY, POSITION,
       e.REPORTS_TO, s.NthSalary
 FROM  XTREME.EMPLOYEE e LEFT OUTER JOIN
       (SELECT Position, NthSalary FROM
            (SELECT Position, SALARY NthSalary, RANK()
                  OVER (PARTITION BY Position ORDER BY Salary DESC,
                  Employee_Id) N
               FROM Employee)
          WHERE N=2) s
 USING (position)
 ORDER BY POSITION, e.REPORTS_TO
```

NOTE

For Oracle 8i, the join syntax must be changed.

Nth Smallest To get the Nth smallest value, just change the sort order to ascending:

```
SELECT e.EMPLOYEE_ID, e.FIRST_NAME, e.SALARY, POSITION,
       e.REPORTS_TO, s.NthSalary
 FROM  XTREME.EMPLOYEE e LEFT OUTER JOIN
       (SELECT Position, NthSalary FROM
            (SELECT Position, Salary NthSalary, RANK()
                  OVER (PARTITION BY Position ORDER BY Salary ASC,
                  Employee_Id) N
               FROM Employee)
          WHERE N=2) s
 USING (Position)
 ORDER BY POSITION, e.REPORTS_TO
```

Mode To get the mode, you can create a SQL Command with a query like the following. Because there may be multiple modal values, the minimum is chosen. This is consistent with the Crystal Reports Mode function.

Note that this query uses the subquery factoring clause of the Oracle SELECT command.

```
SELECT e.EMPLOYEE_ID, e.FIRST_NAME, e.SALARY, POSITION,
       e.REPORTS_TO, s.Min_Modal_Salary
 FROM  XTREME.EMPLOYEE e LEFT OUTER JOIN
 (WITH Counts AS
      (SELECT Position, Salary, COUNT(Salary) M
         FROM Employee
         GROUP BY Position, Salary),
     MaxCounts AS
      (SELECT Position, MAX(M) MaxM
         FROM Counts
         GROUP BY Position)
SELECT Counts.Position, MIN(Counts.Salary) Min_Modal_Salary
  FROM Counts, MaxCounts
 WHERE Counts.Position=MaxCounts.Position
   AND Counts.M=MaxCounts.MaxM
 GROUP BY Counts.Position) s
 USING (Position)
```

NOTE

The preceding query will not work in Oracle 8i.

Nth Most Frequent   To get the Nth most frequent value, you can create a SQL Command with a query like the following. Again, because there may be multiple values that occur with Nth frequency, the minimum is chosen. This is consistent with the Crystal Reports NthMostFrequent function.

```
SELECT e.EMPLOYEE_ID, e.FIRST_NAME, e.SALARY, POSITION,
       e.REPORTS_TO, f.NthMostFrequent
 FROM  XTREME.EMPLOYEE e LEFT OUTER JOIN
 (WITH Ranks AS
      (SELECT Position, Salary,
              RANK() OVER (PARTITION BY Position ORDER BY Salary) R
         FROM Employee),
     RankCounts AS
      (SELECT Position, R, COUNT(R) N
         FROM Ranks
         GROUP BY Position, R)
 SELECT DISTINCT Position, MIN(Ranks.Salary) NthMostFrequent
   FROM Ranks JOIN RankCounts
  USING (Position, R)
  WHERE N=2
  GROUP BY Position) f
USING (Position)
```

NOTE

The preceding query will not work in Oracle 8i.

Financial

Equivalents of the Crystal Financial functions created as Oracle functions can be created, but they are too complex for inclusion here.

Strings

Note that none of the Crystal Reports String Functions converts to its Oracle equivalent automatically when used in record selection formulas.

Table 6-9 lists all available Crystal string functions shown in the illustration and gives SQL Expression substitutes.

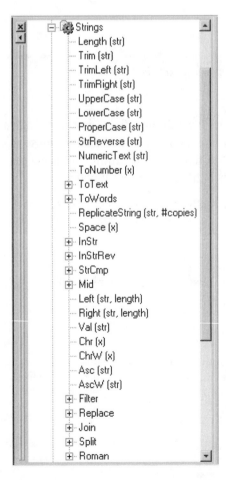

Function	Formula	SQL Expression
Length	Length ({ORDERS.COURIER_WEBSITE})	LENGTH ("ORDERS"."COURIER_WEBSITE")
Trim	Trim ({ORDERS.COURIER_WEBSITE})	TRIM ("ORDERS"."COURIER_WEBSITE")
TrimLeft	TrimLeft ({ORDERS.COURIER_WEBSITE})	LTRIM ("ORDERS"."COURIER_WEBSITE")
TrimRight	TrimRight ({ORDERS.COURIER_WEBSITE})	RTRIM ("ORDERS"."COURIER_WEBSITE")
UpperCase	UpperCase ({ORDERS.COURIER_WEBSITE})	UPPER ("ORDERS"."COURIER_WEBSITE")
LowerCase	LowerCase ({ORDERS.COURIER_WEBSITE})	LOWER ("ORDERS"."COURIER_WEBSITE")
ProperCase	ProperCase ({ORDERS.COURIER_WEBSITE})	INITCAP ("ORDERS"."COURIER_WEBSITE")
StrReverse	StrReverse ({ORDERS.COURIER_WEBSITE})	No Equivalent
NumericText	NumericText ({CUSTOMER.POSTAL_CODE})	NVL2 (TRANSLATE ("CUSTOMER"."POSTAL_CODE",'ABCDEFGHIJ KLMNOPQRSTUVWXYZ0123456789', 'ABCDEFGHIJKLMNOPQRSTUVWXYZ'), 'False', 'True')
ToNumber	ToNumber ({EMPLOYEE.SSN})	TO_NUMBER ("EMPLOYEE"."SSN")
ToText	ToText ({ORDERS.ORDER_AMOUNT})	TO_CHAR ("ORDERS"."ORDER_AMOUNT", 'FM999,990.00')
ToWords	ToWords ({ORDERS.ORDER_AMOUNT})	No Equivalent
ReplicateString	ReplicateString ('x',3)	LPAD ('x', 3, 'x')
Space	Space (3)	LPAD (' ', 3, ' ')
InStr	InStr ({EMPLOYEE.LAST_NAME}, 'a')	INSTR ("EMPLOYEE"."LAST_NAME", 'a')
	InStr (3, {EMPLOYEE.LAST_NAME}, 'a')	INSTR ("EMPLOYEE"."LAST_NAME", 'a', 3)
	InStr ({EMPLOYEE.LAST_NAME}, 'a', 1)	INSTR (UPPER("EMPLOYEE"."LAST_NAME"), UPPER ('a'))
InStrRev	InStrRev ({EMPLOYEE.LAST_NAME}, 'a')	INSTR ("EMPLOYEE"."LAST_NAME", 'a', -1)
StrCmp	StrCmp ({EMPLOYEE.LAST_NAME}, {EMPLOYEE.FIRST_NAME})	CASE WHEN "EMPLOYEE"."LAST_NAME" > "EMPLOYEE"."FIRST_NAME" THEN 1 WHEN "EMPLOYEE"."LAST_NAME" < "EMPLOYEE"."FIRST_NAME" THEN -1 ELSE 0 END
Mid	Mid ({EMPLOYEE.LAST_NAME}, 2, 3)	SUBSTR ("EMPLOYEE"."LAST_NAME", 2, 3)

Table 6-9   *String Functions*

Function	Formula	SQL Expression
Left	Left ({EMPLOYEE.LAST_NAME}, 3)	SUBSTR ("EMPLOYEE"."LAST_NAME", 1, 3)
Right	Right ({EMPLOYEE.LAST_NAME}, 3)	SUBSTR ("EMPLOYEE"."LAST_NAME", LENGTH ("EMPLOYEE"."LAST_NAME") -2, 3)
Val	Val ({EMPLOYEE.SSN})	TO_NUMBER (TRANSLATE("EMPLOYEE"."SSN", '0123456789ABCDEFGHIJKLMNOPQRSTUVWXYZ- ', '0123456789'))
Chr	Chr (65)	CHR (65)
ChrW	ChrW (65)	NCHR (65) (9*i* only)
Asc	Asc ('A')	ASCII ('A')
AscW	AscW ('A')	No equivalent
Filter	An array function	No equivalent
Replace	Replace ({EMPLOYEE.LAST_NAME}, 'a', '4')	REPLACE ("EMPLOYEE"."LAST_NAME", 'a', '4')
Join	An array function	No equivalent
Split	Returns an array	No equivalent
Roman	Roman ({EMPLOYEE.EMPLOYEE_ID})	TO_CHAR ("EMPLOYEE"."EMPLOYEE_ID", 'RN')
+	{EMPLOYEE.FIRST_NAME} + {EMPLOYEE.LAST_NAME}	CONCAT ("EMPLOYEE"."FIRST_NAME", "EMPLOYEE"."LAST_NAME")

Table 6-9   *String Functions* (continued)

Date and Time

None of the Crystal Reports Date and Time functions converts to its Oracle equivalent automatically when used in record selection formulas.

Table 6-10 lists all available Crystal date and time functions, shown in the illustration, and gives SQL Expression substitutes.

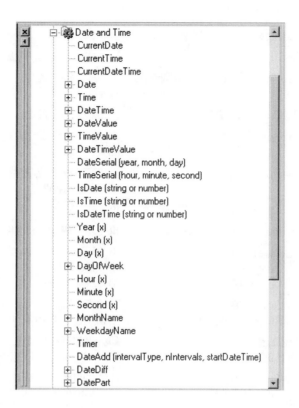

Function	Formula	SQL Expression
CurrentDate	CurrentDate	TRUNC(SYSDATE) TRUNC(CURRENT_DATE) (9*i* only)
CurrentTime	CurrentTime	Time portion of SYSDATE or CURRENT_DATE.
CurrentDateTime	CurrentDateTime	SYSDATE CURRENT_DATE (9*i* only)
Date	Date ({EMPLOYEE.BIRTH_DATE})	TRUNC ("EMPLOYEE"."BIRTH_DATE")
	Date (2003, 2, 20)	TO_DATE ('2003/02/20', 'YYYY/MM/DD')
Time	Time ({ORDERS.SHIP_DATE})	TO_DATE ("ORDERS"."SHIP_DATE", 'HH:MI:SS')

Table 6-10   *Date and Time Functions*

Function	Formula	SQL Expression
	Time (12,0,0)	TO_DATE ('12:00:00','HH:MI:SS')
DateTime	DateTime (Date (2003, 02, 20), Time (12, 0, 0))	TO_DATE ('2003/02/20 12:00:00', 'YYYY/MM/DD HH:MI:SS')
	DateTime (2003,2,20)	TO_DATE ('2003/02/20', 'YYYY/MM/DD')
	DateTime (2003,2,20,12,0,0)	TO_DATE ('2003/02/20 12:00:00', 'YYYY/MM/DD HH:MI:SS')
DateValue	DateValue (50)	TO_DATE ('1999/12/30 00:00:00', 'YYYY/MM/DD HH24:MI:SS') + 50
	DateValue ("September 20, 2003")	TO_DATE ('September 20, 2003, 'Month DD, YYYY')
	DateValue ({EMPLOYEE.BIRTH_DATE})	TO_DATE ("EMPLOYEE"."BIRTH_DATE")
	DateValue (1999, 9, 20)	TO_DATE (TO_CHAR(2000, '0000') || '/' || TO_CHAR(9, '00') || '/' || TO_CHAR(20, '00'), 'YYYY/MM/DD')
DateSerial	DateSerial (2003, 2, 20 – {EMPLOYEE.EMPLOYEE_ID})	TO_DATE ('2003/02/20', 'YYYY/MM/DD') – "EMPLOYEE"."EMPLOYEE_ID"
	DateSerial (2003, 2 – {EMPLOYEE.EMPLOYEE_ID}, 20)	ADD_MONTHS (TO_DATE('2003/02/20', 'YYYY/MM/DD'), – "EMPLOYEE"."EMPLOYEE_ID")
	DateSerial (2003 – {EMPLOYEE.EMPLOYEE_ID}, 2, 20)	ADD_MONTHS (TO_DATE('2003/02/20', 'YYYY/MM/DD'), – ("EMPLOYEE"."EMPLOYEE_ID" * 12))
IsDate	IsDate ('02/19/2002')	No equivalent
IsTime	IsTime ('12:00 AM')	No equivalent
IsDateTime	IsDateTime ('02/19/2002 12:00 AM')	No equivalent
Year	Year ({EMPLOYEE.BIRTH_DATE})	EXTRACT (YEAR FROM "EMPLOYEE"."BIRTH_DATE") or TO_NUMBER (TO_CHAR ("EMPLOYEE"."BIRTH_DATE", 'YYYY'))
Month	Month ({EMPLOYEE.BIRTH_DATE})	EXTRACT (MONTH FROM "EMPLOYEE"."BIRTH_DATE") or TO_NUMBER (TO_CHAR ("EMPLOYEE"."BIRTH_DATE", 'MM'))

Table 6-10   *Date and Time Functions* (continued)

Function	Formula	SQL Expression
Day	Day ({EMPLOYEE.BIRTH_DATE})	EXTRACT (DAY FROM "EMPLOYEE"."BIRTH_DATE") or TO_NUMBER (TO_CHAR ("EMPLOYEE"."BIRTH_DATE", 'DD'))
DayOfWeek	DayOfWeek ({EMPLOYEE.BIRTH_DATE})	TO_NUMBER (TO_CHAR ("EMPLOYEE"."BIRTH_DATE", 'D'))
Hour	Hour ({ORDERS.SHIP_DATE})	TO_NUMBER (TO_CHAR ("ORDERS"."SHIP_DATE", 'HH24'))
Minute	Minute ({ORDERS.SHIP_DATE})	TO_NUMBER (TO_CHAR ("ORDERS"."SHIP_DATE", 'MI'))
Second	Second ({ORDERS.SHIP_DATE})	TO_NUMBER (TO_CHAR ("ORDERS"."SHIP_DATE", 'SS'))
MonthName	MonthName (Month ({EMPLOYEE.BIRTH_DATE}))	TO_CHAR ("EMPLOYEE"."BIRTH_DATE", 'Month')
WeekdayName	WeekdayName (DayOfWeek ({EMPLOYEE.BIRTH_DATE}))	TO_CHAR ("EMPLOYEE"."BIRTH_DATE", 'Day')
WeekdayName	WeekdayName (DayOfWeek ({EMPLOYEE.BIRTH_DATE}), True)	TO_CHAR ("EMPLOYEE"."BIRTH_DATE", 'Dy')
Timer	Timer	(SYSDATE − TRUNC (SYSDATE))*24*60*60
DateAdd yyyy, q, m	DateAdd ('yyyy', 21, {EMPLOYEE.BIRTH_DATE})	ADD_MONTHS ("EMPLOYEE"."BIRTH_DATE", 21*12)
	DateAdd ('q', 2, {EMPLOYEE.BIRTH_DATE})	ADD_MONTHS ("EMPLOYEE"."BIRTH_DATE", 2*3)
	DateAdd ('m', 2, {EMPLOYEE.BIRTH_DATE})	ADD_MONTHS ("EMPLOYEE"."BIRTH_DATE", 2)
DateAdd Y, d, w	DateAdd ('y', 30, {EMPLOYEE.BIRTH_DATE})	"EMPLOYEE"."BIRTH_DATE" + 30
	DateAdd ('d', 30, {EMPLOYEE.BIRTH_DATE})	"EMPLOYEE"."BIRTH_DATE" + 30
	DateAdd ('m', 2, {EMPLOYEE.BIRTH_DATE})	"EMPLOYEE"."BIRTH_DATE" + 30
DateAdd ww	DateAdd ('ww', 3, {EMPLOYEE.BIRTH_DATE})	"EMPLOYEE"."BIRTH_DATE" + 3*7

Table 6-10   *Date and Time Functions* (continued)

Function	Formula	SQL Expression
DateAdd h	DateAdd ('h', 6, {EMPLOYEE.BIRTH_DATE})	"EMPLOYEE"."BIRTH_DATE" + (6/24)
DateAdd n	DateAdd ('n', 30, {EMPLOYEE.BIRTH_DATE})	"EMPLOYEE"."BIRTH_DATE" + (30/(24*60))
DateAdd s	DateAdd ('s', 30, {EMPLOYEE.BIRTH_DATE})	"EMPLOYEE"."BIRTH_DATE" + (30/(24*60*60))
DateDiff yyy	DateDiff ('yyyy', {EMPLOYEE.BIRTH_DATE}, CurrentDate)	EXTRACT (YEAR FROM SYSDATE) – EXTRACT (YEAR FROM "EMPLOYEE"."BIRTH_DATE")
DateDiff q	DateDiff ('q', {EMPLOYEE.BIRTH_DATE}, CurrentDate)	(EXTRACT (YEAR FROM SYSDATE) * 4 + CEIL (EXTRACT (MONTH FROM SYSDATE) / 3)) – (EXTRACT (YEAR FROM "EMPLOYEE"."BIRTH_DATE") * 4 + CEIL (EXTRACT(MONTH FROM "EMPLOYEE"."BIRTH_DATE") / 3))
DateDiff m	DateDiff ('m', {EMPLOYEE.BIRTH_DATE}, CurrentDate)	(EXTRACT (YEAR FROM SYSDATE) * 12 + EXTRACT (MONTH FROM SYSDATE)) – (EXTRACT (YEAR FROM "EMPLOYEE"."BIRTH_DATE") * 12 + EXTRACT (MONTH FROM "EMPLOYEE"."BIRTH_DATE"))
DateDiff D, y	DateDiff ('d', {EMPLOYEE.BIRTH_DATE}, CurrentDate)	TRUNC (SYSDATE – "EMPLOYEE"."BIRTH_DATE")
DateDiff w	DateDiff ('w', {EMPLOYEE.BIRTH_DATE}, CurrentDate)	FLOOR ((SYSDATE – "EMPLOYEE"."BIRTH_DATE") / 7)
DateDiff ww		No Equivalent
DateDiff h	DateDiff ('h', {EMPLOYEE.BIRTH_DATE}, CurrentDateTime)	TRUNC ((SYSDATE – "EMPLOYEE"."BIRTH_DATE") * 24)
DateDiff n	DateDiff ('n', {EMPLOYEE.BIRTH_DATE}, CurrentDateTime)	TRUNC ((SYSDATE – "EMPLOYEE"."BIRTH_DATE") * 24 * 60)
DateDiff s	DateDiff ('s', {EMPLOYEE.BIRTH_DATE}, CurrentDateTime)	TRUNC((SYSDATE – "EMPLOYEE"."BIRTH_DATE") * 24 * 60 * 60)
DatePart y	DatePart ('yyyy', {ORDERS.ORDER_DATE})	TO_NUMBER (TO_CHAR("ORDERS"."ORDER_DATE", 'YYYY'))

Table 6-10   *Date and Time Functions* (continued)

Function	Formula	SQL Expression
DatePart q	DatePart ('q', {ORDERS.ORDER_DATE})	TO_NUMBER (TO_CHAR ("ORDERS"."ORDER_DATE", 'Q'))
DatePart m	DatePart ('m', {ORDERS.ORDER_DATE})	TO_NUMBER (TO_CHAR ("ORDERS"."ORDER_DATE", 'MM'))
DatePart y	DatePart ('y', {ORDERS.ORDER_DATE})	TO_NUMBER (TO_CHAR ("ORDERS"."ORDER_DATE", 'DDD'))
DatePart d	DatePart ('d', {ORDERS.ORDER_DATE})	TO_NUMBER (TO_CHAR ("ORDERS"."ORDER_DATE", 'DD'))
DatePart w	DatePart ('w', {ORDERS.ORDER_DATE})	TO_NUMBER (TO_CHAR ("ORDERS"."ORDER_DATE", 'D'))
DatePart ww	DatePart ('ww', {ORDERS.ORDER_DATE})	CEIL((TO_CHAR ("ORDERS"."ORDER_DATE", 'DDD') + TO_CHAR (TO_DATE (TO_CHAR ("ORDERS"."ORDER_DATE", 'YYYY') || '/01/01', 'YYYY/MM/DD'), 'D') −1) / 7)
DatePart h	DatePart ('h', {ORDERS.ORDER_DATE})	TO_CHAR ("ORDERS"."ORDER_DATE", 'HH24')
DatePart n	DatePart ('n', {ORDERS.ORDER_DATE})	TO_CHAR ("ORDERS"."ORDER_DATE", 'MI')
DatePart s	DatePart ('s', {ORDERS.ORDER_DATE})	TO_CHAR ("ORDERS"."ORDER_DATE", 'SS')
	No equivalent	LAST_DAY
	No equivalent	NEXT_DAY

Table 6-10   *Date and Time Functions* (continued)

Date Ranges

The Date Range functions return ranges. Returning ranges is not possible in a SQL Expression.

Arrays

The Array functions return arrays. Returning arrays is not possible in a SQL Expression.

Ranges

The Range functions return Boolean values. Returning Boolean values is not possible in a SQL Expression.

Type Conversion

Crystal formula syntax includes several type conversion functions as shown in the following illustration. Table 6-11 lists them and gives SQL Expression substitutes.

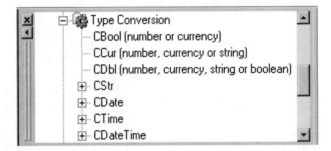

Programming Shortcuts

Note that none of the Crystal Reports Programming Shortcuts functions converts to its Oracle equivalent automatically when used in record selection formulas unless no database fields are included.

Function	Formula	SQL Expression
CBool		No equivalent
CCur	CCur ('$200.20')	TO_NUMBER('$200.20', '$999.99')
CDbl	CDbl ('$200.20')	TO_NUMBER('$200.20', '$999.99')
CStr		Equivalent to ToText; see the "Strings" section for details
CDate		Equivalent to Date; see the "Date and Time" section for details
CTime		Equivalent to Time; see the "Date and Time" section for details
CDateTime		Equivalent to Time; see the "Date and Time" section for details

Table 6-11   *Type Conversion Functions*

Table 6-12 lists all available Crystal programming shortcuts, shown in the illustration, and gives Oracle SQL Expression substitutes.

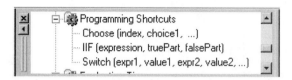

NOTE

For the Switch, Choose, and IIF functions, if all of the field references contained within the function calls refer to parameter fields and not to database fields, the expression will be simplified and included in the database query.

Evaluation Time

The evaluation time functions deal with the Crystal Reports processing passes. All Oracle processing will happen in Pass 1, during the WhileReadingRecords phase.

Print State

Crystal Reports contains many Print State functions as shown in the next illustration. Some Print State functions are applicable to the report itself and have no Oracle equivalents. These functions are PageNumber, TotalPageCount, PageNofM, GroupNumber, RecordSelection, GroupSelection, InRepeatedGroupHeader, and DrillDownGroupLevel. They are not shown in the following table. RecordNumber, OnFirstRecord, and OnLastRecord have Oracle equivalents that are applicable in

Function	Formula	SQL Expression
Choose	Choose (DatePart ('q', {ORDERS.ORDER_DATE}), 'First Quarter', 'Second Quarter', 'Third Quarter', 'Fourth Quarter')	DECODE (TO_CHAR("ORDERS"."ORDER_DATE", 'Q'), 1, 'First Quarter', 2, 'Second Quarter', 3, 'Third Quarter', 4, 'Fourth Quarter')
IIF	IIF ({ORDERS.REQUIRED_DATE} < {ORDERS.ORDER_DATE}, 'Problem', 'OK')	CASE WHEN "ORDERS"."REQUIRED_DATE" < "ORDERS"."ORDER_DATE" THEN 'Problem' ELSE 'OK' END
Switch	Switch ({ORDERS.ORDER_AMOUNT} > 5000, "large", {ORDERS.ORDER_AMOUNT} > 1000, "medium", True, "small")	CASE WHEN "ORDERS"."ORDER_AMOUNT" > 5000 THEN 'large' WHEN "ORDERS"."ORDER_AMOUNT" > 1000 THEN 'medium' ELSE 'small' END

Table 6-12 *Programming Shortcut Functions*

some circumstances, but not all circumstances. Print State functions that have Oracle equivalents are shown in Table 6-13.

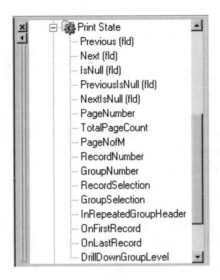

Function	Formula	SQL Expression
Previous (fld)	Previous ({EMPLOYEE.LAST_NAME})	LAG("EMPLOYEE"."LAST_NAME") OVER (ORDER BY "EMPLOYEE"."EMPLOYEE_ID")
Next (fld)	Next ({EMPLOYEE.LAST_NAME})	LEAD("EMPLOYEE"."LAST_NAME") OVER (ORDER BY "EMPLOYEE"."EMPLOYEE_ID")
IsNull (fld)	IsNull ({EMPLOYEE.SUPERVISOR_ID})	CASE WHEN "EMPLOYEE"."SUPERVISOR_ID" IS NULL THEN 'True' ELSE 'False' END
PreviousIsNull (fld)	PreviousIsNull ({EMPLOYEE.SUPERVISOR_ID})	CASE WHEN LAG ("EMPLOYEE"."SUPERVISOR_ID") OVER (ORDER BY "EMPLOYEE"."EMPLOYEE_ID") IS NULL THEN 'True' ELSE 'False' END
NextIsNull (fld)	NextIsNull ({EMPLOYEE.SUPERVISOR_ID})	CASE WHEN LEAD ("EMPLOYEE"."SUPERVISOR_ID") OVER (ORDER BY "EMPLOYEE"."EMPLOYEE_ID") IS NULL THEN 'True' ELSE 'False' END
RecordNumber	RecordNumber	ROWNUM

Table 6-13   *Print State Functions*

Function	Formula	SQL Expression
OnFirstRecord	OnFirstRecord	CASE FIRST_VALUE ("EMPLOYEE"."EMPLOYEE_ID") OVER (ORDER BY "EMPLOYEE"."SUPERVISOR_ID", "EMPLOYEE"."EMPLOYEE_ID") WHEN "EMPLOYEE"."EMPLOYEE_ID" THEN 'True' ELSE 'False' END (9*i* only)
OnLastRecord	OnLastRecord	CASE LAST_VALUE ("EMPLOYEE"."EMPLOYEE_ID") OVER (ORDER BY "EMPLOYEE"."SUPERVISOR_ID", "EMPLOYEE"."EMPLOYEE_ID" ROWS BETWEEN UNBOUNDED PRECEDING AND UNBOUNDED FOLLOWING) WHEN "EMPLOYEE"."EMPLOYEE_ID" THEN 'True' ELSE 'False' END (9*i* only)

Table 6-13   *Print State Functions* (continued)

Document Properties

The Document Properties functions concern report specific values and have no Oracle equivalents.

Alerts

The Alert functions concern report specific values and have no Oracle equivalents.

Note that Oracle contains a Publish/Subscribe feature that allows messages to be sent to users when defined conditions are met in the database.

Additional Functions

Oracle equivalents for Crystal's Additional functions can be created as Oracle functions if desired.

Running Totals

Crystal Running Totals can be moved to the server for processing by using Oracle's Windowing Aggregate Functions. For a full discussion of this capability, see the section "Reporting Aggregate Functions" in Chapter 4.

For an example, create a Crystal Running Total, as shown in Figure 6-7, for a report that uses the EMPLOYEE table and is grouped by EMPLOYEE.POSITION and sorted by EMPLOYEE.REPORTS_TO.

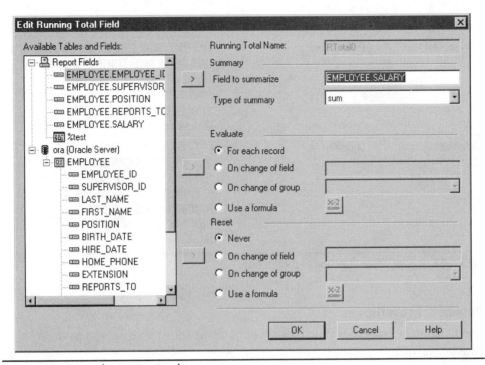

Figure 6-7 *Crystal Running Total 1*

Put the running total field on the report, and then create a SQL Expression using the following code:

```
SUM("EMPLOYEE"."SALARY")
OVER (ORDER BY "EMPLOYEE"."POSITION","EMPLOYEE"."REPORTS_TO"
     ROWS UNBOUNDED PRECEDING)
```

Put the SQL Expression field on the report and compare its values to the Running Total. They should match.

Next, modify the Running Total so that it resets for each EMPLOYEE.POSITION group, as shown in Figure 6-8.

Modify the SQL Expression as shown:

```
SUM("EMPLOYEE"."SALARY")
OVER (PARTITION BY "EMPLOYEE"."POSITION"
     ORDER BY "EMPLOYEE"."POSITION","EMPLOYEE"."REPORTS_TO"
     ROWS UNBOUNDED PRECEDING)
```

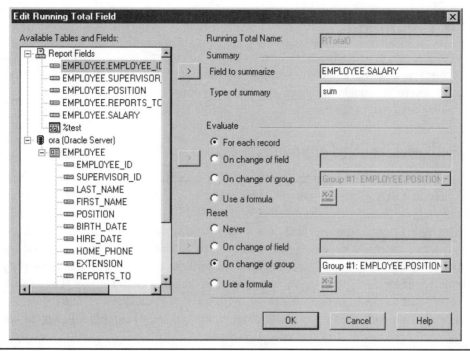

Figure 6-8   *Crystal Running Total 2*

Again, the values should match.

For a conditional running total, modify the running total field to evaluate only if the salary is greater than $35,000. The formula in the Evaluate section should be as follows:

```
{EMPLOYEE.SALARY}>=35000
```

Modify the SQL Expression as follows:

```
SUM(CASE WHEN "EMPLOYEE"."SALARY">=35000 THEN "EMPLOYEE"."SALARY"
        ELSE 0 END)
OVER (PARTITION BY "EMPLOYEE"."POSITION"
     ORDER BY "EMPLOYEE"."POSITION","EMPLOYEE"."REPORTS_TO"
     ROWS UNBOUNDED PRECEDING)
```

The results should match.

SQL Commands

Crystal Reports constructs a SQL query for the developer from choices that are made in wizards or elsewhere in the development environment. Crystal Reports 9 allows the user to create a query by simply typing in a command that is valid for the particular database in the connection. This feature is called a SQL Command.

SQL Allowed in SQL Commands

Crystal documentation states only that any SQL acceptable to the database can be executed in a SQL Command object. This is not very detailed information. So what exactly *can* be done in a Crystal SQL Command?

The SQL Command must result in a dataset or an opened REF Cursor. There are two types of statement structures that work from SQL Commands for Oracle. The first is any valid Oracle SELECT statement, no matter how complex, entered as the only command. Entering multiple commands one after the other causes errors. The second structure that works is an anonymous PL/SQL block that calls a REF Cursor stored procedure. Using the second structure, other commands may be executed after the call to the stored procedure. The syntax is shown next:

```
BEGIN
   Stored_Proc([Parameters]);
   Other statements
END;
```

Experimentation determined that the call to the stored procedure must come first, otherwise an error results. The other statements must not open another REF Cursor, but they can do Inserts, Deletes, Updates, and so on.

I do not recommend making database changes via SQL Commands, but using SQL Commands to take advantage of Oracle Select options that are not available in Crystal wizards can be very powerful. Oracle SQL has many options that are not available or not translatable via normal Crystal operations, but these special features can be used in SQL Commands, views, or stored procedures and may be useful in certain situations. See Chapter 3 and Chapter 4 for details on Oracle SQL that may be used in SQL Commands.

Some drivers may require that you call a stored procedure from a SQL Command because they do not display the stored procedures in the Database Expert. In that case, the following syntax will call the procedure:

```
{CALL ProcSchema.ProcPackage.ProcName(Param1, Param2,…)}
```

Do not include the REF Cursor parameter in the list.

Optimizing SQL Commands

The ability to use SQL Commands in Crystal Reports gives you the power to fully utilize the query capabilities of Oracle. Because you can write any valid SELECT statement, you can customize the query to return only the data you require, which is always the most important optimization goal. However, as with any power, it can be easily abused.

You must never return more columns in a SQL Command than will be used in the report directly or that are needed for computations. Ideally, you should embed the computations in the query too. When Crystal constructs the query for you, it returns only those fields that are used in the report. If you write a SQL Command, every column in the Select list will be returned, whether or not you use it in the report.

For example, create a report based on this SQL Command:

```
SELECT * FROM Employee
```

Include the Employee_ID, Supervisor_ID, Last_Name, First_Name, Position, and Birth_Date on the report. Run the report and then look at Report | Performance Information and choose Performance Timing. You will see something like the results shown in Figure 6-9.

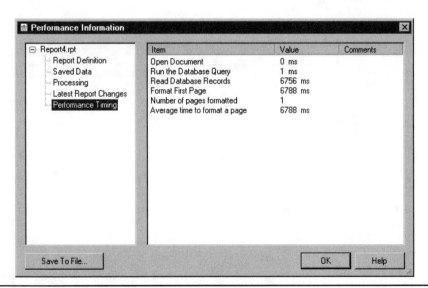

Figure 6-9   *Performance Timing for selecting all fields*

Now change the SQL Command as shown:

```
SELECT Employee_ID, Supervisor_Id, Last_Name, First_Name,
       Position, Birth_Date
FROM Employee
```

Run the report and view the Performance Information again. You will see a much improved processing time, similar to that in Figure 6-10.

The large performance gain this example shows is due to the large BLOB and CLOB fields in the Employee table, which are returned in the first query even though they are not used.

SQL Command Parameters

When using SQL Commands, you have the capability to create parameters. These parameters can be both less powerful and more powerful than regular Crystal report parameters. They must be simple types such as string, number, or date, but they cannot be multivalued in the typical sense. SQL Command parameters are converted to strings and added to the database query before it is sent to the server. Because of this, you can do things with these parameters that are similar to constructing the query programmatically.

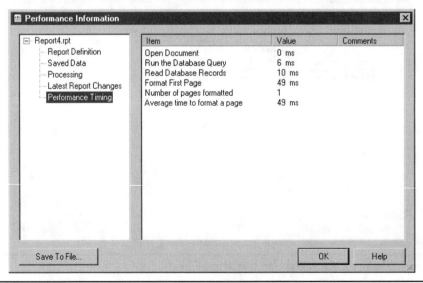

Figure 6-10   *Performance Timing for selecting specific fields*

For example, say that you want to allow your users to add their own filtering criteria. Create a SQL Command with a string parameter as shown:

```
SELECT Employee_ID, Supervisor_Id, Last_Name, First_Name,
       Position, Birth_Date
FROM Employee
WHERE {?Where_Clause}
```

As long as the user enters a valid WHERE clause, the query will execute and return only the rows that the user needs. Try entering 'Employee_Id IN (1,2,3)' in the prompt.

Schema-Specific Queries

Imagine that you are in an environment where each user has a copy of an application's tables. In this case, the schema needs to change for each user who runs the report. This is difficult to accomplish in Crystal because the schema qualifier is embedded in the report definition. Here is a solution using a SQL Command:

```
SELECT Employee_ID, Supervisor_Id, Last_Name, First_Name,
       Position, Birth_Date
FROM Employee
```

Because no schema qualifier is listed in the query, Oracle will resolve the table reference as usual, first looking in the schema of the logged in user.

This chapter covered optimization techniques that can be used in the Crystal Reports designer. The next chapter will cover optimization techniques that can be employed on the Oracle database to enhance report efficiency.

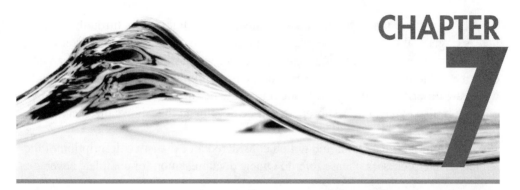

Optimizing:
The Oracle Side

A ny query that returns data and runs against Oracle goes through three general steps. First, the query is parsed and an execution plan is determined, then it is executed, and finally the caller fetches the results. This chapter describes Oracle optimizers and execution plans. Optimizer hints useful to a report writer are described, and effective indexing strategies are covered. The use of stored outlines is also explained. A subreport will be developed that shows the execution plan for a report query.

Material in this chapter should not be considered an exhaustive description of the related Oracle processes. Please refer to Oracle documentation for complete coverage.

Oracle Optimizers

A general knowledge of the Oracle optimizers is required in order to understand execution plan optimization. Though the argument could be made that optimization is the domain of the DBA only, it would be shortsighted. The report developer can contribute much toward the creation of reusable, resource-efficient, optimized queries. The DBA's outlook is the entire system; the report developer can concentrate on a much smaller portion of that system, namely the report query.

Oracle has two optimizers, the older rule-based optimizer, and the newer cost-based optimizer. These optimizers are responsible for generating an execution plan for each query. The execution plan is a set of steps that the DBMS will follow to get the data required by the query. The default optimizer for the instance is set using the OPTIMIZER_MODE initialization parameter. The default value for OPTIMIZER_ MODE for Oracle 8*i* and Oracle 9*i* is CHOOSE. The instance's optimizer mode can be overridden for a session by using ALTER SESSION, or for a particular query by using optimizer hints in the statement.

Rule-Based

The rule-based optimizer makes decisions about the optimal execution plan for a given query based on a set of rules. A full discussion of these rules is outside the scope of this book, but the type of information that is stored in the database dictionary drives them. The rules are based on information about table definitions, index definitions, clustering, and so on in combination with the requirements of the query. No matter what data is stored in the database, the rule-based optimizer will always make the same decision. The rule-based optimizer will be used if the OPTIMIZER_MODE is set to RULE, or if no database statistics are available.

Cost-Based

The cost-based optimizer uses database statistics such as the number of rows in a table and the key spread, in combination with object definitions, to determine the optimal execution plan. The cost-based optimizer will calculate a cost for each possible execution plan and choose the least costly. In order to function, the cost-based optimizer requires that database statistics are available. The cost-based optimizer will be used if the OPTIMIZER_MODE is set to CHOOSE and at least one table in the query has statistics calculated for it. For the CHOOSE optimizer mode, the cost-based optimizer will choose the best execution plan that returns all rows. If the optimizer mode is set to FIRST_ROWS_n or ALL_ROWS, the cost-based optimizer will be used whether or not statistics exist. ALL_ROWS will optimize for total throughput, whereas FIRST_ROWS_n will optimize for the speediest return of the first n rows, where n can be 1, 10, 100, or 1000. The FIRST_ROWS optimizer mode exists for backward compatibility.

Gathering Statistics

Gathering database statistics is the domain of the DBA, and there are multiple methods in which to do this. Shown next is Oracle 9*i* sample code for gathering statistics for the XTREME schema that uses the DBMS_STATS package. A report developer would not usually be gathering statistics. This topic is mentioned for two reasons. One, if you see unexpected results when viewing execution plans, you will have the background to realize that statistics may be stale. Two, this script should be run so that the examples later in the book will work. Statistics should be gathered regularly so that the cost-based optimizer can make valid decisions.

```
BEGIN
DBMS_STATS.GATHER_SCHEMA_STATS(
   OWNNAME=>'XTREME',
   ESTIMATE_PERCENT=>DBMS_STATS.AUTO_SAMPLE_SIZE,
   CASCADE=>TRUE,
   OPTIONS=>'GATHER AUTO',
   METHOD_OPT=>'FOR ALL INDEXED COLUMNS');
-- Skewed column ORDERS.SHIPPED
DBMS_STATS.GATHER_TABLE_STATS(
   OWNNAME=>'XTREME', TABNAME=>'ORDERS',
   ESTIMATE_PERCENT=>DBMS_STATS.AUTO_SAMPLE_SIZE,
   CASCADE=>TRUE,
   METHOD_OPT=>'FOR COLUMNS SIZE AUTO SHIPPED');
END;
```

Here is a script for Oracle 8*i*:

```
BEGIN
DBMS_STATS.GATHER_SCHEMA_STATS(
    OWNNAME=>'XTREME',
    CASCADE=>TRUE,
    OPTIONS=>'GATHER',
    METHOD_OPT=>'FOR ALL INDEXED COLUMNS');
-- Skewed column ORDERS.SHIPPED
DBMS_STATS.GATHER_TABLE_STATS(
    OWNNAME=>'XTREME', TABNAME=>'ORDERS',
    CASCADE=>TRUE,
    METHOD_OPT=>'FOR COLUMNS SIZE 100 SHIPPED');
END;
```

Execution Plans

An execution plan is the systematic process that Oracle will go through to retrieve the data required to satisfy the query. For a query backing a report, data retrieval will usually be the most time-consuming and resource-intensive portion of the process. The parser checks the syntax and verifies the existence of objects and may rewrite queries containing views, subqueries, or IN clauses. It may also convert a query to use an existing materialized view instead of base tables. The parser then determines an optimal access path, from which it produces an execution plan.

The optimizer goal as shown in an execution plan can be CHOOSE or RULE. If the COST field is populated, the cost-based optimizer was used. If it is null, the rule-based optimizer was used.

Displaying Execution Plans

Execution plans can be displayed using the Explain Plan directive in SQL*Plus, Oracle trace files, or they can be queried from the dynamic performance views. The "Execution Plan Subreport" section later in this chapter shows how to use a Crystal subreport to display the actual execution plan used in the report. In this section, Explain Plan will be used to demonstrate what execution plans look like. To use Explain Plan, you must have access to a PLAN_TABLE. The SQL script UTLXPLAN.SQL, usually found in the Oracle_Home\RDBMS\Admin directory and included in the download files for this chapter, creates the PLAN_TABLE. The PLAN_TABLE for the XTREME schema was created in Chapter 1 with the other schema objects.

To populate the PLAN_TABLE, run a statement of the following form from a SQL*Plus prompt:

```
EXPLAIN PLAN FOR <<SQL Statement>>
```

See Oracle documentation for a full description of the EXPLAIN PLAN statement. The plan can be put into a table other than the PLAN_TABLE or identified with a statement_id using other available options.

To display the execution plan, you can use a supplied PL/SQL package (9*i*), a supplied database script, or you can query the PLAN_TABLE directly as shown:

```
SELECT id, cardinality "Rows",
       SUBSTR(lpad(' ',level-1)
       ||operation||' '||options||' '||object_name, 1, 40) Plan,
       SUBSTR(optimizer,1,10) Optimizer, cost, bytes
 FROM PLAN_TABLE
WHERE timestamp=(SELECT MAX(timestamp) FROM plan_table)
CONNECT BY prior id = parent_id
  AND prior timestamp = timestamp
 START WITH id = 0
ORDER BY id;
```

To use the PL/SQL package for 9*i*, run the following:

```
SELECT plan_table_output
  FROM TABLE(DBMS_XPLAN.DISPLAY('plan_table',null,'all'));
```

See Figure 7-1 for a complete example. See Oracle documentation for a full description of the DBMS_XPLAN package.

To use the supplied SQL scripts, run UTLXPLS.SQL for nonpartitioned queries or UTLXPLP.SQL for partitioned queries. These scripts can be found in the Oracle_Home\RDBMS\Admin directory or in the download files for this chapter.

The order of steps in the execution plan in the display is not the order in which those steps are actually executed. The execution starts at the leaf nodes and works up from there. The predicate information section shows the actual joining and filtering conditions from the query.

Access Methods

The execution plan will tell you what table access methods will be used. There are several possible methods of table access, including full table scan, index lookup, and ROWID.

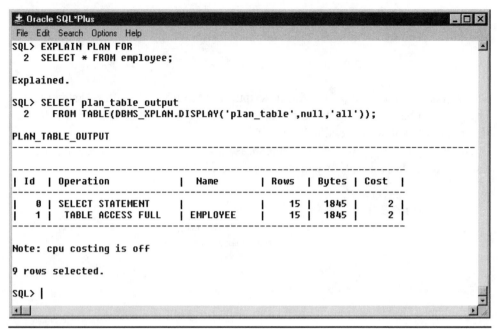

Figure 7-1   *DBMS_XPLAN example*

Full Table Scan

A full table scan means that the entire table is read up to the high water mark, which is the last block that had data written to it. If a table is highly unstable, it should be reorganized frequently to ensure that the high water mark is conservative. Full table scans use multiblock IO, and how many blocks are read is determined by the system parameter DB_FILE_MULTIBLOCK_READ_COUNT. Blocks read in a full table scan are placed at the least recently used end of the buffer cache and will be aged out of the cache quickly. Figure 7-1 shows an execution plan with a full table scan.

Index Lookup

Index lookup uses an index to look up the necessary ROWIDs and then reads the rows from the table using the ROWID. Index lookups use single block IO. If all of the required columns are in the index, no table access will be performed. If the ORDER BY clause of the query matches the index used, no sort will be required.

NOTE

All the following examples use Oracle 9i. 8i results would be similar.

Index Unique Scan   The Index unique scan looks up a single index value. All columns of the index must be used in the WHERE clause of the query with equality operators.

```
SQL> EXPLAIN PLAN FOR
  2   SELECT * FROM employee
  3   WHERE employee_id=5;


Explained.


SQL> SELECT plan_table_output
  2     FROM TABLE(DBMS_XPLAN.DISPLAY('plan_table',null,'all'));


PLAN_TABLE_OUTPUT
----------------------------------------------------------------------
| Id  | Operation                   | Name         |Rows |Bytes|Cost|
----------------------------------------------------------------------
|   0 | SELECT STATEMENT            |              |    1|  123|  1 |
|   1 |  TABLE ACCESS BY INDEX ROWID| EMPLOYEE     |    1|  123|  1 |
|*  2 |   INDEX UNIQUE SCAN         | EMPLOYEE_PK  |   15|     |    |
----------------------------------------------------------------------

Predicate Information (identified by operation id):
---------------------------------------------------
   2 - access("EMPLOYEE"."EMPLOYEE_ID"=5)


Note: cpu costing is off
```

Index Range Scan   The index range scan method looks up a range of key values. One or more of the leading columns of the index must be used in the query. Rows are returned in index order.

```
SQL> EXPLAIN PLAN FOR
  2   SELECT * FROM orders
  3   WHERE order_id > 3150;


Explained.
```

```
SQL> SELECT plan_table_output
  2    FROM TABLE(DBMS_XPLAN.DISPLAY('plan_table',null,'all'));


PLAN_TABLE_OUTPUT
-----------------------------------------------------------------
| Id  | Operation                    | Name      | Rows |Bytes|Cost|
-----------------------------------------------------------------
|   0 | SELECT STATEMENT             |           |   30| 2310|   3|
|   1 |  TABLE ACCESS BY INDEX ROWID| ORDERS    |   30| 2310|   3|
|*  2 |   INDEX RANGE SCAN           | ORDERS_PK |   30|     |   2|
-----------------------------------------------------------------

Predicate Information (identified by operation id):
---------------------------------------------------

   2 - access("ORDERS"."ORDER_ID">3150)


Note: cpu costing is off
```

Index Range Scan Descending   Index range scan descending is used when an ORDER BY DESC clause that can use an index is in the query; it is identical to an index range scan except that data is returned in descending index order.

```
SQL> EXPLAIN PLAN FOR
  2    SELECT * FROM orders
  3    WHERE order_id > 3150
  4    ORDER BY order_id DESC;


Explained.


SQL> SELECT plan_table_output
  2    FROM TABLE(DBMS_XPLAN.DISPLAY('plan_table',null,'all'));


PLAN_TABLE_OUTPUT
-----------------------------------------------------------------
| Id  | Operation                     | Name      | Rows|Bytes|Cost|
-----------------------------------------------------------------
|   0 | SELECT STATEMENT              |           |   30| 2310|   3|
|   1 |  TABLE ACCESS BY INDEX ROWID  | ORDERS    |   30| 2310|   3|
|*  2 |   INDEX RANGE SCAN DESCENDING | ORDERS_PK |   30|     |   2|
-----------------------------------------------------------------
Predicate Information (identified by operation id):
---------------------------------------------------

   2 - access("ORDERS"."ORDER_ID">3150)
       filter("ORDERS"."ORDER_ID">3150)


Note: cpu costing is off
```

Index Skip Scans   Index skip scanning allows indexes to be searched even when the leading columns are not used. This can be faster than scanning the table itself. In the following example, the index ORDERS_SHIPPED_DATE is on columns SHIPPED and SHIP_DATE. SHIPPED, which is the first field in the index, is not used in the query, so the index is skip scanned.

NOTE

Skip scanning is a new feature of Oracle 9i.

```
SQL> EXPLAIN PLAN FOR
  2   SELECT * FROM orders
  3   WHERE ship_date=To_DATE('01/12/2000','mm/dd/yyyy');

Explained.

SQL> SELECT plan_table_output
  2      FROM TABLE(DBMS_XPLAN.DISPLAY('plan_table',null,'all'));

PLAN_TABLE_OUTPUT
-----------------------------------------------------------------
|Id|Operation                  | Name               |Rows|Bytes|Cost|
-----------------------------------------------------------------
| 0|SELECT STATEMENT           |                    | 3 | 231 | 5 |
| 1| TABLE ACCESS BY INDEX ROWID|ORDERS             | 3 | 231 | 5 |
|*2|  INDEX SKIP SCAN          |ORDERS_SHIPPED_DATE| 1 |     | 3 |
-----------------------------------------------------------------
Predicate Information (identified by operation id):
-----------------------------------------------------------------
   2 - access("ORDERS"."SHIP_DATE"=TO_DATE('2000-01-12 00:00:00',
 'yyyy-mm-dd hh24:mi:ss'))
       filter("ORDERS"."SHIP_DATE"=TO_DATE('2000-01-12 00:00:00',
 'yyyy-mm-dd hh24:mi:ss'))

Note: cpu costing is off
```

Index Full Scan   Index full scanning reads the entire index in order. It might be used instead of a full table scan if the rows need to be returned in index order, but it uses single block IO and can be inefficient.

Index Fast Full Scan Index fast full scanning reads the entire index but not in order. It is used only by the cost-based optimizer and uses multiblock IO. It can be used for parallel execution and when the first column of the index is not needed in the query. In the following example, the query returns only the SHIP_DATE column, so even though SHIP_DATE is the second field in the ORDERS_SHIPPED_DATE index, it is faster to read the index than it would be to read the entire ORDERS table.

```
SQL> EXPLAIN PLAN FOR
  2  SELECT DISTINCT ship_date FROM orders;

Explained.

SQL> SELECT plan_table_output
  2      FROM TABLE(DBMS_XPLAN.DISPLAY('plan_table',null,'all'));

PLAN_TABLE_OUTPUT
---------------------------------------------------------------------
| Id  | Operation           | Name                 |Rows|Bytes|Cost|
---------------------------------------------------------------------
|   0 | SELECT STATEMENT    |                      | 731| 5848|  10|
|   1 |   SORT UNIQUE       |                      | 731| 5848|  10|
|   2 |    INDEX FAST FULL SCAN| ORDERS_SHIPPED_DATE |2192|17536|   4|
---------------------------------------------------------------------

Note: cpu costing is off
```

ROWID

Using this method, the block with the specified ROWID is read. This is the fastest access method, although it is rare that a query is written explicitly to use a ROWID. This method is most commonly used implicitly with an index lookup. See the index unique scan example in the preceding section.

Joins

The join order is very important in determining an optimal execution plan. If there are more than two tables in a query, the joins will happen in a particular order. First, the first table and the second table will be joined and any filtering conditions that apply to them will be made. Then the third table will be joined to the result of the first join, and so on. The fewer records returned by the first join, the fewer records any subsequent joins have to deal with. The optimizer will determine a join order, but this may be overridden with the ORDERED optimizer hint.

There are three types of joins: the sort merge join, the nested loops join, and the hash join. In addition to the normal join types, a Cartesian product can also be returned.

Sort Merge Join

When two tables are joined using a sort merge join, each table is independently sorted if it is not already sorted on the join fields, and then the two sorted datasets are merged. An Explain Plan includes table access statements and then a merge join statement. Due to the required sorting, this is not an efficient join method.

```
SQL> EXPLAIN PLAN FOR
  2  SELECT order_id, SUM(order_amount),
  3         SUM(unit_price*quantity) test_amount
  4  FROM orders JOIN orders_detail USING (order_id)
  5  WHERE order_id>3150
  6  GROUP BY order_id;

Explained.

SQL> SELECT plan_table_output
  2      FROM TABLE(DBMS_XPLAN.DISPLAY('plan_table',null,'all'));
```

```
PLAN_TABLE_OUTPUT
```

Id	Operation	Name	Rows	Bytes	Ct
0	SELECT STATEMENT		29	609	8
1	SORT GROUP BY NOSORT		29	609	8
2	MERGE JOIN		29	609	8
3	TABLE ACCESS BY INDEX ROWID	ORDERS	30	270	3
*4	INDEX RANGE SCAN	ORDERS_PK	30		2
*5	SORT JOIN		50	600	5
6	TABLE ACCESS BY INDEX ROWID	ORDERS_DETAIL	50	600	3
*7	INDEX RANGE SCAN	ORDERS_DETAIL_ORDER_ID_INDEX	1		2

```
Predicate Information (identified by operation id):
---------------------------------------------------

   4 - access("ORDERS"."ORDER_ID">3150)
   5 - access("ORDERS"."ORDER_ID"="ORDERS_DETAIL"."ORDER_ID")
       filter("ORDERS"."ORDER_ID"="ORDERS_DETAIL"."ORDER_ID")
   7 - access("ORDERS_DETAIL"."ORDER_ID">3150)

Note: cpu costing is off
```

Nested Loops

In nested loop joins, the rows meeting the filtering criteria for the first table are returned. Then, for each row in that result, table two is probed for the matching rows. The number of rows returned by the first table and the speed of access to the second table determines the efficiency of nested loops.

```
SQL> EXPLAIN PLAN FOR
  2    SELECT order_id, SUM(order_amount),
  3           SUM(unit_price*quantity) test_amount
  4    FROM orders JOIN orders_detail USING (order_id)
  5    WHERE order_id=3150
  5    GROUP BY order_id;

Explained.

SQL> SELECT plan_table_output
  2      FROM TABLE(DBMS_XPLAN.DISPLAY('plan_table',null,'all'));

PLAN_TABLE_OUTPUT
---------------------------------------------------------------------
```

Id	Operation	Name	Rows	Bytes	Cst
0	SELECT STATEMENT			1	21	4
1	SORT GROUP BY NOSORT			1	21	4
2	NESTED LOOPS			2	42	4
3	TABLE ACCESS BY INDEX ROWID	ORDERS		1	9	2
*4	INDEX UNIQUE SCAN	ORDERS_PK	2192		1
5	TABLE ACCESS BY INDEX ROWID	ORDERS_DETAIL		2	24	2
*6	INDEX RANGE SCAN	ORDERS_DETAIL_ORDER_ID_INDEX	2		1

```
Predicate Information (identified by operation id):
---------------------------------------------------------------------
   4 - access("ORDERS"."ORDER_ID"=3150)
   6 - access("ORDERS_DETAIL"."ORDER_ID"=3150)
Note: cpu costing is off
```

Hash Join

Only the cost-based optimizer uses hash joins. The data source with the fewest rows is determined, and a hash table and a bitmap are created. The second table is then hashed and matches are looked for.

```
SQL> EXPLAIN PLAN FOR
  2  SELECT employee_id, first_name, last_name
  3  city, country
  4  FROM employee JOIN employee_addresses USING (employee_id);

Explained.

SQL> SELECT plan_table_output
  2    FROM TABLE(DBMS_XPLAN.DISPLAY('plan_table',null,'all'));

PLAN_TABLE_OUTPUT
-----------------------------------------------------------------
```

Id	Operation	Name	Rows	Bytes	Cost
0	SELECT STATEMENT		15	405	5
* 1	HASH JOIN		15	405	5
2	TABLE ACCESS FULL	EMPLOYEE	15	270	2
3	TABLE ACCESS FULL	EMPLOYEE_ADDRESSES	15	135	2

```
Predicate Information (identified by operation id):

   1 - access("EMPLOYEE"."EMPLOYEE_ID"="EMPLOYEE_ADDRESSES"."EMPLOYEE_ID")

Note: cpu costing is off
```

Cartesian Product

Cartesian products are usually caused by a mistake in coding the query. They occur when no join conditions are defined and result in each row of the second table being joined to each row of the first table.

```
SQL> EXPLAIN PLAN FOR
  2  SELECT contact_first_name, contact_last_name
  3  first_name, last_name
  4  FROM customer, employee;

Explained.

SQL> SELECT plan_table_output
  2    FROM TABLE(DBMS_XPLAN.DISPLAY('plan_table',null,'all'));
```

```
PLAN_TABLE_OUTPUT
--------------------------------------------------------------------
| Id  | Operation            | Name     | Rows | Bytes | Cost  |
--------------------------------------------------------------------
|  0  | SELECT STATEMENT     |          | 4050 | 93150 |    47 |
|  1  |  MERGE JOIN CARTESIAN|          | 4050 | 93150 |    47 |
|  2  |   TABLE ACCESS FULL  | EMPLOYEE |   15 |   120 |     2 |
|  3  |   BUFFER SORT        |          |  270 |  4050 |    45 |
|  4  |    TABLE ACCESS FULL | CUSTOMER |  270 |  4050 |     3 |
--------------------------------------------------------------------
```

Note: cpu costing is off

Operations

Three operations may appear in execution plans: sort, filter, and view. Sorts are
expensive operations but may be needed due to ORDER BY clauses, GROUP BY
clauses, or sort merge joins. Filtering may occur due to partition elimination or the
use of functions like MIN or MAX.

Views

If the view operation shows up in an execution plan, the view used by the query
will not be broken down to its base tables but will instead be selected from directly.
No in-line views can be broken down, so they will always show up with the view
operation in the execution plan. A view operation in the execution plan means that
the view will be instantiated, which is usually a costly operation.

Bind Variables

If you execute a query containing bind variables in Oracle 9*i,* the optimizer will peek
at the initial value of the bind variable and produce an execution plan appropriate for
that value. The same plan will be used for later executions. If the query contains bind
variables, the optimizer assumes that the execution plan should stay constant no matter
what the value of the bind variable. Only Crystal Reports backed by stored procedures
will contain bind variables, unless CURSOR_SHARING is enabled.

Other

Other execution plan possibilities, such as parallel queries, remote queries, and partition
views, are not covered here. See Oracle documentation for more information.

Execution Plan Subreport

A subreport that displays the execution plan for a report query and that can be inserted into any report facilitates optimization of the report. The actual execution plan used to process a query is stored in the dynamic performance view V$SQL_PLAN, so it is available to report on as long as it has not aged out of the library cache.

To query V$SQL_PLAN for the execution plan, you must know the address and hash_value for the related cursor. The V$SESSION dynamic performance view contains the current and previous address and hash_value for statements executed by session ID, and the function USERENV('SESSIONID') returns the *audit* session ID for the current session. Putting these facts together, you can create a subreport using the V$SQL_PLAN and V$SESSION views, add a SQL Expression to the main report that returns the audit session ID, and link the subreport to the main report using the audit session ID.

However, there are a couple of open issues to resolve before continuing. First, how should V$SQL_PLAN and V$SESSION be linked? Via experimentation, it appears that the cursor for the main report is closed before the subreport is executed, which results in the current address and hash_values being zero and the values of interest to you being moved into the corresponding previous fields. Therefore, the database link between V$SQL_PLAN and V$SESSION should use the V$SESSION PREV_SQL_ADDR and PREV_HASH_VALUE.

NOTE

For reports backed by stored procedures, the main report cursor is not closed before the subreport is executed, so the database link between V$SQL_PLAN and V$SESSION should use the V$SESSION SQL_ADDRESS and SQL_HASH_VALUE. Also note that the subreport will display information only about the last SQL statement executed by the procedure.

There is a second issue. If you use the same database connection to log in to the subreport that you used for the main report, the main report and the subreport will use the same database session. This causes the subreport to run, exactly as the main report would, and to complete its query execution, which leaves the SQL_HASH_VALUE at zero and the session INACTIVE, and the PREV_HASH_VALUE will be the hash value of the query connected to the subreport, not the query connected to the main report. You will have to ensure that the main report and the subreport use different sessions in order to avoid losing the hash value for the main report. Using more than one session per report should be avoided in most circumstances. This situation is an exception and should be used only during development or optimization.

Crystal Reports will not allow more than one logon to the same data source. However, convincing Crystal that two data sources are different is easy. If you are using ODBC, simply create two ODBC Datasource names that point to the same database. If you are using the native driver, it is no more difficult but may require the assistance of your DBA. In short, you must create two TNS names that point to the same database. Here is an extract from a TNSNames.ora file showing two TNS names that point to the same database:

```
ORA.HOME =
  (DESCRIPTION =
    (ADDRESS_LIST =
      (ADDRESS = (PROTOCOL = TCP)(HOST = server)(PORT = 1521))
    )
    (CONNECT_DATA =
      (SERVICE_NAME = ORA.HOME)
    )
  )

ORA2.HOME =
  (DESCRIPTION =
    (ADDRESS_LIST =
      (ADDRESS = (PROTOCOL = TCP)(HOST = server)(PORT = 1521))
    )
    (CONNECT_DATA =
      (SERVICE_NAME = ORA.HOME)
    )
  )
```

Of course, you could also use a native connection for the main report and an ODBC connection for the subreport, or some other driver combination, to ensure two sessions.

A subreport for displaying the execution plan is available for download as Chapter 7\ Show SQL Plan Subreport. The subreport is set up to use the ORA2 native connection created in Chapter 1. To run this subreport, the user must have SELECT privileges on the V$SESSION, V$SQL_PLAN, and V$SQL_Workarea dynamic performance views. The role XTREME_REPORTER has been granted these privileges and given to the user XTREME. If you need to grant the privileges directly to a user, use the following syntax:

```
GRANT SELECT ON V_$Session TO <user id>;
GRANT SELECT ON V_$SQL_Plan TO <user id>;
GRANT SELECT ON V_$SQL_Workarea TO <user id>;
```

To demonstrate using the plan subreport, open the Crystal Sample Reports\General Business\Account Statement report. Create a SQL Expression named AUDSID using the following code:

```
USERENV('SESSIONID')
```

The report footer section is hidden, but the subreport will be put in that section, so show it. Next, choose Insert | Subreport. Select the Choose A Report radio button and browse to Chapter 7\Show SQL Plan Subreport. See Figure 7-2.

Next, select the Link tab. Move %AUDSID from the Available Fields list into the Field(s) To Link To list. Set the Subreport Parameter Field To Use box to ?AUDSID (note that this should be ?AUDSID, not ?PM-%AUDSID). Clear the Select Data In Subreport Based On Field checkbox. The dialog box should look like Figure 7-3. Click OK and place the subreport in the report footer section.

Run the report. Log in to ORA2 if necessary. Because ORA2 is exactly the same database as ORA, the XTREME user can log on to both connections. Scroll to the last page of the report to view the plan subreport, as shown in Figure 7-4. This report is available as Chapter 7\Account Statement with Plan Subreport.

The subreport uses Crystal's hierarchical grouping, so the fields are indented a few characters to highlight children. The lightly shaded rows in the subreport show

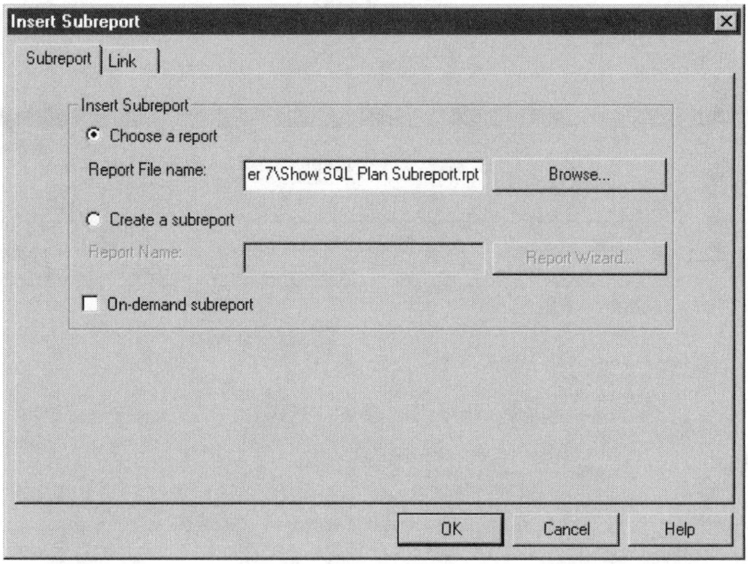

Figure 7-2   *Link tab*

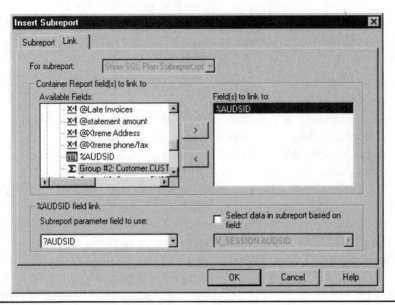

Figure 7-3 *Insert Subreport dialog*

the actual filtering or joining conditions. The darker shaded rows show the SQL work area or PGA usage. Only some operations, such as sorting, require use of a work area. See the "PGA" section later in this chapter for more information about memory usage by work areas.

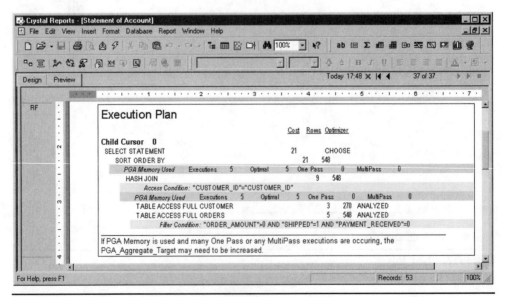

Figure 7-4 *Statement of Account execution plan*

NOTE

When using this subreport with a report based on a stored procedure, modify the stored procedure to return the audit session ID in addition to the other required fields to use for linking, and modify the links in the subreport to use the SQL_ADDRESS and SQL_HASH_VALUE.

NOTE

This subreport works only for Oracle 9i. The V$SQL_PLAN and V$SQL_Workarea dynamic performance views do not exist in previous versions. The subreport works for all connection types, but be aware when changing the database location to an OLE DB type that the table aliases are slightly different for the dynamic performance views, so you must do a table-by-table change.

Optimizing the Environment

This chapter is concerned primarily with optimizing a single particular query. Optimizing the overall system is generally beyond the intended scope. However, it must be recognized that instance level parameters and resource consumption by other processes affect the performance of an individual query. Ideally, before attempting to optimize individual statements, the Oracle environment will be evaluated, decisions will be made about setting initialization parameters that influence query performance and memory usage, unnecessary anonymous PL/SQL blocks will be eliminated, and frequently used objects will be identified and pinned in memory.

Optimizer Initialization Parameters

The values of several initialization parameters affect the cost that the cost-based optimizer computes. Modifying these parameters can change the execution plan by causing some access methods to be more expensive than others. These parameters will affect all database queries, so care must be taken to ensure that improving reporting performance does not result in unacceptably degrading other areas.

CURSOR_SHARING

The CURSOR_SHARING parameter affects how statements are parsed. See Chapter 8 for a full description of this parameter.

DB_FILE_MULTIBLOCK_READ_COUNT

This parameter determines the number of blocks read in any multiblock read operation. Full table scans and index fast full scans use multiblock IO. The higher the value of DB_FILE_MULTIBLOCK_READ_COUNT, the more likely it will be that the optimizer will choose to do full table scans or index fast full scans instead of using other access methods.

HASH_AREA_SIZE

The size of this parameter affects the cost of a hash join operation. The larger the HASH_AREA_SIZE, the less costly a hash join will be. See the "PGA" section for details on setting this parameter.

HASH_JOIN_ENABLED

If this parameter is TRUE, the cost-based optimizer will consider using hash join operations. If it is FALSE, no hash joins will be done. The default value for this parameter for Oracle 8*i* and 9*i* is TRUE.

OPTIMIZER_INDEX_CACHING

This parameter influences the cost of index probing in nested loop operations and tells the optimizer to assume a particular percentage of index blocks are cached. A value of 100 indicates that the entire index is in the buffer cache. The default value for this parameter in Oracle 8*i* and 9*i* is 0.

OPTIMIZER_INDEX_COST_ADJ

This parameter reduces the estimated cost of index probing. A value of 100 means to use the normal cost. A value of 50 means to treat an index probe as if it costs 50 percent of the normal cost.

OPTIMIZER_MAX_PERMUTATIONS

This parameter controls the maximum number of join permutations that the cost-based optimizer will consider. Reducing it may reduce the parse time for queries containing many tables, but it may also cause the true optimal plan to never be considered.

OPTIMIZER_MODE

The OPTIMIZER_MODE parameter was covered in the "Oracle Optimizers" section. Oracle recommends using the cost-based optimizer.

PARTITION_VIEW_ENABLED

This parameter is useful when your environment contains partitioned tables. If it is TRUE, the optimizer will scan only the needed partitions based on join conditions or WHERE clauses.

QUERY_REWRITE_ENABLED

If TRUE, the optimizer will consider transparently rewriting queries to take advantage of existing materialized views. See Chapter 9 for an in-depth description. This parameter also determines whether function-based indexes are used; see the "Function-Based Index" section for more information.

SORT_AREA_SIZE

The larger the value of SORT_AREA_SIZE, the less the optimizer will estimate the cost of sort operations to be. See the "PGA" section for information about setting this parameter.

STAR_TRANSFORMATION_ENABLED

Setting the STAR_TRANSFORMATION_ENABLED optimizer parameter to TRUE enables the optimizer to cost star transformations using combinations of bitmap indexes. Star queries are used in a data warehouse environment where dimension and fact tables exist with bitmap indexes on those tables.

Memory Allocation

Memory use by an Oracle instance is divided among several caches or pools. Optimizing memory usage depends on allocating available memory to the pools in a manner that will produce the best overall performance. In-depth coverage of memory optimization is outside the scope of this book, but an overview is given to help the report writer understand how queries use server resources.

Buffer Cache

The buffer cache is where blocks of data are stored once they have been read from disk. All source data for a query is returned from the buffer cache. If a query requires data that is not already in the buffer cache, it is read from disk into the buffer cache for use. Queries should be optimized to require as few blocks as possible from the buffer cache, and the environment should be configured so that frequently used data can be found in the buffer cache, to avoid disk reads. The Crystal side optimization goal of returning as few records as possible will help optimize buffer cache use. The DBA will tune the buffer cache using tools such as the V$DB_CACHE_ADVICE and V$SYSSTAT dynamic performance views and monitor it over time.

Data in the buffer cache is aged out using a least recently used algorithm. As new data is placed at the most recently used end of the list, blocks at the least recently used end are dropped. Blocks read for full table scans and fast full index scans are an exception: they are placed at the least recently used end of the list with the rationale that the data will probably not be needed by other queries, should be aged out quickly, and should not force other blocks to be aged out.

The buffer cache can be segmented by using a KEEP or RECYCLE pool along with the DEFAULT pool. The KEEP and RECYCLE pools behave in exactly the same way as the DEFAULT pool because they all use a least recently used algorithm for aging blocks. However, the intention should be to store frequently accessed small segments in the KEEP pool and size the KEEP pool so that it is large enough to hold those items without aging them out. Large segments that are used infrequently should be stored in the RECYCLE pool where they will not cause undesired aging out in the DEFAULT or KEEP pools. The desired pool is set using the BUFFER_POOL keyword of the STORAGE clause for tables, indexes, and clusters. In a reporting environment, you might want to set the BUFFER_POOL to KEEP for small, frequently used lookup tables or frequently used indexes. You might also want to set the BUFFER_POOL to RECYCLE for large tables that are commonly accessed via full table scans.

Shared Pool and Large Pool

The shared pool contains the library cache, the dictionary cache, and other data. The dictionary cache stores data dictionary information, such as the column names that belong to a table, and is used heavily as almost every operation must verify catalog information. The library cache stores SQL statements, PL/SQL code, and their executable forms. Crystal Reports reads from the dictionary cache to create the table and field lists shown in the Database Expert. When Crystal Reports executes a query, that query is parsed using the dictionary cache, and the executable form is stored in the library cache. The dictionary and library caches, like other Oracle memory structures, use a least recently used algorithm to age items out of the cache. Oracle will dynamically resize the dictionary cache and library cache within the limits set for the shared pool.

The large pool can be created for use by the shared server, parallel query, or Recovery Manager to segregate those processes from other shared pool processes.

Reduce Parsing   The DBA will tune and monitor the shared pool. However, there are several things that report writers can do to help optimize use of the library cache. See Chapter 8 for more information.

Pin Frequently Used Cursors or PL/SQL Packages   Objects may be pinned in the shared pool so that they are never aged out. This can be useful if large objects are causing many other objects to be aged out due to lack of contiguous space. Pinning should be done immediately after instance startup both so that the pinned objects do not contribute to memory fragmentation and to guarantee their place in memory before any user might call them; this will eliminate any extra wait time on first execution.

Pinning is done using the DBMS_SHARED_POOL.KEEP procedure. Several object types may be pinned, including sequences and triggers, but report writers will be primarily concerned with SQL cursors and PL/SQL packages or procedures. If your most frequently used reports are based on stored procedures, and those stored procedures are in a package, pinning that package may be advantageous.

A procedure or package is pinned by executing a statement like the following:

```
DBMS_SHARED_POOL.KEEP(<<package or procedure name>>);
```

Pinning SQL cursors is more complex. The SQL cursor must exist in the shared pool, so it must have been previously parsed. You must determine the address and hash value of the cursor. Then you can pin the cursor using the following format:

```
DBMS_SHARED_POOL.KEEP(<<address.hash_value>>);
```

If you need to pin a cursor that is backing a report, it would be simpler to put that query in a stored procedure and pin the procedure or the package that contains it.

Eliminate Large Anonymous PL/SQL Blocks   Avoid an environment where large anonymous PL/SQL blocks are regularly executed. Large anonymous blocks are not likely to be sharable; hence, they will consume more space in the shared pool. If many similar blocks are being executed ad hoc or from scripts, consider creating PL/SQL parameterized procedures to reduce parsing and memory consumption. An anonymous block will be executed when a Crystal SQL Command is used that has multiple statements in it.

Qualify Object Names with the Schema Owner   When using SQL Commands, qualify the table or view name with the owner name whenever possible. Use XTREME .EMPLOYEE rather than EMPLOYEE. This will reduce the space used in the dictionary cache and speed the parsing process because the parser will not have to determine the proper schema.

PGA

Oracle 9*i* introduced automated management of several parameters that affect SQL execution for dedicated sessions, including HASH_AREA_SIZE, CREATE_BITMAP_ AREA_SIZE and SORT_AREA_SIZE. Setting the PGA_AGGREGATE_TARGET to a value other than zero will cause the *_AREA_SIZE parameter values to be ignored for dedicated sessions in favor of dynamic manipulation by Oracle.

With the PGA_AGGREGATE_TARGET set, Oracle 9*i* will dynamically adjust the amount of memory allocated to the various work areas to optimize performance.

The goal is to have as many executions as possible using an optimal work area size. One pass executions are usually acceptable but not as fast as optimal executions. Multipass executions should be avoided. The DBA should use the V$PGA_TARGET_ ADVICE and the V$PGA_TARGET_ADVICE_HISTOGRAM to tune the PGA_AGGREGATE_TARGET parameter. The report writer can view work area usage in the execution plan subreport developed in the "Execution Plan Subreport" section. If you see reports running with multipass executions, consult your DBA.

Parallel Execution

Explaining the full details of parallel execution is beyond the scope of this book, but report writers should be aware of the possibility of parallel execution, especially when querying large tables. Parallel execution can improve the performance of large queries by distributing the work across multiple server processes. However, parallel execution requires more memory and CPU resources.

Certain initialization parameters must be set to enable a parallel execution environment, and there are two possible methods of implementing parallel query execution. The DBA can set the PARALLEL option on tables and indexes to cause parallel execution for all operations against those objects. Alternatively, a SELECT statement can be written with the PARALLEL hint, which will force parallel execution for that particular query.

Table Partitioning

Table partitioning breaks the physical storage of tables into chunks or partitions that are transparent to any user querying the database. Users do not need to know anything about the partition status of any tables. However, if a table is partitioned and a query requires data only from some partitions, the query performance may be improved. The report writer has no direct method of creating partitioned tables because that is a function of the DBA and must be done at table creation. However, the report writer should be aware that tables can be partitioned and that partitioning may improve query performance on large tables or indexes.

There are several types of partitioning; a common type is partitioning by date. Suppose that in the sample data, the Orders table was very large. If you partitioned it by Order_Date or a range of Order_Dates, then reports that were always run for today or this month would probably see a performance gain.

Dynamic Sampling

Dynamic sampling is a new feature of Oracle 9*i* release 2. Dynamic sampling allows the optimizer to sample data from tables to make estimates about cardinality and selectivity. This can be helpful in situations where there are no statistics gathered, the statistics are old, or the statistics are not desirable for some other reason. The optimizer determines whether dynamic sampling would be useful for each query, and the level of sampling is controlled by the initialization parameter OPTIMIZER_ DYNAMIC_SAMPLING. The optimizer hint DYNAMIC_SAMPLING customizes the sampling for a particular query.

Optimizing the Execution Plan

Optimizing an execution plan can involve several methods. This section covers various general tips to improve query performance, as well as optimizer hints that can be set for an individual query, indexing to improve performance, and using stored outlines.

Tips

Some general tips for optimization of execution plans are to make sure that statistics have been gathered appropriately so that the cost-based optimizer has up-to-date information and to use the execution plan subreport or Explain Plan to view the execution plan for a report query, then check the plan for any of the following conditions.

Eliminate Cartesian Products

If the execution plan shows a Cartesian product, there is probably a missing table linking condition. On rare occasions, a Cartesian product can be intentional and necessary.

Avoid Full Table Scans

Full table scans should be avoided unless the tables are small, the query returns more than 5 percent to 10 percent of the rows, you are using parallel execution, or in some cases where a hash join is used. For some reports, a large portion of rows will be returned, so full table scans may be appropriate.

Join Order

An important tuning goal is to filter out as many records as you can as soon as possible in the execution plan. Review the execution plan from the leaf operations to the final operations. Verify that the data source with the most selective filter is used first, followed by the source with the next most selective filter, and so on.

Optimal Join Method

The optimal join method, when a small number of rows will be returned, is usually nested loops. Other methods might be more appropriate when larger numbers of rows are returned.

Appropriate Table Access Methods

For tables that have filtering conditions in the WHERE clause, if that filtering will return a small number of rows from the table, you should expect to see the use of an index. If an index is not being used in this circumstance, then you should investigate why. If there is no filtering or the filtering is not very selective, you might expect to see a full table scan.

Use Equijoins

Equijoins, joins based on equality conditions, are more efficient than nonequijoins, which are fairly uncommon but necessary for some queries. If you see a join condition containing anything other than an equal sign, verify that it is appropriate.

Avoid Expressions in Join Conditions and WHERE Clauses

If the join condition or filter condition contains an expression instead of a simple column name, indexes cannot be used unless the expression has an equivalent function-based index. Be aware of implicit type conversions where Oracle will rewrite the query to contain the appropriate conversion function. For instance, if you have a filtering condition such as the following where ColA is VARCHAR2:

```
WHERE ColA=100
```

Oracle will convert it as shown and no index can be used:

```
WHERE TO_NUMBER(ColA)=100
```

To avoid this, rewrite the condition as shown next, assuming the format string is appropriate and any index on ColA can be used:

```
WHERE ColA=TO_CHAR(100,'L99G999D99MI')
```

When functions such as NVL are used in filtering conditions, they can sometimes be rewritten to avoid the use of the function. For example, the following condition:

```
WHERE NVL(Col1,100)=100
```

can be rewritten as shown to preserve the use of indexes:

```
WHERE (Col1=100 OR Col1 IS NULL)
```

Use Views Appropriately

When a view is used in a query, verify that it is necessary. For instance, if a view containing joins is used but all fields in the SELECT clause are from one table only, it would be more efficient to use the underlying table. There are some organizations in which views are used to insulate the reports from changes in the underlying database. In this case, views should be available that are based on single tables, in addition to any special purpose views containing joins. The single table views should then be used for reports on individual tables, and the optimizer will rewrite the query to use the table.

Avoid Joining Views

The optimizer will attempt to rewrite views to use underlying tables when possible, but using a query that joins views may make this rewrite impossible. In this case, a view may have to be instantiated to complete the query, which will cause heavy resource usage. If you have a report that contains a view joined to another view, it's better to create a new view containing the data you need and eliminate the view joins.

Use CASE Statements

This tip is not strictly about optimizing an execution plan. Sometimes multiple queries are used to return different aggregations of the same data. For instance, say that you need the count of employees whose salary is less than $30,000, and you also need the count of employees whose salary is between $30,000 and $60,000. Instead of creating two queries, one query with a CASE statement could be used, reducing the number of times that the same data needs to be read.

Optimizer Hints

Optimizer hints are keywords embedded in the SELECT statement that direct the optimizer to use a particular join order, join method, access path, or parallelization. The hint follows the SELECT statement. If a query is compound, with multiple SELECT statements, each can have its own hint. Optimizer hints can be used in SQL Commands, stored procedures, and view definitions.

Only commonly used hints for SELECT statements are covered.

The syntax for specifying hints is shown next:

```
SELECT /*+ hint [text] [hint[text]]... */
```

Optimizer Mode Hints

Optimizer mode hints are those hints that influence how the cost-based optimizer will cost the statement. Note that if the FIRST_ROWS, FIRST_ROWS(n), or ALL_ROWS optimizer hints are used, the cost-based optimizer will be used even if statistics do not exist.

FIRST_ROWS(n)

```
SELECT /*+ FIRST_ROWS(n) */ …
```

The FIRST_ROWS(n) hint tells the optimizer to pick the execution plan that returns the first n rows the fastest. N can be any positive integer. This differs from the corresponding First Rows optimizer mode that allows a limited set of values for n. The FIRST_ROWS(n) hint will be ignored if the statement contains any operation that requires returning all rows before selecting the first n. Such operations include GROUP BY, ORDER BY, aggregation, UNION, and DISTINCT. FIRST_ROWS(n) has limited usage for Crystal Reports queries because few report queries lack at least an ORDER BY clause.

NOTE

The FIRST_ROWS(n) optimizer hint is new in Oracle 9i.

FIRST_ROWS   FIRST_ROWS is equivalent to FIRST_ROWS(1).

ALL_ROWS

```
SELECT /*+ ALL_ROWS */ …
```

The ALL_ROWS hint causes the optimizer to optimize for maximum throughput, to return all rows as fast as possible.

CHOOSE

```
SELECT /*+ CHOOSE */ …
```

The CHOOSE hint tells Oracle to use the cost-based optimizer if any table in the query has statistics and to use the rule-based optimizer if no statistics exist.

RULE

```
SELECT /*+ RULE */ …
```

The RULE hint instructs Oracle to use the rule-based optimizer even if statistics exist.

Access Path Hints

Access path hints tell the optimizer which access path it should use. If the hinted access path is unavailable, the hint is ignored. For these hints, the table name must be given. If an alias for the table name exists, the alias should be used in the hint.

FULL

```
SELECT /*+ FULL (table_name or alias) */ …
```

The FULL hint forces a full table scan. A full table scan can be more efficient than an index scan if a large portion of the table rows need to be returned because of the way data is read for a full table scan versus an index scan. In a full table scan, multiple blocks are read simultaneously. In an index scan, one block is read at a time. Whether using a full scan is better than an index scan depends on many things, including the speed of the hardware, the DB_FILE_MULTIBLOCK_READ_COUNT, the DB_BLOCK_SIZE, and the way the index values are distributed. If your query returns more than 5 to 10 percent of the rows and the optimizer chooses to use an index, you may want to investigate the results of forcing a full table scan.

ROWID

```
SELECT /*+ ROWID (table_name or alias) */ …
```

A ROWID hint forces the table to be scanned by ROWID.

INDEX

```
SELECT /*+ INDEX (table_name or alias [index_name1
                                  [index_name2…]]) */ …
```

The INDEX hint forces an index scan on the table listed. If no index names are given, the optimizer will use the index with the least cost. If one index name is given, the optimizer will use that index. If multiple index names are given, the optimizer will use the index from the list that has the least cost.

INDEX_ASC

```
SELECT /*+ INDEX_ASC (table_name or alias [index_name1
                                  [index_name2...]]) */ …
```

The INDEX_ASC hint is currently identical to the INDEX hint. It forces an index scan in ascending order.

INDEX_COMBINE

```
SELECT /*+ INDEX_COMBINE (table_name or alias
                          [bitmap_index_name1
                          [bitmap_index_name2...]]) */ …
```

INDEX_COMBINE is similar to INDEX but forces a bitmap index to be used.

INDEX_JOIN

```
SELECT /*+ INDEX_JOIN (table_name or alias
                        [join_index_name1
                        [join_index_name2...]]) */ …
```

INDEX_JOIN forces the optimizer to use an index join on the listed tables.

INDEX_DESC

```
SELECT /*+ INDEX_DESC (table_name or alias [index_name1
                                  [index_name2...]]) */ …
```

INDEX_DESC is similar to INDEX, but if the statement requires a range scan, the INDEX_DESC hint will force the range to be scanned in reverse order.

INDEX_FFS

```
SELECT /*+ INDEX_FFS (table_name or alias [index_name1
                                  [index_name2...]]) */ …
```

INDEX_FFS forces a fast full index scan instead of a full table scan.

NO_INDEX

```
SELECT /*+ NO_INDEX (table_name or alias [index_name1
                                  [index_name2...]]) */ …
```

NO_INDEX removes the listed indexes from the compiler's consideration. If no index names are given, none of the available indexes will be used. If one or more index names are given, only those indexes will not be considered and any other existing indexes can be used.

CLUSTER

```
SELECT /*+ CLUSTER(table_name or alias) */ …
```

The CLUSTER hint forces a cluster scan of the specified table. This hint can only be used with tables that are part of a cluster.

HASH

```
SELECT /*+ HASH(table_name or alias) */ …
```

The HASH hint forces a hash scan of the specified table. This hint can only be used with tables that are part of a cluster.

AND_EQUAL

```
SELECT /*+ AND_EQUAL(table_name or alias index_name1 index_name2
[[index_name3 [index_name4]] [index_name5]]) */ …
```

The AND_EQUAL hint forces the optimizer to combine index scans for the listed table using from two to five of its single column indexes.

Join Order Hints

Join order hints let you tell the optimizer in what order the tables should be joined.

ORDERED

```
SELECT /*+ ORDERED */ …
```

ORDERED forces the optimizer to join the tables in the order they are listed in the FROM clause. Using the new Oracle 9*i* join syntax, the same result can be obtained without using hints.

STAR

```
SELECT /*+ STAR */ …
```

The STAR hint forces a star query plan to be used, if possible. This hint is used in data warehouse environments.

Join Operation Hints

The join operation hints suggest join methods for tables in the query.

Several special purpose join operation hints are not covered here, including DRIVING_SITE, HASH_AJ, MERGE_AJ, NL_AJ, HASH_SJ, MERGE_SJ, and NL_SJ. For information about these hints, refer to Oracle documentation.

USE_NL

```
SELECT /*+ ORDERED USE_NL (table_name or alias) */ …
```

The USE_NL hint forces a nested loop join and may cause the first rows of a query to be returned faster than they would be if a merge join was used. The ORDERED hint should always be used with this hint, and the table listed in the hint must be the inner table of a nested loop join.

USE_MERGE

```
SELECT /*+ USE_MERGE (table_name or alias) */ …
```

The USE_MERGE hint forces a merge join of the given table and may cause the entire query result to be returned faster than if a nested table join was used. The ORDERED hint should always be used with this hint, and the table listed in the hint will be merged to the result set of any joins preceding it in the order.

USE_HASH

```
SELECT /*+ USE_HASH (table_name or alias) */ …
```

The USE_HASH hint will force the listed table to be joined using a hash join.

LEADING

```
SELECT /*+ LEADING (table_name or alias) */ …
```

The LEADING hint forces the table listed to be first in the join order. LEADING is overridden by an ORDERED hint.

Parallel Hints

The work involved in processing a query can be broken into pieces, and the pieces can be executed simultaneously. This is called parallel execution. Parallel query execution is used if the tables involved in the query have their parallel option set or if a parallel hint is in the query, assuming that other initialization parameters that govern parallel execution are set.

Note that parallel execution is not the same thing as partitioning. Partitioned tables are broken into pieces for storage and can influence query execution because only required partitions may need to be read. Parallel execution, however, refers to the number of server processes that are working on the query.

PARALLEL

```
SELECT /*+ PARALLEL(table_name or alias[,degree_of_parallelism]) */ …
```

If no degree of parallelism is given, the system default based on initialization parameters will be used.

NOPARALLEL

```
SELECT /*+ NOPARALLEL(table_name or alias) */ …
```

If a table is used that has its parallel option set, this hint will override that and cause the query to execute without parallelism.

Three other parallel hints exist: PQ_DISTRIBUTE allows you to fine-tune the distribution of parallel join operations among query servers; PARALLEL_INDEX can be used with partitioned indexes to set the number of Oracle Real Application Cluster instances and the number of query servers working on those instances; and NO_PARALLEL_INDEX instructs the optimizer to not use a parallel index scan on the listed table and/or index.

Other Hints

There are several other hints that do not fit into the preceding categories. A few of them are covered here. See Oracle documentation for any that you do not find here.

CACHE

```
SELECT /*+ CACHE (table_name or alias) */ …
```

As discussed previously, when a full table scan is performed, the blocks read are placed at the least recently used end of the buffer so that they will age out quickly. The CACHE hint, however, causes the blocks to be placed at the most recently used end so that they will not age out quickly. This might be useful for small lookup tables that are read frequently with full table scans, but small tables are automatically cached in Oracle 9*i* release 2.

CURSOR_SHARING_EXACT

```
SELECT /*+ CURSOR_SHARING_EXACT */ …
```

If the CURSOR_SHARING initialization parameter is set to FORCE or SIMILAR, using the CURSOR_SHARING_EXACT hint will override that behavior for the query containing the hint.

> **NOTE**
> *CURSOR_SHARING_EXACT is new in Oracle 9i.*

DYNAMIC_SAMPLING

```
SELECT /*+ DYNAMIC_SAMPLING ([table_name or alias] sampling_level) */ …
```

The DYNAMIC_SAMPLING hint allows the optimizer to gather sample statistics for the query to help in determining cardinality and selectivity. If a table name is supplied, the sampling will be done only for that table. If no table name is supplied, sampling is done for the whole query, as indicated by the sampling level. The sampling level is a number from 0 to 10: 0 turns off sampling; 1 is the default value and indicates that sampling will be done on unanalyzed, nonindexed tables that are joined to other tables or used in subqueries and that have more than 32 blocks of data. Thirty-two blocks will be sampled. Setting the sampling level higher makes the sampling more aggressive and more likely. See Oracle documentation for a full description of the levels.

> **NOTE**
> *The DYNAMIC_SAMPLING hint is new in Oracle 9i.*

Indexing

Proper database indexing is a complex topic and has widespread effects. The DBA, application developers, and report writers must coordinate indexing decisions so that end users get the best overall performance. A report writer might commonly notice that the query execution plan does not use an index where expected. The report writer would then discuss the matter with the DBA and/or the application developers, so that an optimal indexing decision could be made.

There are several key places where indexing will speed query execution. Indexing the columns used in WHERE clauses will speed query execution. Indexing the columns used to join tables will also speed query execution. Reordering columns in concatenated indexes so that the most selective fields are first may speed query execution. If an index is not selective, adding a column to it may increase its selectivity (the selectivity of an index refers to the number of rows with the same value). The fewer the number of rows with the same value, the higher the selectivity of the index.

Nonselective indexes probably will not affect SELECT performance because the optimizer will probably not use them, but they will be detrimental to data manipulation statements. The DBA should monitor index usage and drop any unnecessary unused indexes. Be aware that indexing will have a negative impact on DML operations, so avoid indexing columns that are frequently updated.

B-tree Index

The default Oracle index is a B-tree index. B-tree indexes should be used in most cases where indexing is required and cardinality is high.

Function-Based Index

Function-based indexes allow you to create indexes on expressions. This speeds query execution when an expression is used often in the WHERE clause or ORDER BY clause. For example, consider the Last_Name column in the Employee table. A regular index created on Last_Name would be useful when a SELECT statement with the following WHERE clause was issued:

```
SELECT
...
WHERE Last_Name='King';
```

That index would be useless if the query was as follows:

```
SELECT
...
WHERE UPPER(Last_Name)='KING';
```

However, if a function-based index was created on the expression UPPER(Last_Name), it could be used in the previous query.

The database initialization parameter, QUERY_REWRITE_ENABLED must be true, or the equivalent session parameter must be true for function-based index use. By default, function-based indexes can only be created for built-in functions. To enable the use of user-defined functions, you must set the QUERY_REWRITE_INTEGRITY parameter to something other than its default value of ENFORCED.

Function-based indexes precompute expressions that are commonly used in WHERE clauses. Suppose that the month of order is used in many reports, so that many reports have clauses like the following two:

```
WHERE Extract(Month from Order_Date) = :Order_Month

ORDER BY Extract(Month from Order_Date)
```

A function-based index on the expression Extract(Month from Order_Date) would improve query performance.

Index Organized Tables

Index organized tables are Oracle tables where the entire row data is stored in the index. Hence, the entire table, not just the index, is always in physical order by the primary key. This structure is similar to some desktop databases such as Access or Paradox, where the rows are maintained in primary key order when inserts, deletes, or updates are made. Index organized tables can speed query execution if many queries use exact match or range searches of the primary key.

Bitmap Index

A bitmap index is appropriate for table columns with few distinct values and a large number of rows, but it can be costly to keep updated if there is frequent, nonbulk updating. Bitmap indexes are frequently used in data warehousing environments, where they help speed the processing of queries with complex WHERE clauses. In the XTREME sample data, a column such as Customer.Country is a candidate for a bitmap index because it has few distinct values.

Bitmap indexes require less storage than B-tree indexes. Bitmap indexes on single columns can be combined for use in WHERE clauses that use more than one bitmap indexed column. Bitmap indexes cannot be used to enforce referential integrity constraints.

Bitmap Join Index

Bitmap join indexes are used in data warehousing environments to effectively prejoin tables. The bitmap join index contains entries for the join columns and the ROWIDs of the corresponding rows.

NOTE

Bitmap join indexes are new in Oracle 9i.

Other Index Types

Other indexing methods are available. Domain indexes are indexes built using a user-defined index type. Domain indexes are usually supplied as part of an Oracle cartridge and enable indexing of complex user-defined data types. Clusters and hash clusters speed access to tables that are frequently queried together via joins.

Stored Outlines

An execution plan can be stored so that the SQL statement will always use that plan. If a stored outline exists, the cost-based optimizer will use it even if current conditions dictate a different plan. Stored outlines should be used with care, however, because they can result in performance degradation over time. See Oracle documentation for more detail on creating and using stored outlines.

This chapter described the Oracle optimizers and execution plans. A subreport for displaying report query execution plans was created, and tips were given for optimizing the execution plan. The next chapter will explain SQL statement parsing and the impact of parsing on a reporting environment and give suggestions for parse reduction.

Optimizing: Reducing Parses

IN THIS CHAPTER:

Reducing parses can be an important part of optimizing the use of database resources and, hence, the reporting environment. Developers, including report developers, can reduce parses with little or no help from the DBA because parse reduction is almost entirely dependent on the way in which queries are constructed. The DBA may point out queries that appear to be causing memory or scalability problems, but modifying those queries, or optimizing them in the first place, is the job of the developer.

Reducing parses is especially important when optimizing transaction processing systems. Typically, in a transaction processing system, there will be many queries that return little or no data, so the proportion of time spent parsing to the time spent fetching can be significant.

In a reporting environment, each query usually returns a large amount of data so the proportion of the parsing time to the total processing time is smaller, and perhaps, in some cases, insignificant. However, it does not change the fact that each parsed cursor requires memory and uses CPU resources. A more important benefit may be the increased scalability made possible by reducing memory use in the shared pool and reducing CPU usage for parsing, rather than speed enhancement for any particular query.

Description of Parsing

SQL statements issued against an Oracle database are parsed and stored in a global memory area called the library cache, which is a component of the shared pool. Parsing is the operation of converting SQL text to an executable version and involves allocation of memory, validation of the SQL statement, and the creation of an execution plan. Parsing does not include actually getting the data and returning it.

Parsing consists of several steps: syntax checking, semantic analysis, check for existence in the shared pool, optimization, and plan generation. Only after the syntax checking and semantic analysis steps can a check be made to see if the SQL statement already exists in the shared pool. At that point, the statement has been checked for syntactic correctness and had any unqualified references resolved. A hard parse occurs when no match is found in the shared pool considering both the text of the statement and any environment settings that affect execution plans. In that case, the final two steps must occur. The statement must be optimized and a new plan will be generated for it. A soft parse is said to occur when the final two steps are not required.

SQL statements are maintained in the shared pool using a least recently used algorithm so they will age out over time. SQL statements stored in the shared pool can be shared by many users and across sessions. Assuming that the CURSOR_ SHARING parameter is set to its default of EXACT, to be considered identical, two statements must contain exactly the same text, character for character, including spaces, case, and comments. In addition, the environment of the sessions issuing the statements must be the same. For example, if one session is using the cost-based optimizer, so must the other session. In addition, if the objects in the statements are not explicitly qualified with a schema name, they must refer to an object in the same schema. If the SQL statements contain bind variables, the bind variables must have the same names, datatypes, and lengths.

Reducing Hard Parsing

The reduction of hard parsing is accomplished by making changes that will increase the number of reusable statements. You can do this by implementing bind variables or modifying instance parameters.

Looking at Oracle's V$SQL Dynamic Performance View

Oracle has a built-in view called V$SQL. This view contains each of the SQL statements that are currently in the library cache and includes statistics on the number of executions and parses of each SQL statement.

A very simple report, Supplier.rpt, is available for download in the Chapter 8 files. It uses the Suppliers table and has one parameter for inputting the desired supplier. The SQL query that Crystal Reports sends to Oracle is shown here if this report is run for supplier number 2:

```
SELECT  "SUPPLIER"."SUPPLIER_ID",  "SUPPLIER"."SUPPLIER_NAME",
        "SUPPLIER"."COUNTRY",  "SUPPLIER"."PHONE"
  FROM    "XTREME"."SUPPLIER" "SUPPLIER"
  WHERE   "SUPPLIER"."SUPPLIER_ID"=2
```

Another report is included called Chapter 8\Show_SQL_Stats.rpt. (Use Show_ SQL_Stats_8i.rpt for Oracle 8*i*.) Show_SQL_Stats takes a SQL statement (or the initial part of a SQL statement) and displays the V$SQL statistics for that statement. In order to run Show_SQL_Stats, you must have the SELECT privilege on the V$SQL dynamic performance view. Since V$SQL is a synonym, to grant access to it, you must grant access to the actual table name (which is V_$SQL) as follows:

```
GRAND SELECT ON V_$SQL TO xtreme;
```

Run the Supplier report several times. Use the same parameter value a few times and also several different parameter values. On the last run, choose Database | Show SQL Query and copy the text, up to the equal sign, to the clipboard. Then run the Show_SQL_Stats report, pasting the previously saved SQL statement into the parameter prompt. The resulting report will look something like Figure 8-1.

Crystal Parameters and Parsing

Note that the Show_SQL_Stats report will show a different hash value for each different parameter value that was supplied for the Supplier report. This tells you that Oracle considers the query for Supplier=5 to be a completely different query than the one for Supplier=1, which results in a new hard parse for each value sent from Crystal Reports. Each query consumes memory.

The first detail line in the Show_SQL_Stats report displays the memory usage and optimizer values for the query. The second detail line displays the totals for a particular query. It shows the number of times the query was executed, total CPU time, elapsed time, disk reads, buffer gets, and rows processed. The third detail line, starting with Per Execution, computes the average values for each of those variables per execution. The first execution for any query will include the hard parse and hence

SQL Statistics

Hash Value 915,366,722   **Address 65B50250**
Child Cursor 0

	Memory			Optimizer		
Sharable	Persistent	Runtime	Mode	Cost	First Loaded At	
7,763	748	1,912	CHOOSE	1	2003-06-18/16:50:39	

Executions	Loads	CPU Time	Elapsed Time	Disk Reads	Buffer Gets	Rows	Sorts
1	1	0	868	0	2	1	0
Per Execution	1.00	0	868	0	2	1	0

```
SELECT "SUPPLIER"."SUPPLIER_ID", "SUPPLIER"."SUPPLIER_NAME",
"SUPPLIER"."COUNTRY", "SUPPLIER"."PHONE" FROM  "XTREME"."SUPPLIER" "SUPPLIER"
WHERE "SUPPLIER"."SUPPLIER_ID"=5
```

Hash Value 1,391,335,719   **Address 65B27C78**
Child Cursor 0

	Memory			Optimizer		
Sharable	Persistent	Runtime	Mode	Cost	First Loaded At	
8,419	748	1,912	CHOOSE	1	2003-06-18/16:50:17	

Executions	Loads	CPU Time	Elapsed Time	Disk Reads	Buffer Gets	Rows	Sorts
3	1	0	46,986	4	8	3	0
Per Execution	0.33	0	15,662	1	3	1	0

```
SELECT "SUPPLIER"."SUPPLIER_ID", "SUPPLIER"."SUPPLIER_NAME",
"SUPPLIER"."COUNTRY", "SUPPLIER"."PHONE" FROM  "XTREME"."SUPPLIER" "SUPPLIER"
WHERE "SUPPLIER"."SUPPLIER_ID"=1
```

Figure 8-1   *Example SQL stats results*

will consume more CPU time, and other resources, than subsequent executions. Other variations in the statistics can be due to other conditions on the database. For example, the data required for the query may or may not be in the buffer cache.

NOTE

The CPU_Time and Elapsed_Time fields in V$SQL did not exist prior to Oracle 9i, and are therefore omitted from the 8i version of the report.

The Loads column shows the number of times the query was loaded, or parsed. This number will increment only when Oracle needs to reparse the query. It might need to reparse if the query has been aged out of the library cache, the library cache has been cleared for some other reason, or a session parameter that affects the execution plan has been changed.

Subreport for SQL Statistics

The Show_SQL_Stats report is useful but somewhat awkward to use because you must paste or type in a very long string containing the SQL text of a query that has been executed previously. It would be convenient if the SQL statistics could be generated directly in the report in question as a subreport, without requiring any parameter from the user. You cannot insert the existing Show_SQL_Stats report as a subreport into the Supplier report, however, because that would require linking on the SQL query text, which is not possible in Crystal Reports. This means that another method to tie the main report query to the SQL statistics query must be implemented.

The V$Session dynamic performance view contains information about the current session, including the hash value of the query currently being executed and the hash value of the previously executed statement. If you link V$Session to V$SQL, you can determine which SQL query is being executed by which session. Then the only missing piece is determining the session ID of the main report.

NOTE

Much of the following discussion is identical to that covered in Chapter 7 regarding the linking of the execution plan subreport.

The Oracle function USERENV(SessionID) will return the audit session ID for the current session and can be used to link the main report to the SQL statistics subreport. Note that Crystal will execute the main report first and then any subreports. Because the query backing the main report is finished before the query for the subreport is run, the main report session will have no currently executing SQL during subreport execution, its SQL_Hash_Value will be 0, its session will be INACTIVE, and its Prev_Hash_Value will contain the hash value for the main report's query. This allows you to use the Prev_Hash_Value to link V$Session to V$SQL.

However, there is another complication. If you use the same database connection to log in to the subreport that you used for the main report, the main report and the subreport will be using the same database session. Then, running the subreport, as with the main report, will complete its query execution, leaving the SQL_Hash_Value 0. The session will be INACTIVE, and the Prev_Hash_Value will be the hash value of the query connected to the subreport, not the query connected to the main report.

To address this problem, you will have to ensure that the main report and the subreport use different sessions. Using more than one session per report should be avoided in most circumstances, but this situation is an exception and these guidelines should be used only during the development or optimization phases.

As we already discussed in Chapter 7, Crystal Reports will not allow more than one login to the same data source. However, convincing Crystal that two data sources are different is easy. If you are using ODBC, simply create two ODBC Data Source Names that point to the same database. If you are using the native driver, remember that you must create two TNS names that point to the same database. Here is an extract from a TNSNames.ora file showing two TNS names that point to the same database:

```
ORA.HOME =
  (DESCRIPTION =
    (ADDRESS_LIST =
      (ADDRESS = (PROTOCOL = TCP)(HOST = server)(PORT = 1521))
    )
    (CONNECT_DATA =
      (SERVICE_NAME = ORA.HOME)
    )
  )


ORA2.HOME =
  (DESCRIPTION =
    (ADDRESS_LIST =
      (ADDRESS = (PROTOCOL = TCP)(HOST = server)(PORT = 1521))
    )
    (CONNECT_DATA =
      (SERVICE_NAME = ORA.HOME)
    )
  )
```

Of course, you could also use a native connection for the main report and an ODBC connection for the subreport, or some other combination, to ensure two sessions.

Now you can modify the Show_SQL_Stats report so that it can be used as a subreport. Save Show_SQL_Stats as Show_SQL_Stats_Subreport. In order to run the new subreport, you must have the SELECT privilege on the V$SESSION dynamic performance view. Because V$SESSION is a synonym, to grant access to V$SESSION, you must grant access to the actual table name, V_$SESSION, as follows:

```
GRANT SELECT ON V_$SESSION TO xtreme;
```

Go to the Database Expert and add the V$Session dynamic performance view—you will find it in the PUBLIC folder if you have enabled Synonyms. Link from the Prev_SQL_Addr in V_Session to Address in V_SQL, and from Prev_Hash_Value in V_Session to Hash_Value in V_SQL, as shown in Figure 8-2.

Modify the report to use whichever secondary data source you want to use, using the Database | Set Datasource Location dialog (this will prevent problems when adding this subreport to other reports). Remove the existing Selection formula that is dependent on the SQL text parameter. Delete the {?SQL Text} parameter and add a parameter for the audit ID, as shown in Figure 8-3.

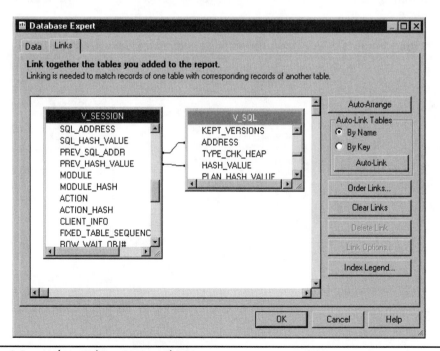

Figure 8-2 *Linking V$Session to V$SQL*

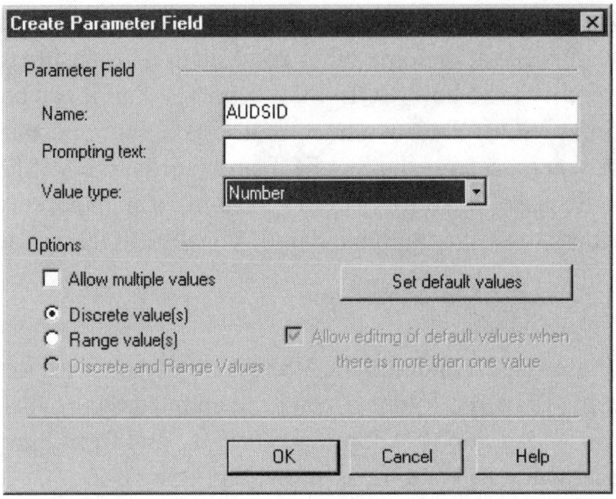

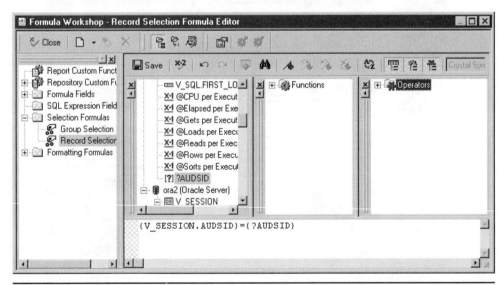

Figure 8-3   *AUDSID parameter*

Add a selection formula that uses the audit ID parameter, as shown in Figure 8-4. Add some of the V$Session fields to the report, if desired, as shown in Figure 8-5.

Figure 8-4   *AUDSID selection formula*

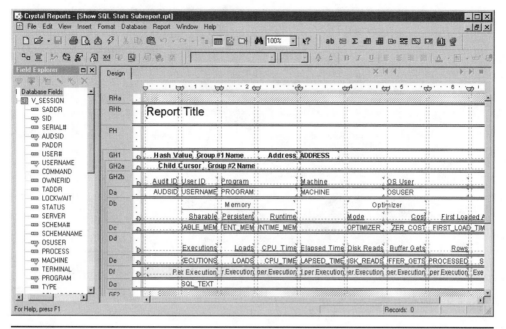

Figure 8-5   *Add V$Session fields*

Save the report. This completed report is available for download as Chapter 8\Show SQL Stats Subreport.rpt and Chapter 8\Show SQL Stats Subreport 8i.rpt for Oracle 8*i*.

Open the Supplier report and create a SQL Expression field called AUDSID with the following definition:

```
USERENV('SESSIONID')
```

Insert a subreport. Select Choose a Report and browse to the location of Show SQL Stats Subreport (or Show SQL Stats Subreport 8*i*). On the Link tab, choose the main report's SQL Expression field, %AUDSID, as the field to link to. Choose the subreport's parameter field, ?AUDSID from the Subreport Parameter Field To Use list (see Figure 8-6).

Place the subreport in the report footer section of the main report. Right-click the subreport and choose Format Subreport. On the Subreport tab, set the Subreport Name to SQL Statistics, as shown in Figure 8-7. This completed report is available as Chapter 8\Supplier with Statistics.rpt or Chapter 8\Supplier with Statistics 8i.rpt.

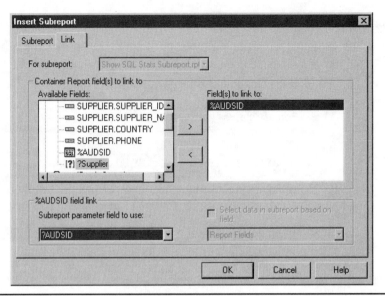

Figure 8-6 *Linking the SQL stats subreport*

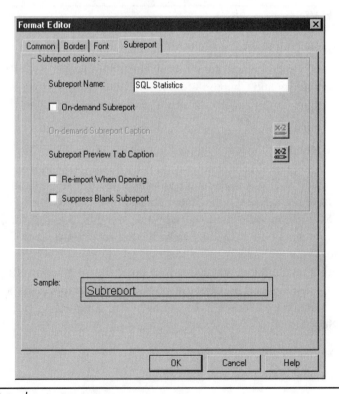

Figure 8-7 *Set subreport name*

Run the report. The SQL Statistics data should appear as shown in Figure 8-8.

Now you have a subreport that can be added to any report you like, if you need to see the report's SQL statistics. The only modification required to the main report is the addition of the SQL Expression field %AUDSID that contains the audit session ID needed for linking.

Oracle Bind Variables

One of Oracle's recommendations for parse reduction is to use bind variables. Bind variables replace the literal values that change from query to query. In the example, you would send your Supplier query to Oracle with a bind variable such as in the following:

```
SELECT  "SUPPLIER"."SUPPLIER_ID", "SUPPLIER"."SUPPLIER_NAME",
        "SUPPLIER"."COUNTRY", "SUPPLIER"."PHONE"
FROM    "XTREME"."SUPPLIER" "SUPPLIER"
WHERE   "SUPPLIER"."SUPPLIER_ID"= :Supp
```

If you could do this, Oracle will consider the SQL statement to be the same, no matter what value was entered for the :Supp bind variable.

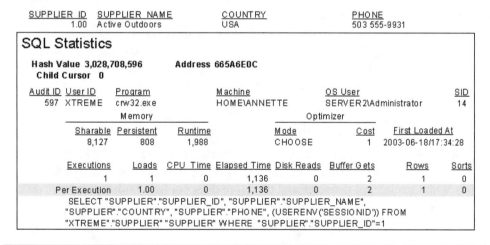

Figure 8-8 *Supplier with SQL stats subreport*

Note that there is a possible tradeoff to the benefits of using bind variables: the cost-based optimizer can make better decisions about how to access the required data if it knows the actual value. For instance, say that a table has 100,000 rows. The value of a field called Country is "USA" for 90,000 rows, and "CAN" for 5 rows, and there is an index on Country. If a query containing WHERE country="USA" were submitted, the cost-based optimizer would generate an execution plan using a full table scan. If a query containing WHERE country="CAN" were submitted, then the cost-based optimizer would generate an execution plan using the index on Country. In Oracle 9*i,* if a query with a bind variable for Country is submitted, the cost-based optimizer will peek at the value of the bind variable on the first execution and choose an execution plan appropriate for that value. It will then use that execution plan, no matter what future values the bind variable takes on. In Oracle 8*i*, the optimizer will assume a level distribution of values. When attempting to optimize or reduce parsing, you should consider the expense of skewness in selection columns in relation to the expense of reparsing.

Skewness and selectivity are both measures of data variation in a field. Selectivity is a measure of the number of different values that a field might contain. In the example discussed, the selectivity is at least 3/100,000 given that there are at least three different values for Country; "USA", "CAN", and something else. Selectivity gives no information about the distribution of the different values, only the count of the different values over the total. If each of the different values showed up an equal number of times, then the field would not be skewed, which is what the 8*i* optimizer assumes. If one value showed up a much larger number of times than another value, then the field would be skewed to that value. That skewness is what causes the problem when using bind variables because it indicates different access methods for values that show up in a large portion of the rows (full table scan), versus values that show up in only a small portion of the rows (use index).

SQL Commands and Parsing

Do Crystal Reports parameterized SQL Commands create queries with bind variables? No. Unfortunately, creating a SQL Command with parameters does not generate a query with Oracle bind variables and therefore does not help with reparsing. You can verify this by creating such a SQL Command and using the SQL Statistics subreport.

Create a new report with a SQL Command like the following, including the Supplier ID parameter:

```
SELECT "SUPPLIER"."SUPPLIER_ID", "SUPPLIER"."SUPPLIER_NAME",
       "SUPPLIER"."COUNTRY", "SUPPLIER"."PHONE",
```

```
        (USERENV('SESSIONID')) AUDSID
 FROM   "XTREME"."SUPPLIER" "SUPPLIER"
 WHERE  "SUPPLIER"."SUPPLIER_ID"={?Supplier ID}
```

Place the Supplier_ID, Supplier_Name, Supplier.Country, and Supplier.Phone on the report. Add the SQL Statistics subreport, linking it on Supplier.AUDSID, and run the report.

In Figure 8-9 you will see that even though the report is based on a parameterized SQL Command, the query being sent to Oracle by Crystal Reports still has the literal value for the parameter embedded in it. Running the report with different Supplier_IDs will show different hash values and therefore different SQL statements that each requires parsing. This report is available for download as Chapter 8\Supplier SQL Command with Statistics.rpt or Chapter 8\Supplier SQL Command with Statistics 8i.rpt.

Stored Procedures and Parsing

To investigate parsing and stored procedures, create the following stored procedure:

```
CREATE OR REPLACE  PACKAGE "XTREME"."SUPPLIER_RPTS"  AS

TYPE Supp_Rpt_Rec_Type IS RECORD
   (Supplier_ID    Supplier.Supplier_ID%TYPE,
    Supplier_Name Supplier.Supplier_Name%Type,
    Country        Supplier.Country%Type,
    Phone          Supplier.Phone%Type,
    AUSID          number);

TYPE Supp_Rpt_Type IS REF CURSOR RETURN Supp_Rpt_Rec_Type;

PROCEDURE Supplier_Report
   (Supp_Rpt_Cur IN OUT Supp_Rpt_Type,
    Supplier     IN    Supplier.Supplier_Id%TYPE);

END SUPPLIER_RPTS;
/
CREATE OR REPLACE  PACKAGE BODY "XTREME"."SUPPLIER_RPTS"  AS

PROCEDURE Supplier_Report
   (Supp_Rpt_Cur IN OUT Supp_Rpt_Type,
    Supplier     IN    Supplier.Supplier_Id%TYPE)
IS
  BEGIN
```

```
   Open Supp_Rpt_Cur for
      Select Supplier_ID, Supplier_Name,
             Country, Phone, userenv('sessionid') AUDSID
        from Supplier
       where Supplier_ID=Supplier;
   END Supplier_Report;

END SUPPLIER_RPTS;
```

Now create a report based on this stored procedure, add the Show_SQL_Stats_ Subreport, and link it to the AUDSID. Run the report.

No data shows up in the subreport. This is because, due to the manner in which the stored procedure is executed, the hash value for the main report query is still stored in the SQL_Hash_Value and has not been moved to the Prev_Hash_Value. Modify the links in the subreport to use SQL_Address and SQL_Hash_Value instead of Prev_SQL_Addr and Prev_Hash_Value (see Figure 8-10).

Refresh the report and the SQL Statistics will be populated, as shown in Figure 8-11. Note that the SQL text now contains a bind variable. Run the report with different Supplier IDs. You will see that the SQL statement does not change, so no reparsing is required. Using stored procedures guarantees that no reparsing is required due to changing parameter values. This report is available as Chapter 8\Supplier Stored Procedure with Statistics.rpt or Chapter 8\Supplier Stored Procedure with Statistics 8i.rpt.

Supplier

SUPPLIER ID	SUPPLIER NAME	COUNTRY	PHONE
2.00	Triumph	USA	313 555-5735

SQL Statistics

Hash Value 64,173,633   **Address** 665C1364
Child Cursor 0

Audit ID	User ID	Program	Machine	OS User	SID
599	XTREME	crw32.exe	HOME\ANNETTE	SERVER2\Administrator	15

	Memory			Optimizer	

	Sharable	Persistent	Runtime	Mode		Cost	First Loaded At
	8,657	808	1,988	FIRST_ROWS		1	2003-06-18/18:10:55

	Executions	Loads	CPU Time	Elapsed Time	Disk Reads	Buffer Gets	Rows	Sorts
	2	1	0	1,359	0	4	2	0
Per Execution		0.50	0	680	0	2	1	0

```
SELECT /*+ FIRST_ROWS */
   "SUPPLIER"."SUPPLIER_ID", "SUPPLIER"."SUPPLIER_NAME", "SUPPLIER"."COUNTRY",
   "SUPPLIER"."PHONE", (USERENV('SESSIONID')) AUDSID
   FROM  "XTREME"."SUPPLIER" "SUPPLIER"
   WHERE "SUPPLIER"."SUPPLIER_ID"=2
```

Figure 8-9   *Supplier with SQL Command*

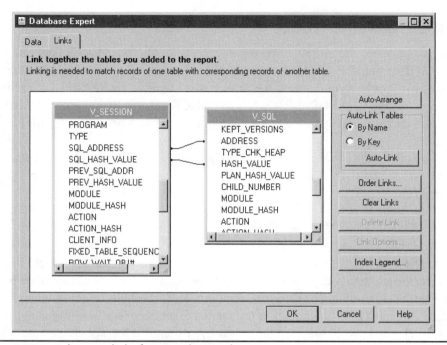

Figure 8-10   *Subreport links for stored procedure*

Supplier

SUPPLIER ID	SUPPLIER NAME	COUNTRY	PHONE
2.00	Triumph	USA	313 555-5735

SQL Statistics

Hash Value 462,512,067   **Address 6677817C**
Child Cursor 0

Audit ID	User ID	Program	Machine	OS User	SID
601	XTREME	crw32.exe	HOME\ANNETTE	SERVER2\Administrator	14

	Memory			Optimizer	
Sharable	Persistent	Runtime	Mode	Cost	First Loaded At
14,166	828	1,992	CHOOSE	1	2003-06-18/18:19:01

Executions	Loads	CPU Time	Elapsed Time	Disk Reads	Buffer Gets	Rows	Sorts
2	1	0	1,649	0	4	1	0
Per Execution	0.50	0	825	0	2	1	0

SELECT Supplier_ID, Supplier_Name,   Country, Phone, userenv('sessionid') AUDSID   from
Supplier   where Supplier_ID=:b1

Figure 8-11   *Stored procedure SQL stats*

CURSOR_SHARING=FORCE

Prior to Oracle 9*i*, the initialization parameter CURSOR_SHARING could be set to EXACT or FORCE. EXACT was and still is the default value; it ensures that cursors will not be shared unless the SQL text is identical, as described in earlier sections. Setting CURSOR_SHARING to FORCE ensures that cursors will be shared if they differ only in the value of literals that could be replaced with bind variables.

To see the results of setting CURSOR_SHARING equal to FORCE, set CURSOR_SHARING as shown. You must have ALTER SYSTEM privileges to change environment settings.

```
ALTER SYSTEM SET CURSOR_SHARING=FORCE;
```

Run the Supplier with Statistics or Supplier with Statistics 8*i* report twice; first with Supplier=1, then with Supplier=2. After the second run, you should see something like Figure 8-12. Notice that the literals in the SQL text have been replaced with system-generated bind variables. On the second execution, Oracle recognized that the second query was identical to the first query except for literals, so the parser

Supplier

SUPPLIER ID	SUPPLIER NAME	COUNTRY	PHONE
2.00	Triumph	USA	313 555-5735

SQL Statistics

Hash Value 3,300,332,828   **Address 6678ECF8**
Child Cursor 0

Audit ID	User ID	Program	Machine	OS User	SID
601	XTREME	crw32.exe	HOME\ANNETTE	SERVER2\Administrator	14

	Memory			Optimizer		
Sharable	Persistent	Runtime	Mode		Cost	First Loaded At
40,011	848	1,988	CHOOSE		1	2003-06-18/18:29:01

Executions	Loads	CPU Time	Elapsed Time	Disk Reads	Buffer Gets	Rows	Sorts
1	1	0	610	0	2	1	0
Per Execution	1.00	0	610	0	2	1	0

```
SELECT "SUPPLIER"."SUPPLIER_ID", "SUPPLIER"."SUPPLIER_NAME",
"SUPPLIER"."COUNTRY", "SUPPLIER"."PHONE", (USERENV(:"SYS_B_0")) FROM
"XTREME"."SUPPLIER" "SUPPLIER" WHERE "SUPPLIER"."SUPPLIER_ID"=:"SYS_B_1"
```

Figure 8-12 *Supplier report results 1*

replaced these literals with bind variables and parsed the new query. At this point, both queries have been hard parsed, so no reparsing resources have been saved.

Now run the report with Supplier=3. Notice, as shown in Figure 8-13, that the query has not changed and the execution count has increased. On each subsequent query execution, no reparsing will be required.

Setting CURSOR_SHARING=FORCE seems like a good option for reporting environments where many reports are run that differ only in the parameter value chosen. However, there is one downside to this option.

To help you investigate, we have created a second subreport as described in Chapter 7. This subreport, called Show SQL Plan Subreport.rpt, shows the execution plan for the main report query. To run it, you must be using Oracle 9*i* and have the SELECT privilege on the V$SQL_PLAN dynamic performance view:

```
GRANT SELECT ON V_$SQL_PLAN TO xtreme;
```

First, set CURSOR_SHARING back to EXACT:

```
ALTER SYSTEM SET CURSOR_SHARING=EXACT;
```

If statistics have not been gathered, as shown in Chapter 7, do so now. Then open the Orders report (or Orders 8*i*), and run it for Shipped=1. Scroll to the end of the report, as shown in Figure 8-14.

Supplier

SUPPLIER ID	SUPPLIER NAME	COUNTRY	PHONE
3.00	Guardian	Japan	81 3 3555-5011

SQL Statistics

Hash Value 3,300,332,828   **Address 6678ECF8**
Child Cursor 0

Audit ID	User ID	Program	Machine	OS User	SID
601	XTREME	crw32.exe	HOME\ANNETTE	SERVER2\Administrator	14

	Memory			Optimizer	

	Sharable	Persistent	Runtime	Mode	Cost	First Loaded At
	40,011	848	1,988	CHOOSE	1	2003-06-18/18:29:01

	Executions	Loads	CPU Time	Elapsed Time	Disk Reads	Buffer Gets	Rows	Sorts
	2	1	0	866	0	4	2	0
Per Execution		0.50	0	433	0	2	1	0

```
SELECT "SUPPLIER"."SUPPLIER_ID", "SUPPLIER"."SUPPLIER_NAME",
"SUPPLIER"."COUNTRY", "SUPPLIER"."PHONE", (USERENV(:"SYS_B_0")) FROM
"XTREME"."SUPPLIER" "SUPPLIER" WHERE "SUPPLIER"."SUPPLIER_ID"=:"SYS_B_1"
```

Figure 8-13 *Supplier report results 2*

Orders

ORDER	ORDER AMO	CUSTOMER	EMPLOYEE	REQUIRED	SHIP DATE	SHIP VIA	PO#	PAYMENT

SQL Statistics

Hash Value 939,196,079   Address 66F49E50
Child Cursor 0

Audit ID	User ID	Program	Machine	OS User	SID
611	XTREME	crw32.exe	HOME\ANNETTE	SERVER2\Administrator	16

	Memory			Optimizer		
Sharable	Persistent	Runtime	Mode	Cost	First Loaded At
10,688	1,228	2,512	CHOOSE	4	2003-06-19/11:56:31

Executions	Loads	CPU Time	Elapsed Time	Disk Reads	Buffer Gets	Rows	Sorts
1	1	46,875	94,998	30	193	2,122	0
Per Execution	1.00	46,875	94,998	30	193	2,122	0

SELECT "ORDERS"."ORDER_ID", "ORDERS"."ORDER_AMOUNT", "ORDERS"."CUSTOMER_ID",
"ORDERS"."EMPLOYEE_ID", "ORDERS"."ORDER_DATE", "ORDERS"."REQUIRED_DATE",
"ORDERS"."SHIP_DATE", "ORDERS"."SHIP_VIA", "ORDERS"."PO#",
"ORDERS"."PAYMENT_RECEIVED", "ORDERS"."SHIPPED", (USERENV('SESSIONID')) FROM
"XTREME"."ORDERS" "ORDERS" WHERE "ORDERS"."SHIPPED"=1

Execution Plan

OPERATION	OPTIONS	OBJECT NAME	COST	CARDINALITY
0.00				
SELECT STATEMENT			4	
TABLE ACCESS	FULL	ORDERS	4	2,122

Figure 8-14   *Orders report results 1*

Notice that the execution plan includes a full table scan of the orders table. (The execution plan subreport is not available in the 8*i* version.)

Now run the report again for Shipped=0. Your results should look similar to Figure 8-15. Notice that the execution plan shows table access by an index.

The two different parameter values generate two different execution plans because of the skewness of the Shipped column data. There are 2,192 total rows in the Orders table. Of those 2,192 rows, only 70 contain a 0, or Not Shipped, value in the Shipped column; the other 2,122 rows contain a 1, or Shipped, value. Thus, it is more efficient to use a full table scan when the query is going to return a large portion of the rows and more efficient to use an index when the query is going to return a small portion of the rows.

Note that the cost-based optimizer can only make decisions based on the skewness of column data if histograms have been created for those columns. The statistics gathering in Chapter 7 created a histogram for the Shipped column.

So, what will happen in this case if you set CURSOR_SHARING equal to FORCE?

In Crystal, log off all database connections, then flush the shared pool to remove the already parsed queries with literal parameter values:

```
ALTER SYSTEM FLUSH SHARED_POOL
```

Next, set CURSOR_SHARING to FORCE:

```
ALTER SYSTEM SET CURSOR_SHARING=FORCE;
```

Run the report for Shipped=1. Notice, as shown in Figure 8-16, that the literals have been replaced with bind variables and the execution plan involves a full table scan.

Run the report for Shipped=0. Notice, as shown in Figure 8-17, that the same query is executed a second time and that the execution plan is still doing a full table scan even though using an index would be less costly.

As you can see, the drawback to setting CURSOR_SHARING=FORCE is that the optimizer will share the cursor even when it does not produce an optimal execution plan.

CURSOR_SHARING=SIMILAR

A possible value of SIMILAR for the CURSOR_SHARING parameter was introduced in Oracle 9*i* to minimize the problems caused by the FORCE value and yet retain its positive aspects. Setting CURSOR_SHARING=SIMILAR tells Oracle to share cursors if SQL statements differ only in literals *and* their execution plans are the same.

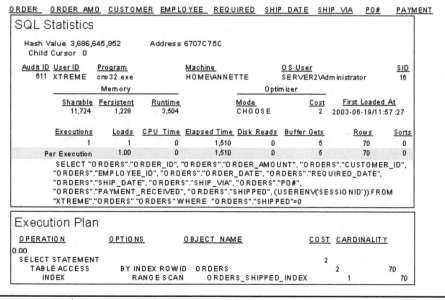

Figure 8-15 *Orders report results 2*

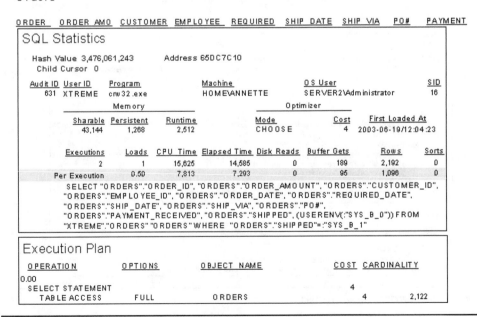

Figure 8-16 *Orders report results 3*

Orders

ORDER	ORDER AMO	CUSTOMER	EMPLOYEE	REQUIRED	SHIP DATE	SHIP VIA	PO#	PAYMENT

SQL Statistics

Hash Value 3,476,061,243   Address 65DC7C10
Child Cursor 0

Audit ID	User ID	Program	Machine	OS User	SID
631	XTREME	crw32.exe	HOME\ANNETTE	SERVER2\Administrator	16

| | | Memory | | Optimizer | |

Sharable	Persistent	Runtime	Mode	Cost	First Loaded At
43,144	1,268	2,512	CHOOSE	4	2003-06-19/12:04:23

	Executions	Loads	CPU Time	Elapsed Time	Disk Reads	Buffer Gets	Rows	Sorts
	2	1	15,625	14,585	0	189	2,192	0
Per Execution	0.50		7,813	7,293	0	95	1,096	0

SELECT "ORDERS"."ORDER_ID", "ORDERS"."ORDER_AMOUNT", "ORDERS"."CUSTOMER_ID",
"ORDERS"."EMPLOYEE_ID", "ORDERS"."ORDER_DATE", "ORDERS"."REQUIRED_DATE",
"ORDERS"."SHIP_DATE", "ORDERS"."SHIP_VIA", "ORDERS"."PO#",
"ORDERS"."PAYMENT_RECEIVED", "ORDERS"."SHIPPED", (USERENV(:"SYS_B_0")) FROM
"XTREME"."ORDERS" "ORDERS" WHERE "ORDERS"."SHIPPED"=:"SYS_B_1"

Execution Plan

OPERATION	OPTIONS	OBJECT NAME	COST	CARDINALITY
0.00				
SELECT STATEMENT			4	
TABLE ACCESS	FULL	ORDERS	4	2,122

Figure 8-17 *Orders report results 4*

NOTE

SIMILAR is only available in Oracle 9i.

To see what will happen with our Orders report if you set CURSOR_SHARING equal to SIMILAR, log off all database connections in Crystal and flush the shared pool to remove the already parsed queries:

```
ALTER SYSTEM FLUSH SHARED_POOL
```

Then set CURSOR_SHARING to SIMILAR:

```
ALTER SYSTEM SET CURSOR_SHARING=SIMILAR;
```

Run the report for Shipped=1. Notice that, as shown in Figure 8-18, the literals have been replaced with bind variables, and the execution plan performs a full table scan, just as when CURSOR_SHARING was set to FORCE.

Orders

ORDER	ORDER AMO	CUSTOMER	EMPLOYEE	REQUIRED	SHIP DATE	SHIP VIA	PO#	PAYMENT

SQL Statistics

Hash Value 3,476,061,243   Address 65E2F2AC
Child Cursor 0

Audit ID	User ID	Program		Machine		OS User		SID
651	XTREME	crw32.exe		HOME\ANNETTE		SERVER2\Administrator		16
		Memory			Optimizer			

	Sharable	Persistent	Runtime		Mode		Cost	First Loaded At
	42,996	1,268	2,512		CHOOSE		4	2003-06-19/12:08:29

	Executions	Loads	CPU Time	Elapsed Time	Disk Reads	Buffer Gets	Rows	Sorts
	1	1	15,625	12,168	0	158	2,122	0
Per Execution	1.00		15,625	12,168	0	158	2,122	0

```
SELECT "ORDERS"."ORDER_ID", "ORDERS"."ORDER_AMOUNT", "ORDERS"."CUSTOMER_ID",
"ORDERS"."EMPLOYEE_ID", "ORDERS"."ORDER_DATE", "ORDERS"."REQUIRED_DATE",
"ORDERS"."SHIP_DATE", "ORDERS"."SHIP_VIA", "ORDERS"."PO#",
"ORDERS"."PAYMENT_RECEIVED", "ORDERS"."SHIPPED", (USERENV(:"SYS_B_0")) FROM
"XTREME"."ORDERS" "ORDERS" WHERE "ORDERS"."SHIPPED"=:"SYS_B_1"
```

Execution Plan

OPERATION	OPTIONS	OBJECT NAME	COST	CARDINALITY
0.00				
SELECT STATEMENT			4	
TABLE ACCESS	FULL	ORDERS	4	2,122

Figure 8-18   *Orders report results 5*

Now run the report for Shipped=0. Notice, as shown in Figures 8-19 and 8-20, you now have two Child Cursors. This happened because the two queries that you executed have the same SQL text, including the substitution of bind variables for literals, but they have two different execution plans.

Because CURSOR_SHARING is set to SIMILAR, Oracle considers the execution plan as well as the SQL text before determining statement equality. In this case, Child Cursor 1 is the one that was actually executed, as seen by examining the Loads and Executions columns for each child cursor. This is the desired outcome because Child Cursor 1 uses the index for table access.

Setting CURSOR_SHARING=SIMILAR seems to be the optimal process. However, there is a performance hit, as extra work is required to determine the similar statements and to compare their execution plans.

SQL Statistics

Hash Value 3,476,061,243   **Address 65E2F2AC**
Child Cursor 0

Audit ID	User ID	Program		Machine		OS User		SID
651	XTREME	crw32.exe		HOME\ANNETTE		SERVER2\Administrator		16
		Memory				Optimizer		

Sharable	Persistent	Runtime	Mode	Cost	First Loaded At
42,996	1,268	2,512	CHOOSE	4	2003-06-19/12:08:29

Executions	Loads	CPU Time	Elapsed Time	Disk Reads	Buffer Gets	Rows	Sorts
1	1	15,625	12,168	0	158	2,122	0
Per Execution	1.00	15,625	12,168	0	158	2,122	0

```
SELECT "ORDERS"."ORDER_ID", "ORDERS"."ORDER_AMOUNT", "ORDERS"."CUSTOMER_ID",
"ORDERS"."EMPLOYEE_ID", "ORDERS"."ORDER_DATE", "ORDERS"."REQUIRED_DATE",
"ORDERS"."SHIP_DATE", "ORDERS"."SHIP_VIA", "ORDERS"."PO#",
"ORDERS"."PAYMENT_RECEIVED", "ORDERS"."SHIPPED", (USERENV(:"SYS_B_0")) FROM
"XTREME"."ORDERS" "ORDERS" WHERE "ORDERS"."SHIPPED"=:"SYS_B_1"
```

Child Cursor 1

Audit ID	User ID	Program		Machine		OS User		SID
651	XTREME	crw32.exe		HOME\ANNETTE		SERVER2\Administrator		16
		Memory				Optimizer		

Sharable	Persistent	Runtime	Mode	Cost	First Loaded At
43,560	1,268	3,504	CHOOSE	2	2003-06-19/12:08:29

Executions	Loads	CPU Time	Elapsed Time	Disk Reads	Buffer Gets	Rows	Sorts
1	1	0	1,036	0	5	70	0
Per Execution	1.00	0	1,036	0	5	70	0

```
SELECT "ORDERS"."ORDER_ID", "ORDERS"."ORDER_AMOUNT", "ORDERS"."CUSTOMER_ID",
"ORDERS"."EMPLOYEE_ID", "ORDERS"."ORDER_DATE", "ORDERS"."REQUIRED_DATE",
"ORDERS"."SHIP_DATE", "ORDERS"."SHIP_VIA", "ORDERS"."PO#",
"ORDERS"."PAYMENT_RECEIVED", "ORDERS"."SHIPPED", (USERENV(:"SYS_B_0")) FROM
"XTREME"."ORDERS" "ORDERS" WHERE "ORDERS"."SHIPPED"=:"SYS_B_1"
```

Figure 8-19   *Orders report results 6: SQL Statistics*

```
Execution Plan
    OPERATION          OPTIONS          OBJECT NAME              COST  CARDINALITY
0.00
    SELECT STATEMENT                                              4
        TABLE ACCESS    FULL             ORDERS                   4        2,122
1.00
    SELECT STATEMENT                                              2
        TABLE ACCESS    BY INDEX ROWID   ORDERS                   2          70
            INDEX       RANGE SCAN       ORDERS_SHIPPED_INDEX     1          70
```

Figure 8-20   *Orders report results 6: Execution Plan*

Choosing a Parse Reduction Method

Reducing parsing is always desirable. However, the proportional benefit of reduced parsing depends on the resource usage for parsing versus the resource usage for all other phases of execution. This varies depending on the query. Parse reduction benefits also depend on the server environment, including how much memory is available for the shared pool and how extensive your available CPU resources are.

Table 8-1 summarizes the pros and cons of the methods we have discussed for hard parse reduction.

Which, if any, of these methods that you employ, will depend on your particular environment and reports. If you have an environment that is experiencing memory shortages or scalability problems and you determine that these problems are due to many similar statements existing in the shared pool, you will want to employ one or all of these methods to alleviate those problems.

If your aim is to create an optimized reporting environment up front, you will need to make a system level decision about setting the CURSOR_SHARING parameter, and a report-by-report decision about a parse reducing method.

Method	Pro	Con
Stored procedures	No extra work involved in parsing	Doesn't always use optimal execution plan based on column skewness
CURSOR_SHARING=FORCE	Less extra work involved in parsing than CURSOR_SHARING=SIMILAR	Doesn't always use optimal execution plan based on column skewness Some extra work involved in parsing
CURSOR_SHARING=SIMILAR (9*i* only)	Always uses optimal execution plan based on column skewness	More extra work involved in parsing than CURSOR_SHARING=FORCE Only available in 9*i*

Table 8-1   *Choosing a Parse Reduction Method*

If you know that a majority of your reports are executed repeatedly with different parameter values, and that the selection fields involved are not highly skewed, your optimal choice would be to create a stored procedure to back up each report. This would ensure minimal parsing and cause no overhead. Your second choice, which would not require any rewrites to existing reports, would be to set CURSOR_SHARING equal to FORCE. Doing this would also ensure minimal parsing but add a small amount of overhead. If you are concerned that your environment contains some reports that use a skewed field for selection or sorting, you should set CURSOR_SHARING equal to SIMILAR. Though SIMILAR causes more overhead than FORCE, it is still a small amount and well worth the tradeoff of reduced hard parses.

Of course, the CURSOR_SHARING parameter will affect all queries made against the server and not just those that support reporting. You must weigh the reporting benefits of setting this parameter against any problems caused to nonreporting processes.

Once you make your decision about the system level setting for the CURSOR_SHARING parameter, you will still need to evaluate each report to determine its optimal cursor sharing method. If CURSOR_SHARING is set to EXACT, your only report level option will be whether to use a stored procedure or not. If you use a stored procedure, the SQL statement will be reused in every case. If you do not use a stored procedure, each time the parameter values change, a new cursor will be parsed.

For an individual report, to override CURSOR_SHARING being set to SIMILAR or FORCE at the system level, you can use the CURSOR_SHARING_EXACT optimizer hint. (See the "Optimizer Hints" section in Chapter 7 for details on how to use optimizer hints.) This gives you the option of using a stored procedure or the hint. Either will ensure no reparsing, although they will not account for column skewness.

Caching Cursors

As with any optimization attempt, improving one process can reveal issues with another process. Reducing hard parses will, by definition, create more soft parsing. Soft parsing is significantly less resource intensive than hard parsing, so this is a desirable outcome. However, you can go one step further and attempt to reduce the impact of soft parsing as well.

A normal soft parse consists of a syntax check, a semantics check, and a search of the shared pool to find the already optimized statement and its execution plan. The session cursor cache, if enabled, saves pointers to the shared pool of parsed versions of the session's SQL statements. The initialization parameter that sets the number of cursors saved is the Session_Cached_Cursors parameter. If a cursor is needed again by a session and exists in the cursor cache, some resources that would otherwise have been required by the parse will be saved.

The default value of Session_Cached_Cursors is zero, and they can be set either dynamically for a given session using the ALTER SESSION command, or in the initialization file to change the default for all database sessions. They cannot be changed dynamically at the ALTER SYSTEM level. Because there is no method with which to issue an ALTER SESSION command from Crystal Reports (except with dynamic SQL in a stored procedure), you must change the Session_Cached_ Cursors parameter at the database level.

Determining what Session_Cached_Cursors should be set to will require the assistance of your DBA. If Session_Cached_Cursors is set to a value greater than 0 and a given SQL statement has been parsed at least three times, a pointer to it will be added to the session's cursor cache when the session next makes a parse call. Then, the next time that a parse call for that statement is made, a cache hit will occur and the soft parse will be eliminated. Setting Session_Cached_Cursors requires some memory; however, because it stores only pointers, this memory requirement is quite low. Oracle recommends starting with a value of 50 and monitoring "session cursor cache hits" to adjust the value on an ongoing basis. Ideally, your DBA will be monitoring SQL statistics and will know approximately how many statements have large numbers of soft parses on an ongoing basis.

Session_Cached_Cursors is a per session parameter. The value of setting it will depend on your reporting environment and how sessions are maintained. Each log off/log on from Crystal Reports will create a new session. However, the parse count is maintained for each statement across all sessions, so each session knows how many times a given statement has been parsed and can cache it immediately if it has already been parsed three times by any other session.

For the examples, Session_Cached_Cursors was set to 50 and the database was restarted.

To investigate the impact of setting Session_Cached_Cursors, a new subreport has been created. This subreport displays session statistics and is called Show Session Stats Subreport.rpt (Show Session Stats Subreport 8i.rpt). The subreport uses the V$Session, V$SesStat, and V$StatName dynamic performance views. The user must have SELECT privileges on these views in order to use the subreport.

The Show Session Stats Subreport was added to the Orders report and the new report is named Chapter 8\Orders with Session Stats.rpt or Chapter 8\Orders with Session Stats 8i.rpt. Open Orders with Session Stats. Run the report for Shipped=1 and scroll to the last page.

As shown in Figure 8-21, the Session Statistics show many parses, some hard, some soft, as well as some cache hits. This is because the Session Statistics displays

SQL Statistics

Hash Value 3,476,061,243   **Address 67136EBC**
Child Cursor 0

Audit ID	User ID	Program	Machine	OS User	SID
695	XTREME	crw32.exe	HOME\ANNETTE	SERVER2\Administrator	10
		Memory		Optimizer	

	Sharable	Persistent	Runtime	Mode	Cost	First Loaded At
	42,968	1,268	2,512	CHOOSE	4	2003-06-19/14:21:30

	Executions	Loads	CPU Time	Elapsed Time	Disk Reads	Buffer Gets	Rows	Sorts
	1	1	15,625	11,843	0	158	2,122	0
Per Execution		1.00	15,625	11,843	0	158	2,122	0

```
SELECT "ORDERS"."ORDER_ID", "ORDERS"."ORDER_AMOUNT", "ORDERS"."CUSTOMER_ID",
"ORDERS"."EMPLOYEE_ID", "ORDERS"."ORDER_DATE", "ORDERS"."REQUIRED_DATE",
"ORDERS"."SHIP_DATE", "ORDERS"."SHIP_VIA", "ORDERS"."PO#",
"ORDERS"."PAYMENT_RECEIVED", "ORDERS"."SHIPPED", (USERENV(:"SYS_B_0")) FROM
"XTREME"."ORDERS" "ORDERS" WHERE "ORDERS"."SHIPPED"=:"SYS_B_1"
```

Execution Plan

Operation	Options	Object Name	Cost	Rows	Optimizer
Child Cursor 0					
SELECT STATEMENT			4		CHOOSE
TABLE ACCESS	FULL	ORDERS	4	2,122	ANALYZED

Session Statistics

	Cache Hits	Parse Counts			Parse Times			Session Cursor Cache Count	Current Open Cursors	Queries Parallelized
		Soft	Hard	Total	CPU	Waiting	Elapsed			
	14	52	17	69	5	0	5	0	1	0

Figure 8-21   *Orders with Session Stats 1*

the totals for the session, whereas the SQL Statistics show the values for only one SQL command. Presumably, Crystal Reports has issued several queries as part of its initialization for the report. Some of these probably queried the database dictionary, for instance, to retrieve the table names. In any case, it is the change in the Session Statistics values that you are interested in. You may see different totals for the Session Statistics as you run the examples, but the change in the values should be the same as stated here.

Now run the report again with the same parameter value.

Notice, as shown in Figure 8-22, that the executions increased by 1, loads stayed the same, and soft parses increased by 1.

SQL Statistics

Hash Value 3,476,061,243   Address 67136EBC
Child Cursor 0

Audit ID	User ID	Program	Machine	OS User	SID
695	XTREME	crw32.exe	HOME\ANNETTE	SERVER2\Administrator	10
		Memory		Optimizer	

	Sharable	Persistent	Runtime	Mode	Cost	First Loaded At
	42,968	1,268	2,512	CHOOSE	4	2003-06-19/14:21:30

	Executions	Loads	CPU Time	Elapsed Time	Disk Reads	Buffer Gets	Rows	Sorts
	2	1	15,625	17,149	0	205	4,244	0
Per Execution	0.50		7,813	8,575	0	103	2,122	0

```
SELECT "ORDERS"."ORDER_ID", "ORDERS"."ORDER_AMOUNT", "ORDERS"."CUSTOMER_ID",
"ORDERS"."EMPLOYEE_ID", "ORDERS"."ORDER_DATE", "ORDERS"."REQUIRED_DATE",
"ORDERS"."SHIP_DATE", "ORDERS"."SHIP_VIA", "ORDERS"."PO#",
"ORDERS"."PAYMENT_RECEIVED", "ORDERS"."SHIPPED", (USERENV("SYS_B_0")) FROM
"XTREME"."ORDERS" "ORDERS" WHERE "ORDERS"."SHIPPED"=":SYS_B_1"
```

Execution Plan

Operation	Options	Object Name	Cost	Rows	Optimizer
Child Cursor 0					
SELECT STATEMENT			4		CHOOSE
TABLE ACCESS	FULL	ORDERS	4	2,122	ANALYZED

Session Statistics

						Session Cursor Cache Count	Current Open Cursors	Queries Parallelized
Cache Hits	Parse Counts			Parse Times				
	Soft	Hard	Total	CPU	Waiting	Elapsed			
14	53	17	70	5	0	5	0	1	0

Figure 8-22   *Orders with Session Stats 2*

Now run the report again with the same parameter values. You will notice, as shown in Figure 8-23, that executions increased by 1 again, loads stayed the same, and soft parses also increased by 1 again.

Run the report again with the same parameter values. In the fourth run, you will see that executions increased by 1, loads stayed the same, and the cache hit increased along with the soft parses, as shown in Figure 8-24. This demonstrates session cursor caching in action. On the fourth and subsequent runs, the parsed statement will be drawn from the cache.

Note that the SID for the current session as shown in the SQL Statistics subreport is 10. Log off of all connected databases, and rerun the report with the same parameter values.

SQL Statistics

Hash Value 3,476,061,243 **Address 67136EBC**
Child Cursor 0

Audit ID	User ID	Program	Machine	OS User	SID
695	XTREME	crw82.exe	HOME\ANNETTE	SERVER2\Administrator	10

| | | | Optimizer | | |
| Memory | | | | | |

	Sharable	Persistent	Runtime	Mode	Cost	First Loaded At
	42,968	1,268	2,512	CHOOSE	4	2003-06-19/14:21:30

	Executions	Loads	CPU Time	Elapsed Time	Disk Reads	Buffer Gets	Rows	Sorts
	3	1	15,625	22,408	0	252	6,366	0
Per Execution		0.33	5,208	7,469	0	84	2,122	0

SELECT "ORDERS"."ORDER_ID", "ORDERS"."ORDER_AMOUNT", "ORDERS"."CUSTOMER_ID",
"ORDERS"."EMPLOYEE_ID", "ORDERS"."ORDER_DATE", "ORDERS"."REQUIRED_DATE",
"ORDERS"."SHIP_DATE", "ORDERS"."SHIP_VIA", "ORDERS"."PO#",
"ORDERS"."PAYMENT_RECEIVED", "ORDERS"."SHIPPED", (USERENV(:"SYS_B_0")) FROM
"XTREME"."ORDERS" "ORDERS" WHERE "ORDERS"."SHIPPED"=:"SYS_B_1"

Execution Plan

Operation	Options	Object Name	Cost	Rows	Optimizer
Child Cursor 0					
SELECT STATEMENT			4		CHOOSE
TABLE ACCESS	FULL	ORDERS	4	2,122	ANALYZED

Session Statistics

						Session Cursor Cache Count	Current Open Cursors	Queries Parallelized
Cache Hits	Parse Counts			Parse Times				
	Soft	Hard	Total	CPU	Waiting	Elapsed			
14	54	17	71	5	0	5	0	1	0

Figure 8-23   *Orders with Session Stats 3*

SQL Statistics

Hash Value 3,476,061,243 **Address 67136EBC**
Child Cursor 0

Audit ID	User ID	Program	Machine	OS User	SID
695	XTREME	crw82.exe	HOME\ANNETTE	SERVER2\Administrator	10

| | | | Optimizer | | |
| Memory | | | | | |

	Sharable	Persistent	Runtime	Mode	Cost	First Loaded At
	42,968	1,268	2,512	CHOOSE	4	2003-06-19/14:21:30

	Executions	Loads	CPU Time	Elapsed Time	Disk Reads	Buffer Gets	Rows	Sorts
	4	1	62,500	28,074	0	299	8,488	0
Per Execution		0.25	15,625	7,019	0	75	2,122	0

SELECT "ORDERS"."ORDER_ID", "ORDERS"."ORDER_AMOUNT", "ORDERS"."CUSTOMER_ID",
"ORDERS"."EMPLOYEE_ID", "ORDERS"."ORDER_DATE", "ORDERS"."REQUIRED_DATE",
"ORDERS"."SHIP_DATE", "ORDERS"."SHIP_VIA", "ORDERS"."PO#",
"ORDERS"."PAYMENT_RECEIVED", "ORDERS"."SHIPPED", (USERENV(:"SYS_B_0")) FROM
"XTREME"."ORDERS" "ORDERS" WHERE "ORDERS"."SHIPPED"=:"SYS_B_1"

Execution Plan

Operation	Options	Object Name	Cost	Rows	Optimizer
Child Cursor 0					
SELECT STATEMENT			4		CHOOSE
TABLE ACCESS	FULL	ORDERS	4	2,122	ANALYZED

Session Statistics

						Session Cursor Cache Count	Current Open Cursors	Queries Parallelized
Cache Hits	Parse Counts			Parse Times				
	Soft	Hard	Total	CPU	Waiting	Elapsed			
15	55	17	72	5	0	5	0	1	0

Figure 8-24   *Orders with Session Stats 4*

Notice, as shown in Figure 8-25, that the SID changed to 12. The SID may or may not change when you run the examples, but be aware that even if the session ID stays the same after relogin, the session is a new session. Also, note that executions increased by 1 and loads stayed level, as expected. However, the cache hits dropped to 0, and soft parses show as 4. Cache hits dropped to 0 because this is the first query that has been run in this session, so no caching has been done yet. Soft parses have been set to 4 because the optimizer must do at least one soft parse for the statement for this session, and it also recognizes that this statement has been parsed at least three times previously by other sessions.

Rerun the report with the same parameter values.

Now you see again, as shown in Figure 8-26, that executions increased by 1 and loads stayed at 1, but this time a cache hit has occurred.

SQL Statistics

Hash Value 3,476,061,243   **Address 67136EBC**
Child Cursor 0

Audit ID	User ID	Program	Machine	OS User	SID
697	XTREME	crw82.exe	HOME\ANNETTE	SERVER2\Administrator	12

	Memory			Optimizer	
Sharable	Persistent	Runtime	Mode	Cost	First Loaded At
42,968	1,268	2,512	CHOOSE	4	2003-06-19/14:21:30

Executions	Loads	CPU Time	Elapsed Time	Disk Reads	Buffer Gets	Rows	Sorts
5	1	78,125	33,292	0	346	10,610	0
Per Execution	0.20	15,625	6,658	0	69	2,122	0

SELECT "ORDERS"."ORDER_ID", "ORDERS"."ORDER_AMOUNT", "ORDERS"."CUSTOMER_ID", "ORDERS"."EMPLOYEE_ID", "ORDERS"."ORDER_DATE", "ORDERS"."REQUIRED_DATE", "ORDERS"."SHIP_DATE", "ORDERS"."SHIP_VIA", "ORDERS"."PO#", "ORDERS"."PAYMENT_RECEIVED", "ORDERS"."SHIPPED", (USERENV(:"SYS_B_0")) FROM "XTREME"."ORDERS" "ORDERS" WHERE "ORDERS"."SHIPPED"=:"SYS_B_1"

Execution Plan

Operation	Options	Object Name	Cost	Rows	Optimizer
Child Cursor 0					
SELECT STATEMENT			4		CHOOSE
TABLE ACCESS	FULL	ORDERS	4	2,122	ANALYZED

Session Statistics

Cache Hits	Parse Counts			Parse Times			Session Cursor Cache Count	Current Open Cursors	Queries Parallelized
	Soft	Hard	Total	CPU	Waiting	Elapsed			
0	4	0	4	0	0	0	2	1	0

Figure 8-25   *Orders with Session Stats 5*

SQL Statistics

Hash Value 3,476,061,243   Address 67136EBC
Child Cursor 0

Audit ID	User ID	Program		Machine		OS User		SID
697	XTREME	crw32.exe		HOME\ANNETTE		SERVER2\Administrator		12

	Memory			Optimizer		
Sharable	Persistent	Runtime		Mode	Cost	First Loaded At
42,968	1,268	2,512		CHOOSE	4	2003-06-19 14:21:30

Executions	Loads	CPU Time	Elapsed Time	Disk Reads	Buffer Gets	Rows	Sorts
6	1	78,125	39,161	0	393	12,732	0
Per Execution	0.17	13,021	6,527	0	66	2,122	0

```
SELECT "ORDERS"."ORDER_ID", "ORDERS"."ORDER_AMOUNT", "ORDERS"."CUSTOMER_ID",
"ORDERS"."EMPLOYEE_ID", "ORDERS"."ORDER_DATE", "ORDERS"."REQUIRED_DATE",
"ORDERS"."SHIP_DATE", "ORDERS"."SHIP_VIA", "ORDERS"."PO#",
"ORDERS"."PAYMENT_RECEIVED", "ORDERS"."SHIPPED", (USERENV(:"SYS_B_0")) FROM
"XTREME"."ORDERS" "ORDERS" WHERE "ORDERS"."SHIPPED"=:"SYS_B_1"
```

Execution Plan

Operation	Options	Object Name	Cost	Rows	Optimizer
Child Cursor 0					
SELECT STATEMENT			4		CHOOSE
TABLE ACCESS	FULL	ORDERS	4	2,122	ANALYZED

Session Statistics

Cache Hits	Parse Counts			Parse Times			Session Cursor Cache Count	Current Open Cursors	Queries Parallelized
	Soft	Hard	Total	CPU	Waiting	Elapsed			
1	5	0	5	0	0	0	2	1	0

Figure 8-26   *Orders with Session Stats 6*

Rerun the report and change the Shipped parameter to 0. As illustrated in Figures 8-27 and 8-28, a new child cursor was created because the execution plan changed, and the changed execution plan forced a hard parse to occur.

However, the cache hits increased anyway, as shown in Figure 8-29. The cache hits increased because the statement was identical to the previous statement even though the execution plan differed.

This chapter covered parse reduction and cursor caching. Parse reduction and cursor caching can be used to optimize the repeated execution of the same or similar report queries in a multiuser environment. Implementing these strategies will improve execution time for a single user and single report, but they will have their greatest impact on improved system scalability.

SQL Statistics

Hash Value 3,476,061,243   **Address 67136EBC**
Child Cursor 0

Audit ID	User ID	Program	Machine	OS User	SID
697	XTREME	crw32.exe	HOME\ANNETTE	SERVER2\Administrator	12
		Memory		Optimizer	

	Sharable	Persistent	Runtime	Mode	Cost	First Loaded At
	42,968	1,268	2,512	CHOOSE	4	2003-06-19/14:21:30

	Executions	Loads	CPU Time	Elapsed Time	Disk Reads	Buffer Gets	Rows	Sorts
	6	1	78,125	39,269	0	393	12,732	0
Per Execution		0.17	13,021	6,545	0	66	2,122	0

```
SELECT "ORDERS"."ORDER_ID", "ORDERS"."ORDER_AMOUNT", "ORDERS"."CUSTOMER_ID",
"ORDERS"."EMPLOYEE_ID", "ORDERS"."ORDER_DATE", "ORDERS"."REQUIRED_DATE",
"ORDERS"."SHIP_DATE", "ORDERS"."SHIP_VIA", "ORDERS"."PO#",
"ORDERS"."PAYMENT_RECEIVED", "ORDERS"."SHIPPED", (USERENV(:"SYS_B_0")) FROM
"XTREME"."ORDERS" "ORDERS" WHERE  "ORDERS"."SHIPPED"=:"SYS_B_1"
```

Child Cursor 1

Audit ID	User ID	Program	Machine	OS User	SID
697	XTREME	crw32.exe	HOME\ANNETTE	SERVER2\Administrator	12
		Memory		Optimizer	

	Sharable	Persistent	Runtime	Mode	Cost	First Loaded At
	43,604	1,268	3,504	CHOOSE	2	2003-06-19/14:21:30

	Executions	Loads	CPU Time	Elapsed Time	Disk Reads	Buffer Gets	Rows	Sorts
	1	1	0	308	0	5	70	0
Per Execution		1.00	0	308	0	5	70	0

```
SELECT "ORDERS"."ORDER_ID", "ORDERS"."ORDER_AMOUNT", "ORDERS"."CUSTOMER_ID",
"ORDERS"."EMPLOYEE_ID", "ORDERS"."ORDER_DATE", "ORDERS"."REQUIRED_DATE",
"ORDERS"."SHIP_DATE", "ORDERS"."SHIP_VIA", "ORDERS"."PO#",
"ORDERS"."PAYMENT_RECEIVED", "ORDERS"."SHIPPED", (USERENV(:"SYS_B_0")) FROM
"XTREME"."ORDERS" "ORDERS" WHERE  "ORDERS"."SHIPPED"=:"SYS_B_1"
```

Figure 8-27   *Orders with Session Stats 7, SQL Statistics*

Execution Plan

Operation	Options	Object Name	Cost	Rows	Optimizer
Child Cursor 0					
SELECT STATEMENT			4		CHOOSE
TABLE ACCESS	FULL	ORDERS	4	2,122	ANALYZED
Child Cursor 1					
SELECT STATEMENT			2		CHOOSE
TABLE ACCESS	BY INDEX ROWI	ORDERS	2	70	ANALYZED
INDEX	RANGE SCAN	ORDERS_SHIPPED_IN	1	70	ANALYZED

Figure 8-28   *Orders with Session Stats 7, Execution Plan*

Session Statistics							Session Cursor Cache Count	Current Open Cursors	Queries Parallelized
Cache Hits	Parse Counts			Parse Times					
	Soft	Hard	Total	CPU	Waiting	Elapsed			
2	5	1	6	0	0	0	2	1	0

Figure 8-29 *Orders with Session Stats 7, Session Statistics*

Chapter 9 will cover various Oracle features that report writers might find useful for special purpose reports, including materialized views to precompute report data, heterogeneous services and external tables to access data outside of Oracle, and flashback queries to report on older data. Modifying database records via Crystal Reports will be touched on briefly.

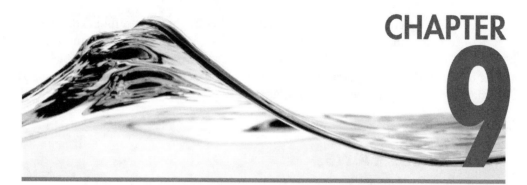

CHAPTER
9

Other Tips

This chapter covers topics that a report writer might find useful in certain circumstances, including materialized views, reporting off non-Oracle data via external tables, and heterogeneous connectivity. Reporting on a past state of the database using Oracle Flashback is also described, as well as modifying the database using stored procedures or Crystal Reports SQL Commands.

Materialized Views

Creating materialized views from SELECT statements is similar to creating regular views. However, the view contents are "materialized"—that is, written to disk. Because materialized views are instantiated, they can be treated, in many respects, like tables. They can have indexes, for instance, and they appear as tables in the Oracle data dictionary and the Crystal Reports Database Expert. (Regular views also appear as tables in the Database Expert, but they are merely stored queries and hold no data, whereas materialized views are stored as tables with their contents maintained automatically by Oracle.)

Materialized views can be refreshed, or brought into sync with their underlying tables, in several different ways according to their definition: If defined as ON COMMIT, they are refreshed automatically when data in the underlying tables is changed. If defined as ON DEMAND, they are refreshed when a command to refresh them is executed. If defined with a refresh schedule, they will be refreshed automatically according to that schedule. Additionally, materialized views can be refreshed using several different methods. They can be "fast" refreshed, which updates the materialized view with changes that have been made to the underlying tables; they can be "complete" refreshed, which re-creates the entire materialized view; or they can be "force" refreshed, which uses a fast refresh if possible and a complete refresh otherwise.

Overview

Materialized views can be very important to report writers. For example, they can speed access to complex datasets by precomputing them. Say that you often need the total order amount by month for various reports, and you are willing to have today's reports reflect the month-to-date total for the current month as of yesterday; that is, you do not require the current month's total to include orders from today. You could create a materialized view that would be refreshed every morning at 1:00 AM. To create the following materialized view, the Xtreme user must have the CREATE MATERIALIZED VIEW system privilege granted directly, not via a role.

```
CREATE MATERIALIZED VIEW XTREME.ORDERS_MONTH_TOTALS_YESTERDAY
BUILD IMMEDIATE
REFRESH COMPLETE
NEXT TRUNC(sysdate+1)+1/24
AS
SELECT EXTRACT(YEAR FROM order_date) AS order_year,
       EXTRACT(MONTH FROM order_date) AS order_month,
       SUM(order_amount) AS month_amount
  FROM orders
 GROUP BY EXTRACT(YEAR FROM order_date),
       EXTRACT(MONTH FROM order_date);
```

The example precomputes an aggregate but could also precompute complex joins.

The CREATE MATERIALIZED VIEW statement has many options. A few will be discussed here; see Oracle documentation for complete coverage.

▶ The BUILD clause can be either IMMEDIATE or DEFERRED. If BUILD
   IMMEDIATE is chosen, the materialized view will be created and populated
   immediately, although in some cases, this may not be desirable. If the time
   or resources involved in creating the view are excessive, the view can be
   DEFERRED. If BUILD DEFERRED is chosen, the view will be created
   and populated at its first refresh time.

▶ The REFRESH clause has several subclauses. The REFRESH type can be
   either FAST, COMPLETE, or FORCE. REFRESH COMPLETE re-creates the
   entire materialized view from its SELECT statement. REFRESH FAST updates
   the materialized view with changes that have been made to the underlying
   tables; it requires that materialized view logs be created for each underlying
   table. REFRESH FORCE will attempt a fast refresh if possible, otherwise it
   will do a complete refresh. FORCE is the default value for the refresh type.

▶ The REFRESH interval can be NEVER, START WITH/NEXT, ON DEMAND,
   or ON COMMIT. If NEVER REFRESH is used, the materialized view can
   never be refreshed. If either or both START WITH or NEXT are used, the
   materialized view will be refreshed on a scheduled basis. The START WITH
   clause requires the date and time of the first refresh. The NEXT clause, as
   used in the preceding example, requires the date and time of all subsequent
   refreshes. If ON DEMAND is chosen, the view can be refreshed with one of
   the DBMS_MVIEW refresh procedures. This option is useful when scheduling
   refreshes along with other batch processes. The ON COMMIT option will
   do a fast refresh of the materialized view when any changes are made to the
   underlying tables and, because of this, materialized view logs must exist. If you

choose ON COMMIT, modifications to the underlying tables will take longer due to the additional work involved in also updating the materialized view.

The following example creates a materialized view that will be refreshed on demand with a DBMS_MVIEW command:

```
CREATE MATERIALIZED VIEW XTREME.ORDERS_MONTH_TOTALS_ONDEMAND
BUILD IMMEDIATE
REFRESH ON DEMAND
AS
SELECT EXTRACT(YEAR FROM order_date) AS order_year,
       EXTRACT(MONTH FROM order_date) AS order_month,
       SUM(order_amount) AS month_amount
  FROM orders
 GROUP BY EXTRACT(YEAR FROM order_date),
       EXTRACT(MONTH FROM order_date);
```

Once this materialized view is created, it can be refreshed at any time with the following command:

```
EXECUTE DBMS_MVIEW.REFRESH('XTREME.ORDERS_MONTH_TOTALS_ONDEMAND');
```

Note that you can specify a list of materialized views to refresh instead of just one, and you can use either of two other refresh procedures, REFRESH_ALL_MVIEWS and REFRESH_DEPENDENT. See Oracle documentation for a full description of these procedures and their syntax.

To enable a fast refresh, which is *required* for the ON COMMIT refresh interval and can be used with the other refresh intervals, you must first create materialized view logs for the underlying tables. These logs keep track of changes to the tables so that they can be applied to the materialized view.

For Oracle 9*i,* first create the log:

```
CREATE MATERIALIZED VIEW LOG
    ON XTREME.ORDERS
TABLESPACE USERS
WITH ROWID, PRIMARY KEY ( ORDER_DATE, ORDER_AMOUNT), SEQUENCE
INCLUDING NEW VALUES;
```

You can then create the materialized view:

```
CREATE MATERIALIZED VIEW XTREME.ORDERS_MONTH_TOTALS_ONCOMMIT
BUILD IMMEDIATE
```

```
REFRESH FAST
ON COMMIT
AS
SELECT EXTRACT(YEAR FROM order_date) AS order_year,
       EXTRACT(MONTH FROM order_date) AS order_month,
       SUM(order_amount) AS month_amount
  FROM orders
 GROUP BY EXTRACT(YEAR FROM order_date),
       EXTRACT(MONTH FROM order_date);
```

For Oracle 8*i*, create the log as follows:

```
CREATE MATERIALIZED VIEW LOG
    ON XTREME.ORDERS
TABLESPACE USERS
WITH ROWID, PRIMARY KEY ( ORDER_DATE, ORDER_AMOUNT)
INCLUDING NEW VALUES;
```

Then create the materialized view as shown:

```
CREATE MATERIALIZED VIEW XTREME.ORDERS_MONTH_TOTALS_ONCOMMIT
BUILD IMMEDIATE
REFRESH FAST
ON COMMIT
AS
SELECT EXTRACT(YEAR FROM order_date) AS order_year,
       EXTRACT(MONTH FROM order_date) AS order_month,
       SUM(order_amount) AS month_amount,
       COUNT(*) AS Row_Count,
       COUNT(order_amount) AS Amount_Count
  FROM orders
 GROUP BY EXTRACT(YEAR FROM order_date),
       EXTRACT(MONTH FROM order_date);
```

Note that each table can have only one materialized view log created for it. If multiple materialized views use the same table for fast refresh, the materialized view log must be defined to contain all the data necessary to enable fast refresh for all of the materialized views that use it.

You have now created three different materialized views. One will be updated on a scheduled basis, one on demand, and one whenever the underlying data changes. Next, we will compare the report processing times for a report using a materialized view versus the base tables. There is a report called Chapter 9\Amount by Order Month Direct.rpt in the download files that displays the total order amount by order month. As shown in the following illustration, its database query uses the base table Orders:

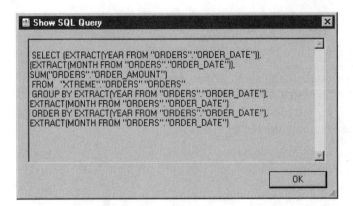

Its performance information is displayed in Figure 9-1.

There is a second report called Chapter 9\Amount by Order Month MV.rpt. As shown in the following illustration, its database query uses a materialized view:

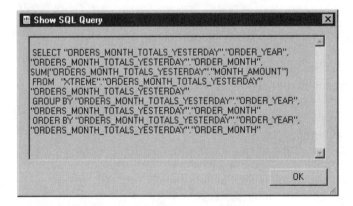

Its performance information is displayed in Figure 9-2.

You can see that the difference in the query runtime is small but still noticeable, improving from 9 milliseconds to 6 milliseconds. You may see different results depending on your environment. This particular materialized view is relatively simple and returns few rows; improvements will be greater when using more complex materialized views.

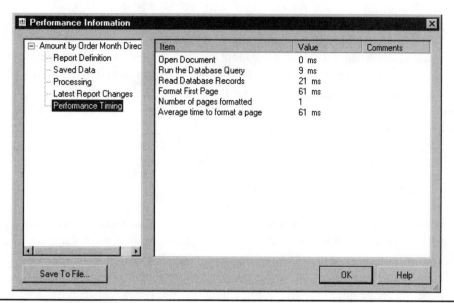

Figure 9-1   *Performance Information for Amount by Order Month Direct*

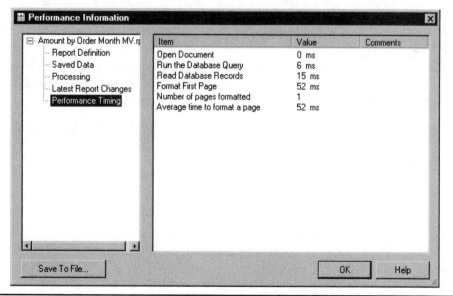

Figure 9-2   *Performance Information for Amount by Order Month MV*

Query Rewrite

Materialized views can also be used in a more transparent manner. Oracle will recognize when a submitted query could be satisfied with an existing materialized view and will transparently rewrite the query to use that materialized view. In this case, the report developer or user need not even know about the existence of materialized views to reap their benefits.

In order to use query rewrite, you must set the initialization parameter QUERY_REWRITE_ENABLED to TRUE using the following syntax:

```
ALTER SYSTEM SET QUERY_REWRITE_ENABLED=TRUE;
```

Note that for some queries to be rewritten, the initialization parameter QUERY_ REWRITE_INTEGRITY may need to be changed from its default value of ENFORCED to either TRUSTED or STALE_TOLERATED.

The owner of the underlying tables must have the QUERY REWRITE system privilege. To create query rewrite enabled materialized views on tables that do not belong to you, you must have the GLOBAL QUERY REWRITE privilege or be granted the QUERY REWRITE object privilege on each underlying table referenced in the view. To grant the QUERY REWRITE privilege, the syntax is as follows:

```
GRANT QUERY REWRITE TO xtreme;
```

You must also create a materialized view with the ENABLE QUERY REWRITE option, and the view must meet the requirements for query rewrite. Here is the syntax to create a materialized view with QUERY REWRITE enabled in 9*i*:

```
CREATE MATERIALIZED VIEW XTREME.ORDERS_MONTH_TOTALS_REWRITE
BUILD IMMEDIATE
REFRESH FAST
ON DEMAND
ENABLE QUERY REWRITE
AS
SELECT EXTRACT(YEAR FROM order_date) AS order_year,
       EXTRACT(MONTH FROM order_date) AS order_month,
       SUM(order_amount) AS month_amount
  FROM xtreme.orders
GROUP BY EXTRACT(YEAR FROM order_date),
       EXTRACT(MONTH FROM order_date);
```

Here is the equivalent for 8*i*:

```
CREATE MATERIALIZED VIEW XTREME.ORDERS_MONTH_TOTALS_REWRITE
BUILD IMMEDIATE
REFRESH FAST
ON DEMAND
ENABLE QUERY REWRITE
AS
SELECT EXTRACT(YEAR FROM order_date) AS order_year,
       EXTRACT(MONTH FROM order_date) AS order_month,
       SUM(order_amount) AS month_amount,
       COUNT(*) AS Row_Count,
       COUNT(order_amount) AS Amount_Count
  FROM xtreme.orders
 GROUP BY EXTRACT(YEAR FROM order_date),
       EXTRACT(MONTH FROM order_date);
```

Oracle recommends that you qualify the object names with their schema when creating materialized views.

You must also gather statistics for the materialized view for it to be considered for use in query rewrite:

```
BEGIN
   DBMS_STATS.GATHER_TABLE_STATS(
     ownname => 'XTREME',
     tabname => 'ORDERS_MONTH_TOTALS_REWRITE');
END;
```

The queries generated by Crystal Reports will not necessarily be rewritten even if it appears that they should be. The difficulty appears to be related to either the aliases or the double quotes that Crystal always includes; you will obtain more consistent results using SQL Commands. Open the Chapter 9\Amount by Order Month Rewrite.rpt report.

NOTE

This report will not work in Oracle 8i because it uses the execution plan subreport.

This report uses the SQL Command shown here:

```
SELECT (EXTRACT(YEAR FROM ORDER_DATE)) ORDER_YEAR,
       (EXTRACT(MONTH FROM ORDER_DATE)) ORDER_MONTH,
       SUM(ORDER_AMOUNT)  ORDER_AMOUNT,
       USERENV('SESSIONID') AUDSID
FROM   XTREME.ORDERS
```

```
GROUP BY EXTRACT(YEAR FROM ORDER_DATE),
         EXTRACT(MONTH FROM ORDER_DATE)
ORDER BY EXTRACT(YEAR FROM ORDER_DATE),
         EXTRACT(MONTH FROM ORDER_DATE)
```

Note that the query uses the Orders table directly, not a materialized view. The AUDSID is included so that the SQL Plan subreport can function. Run the report. The results should be similar to Figure 9-3.

The SQL Plan shows that the query has been rewritten by Oracle to use the Orders_Month_Totals_Rewrite materialized view.

Implementing materialized views that can successfully support query rewrites can be a difficult and complex process. Because the queries that Crystal generates cannot be rewritten, a report writer can use only SQL Commands whose text has been pretested

ORDER YEAR	ORDER MONTH	ORDER AMOUNT
2000	2	92,130.36
2000	12	167,260.28
2000		259,390.64
2001	1	211,265.10
2001	2	240,366.85
2001	3	180,967.89
2001	4	202,186.19
2001	5	217,648.93
2001	6	446,198.19
2001	7	313,481.73
2001	8	219,437.06
2001	9	181,894.82
2001	10	255,488.79
2001	11	241,880.36
2001	12	156,269.27
2001		2,867,085.18
2002	1	253,573.93
2002	2	317,900.02
2002	3	173,797.45
2002	4	183,837.69
2002	5	28,080.43
2002		957,189.52
		4,083,665.34

Execution Plan

			Cost	Rows	Optimizer			
Child Cursor 1								
SELECT STATEMENT			4		CHOOSE			
SORT ORDER BY			4	19				
PGA Memory Used	Executions	1	Optimal	1	One Pass	0	MultiPass	0
TABLE ACCESS FULL			2	19	ANALYZED			
ORDERS_MONTH_TOTALS_REWRITE								

If PGA Memory is used and many One Pass or any MultiPass executions are occuring, the PGA_Aggregate_Target may need to be increased.

Figure 9-3   *Amount by Order Month Rewrite*

for its rewrite capabilities. These restrictions make what should be a transparent process into a clumsy routine.

Freshness Subreport

For those reports that are intentionally written against materialized views, you can create a subreport that will display the last refresh date and time for the materialized view. Open and run Chapter 9\Amount by Order Month MV with Freshness Subreport.rpt. You will see a result similar to that shown in Figure 9-4, with the materialized view refresh time displayed.

Note that this subreport must be modified for each materialized view with which it is used. The selection formula must be changed to indicate the correct materialized view, and there is no way to link the subreport to the main report on the materialized view name.

MONTH	AMOUNT
2	92,130.36
12	167,260.28
2000	259,390.64
1	211,265.10
2	240,366.85
3	180,967.89
4	202,186.19
5	217,648.93
6	446,198.19
7	313,481.73
8	219,437.06
9	181,894.82
10	255,488.79
11	241,880.36
12	156,269.27
2001	2,867,085.18
1	253,573.93
2	317,900.02
3	173,797.45
4	183,837.69
5	28,080.43
2002	957,189.52
	4,083,665.34

The materialized view used in this report was last refreshed on 26-Jun-2003 at 1:00 am.

Figure 9-4   *Amount by Order Month MV with Freshness Subreport*

External Tables

Oracle external tables allow you to query a flat file as if it were a database table. This functionality is usually associated with loading data into data warehouses and eliminating the need for an internal staging table, but it has applications for reporting as well. For example, if you need to include in your report a small amount of data in a comma-delimited file and you have a reason for not loading this data into the database, such as it being unrelated to most other data and not needed for any other purpose, or the database developers are not available to code the load routines.

NOTE

External tables are a new feature of Oracle 9i.

Configuration

The example will use a file of employee IDs and hypothetical salary increases, assuming that a manager wants to analyze the new salaries before committing himself and having the changes made in the database.

Create a directory on the Oracle server to hold the files. Copy Chapter 9\Raises.txt to that directory (Raises.txt is a comma-delimited file containing each employee ID and a proposed percentage increase in salary). Execute the following command, substituting your directory name where appropriate, to create an Oracle directory object. To create a directory object, the user must be a DBA or have the CREATE ANY DIRECTORY privilege.

```
CREATE DIRECTORY EX_TABS AS 'E:\External_Tables';
```

Grant Xtreme the privilege to read from and write to the directory. Write is required to allow the writing of error logs:

```
GRANT READ, WRITE ON DIRECTORY EX_TABS TO xtreme;
```

Create the external table with the following code:

```
CREATE TABLE RAISES (emp_id NUMBER, sal_inc NUMBER)
 ORGANIZATION EXTERNAL (TYPE ORACLE_LOADER DEFAULT DIRECTORY EX_TABS
 LOCATION ('Raises.txt'));
```

Note that the CREATE TABLE statement for the Raises table is very simple because
the default line terminator (NEWLINE) and the default field delimiter (comma) are
used in the file. However, many types of files can be described and used, including those
with fixed width fields, odd terminators, and binary data. See Oracle documentation for
full coverage on creating external tables from files.

Sample Report

Create a new report. You will see that the table Raises appears in the Database Expert
along with the other Oracle tables. You can now use it in your reports just as if it
were a normal database table.

Open the Chapter 9\Proposed Raises.rpt report. Choose Database | Database
Expert and look at the Links tab. As shown in Figure 9-5, the Raises table has been
linked to the Employee table using the Emp_ID field.

Run the report. You will see the report displayed in Figure 9-6, showing that the
external table data has been used.

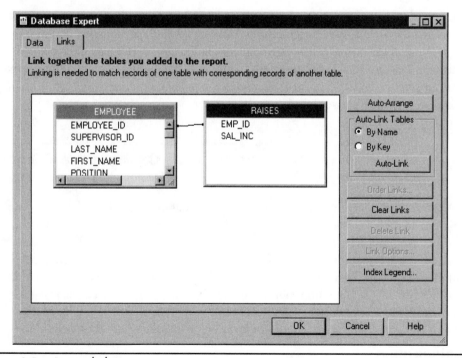

Figure 9-5   *Raises linking*

Proposed Raises

EMPLOYEE ID	LAST NAME	FIRST NAME	SALARY	SAL INC	Raise	Emp Percent of Position	NewSalary
Advertising Specialist							
15.00	Pereira	Laurent	45,000.00	4.00 %	1,800.00	100.00 %	46,800.00
			45,000.00	**4.00 %**	**1,800.00**		**46,800.00**
			Position's portion of total raises.		**5.44 %**		
Business Manager							
10.00	Hellstern	Albert	60,000.00	4.00 %	2,400.00	100.00 %	62,400.00
			60,000.00	**4.00 %**	**2,400.00**		**62,400.00**
			Position's portion of total raises.		**7.26 %**		
Inside Sales Coordinator							
8.00	Callahan	Laura	45,000.00	4.00 %	1,800.00	100.00 %	46,800.00
			45,000.00	**4.00 %**	**1,800.00**		**46,800.00**
			Position's portion of total raises.		**5.44 %**		

Figure 9-6   *Proposed Raises report*

Heterogeneous Services: Generic Connectivity

Heterogeneous services is a mechanism built into Oracle that allows transparent access to data on other database platforms. Heterogeneous services can be implemented in two ways. The first method uses purchased gateways; the second uses generic connectivity. Gateways are purchasable options with highly optimized interfaces to other database platforms such as SQL Server or DB2. Generic connectivity uses ODBC or OLE DB, which is potentially slower but definitely cheaper.

NOTE

For connectivity to other Oracle databases, DB Links can be used. Objects available via DB Links are not recognized by Crystal but can be accessed via SQL Commands or stored procedures.

After setting up heterogeneous services for the database and generic connectivity to particular data sources, you will be able to write queries against those data sources as if they were normal Oracle tables, including joining them to actual Oracle tables. This can be very useful in a reporting environment where you may be required to bring together data from different sources. You can, of course, use Crystal Reports itself for this type of operation, but using Oracle heterogeneous services is usually more efficient.

Configuration

You may use either ODBC or OLE DB to configure heterogeneous services using generic connectivity. The instructions that follow are for ODBC.

NOTE

The examples shown are for Windows only. See Oracle documentation for other platforms.

Several preliminary steps are required. Verify, or have the DBA verify, that Generic Connectivity using ODBC has been installed with the Oracle Universal Installer. If it has not been installed, then install it. Verify that the heterogeneous services tables exist by attempting to query SYS.HS_FDS_CLASS. If they do not exist, create them by running the caths.sql script found in the Oracle_Home\ RDBMS\ADMIN directory logged in as the SYS user. You must also verify that your database server can act as a client to the external data source. If, for instance, you want to connect to an Informix database, you must install the Informix client on the database server and configure it properly, then verify that the appropriate ODBC driver has been installed on the database server and that a system DSN for your data source exists.

For this example, you will use the Crystal XTREME sample ACCESS database, so you will need to copy xtreme.mdb to a directory on your server. The database is installed by Crystal Reports at C:\Program Files\Crystal Decisions\Crystal Reports 9\Samples\En\Databases.

Create a system ODBC DSN called XTREME9DSN, as shown in Figure 9-7, on your server. Set the database location to wherever you copied the file in the previous example. Note that the database can reside anywhere that is network accessible to the server, but the DSN must be created on the server and must be able to connect to the database, wherever it is.

Figure 9-7   *XTREME9DSN Data Source Name configuration*

Heterogeneous services use a special initialization file to map the Oracle service name representing the data source to the ODBC DSN. Under the Oracle home directory in HS\Admin, there will be sample initialization files. Make a copy of the inithsodbc.ora file and call it initXTREME9ODBC.ora. The contents of the file should be as shown here:

```
HS_FDS_CONNECT_INFO = XTREME9DSN
HS_FDS_TRACE_LEVEL = 0
```

Note that other options are available and that tracing can be turned on.

Next, you must modify the tnsnames.ora file on your server to include a service name that can use heterogeneous services. In the following example, the (HS = OK) indicates that this service can use heterogeneous services:

```
XTREME9ODBC =
  (DESCRIPTION =
    (ADDRESS_LIST =
      (ADDRESS = (PROTOCOL = TCP)(HOST = server2)(PORT = 1521))
    )
    (CONNECT_DATA =
      (SID = XTREME9ODBC)
    )
    (HS = OK)
  )
```

Substitute your appropriate host and port and use the name of the heterogeneous services initialization file less the "init" for the SID.

Next, you must modify the listener.ora file on the server to include a new service in the SID_LIST. The program name of hsodbc instructs Oracle to use the programs that implement heterogeneous services for ODBC. The SID_NAME must match what was used in the tnsnames file.

```
(SID_DESC =
  (PROGRAM = hsodbc)
  (SID_NAME = XTREME9ODBC)
  (ORACLE_HOME = E:\oracle\ora92)
)
```

Restart the listener.

Now you can create a database link using the new service. Logged in as Xtreme, execute the following statement:

```
CREATE DATABASE LINK xtreme_link USING 'XTREME9ODBC';
```

If your database requires a user ID and password, the proper authentication type must be set up in the database link. To test the link, execute the following statement:

```
Select "Employee ID" from employee@xtreme_link;
```

Note that because the field names in the Access database contain mixed case and spaces, they must be surrounded by double quotes in the SELECT statement. Note also that attempting to retrieve LOB types in SQL*Plus fails.

Report Example

Suppose that you are in a data warehouse environment and you have loaded your Oracle Xtreme schema from the Xtreme Access database. Now you need to verify that the employee salaries were loaded properly. Heterogeneous connectivity makes this easy.

Crystal Reports does not list or otherwise recognize tables available via Oracle database links. To use this type of data, you must create your own query. Therefore, you must write a SQL Command to display the salary data from the Access database. In addition, linking the results of a SQL Command to a regular table in Crystal fails, so you will have to gather all of the fields required for the report in the SQL Command.

Open Chapter 9\Salary Data Integrity Check.rpt. Note that the SQL Command is as follows:

```
SELECT l."Employee ID", l."Salary" access_salary,
        e.salary oracle_salary
FROM employee@xtreme_link l, employee e
WHERE e.employee_id=l."Employee ID"
```

Run the report. You will see a result like the one shown in Figure 9-8 but, depending on any changes made to the Oracle data, it may or may not match the Access data.

A similar result could be achieved by using two data sources in the Crystal report: one for the Access database and one for the Oracle database. However, there are several benefits to using Oracle generic connectivity over Crystal's multiple database

Salary Data Integrity Check

Employee ID	ACCESS SALARY	ORACLE SALARY	Sal Dif
1.00	40,000.00	40,000.00	0.00
2.00	90,000.00	90,000.00	0.00
3.00	33,000.00	33,000.00	0.00
4.00	35,000.00	35,000.00	0.00
5.00	50,000.00	50,000.00	0.00
6.00	30,000.00	30,000.00	0.00
7.00	37,000.00	37,000.00	0.00
8.00	45,000.00	45,000.00	0.00
9.00	35,000.00	35,000.00	0.00
10.00	60,000.00	60,000.00	0.00
11.00	18,000.00	18,000.00	0.00
12.00	25,000.00	25,000.00	0.00
13.00	75,000.00	75,000.00	0.00
14.00	50,000.00	50,000.00	0.00
15.00	45,000.00	45,000.00	0.00

Figure 9-8   *Salary Data Integrity Check*

reporting capabilities: it centralizes database access, only the server needs the software to be able to connect to the "foreign" databases, and report developers need only Oracle clients and drivers installed.

Using Synonyms

Synonyms can be created for the tables available via a database link. In this case, you can create a synonym such as the following:

```
CREATE SYNONYM XTREME.ACCESS_EMPLOYEE FOR employee@xtreme_link;
```

Then you can query the table as follows:

```
SELECT "Employee ID" FROM access_employee;
```

Creating a synonym also means that the table is now listed in the Crystal Database Expert, at least for the native and Oracle ODBC drivers, and it can be selected from there, as shown in Figure 9-9.

Unfortunately, Crystal converts the characters in the field names to all uppercase and replaces the spaces with underscores when using the native driver. As a result, if you choose the synonym from the Database Expert and then add any of its fields to the report, the generated query will fail because the field names are not correct. The Oracle ODBC driver also fails, even though it appears to treat the field names correctly.

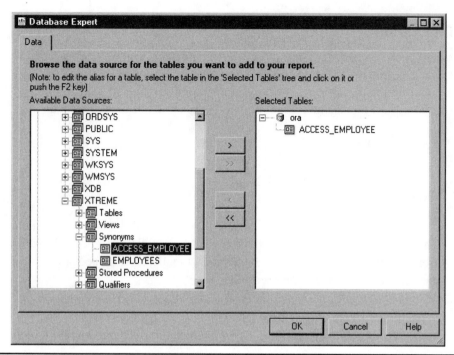

Figure 9-9   *Synonyms for database links in the Database Expert*

Oracle Flashback Query

Oracle Flashback is a database feature that lets you see and report on a version of the database as of a point in the past. There are many potential uses for this feature in a reporting environment. For example, it allows you to write a report that reflects yesterday's statistics even if there has been a change since yesterday. It is also particularly useful for troubleshooting and checking data integrity. For example, say a user complains that they ran the same report on two different days with the same parameters and got different results (in a situation where this would not be the expected behavior) and were at a loss as to how to diagnose the problem. Oracle Flashback lets you run that report as of the previous date without relying on timestamps or other mechanisms built into the database application.

NOTE

Flashback Query is a new feature in Oracle 9i.

Configuration

The Flashback mechanism relies on Oracle UNDO data, which is the information that Oracle optionally stores to roll back the state of the database. Your DBA will need to set up the database for storing some amount of UNDO data. To set up automatic UNDO management, the following steps must be accomplished:

▶ Set the UNDO_RETENTION initialization parameter, which is specified in seconds. The value should be determined considering the tradeoff of space requirements versus depth of UNDO data. To set UNDO_RETENTION to seven days, execute the following statement:

```
ALTER SYSTEM SET UNDO_RETENTION = 604800;
```

▶ The initialization parameter UNDO_MANAGEMENT must be set to AUTO. Note that this parameter cannot be set dynamically, so if it needs to be changed, the database will have to be restarted.

▶ An UNDO tablespace with enough space to contain the UNDO data must exist. If no UNDO tablespace exists, create one with the CREATE UNDO TABLESPACE command.

The user who will execute the Flashback query needs the FLASHBACK privilege. This can be granted on individual tables as shown next. You do not need to be granted the FLASHBACK privilege for tables in your own schema.

```
GRANT FLASHBACK ON xtreme.employee TO <user id>;
```

Flashback can be granted on a system level for any table in the database:

```
GRANT FLASHBACK ANY TABLE TO xtreme;
```

You must also have the EXECUTE privilege on the DBMS_FLASHBACK package if you need to use those procedures:

```
GRANT EXECUTE ON DBMS_FLASHBACK TO xtreme;
```

If you desire to enable Flashback capabilities on LOB columns, additional steps are required. Refer to Oracle documentation for further detail.

SELECT AS OF a Point in the Past

The simplest way to take advantage of Flashback queries is to use the AS OF clause in a SELECT statement. First, make sure that some changed data is available. Run the following UPDATE statement and COMMIT it:

```
UPDATE employee SET Salary = Salary * (1.05);
```

Execute the following to show the new salaries:

```
SQL> SELECT employee_id, salary FROM employee;

EMPLOYEE_ID    SALARY
----------- ----------
          1     42000
          2     94500
          3     34650
          4     36750
          5     52500
```

Then execute the following to show the old salary values:

```
SQL> SELECT employee_id, salary FROM employee AS OF
  2   TIMESTAMP (SYSTIMESTAMP - INTERVAL '60' MINUTE);

EMPLOYEE_ID    SALARY
----------- ----------
          1     40000
          2     90000
          3     33000
          4     35000
          5     50000
```

This query looks at the employee table as it was 60 minutes ago. The AS OF TIMESTAMP clause can be computed as just shown, or a literal or parameter can be used.

Oracle stamps each database change with a System Change Number (SCN). The Flashback query operation always looks at the database as of a certain SCN. To enable the use of the TIMESTAMP option, Oracle keeps track of a TIMESTAMP-to-SCN mapping which it updates every five minutes. Because of this, if you use the TIMESTAMP option, you may be up to five minutes off from the expected database state. In most cases, this is OK. If you are comparing to yesterday, five minutes does not usually matter.

For true precision, you can use the AS OF SCN clause of the SELECT statement. However, to do that, you must know the SCN that you wish to return to. If your reports are embedded in an application, the application can save the SCN as it commits transactions and allow them to be passed to Crystal for reporting. You can then embed reports in applications that show the user the state of the database before the user's most recent changes.

Note that the TIMESTAMP-to-SCN mapping is only maintained for five days worth of data. If the server is down for some length of time, that time is not included in the mappings and would mean that the mapping exists for further in the past than five days. If you need to go further back than five (uptime) days, you must use SCN numbers instead of TIMESTAMPS (and enough UNDO data must exist).

Reporting Using SELECT AS OF

You can use the AS OF clause for reporting based on SQL Commands, stored procedures, or views. The following example is a report based on a view:

```
CREATE OR REPLACE VIEW TODAYS_SALARY_CHANGES
AS
SELECT employee_id, Salary_Now, Salary_Yesterday,
       NVL(Salary_Now,0)-NVL(Salary_Yesterday,0) Salary_Change
 FROM
(SELECT employee_id, salary Salary_Now FROM employee) Now
FULL OUTER JOIN
(SELECT employee_id, salary Salary_Yesterday FROM employee AS OF
  TIMESTAMP (SYSTIMESTAMP - INTERVAL '1' DAY)) Yesterday
 USING (employee_id)
WHERE NVL(Salary_Now,0)<>NVL(Salary_Yesterday,0);
```

To see the effect of the FULL OUTER JOIN, add an employee or delete an employee. Open Chapter 9\Today's Salary Changes.rpt and run it. You will see a result similar to Figure 9-10.

To allow a user to select a particular point in the past, create a parameterized stored procedure. The stored procedure is Salary_Change_Report in the Flashback_Reports package and its core logic is the same as the preceding view with the addition of a parameter for the hours in the past. Open Chapter 9\Salary Change Since X Hours Ago.rpt and run it. You will see a result similar to Figure 9-11.

Today's Salary Changes

EMPLOYEE ID	SALARY NOW	SALARY YESTERDAY	SALARY CHANGE
1.00	42,000.00	40,000.00	2,000.00
2.00	94,500.00	90,000.00	4,500.00
3.00	34,650.00	33,000.00	1,650.00
4.00	36,750.00	35,000.00	1,750.00
5.00	52,500.00	50,000.00	2,500.00
6.00	31,500.00	30,000.00	1,500.00
7.00	38,850.00	37,000.00	1,850.00
8.00	47,250.00	45,000.00	2,250.00
9.00	36,750.00	35,000.00	1,750.00
10.00	63,000.00	60,000.00	3,000.00
11.00	18,900.00	18,000.00	900.00
12.00	26,250.00	25,000.00	1,250.00
13.00	78,750.00	75,000.00	3,750.00
14.00	52,500.00	50,000.00	2,500.00
15.00	47,250.00	45,000.00	2,250.00
100.00	55,000.00		55,000.00
	756,400.00	**668,000.00**	**88,400.00**

Figure 9-10   *Today's Salary Changes*

The SELECT AS OF can also be used with a CREATE TABLE AS SELECT statement to populate temporary tables with past state data for comparison purposes.

Salary Change Since 3.00 Hours Ago

EMPLOYEE ID	SALARY NOW	SALARY BEFORE	SALARY CHANGE
1.00	42,000.00	40,000.00	2,000.00
2.00	94,500.00	90,000.00	4,500.00
3.00	34,650.00	33,000.00	1,650.00
4.00	36,750.00	35,000.00	1,750.00
5.00	52,500.00	50,000.00	2,500.00
6.00	31,500.00	30,000.00	1,500.00
7.00	38,850.00	37,000.00	1,850.00
8.00	47,250.00	45,000.00	2,250.00
9.00	36,750.00	35,000.00	1,750.00
10.00	63,000.00	60,000.00	3,000.00
11.00	18,900.00	18,000.00	900.00
12.00	26,250.00	25,000.00	1,250.00
13.00	78,750.00	75,000.00	3,750.00
14.00	52,500.00	50,000.00	2,500.00
15.00	47,250.00	45,000.00	2,250.00
100.00	55,000.00		55,000.00
	756,400.00	**668,000.00**	**88,400.00**

Figure 9-11   *Salary Change Since X Hours Ago*

DBMS_FLASHBACK

The Oracle-supplied PL/SQL package DBMS_FLASHBACK contains procedures that can be used in PL/SQL programs to work with past state data. If you are writing a stored procedure that requires multiple Flashback queries or that cannot modify the SQL Commands to add the AS OF clause, you can use the DBMS_FLASHBACK subprograms.

The ENABLE_AT_TIME and ENABLE_AT_SCN subprograms put the user's session in Flashback mode for the time or SCN listed. Any queries run after this command are executed and, before DBMS_FLASHBACK.DISABLE is executed, will return data for the time in the past. Cursors can capture the past data; after Flashback is disabled, those cursors will still refer to past data.

The stored procedure Flashback_Reports.Salary_Changes_Report uses the DBMS_FLASHBACK procedures to capture two past salary changes and store them in a temporary table. The temporary table can be created using the following statement:

```
CREATE GLOBAL TEMPORARY TABLE SALARY_CHANGES_TEMP
   (EMPLOYEE_ID     NUMBER(10),
    SALARY_NOW      NUMBER(19, 4),
    SALARY_BEFORE1  NUMBER(19, 4),
    SALARY_BEFORE2  NUMBER(19, 4))
ON COMMIT PRESERVE ROWS;
```

The package body for the procedure is shown here. One cursor is created and then run for the current state of the database and two past states, with the results stored in the temporary table:

```
PROCEDURE Salary_Changes_Report
   (Salary_Changes_Cur  OUT Salary_Changes_Rpt_Type,
    Hours_Past1         IN   NUMBER,
    Hours_Past2         IN   NUMBER)
IS
   TYPE C_Rec_Type IS RECORD
      (Employee_ID  Employee.Employee_ID%Type,
       Salary       Employee.Salary%Type);
   CURSOR C IS SELECT Employee_ID, Salary FROM employee;
   C_Rec C_Rec_Type;
BEGIN
 DELETE FROM Salary_Changes_Temp;
--Now
 OPEN C;
 LOOP
```

```
   FETCH C INTO C_Rec;
   EXIT WHEN C%NOTFOUND;
   INSERT INTO Salary_Changes_Temp(Employee_ID, Salary_Now)
     Values(C_Rec.Employee_id, C_Rec.Salary);
 END LOOP;
 CLOSE C;
 COMMIT;
--t1
 DBMS_FLASHBACK.ENABLE_AT_TIME
   (SYSTIMESTAMP - NUMTODSINTERVAL(Hours_Past1,'HOUR'));
 OPEN C;
 DBMS_FLASHBACK.DISABLE;
 LOOP
   FETCH C INTO C_Rec;
   EXIT WHEN C%NOTFOUND;
   Update Salary_Changes_Temp
     Set Salary_Before1 = C_Rec.Salary
    Where Employee_id = C_Rec.Employee_Id;
 END LOOP;
 CLOSE C;
 COMMIT;
--t2
 DBMS_FLASHBACK.ENABLE_AT_TIME
   (SYSTIMESTAMP - NUMTODSINTERVAL(Hours_Past2,'HOUR'));
 OPEN C;
 DBMS_FLASHBACK.DISABLE;
 LOOP
   FETCH C INTO C_Rec;
   EXIT WHEN C%NOTFOUND;
   Update Salary_Changes_Temp
     Set Salary_Before2 = C_Rec.Salary
    Where Employee_id = C_Rec.Employee_Id;
 END LOOP;
 CLOSE C;
 COMMIT;
--Report Cursor
 OPEN Salary_Changes_Cur FOR
   SELECT Employee_ID, Salary_Now, Salary_Before1,
          NVL(Salary_Now,0)-NVL(Salary_Before1,0) Salary_Change1,
          Salary_Before2,
          NVL(Salary_Before1,0)-NVL(Salary_Before2,0) Salary_Change2,
          USERENV('SESSIONID') AUDSID
     FROM Salary_Changes_Temp;
END Salary_Changes_Report;
```

To visualize the results, you will need to modify the Employee salaries at least twice, at least an hour apart. The salaries have been modified once in the previous section. A script that will make a second modification is shown here:

```
BEGIN
  FOR r IN (SELECT emp_id, sal_inc FROM raises) LOOP
    UPDATE employee
      SET Salary = (1+(r.sal_inc-2)/100)*Salary
    WHERE employee_id = r.emp_id;
  END LOOP;
END;
```

Open the Chapter 9\Salary Changes.rpt report. Run it using parameter choices that will give you two distinct past salaries for the employees. The result will be similar to Figure 9-12.

Oracle Flashback is a wonderful method for querying the past state of the database, as long as you do not need to go very far back and you are not retrieving too much data. Individual users can flash back to different times, and each subquery of a SELECT statement can use a different AS OF date and time. However, you should always be aware of how much of the server resources are being used to implement it for you when using this feature.

Salary Changes

Employee ID	Salary Now	Salary Change	Salary 48 Hours Ago	Salary Change	Salary 120 Hours Ago
1	44,940.00	2,940.00	42,000.00	2,000.00	40,000.00
2	96,390.00	1,890.00	94,500.00	4,500.00	90,000.00
3	35,343.00	693.00	34,650.00	1,650.00	33,000.00
4	37,485.00	735.00	36,750.00	1,750.00	35,000.00
5	54,600.00	2,100.00	52,500.00	2,500.00	50,000.00
6	32,130.00	630.00	31,500.00	1,500.00	30,000.00
7	39,627.00	777.00	38,850.00	1,850.00	37,000.00
8	48,195.00	945.00	47,250.00	2,250.00	45,000.00
9	37,852.50	1,102.50	36,750.00	1,750.00	35,000.00
10	64,260.00	1,260.00	63,000.00	3,000.00	60,000.00
11	19,278.00	378.00	18,900.00	900.00	18,000.00
12	26,775.00	525.00	26,250.00	1,250.00	25,000.00
13	80,325.00	1,575.00	78,750.00	3,750.00	75,000.00
14	56,700.00	4,200.00	52,500.00	2,500.00	50,000.00
15	48,195.00	945.00	47,250.00	2,250.00	45,000.00
100	56,100.00	1,100.00	55,000.00	55,000.00	

Figure 9-12   *Salary Changes*

Updating Data via Crystal Reports

Updating data via Crystal Reports is possible in two ways, though Crystal Reports is not intended as a database modification tool, merely a reporting tool. You can, of course, make database changes using stored procedures. Therefore, if you are using a stored procedure to back a report, you can make any database modifications you desire. The second possibility is to use an anonymous PL/SQL block in a SQL Command. I do not recommend using Crystal Reports for any database modifications with one exception, and that is automating report execution logging.

Via Stored Procedures

To do report execution logging from a stored procedure, you simply need to add a statement that writes the logging information somewhere in the procedure. You can create a separate procedure for this function and call it from all of your report procedures.

Via SQL Commands

To do report execution logging from a SQL Command, you can write the SQL Command similar to the following:

```
BEGIN
    Reports.Supplier_Report({?Supplier});
    Insert into Report_Log
      Values('Reports.Supplier_Report',USER,SYSDATE,
             'Supplier={?Supplier}');
END;
```

Note that there are many restrictions involved in this method. The statement that returns the report data must be a call to a REF Cursor stored procedure; it cannot be a SELECT statement. SELECT statements without INTO clauses are not allowed in PL/SQL blocks. Experimentation has shown any other statements in the block must come *after* the call to the stored procedure; otherwise, an error results. Finally, such calls cannot be made from the native driver.

This chapter has covered several Oracle features that might be of interest to Crystal Report writers, including materialized views, external tables, heterogeneous services, and Flashback queries. The next chapter will develop a generic Oracle database dictionary report.

CHAPTER
10

Data Dictionary Report

U nderstanding the data on which you are required to report is crucial. In an ideal situation, a full, complete, and up-to-date data dictionary will be supplied to you, along with access to the DBA and systems analysts who possess an in-depth knowledge of the structures and their purposes. The real world is rarely ideal.

This chapter presents a complex report example. You will create a data dictionary report for the Crystal Reports sample database that has been moved into Oracle. Because the structure of Oracle data dictionary views is the same no matter what user objects have been created, these instructions can be applied to any Oracle database you choose and will work equally well. Your report will look like the report in the screen shots to follow except that the names of the database objects in the report will differ, and certain object types may or may not exist in your database.

If you complete the steps in this chapter, you will have a good understanding of the Oracle data dictionary views; you will also have a report that you can use to document the objects in any Oracle schema.

Oracle Data Dictionary Views

As mentioned in Chapter 2, the Oracle data dictionary views contain information about the objects that exist in the database. In this chapter, we will look at several of those views in more detail as you use them in our data dictionary report. The ALL_ views will be used in the report because they display all of the objects for which the logged in user has privileges. The DBA_ views are available only to the DBA or a user with the SELECT_CATALOG_ROLE. The USER_ views display only the objects in the logged in user's schema. Your assumption will be that your report users want information on all objects that are available to them.

Report Strategy

The overall structure of the report must be decided before work can begin. This is always a cyclic process and usually requires several iterations to determine the best design that balances easy manipulation in Crystal and query complexity in Oracle. For other than very simple reports, it is recommended that you work out your data requirements using a query tool before starting work in Crystal. Starting a complex report in Crystal without working through the data needs first can lead to over-reliance on Crystal formulas and subreports and can add report complexity. Once you have determined what the query should be, if it can be easily duplicated in Crystal, you can re-create it there. If it cannot be duplicated in Crystal, you will already have created the SQL that can be pasted into a SQL Command or used in a view or stored procedure.

A data dictionary report is particularly difficult to design because you are required to report on many different object types, each having its own characteristics, and many having a hierarchical relationship to other objects. An extensive use of master/detail linked subreports would be the most intuitive approach, but subreports can be inefficient. Using Oracle queries with embedded cursors to display the child data would be efficient but impossible to use in Crystal. You need a query that will return all of the required fields in a form that is easy to format in Crystal.

Before making any design decisions, you must determine the report requirements. Because the report requirement is to document the XTREME sample schema, some database objects types will not be included; for example, there are no triggers or security policies in the XTREME schema. Only a few simple object types exist in the XTREME schema so, although your report will cover them, it would not necessarily be sufficient for more complex object types. The basic objects, such as tables, views, indexes, stored procedures, and table constraints, will be included along with their related column definitions. Most objects of interest to report writers will be included.

There are many ways to organize a report such as this; what follows is the strategy used for this example. For easy use in Crystal, the overall goal will be to get a list of all objects along with their associated grouping values. Then you will join to that list the related fields for each different object type. This will denormalize the data so that each object has one master row of data, but that row will contain all fields of interest for each object type. Therefore, for any given object, the grouping fields will be populated and the fields that belong to that object's type will be populated, but many of the fields that apply only to other object types will be null. You will format the Crystal Report so that fields belonging to different object types are grouped in sections and suppress unnecessary sections. In addition, some object types have lower-level detail such as columns or arguments. That will be the lowest level required and hence the level at which the query will be returned. All higher-level grouping will be done in Crystal.

To start, which objects in the dictionary should be displayed? The object types that will be included in this report are shown in the Group 4 column of Table 10-1, which includes tables or views (including materialized views), constraints, indexes, synonyms, types, sequences, functions, procedures, and database links. You might notice that procedure is listed three times: once for standalone procedures, once for procedures attached to object types (which are often called methods), and once for procedures that belong to packages.

Group 4 is the grouping by object type, Group 5 is the grouping by the name of the database object, and the detail column contains the columns, attributes, or arguments associated with the object. Above Group 4, Group 3 exists so that related objects can be displayed together in the report. For example, a given table will have its constraints and indexes grouped with its basic table information, procedures belonging to object types will be grouped with the type they belong to, and procedures defined in packages will be grouped with the package they belong to. Group 2 is a grouping at the level of the object type of the parent, so that all tables will be grouped together, all synonyms will be grouped together, and so on. The highest level group will be the schema or object owner.

Creating the Query

The dictionary query will be developed in several parts over the following sections. Note that the chapter text contains code for Oracle 9*i*. The logic for 8*i* is identical, and the corresponding code for the end result is provided with the Chapter 10 files.

Group 1	Group 2	Group 3	Group 4	Group 5	Detail
OWNER	PARENT TYPE	PARENT NAME	OBJECT TYPE	OBJECT NAME	COLUMN ID
Schema	Table or view	Table/view name	Table or view	Table/view name	Columns
Schema	Table or view	Table/view name	Constraint	Constraint name	Columns
Schema	Table or view	Table/view name	Index	Index name	Columns
Schema	Synonym	Synonym name	Synonym	Synonym name	No detail
Schema	Type	Type name	Type	Type name	Attributes
Schema	Type	Type name	Procedure	Method name	Arguments
Schema	Sequence	Sequence name	Sequence	Sequence name	No detail
Schema	Function	Function name	Function	Function name	Arguments
Schema	Procedure	Procedure name	Procedure	Procedure name	Arguments
Schema	Package	Package name	Procedure	Package procedure name	Arguments
Schema	DB_Link	DB_Link name	DB_Link	DB_Link name	No detail

Table 10-1   *Dictionary Grouping*

Obtaining All Objects

As mentioned previously, the first task is to create the core list of objects with their grouping values. Unfortunately, there is not a single Oracle data dictionary view containing all of the objects that you need, so you will have to build the list from several views. Start with ALL_OBJECTS, which contains package names but does not contain the package procedures, and then join ALL_OBJECTS to ALL_PROCEDURES to include the packaged procedures.

NOTE

The ALL_PROCEDURES view does not exist in 8i, so the packaged procedure list is obtained from ALL_ARGUMENTS instead.

```
SELECT xo.owner, xo.object_type parent_type,
       xo.object_name parent_name,
       NVL2(xp.procedure_name, 'PROCEDURE',
DECODE(xo.object_type,'TYPE','ATTRIBUTE',xo.object_type))
         object_type,
       NVL(xp.procedure_name, xo.object_name) object_name,
       xo.status,
       DECODE(NVL2(xp.procedure_name,'PROCEDURE',xo.object_type),
         'TYPE','ATTRIBUTE','FUNCTION','ARGUMENT',
         'PROCEDURE','ARGUMENT', 'CONSTRAINT','CONSCOL',
         'COLUMN') detail_type
  FROM all_objects xo
       LEFT JOIN all_procedures xp
         ON (xo.owner=xp.owner
             AND xo.object_name=xp.object_name)
 WHERE xo.object_type IN ('TABLE', 'VIEW', 'SYNONYM',
                          'TYPE', 'SEQUENCE', 'FUNCTION',
                          'PROCEDURE', 'PACKAGE')
   AND xo.generated='N'
```

Note that you include only the object types from ALL_OBJECTS that you are interested in, and only those objects that are not system generated. Indexes will be obtained from the ALL_INDEXES view where the parent object is available. Materialized views are listed twice in ALL_OBJECTS as both materialized views and as tables, so you should include them with the regular tables. There is no filtering done by schema; the report will have a schema parameter so the filter will be added to the query at runtime. The detail_type field has been added to facilitate joining to the detail level data later.

Now you will add unions to your query to add the other object types. Note that after this step, the query can no longer be replicated by Crystal Reports' internal query generation capabilities and must be used in a SQL Command, view, or stored procedure.

```sql
SELECT xo.owner, xo.object_type parent_type,
       xo.object_name parent_name,
       NVL2(xp.procedure_name, 'PROCEDURE',
       DECODE(xo.object_type,'TYPE','ATTRIBUTE',xo.object_type))
         object_type,
       NVL(xp.procedure_name, xo.object_name) object_name,
       xo.status,
       DECODE(NVL2(xp.procedure_name,'PROCEDURE',xo.object_type),
         'TYPE','ATTRIBUTE','FUNCTION','ARGUMENT',
         'PROCEDURE','ARGUMENT', 'CONSTRAINT','CONSCOL',
         'COLUMN') detail_type
  FROM all_objects xo
       LEFT JOIN all_procedures xp
         ON (xo.owner=xp.owner
             AND xo.object_name=xp.object_name)
 WHERE xo.object_type IN ('TABLE', 'VIEW', 'SYNONYM',
                          'TYPE', 'SEQUENCE', 'FUNCTION',
                          'PROCEDURE', 'PACKAGE')
   AND xo.generated='N'
 UNION ALL
SELECT xc.owner, xo.object_type, xc.table_name,
       'CONSTRAINT', xc.constraint_name, xc.status,
       'CONSCOL'
  FROM all_constraints xc
       LEFT JOIN all_objects xo
         ON (xc.owner=xo.owner
             AND xc.table_name=xo.object_name)
 WHERE xc.generated='USER NAME'
 UNION ALL
SELECT owner, table_type, table_name, 'INDEX',
       index_name, status, 'INDEXCOL'
  FROM all_indexes
 WHERE generated='N'
 UNION ALL
SELECT owner, 'DB_LINK', CAST(DB_LINK AS VARCHAR2(30)), 'DB_LINK',
       CAST(DB_LINK AS VARCHAR2(30)), NULL, 'NONE'
  FROM all_db_links
```

NOTE

ALL_CONSTRAINTS must be joined to ALL_OBJECTS to obtain the object that the constraint belongs to.

Object Level Fields

Now you have your complete list of objects and their grouping information. Next, you will turn this list into an inline view and add master level details for each object type. The result will be a very wide record with many columns, where certain columns apply only to certain object types. For tables, views, and materialized views, information will be added from ALL_ALL_TABLES and ALL_TAB_COMMENTS. For materialized views, information will also be added from ALL_MVIEWS. For external tables, information will be added from ALL_EXTERNAL_LOCATIONS and ALL_EXTERNAL_TABLES. For types, information will be added from ALL_TYPES and ALL_COLL_TYPES. For sequences, synonyms, indexes, procedures, constraints, and database links, information will be added from the corresponding ALL_ views. As fields are added, they will be prefixed with a character to distinguish which object type they belong to. This will be useful when developing the report so that related fields can be grouped together in separate sections.

Note that in the following code listing, the inline view subquery is not shown in its entirety but represented by "INLINE VIEW." The entire query is available in Chapter 10\Data_Dict_Master.sql.

```
SELECT o.owner schema, o.parent_type, o.parent_name
       o.object_type, o.object_name, o.status,
       DECODE(a.temporary,'Y','Temporary',NULL) t_temporary,
       SUBSTR(c.comments,1,1000) c_comments,
       a.num_rows t_rowcount,
       a.last_analyzed t_last_analyzed,
       a.partitioned t_partitioned, a.table_type t_table_of_type,
       m.updatable m_updatable,
       m.rewrite_enabled m_rewrite_enabled,
       m.rewrite_capability m_rewrite_capability,
       m.refresh_mode m_refresh_mode,
       m.refresh_method m_refresh_method,
       m.fast_refreshable m_fast_refreshable,
       m.last_refresh_type m_last_refresh_type,
       m.last_refresh_date m_last_refresh_date,
       m.staleness m_staleness,
```

```
        n.location x_location,
        n.directory_name x_directory_name,
        x.type_name x_type_name,
        x.default_directory_name x_default_directory_name,
        x.reject_limit x_reject_limit, x.access_type x_access_type,
        x.access_parameters x_access_parameters,
        t.typecode y_typecode,
        l.coll_type l_coll_type, l.upper_bound l_upper_bound,
        l.elem_type_owner l_elem_type_owner,
        l.elem_type_name l_elem_type_name,
        s.table_owner s_table_owner, s.table_name s_table_name,
        s.db_link s_db_link,
        q.min_value q_min_value, q.max_value q_max_value,
        q.increment_by q_increment_by,
        q.cycle_flag q_cycle_flag, q.order_flag q_order_flag,
        q.cache_size q_cache_size, q.last_number q_last_number,
        p.aggregate p_aggregate, p.parallel p_parallel,
        p.authid p_authid,
        i.index_type i_index_type, i.uniqueness i_uniqueness,
        i.compression i_compression,
        r.constraint_type r_constraint_type,
        r.search_condition r_search_condition,
        r.r_owner r_r_owner,
        r.r_constraint_name r_r_constraint_name,
        r.delete_rule r_delete_rule, r.validated r_validated,
        b.username b_username, b.host b_host, b.created b_created,
        d.column_id, d.column_name, d.data_type, d.data_length,
        d.data_precision, d.data_scale, d.nullable, d.detail_type,
        userenv('SESSIONID') audsid
FROM (INLINE VIEW) o
     LEFT JOIN all_all_tables a
        ON (o.owner=a.owner AND o.object_name=a.table_name)
     LEFT JOIN all_tab_comments c
        ON (o.owner=c.owner AND o.object_name=c.table_name)
     LEFT JOIN all_mviews m
        ON (o.owner=m.owner AND o.object_name=m.mview_name)
     LEFT JOIN all_external_locations n
        ON (o.owner=n.owner AND o.object_name=n.table_name)
     LEFT JOIN all_external_tables x
        ON (o.owner=x.owner AND o.object_name=x.table_name)
     LEFT JOIN all_types t
        ON (o.owner=t.owner AND o.object_name=t.type_name)
     LEFT JOIN all_coll_types l
        ON (o.owner=l.owner AND o.object_name=l.type_name)
```

```
LEFT JOIN all_synonyms s
   ON (o.owner=s.owner AND o.object_name=s.synonym_name)
LEFT JOIN all_sequences q
   ON (o.owner=q.sequence_owner
       AND o.object_name=q.sequence_name)
LEFT JOIN all_procedures p
   ON (o.owner=p.owner
       AND o.parent_object_name=p.object_name
       AND o.object_name=NVL(p.procedure_name,p.object_name))
LEFT JOIN all_indexes i
   ON (o.owner=i.owner AND o.object_name=i.index_name)
LEFT JOIN all_constraints r
   ON (o.owner=r.owner AND o.object_name=r.constraint_name)
LEFT JOIN all_db_links b
   ON (o.owner=b.owner AND o.object_name=b.db_link);
```

Not all fields from every data dictionary view are included. You can add any fields that you desire to the query.

Detail Level

For the detail data, the display fields needed for columns (tables, views, indexes, constraints) are similar to the fields needed for attributes (types) and arguments (procedures), so you will create a subquery that unions all of the different detail types together. One significant difference is in the nullable field, which is filled with the nullable flag for table and view columns, IN/OUT information for arguments, and the attribute type owner for attributes and is left null for indexes and constraints. You will need to modify the report field headings appropriately for each detail type.

```
SELECT owner, table_name parent_name,
       table_name object_name, 'COLUMN' detail_type,
       column_id, SUBSTR(column_name,1,32) column_name,
       data_type, data_length, data_precision, data_scale,
       nullable
  FROM all_tab_columns
UNION ALL
SELECT owner, NVL(package_name, object_name), object_name,
       'ARGUMENT', data_level*100+position,
       DECODE(position,0,object_name,SUBSTR(argument_name,1,32)),
       data_type, data_length, data_precision, data_scale,
       in_out
  FROM all_arguments
```

```
 UNION ALL
SELECT owner, type_name, type_name, 'ATTRIBUTE',
       attr_no, SUBSTR(attr_name,1,32), attr_type_name,
       length, precision, scale, attr_type_owner
  FROM all_type_attrs
 UNION ALL
SELECT index_owner, table_name, index_name,
       'INDEXCOL', column_position,
       SUBSTR(column_name,1,32),
       NULL,NULL,NULL,NULL, descend
  FROM all_ind_columns
 UNION ALL
SELECT owner, table_name, constraint_name, 'CONSCOL',
       position, SUBSTR(column_name,1,32),
       NULL, NULL, NULL, NULL, NULL
  FROM all_cons_columns
```

The argument number is computed from the data_level and position. The zero data_level in the ALL_ARGUMENTS view indicates the actual arguments, so you could have simply filtered out any rows with the data_level not equal to zero and used the position for the column identifier. However, the argument information for the lower levels contains the REF Cursor and the PL/SQL record composition. These define the fields in the REF Cursor for stored procedures and, therefore, the computation will allow you not only to display all of the data, but also to distinguish between the true arguments and the component parts. This computation assumes that there are fewer than 100 arguments.

Final Query

The next step is to join the detail subquery to the main query. There is one complication to overcome concerning this join, however. It is possible and even common for an index to have the same name as the constraint it is implementing. In this situation, this means, for example, the primary key constraint on the employee table has the same owner (XTREME), parent name (EMPLOYEE), and object name (EMPLOYEE_PK) as the associated index. Your solution to this problem will be to add the detail_type column to both the master query and the detail query.

In the following code listing the object inline view is abbreviated as "OBJECT INLINE VIEW," and the detail inline view is abbreviated as "DETAIL INLINE VIEW." Part of the object level select list, along with the object level joins, are also abbreviated. The entire query is available as Chapter 10\Data_Dictionary.sql.

```
SELECT o.owner schema, o.parent_type, o.parent_name,
       o.object_type, o.object_name, o.status,
       …Other Object Level Columns…
       d.column_id, d.column_name, d.data_type, d.data_length,
       d.data_precision,
       d.data_scale, d.nullable, d.detail_type,
       userenv('SESSIONID') audsid
  FROM (OBJECT INLINE VIEW) o
       …Left Joins for Object Level…
       LEFT JOIN (DETAIL INLINE VIEW) d
         ON (o.owner=d.owner AND o.parent_name=d.parent_name
             AND o.object_name=d.object_name
             AND o.detail_type=d.detail_type);
```

For ease of use, the query will be created as a view. The entire view creation statement can be found in Chapter 10\Data Dictionary view.sql.

For Oracle 8*i*, the creation statement is contained in Chapter 10\Data Dictionary view 8i.sql. The 8*i* version uses the older join syntax and lacks references to external tables, as they were not available until 9*i*. Oracle 8*i* does not contain an ALL_PROCEDURES data dictionary view, so the three fields from ALL_PROCEDURES are omitted. In addition, the packaged procedure names are drawn from ALL_ARGUMENTS instead of ALL_PROCEDURES.

Creating the Report

Creating the report involves several steps that will be outlined in the following sections. The significant actions are covered, but extensive formatting, field placement, and so on should be referenced from the report itself. Everything discussed here using 9*i* is directly applicable to 8*i*, except for the lack of the external table fields and the procedure fields.

Preliminary Setup

The Oracle data dictionary is contained in system views that have been given public synonyms. In order to see the data dictionary views from Crystal Reports, the database options need to be modified to show synonyms, as shown in Figure 10-1. Start Crystal Reports, then choose File | Options, and then the Database tab. Make sure Synonyms is checked (the System Tables option need not be checked) and close

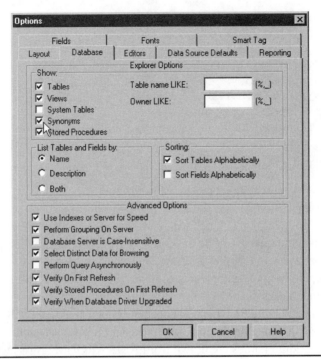

Figure 10-1   *Database options*

the dialog box. The database options can also be modified from the Database Expert by right-clicking a database and choosing Options.

Checking the Show Synonyms option is required if you want to report directly from the system views. In this case, you will be reporting from a view defined in the XTREME schema so this step can be omitted if desired.

Create the Report

Open Crystal Reports and create a new report using the Standard Report Creation Wizard. Choose the XTREME view DATA_DICTIONARY as the only data source. Choose the detail fields shown in Figure 10-2 as the fields to display.

Group on SCHEMA, PARENT_TYPE, PARENT_NAME, OBJECT_TYPE, and OBJECT_NAME, as shown in Figure 10-3, then choose Finish.

On the summaries page remove all summaries, as shown in Figure 10-4.

On the Record Selection page, choose SCHEMA as a filter field and set it equal to XTREME, as shown in Figure 10-5. You will add a parameter for picking a schema later. For now, it is best to create this selection formula to avoid returning all data dictionary objects, which would take quite some time.

Choose Finish, and the report will be displayed.

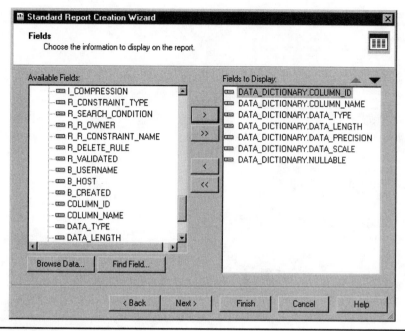

Figure 10-2   *Fields to display*

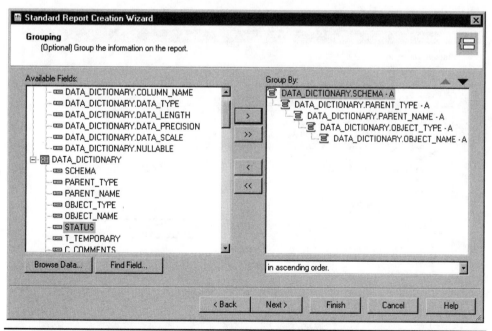

Figure 10-3   *Group by fields*

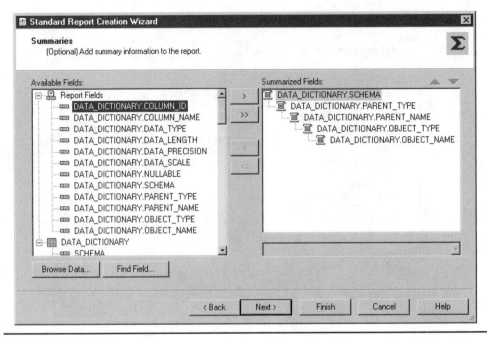

Figure 10-4   *Summaries*

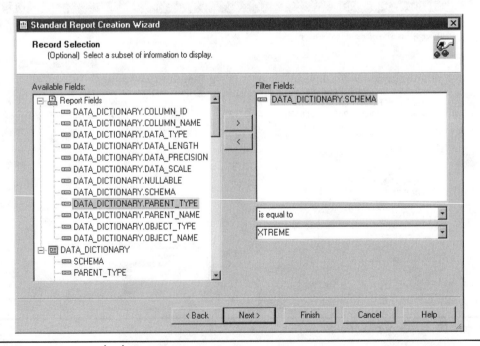

Figure 10-5   *Record selection*

Page Setup

Set the page margins as shown here:

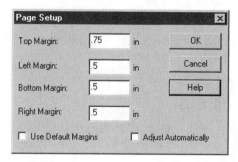

Add the Parameter

Add a parameter field called Schema and modify the record selection formula as shown:

```
{DATA_DICTIONARY.SCHEMA} = {?Schema}
```

When previewing the report set Schema equal to XTREME.

Create Formulas

Create the following formulas using the code shown:

▶ Constraint Type

```
SELECT {DATA_DICTIONARY.R_CONSTRAINT_TYPE}
    CASE 'C': 'Check Constraint'
    CASE 'P': 'Primary Key'
    CASE 'U': 'Unique Key'
    CASE 'R': 'Referential Integrity'
    CASE 'V': 'With Check Option'
    CASE 'O': 'With Read Only'
    DEFAULT : 'Unknown';
```

▶ Detail Column Header

```
SELECT {DATA_DICTIONARY.OBJECT_TYPE}
    CASE 'PROCEDURE', 'FUNCTION' : 'In/Out'
    CASE 'INDEX' : 'Asc/Desc'
    CASE 'CONSTRAINT' : ''
    CASE 'TYPE' : 'Type Owner'
    DEFAULT : 'Nullable';
```

▶ GH3 Continued

```
IF InRepeatedGroupHeader THEN 'Continued' ELSE ''
```

▶   Ref Constraint

```
IF ISNULL({DATA_DICTIONARY.R_DELETE_RULE}) THEN
   'Refers to '+{DATA_DICTIONARY.R_R_OWNER}+'.'
     +{DATA_DICTIONARY.R_R_CONSTRAINT_NAME}
ELSE
   'Refers to '+{DATA_DICTIONARY.R_R_OWNER}+'.'
     +{DATA_DICTIONARY.R_R_CONSTRAINT_NAME}
     +'On Delete ' + {DATA_DICTIONARY.R_DELETE_RULE}
```

Modify the Group Options

Modify the group options for Group 3. Check Repeat Group Header On Each Page.
For Group 4, change the sort order to descending. For Group 5, choose Keep Group
Together.

Populate and Format the Sections

The SCHEMA group name field will be used in the page header so it will appear at the
top of each page. The PARENT_TYPE group name field will also be put in the page
header so that it will include the schema and the main object type. For the object types
that do not have parents, such as database links, functions, procedures, sequences, and
synonyms, the group information for the PARENT_NAME and OBJECT_TYPE
groups will be suppressed. The OBJECT_TYPE group can be suppressed because it
is identical to the PARENT_TYPE. The sections in the OBJECT_NAME group will
be used to display all fields for the various object types, excluding the column level
details. Fields for various object types will be grouped together in sections that can be
suppressed when the current record is for a different object type. You will be putting
what the report considers detail level fields into group headers to effectively suppress
the duplication that was created by joining the object master level information to the
detail inline view.

Split the page header into two sections: PHa and PHb. Split the header section for
Group 5 until you have sections GH5a through GH5u.

Move the detail field headers from the page header into GH5u and then format the
group sections as follows:

▶   PHa
   Contents: Group #1 Name

Contents: Group #2 Name

▶ GH1
Section: Suppress

▶ GH2
Section: Suppress

▶ GH3
Contents: Group #3 Name, Y_TYPECODE, @GH3 Continued

Section: Conditionally suppress when

```
{DATA_DICTIONARY.PARENT_TYPE} IN
  ['FUNCTION','PROCEDURE', 'SEQUENCE', 'SYNONYM', 'DB_LINK']
```

▶ GH4
Contents: Group #4 Name

Section: Conditionally suppress when

```
{DATA_DICTIONARY.PARENT_TYPE} IN
  ['FUNCTION','PROCEDURE', 'SEQUENCE', 'SYNONYM', 'DB_LINK']
```

▶ GH5a
Contents: Group #5 Name, STATUS

▶ GH5b (DB links)
Contents: B_USERNAME, B_HOST, B_CREATED, and text objects for field names

Section: Conditionally suppress when

```
{DATA_DICTIONARY.OBJECT_TYPE}<>'DB_LINK'
```

▶ GH5c (Object comments)
Contents: C_COMMENTS

Section: Suppress blank section

▶ GH5d (Tables/materialized views)
Contents: T_TEMPORARY, T_ROWS, T_LAST_ANALYZED,
T_PARTITIONED, T_TABLE_OF_TYPE, and field names where needed

| GH5d | T_TEMPORAR | Rows: | T_ROW | Analyzed T_LAST_ANA | Partitioned: | T_P | Table Of T_TABLE_OF_TYPE |

Section: Conditionally suppress when

```
{DATA_DICTIONARY.OBJECT_TYPE}<>'TABLE'
```

▶ GH5e (External tables)
Contents: X_DIRECTORY_NAME, X_LOCATION and field names, plus
header text for the external table sections

| GH5e | **External Table** | Directory X_DIRECTORY_NAME | Location X_LOCATION |

Section: Conditionally suppress when

```
ISNULL({DATA_DICTIONARY.X_LOCATION})
```

▶ GH5f (External tables)
Contents: Field headers for external table fields in GH5g

| GH5f | **Type Name** | **Default Directory** | **Reject Limit** | **Access Type** | **Access Parameters** |

Section: Conditionally suppress when

```
ISNULL({DATA_DICTIONARY.X_LOCATION})
```

▶ GH5g (External tables)
Contents: X_TYPE_NAME, X_DEFAULT_DIRECTORY_NAME,
X_REJECT_LIMIT, X_ACCESS_TYPE, X_ACCESS_PARAMETERS

| GH5g | X_TYPE_NAME | X_DEFAULT_DIRECTORY_NA | X_REJECT_LIMIT | X_ACCESS_T | X_ACCESS_PARAMETERS |

Section: Conditionally suppress when

```
ISNULL({DATA_DICTIONARY.X_LOCATION})
```

▶ GH5h (Materialized views)
Contents: M_LAST_REFRESH_DATE, M_STALENESS, plus section header
for materialized views

GH5h				
	Materialized View		Last Refresh Date:	M_LAST_RE[M_STALENESS

Section: Conditionally suppress when

```
ISNULL({DATA_DICTIONARY.M_UPDATABLE})
```

▶ GH5i (Materialized views)
Contents: Field headers for section GH5j

GH5i	Updatable	Rewrite Enabled	Rewrite Capability	Refresh Mode	Refresh Method	Fast Refreshable	Last Refresh Type

Section: Conditionally suppress when

```
ISNULL({DATA_DICTIONARY.M_UPDATABLE})
```

▶ GH5j (Materialized views)
Contents: M_UPDATABLE, M_REWRITE_ENABLED,
M_REFRESH_MODE, M_REFRESH_METHOD,
M_FAST_REFRESHABLE, M_LAST_REFRESH_TYPE

GH5j	_UPDATABLE	RITE_ENA[	WRITE_CAPABILIT[	FRESH_MO[	REFRESH_METHOD	M_FAST_REFRESHABLE	ST_REFRESH_TY

Section: Conditionally suppress when

```
ISNULL({DATA_DICTIONARY.M_UPDATABLE})
```

▶ GH5k (Collection attributes)
Contents: Field headers for GH5l

GH5k	Collection Type	Upper Bound	Element Type Owner	Element Type Name

Section: Conditionally suppress when

```
{DATA_DICTIONARY.OBJECT_TYPE}<>'ATTRIBUTE'
OR
 ({DATA_DICTIONARY.Y_TYPECODE}<>'COLLECTION'
 OR
ISNULL({DATA_DICTIONARY.Y_TYPECODE}))
```

► GH5l (Collection attributes)
Contents: L_COLL_TYPE, L_UPPER_BOUND, L_ELEM_TYPE_OWNER, L_ELEM_TYPE_NAME

Section: Conditionally suppress when

```
{DATA_DICTIONARY.OBJECT_TYPE}<>'ATTRIBUTE'
OR
 ({DATA_DICTIONARY.Y_TYPECODE}<>'COLLECTION'
 OR
ISNULL({DATA_DICTIONARY.Y_TYPECODE}))
```

► GH5m (Synonyms)
Contents: Field headers for GH5n

Section: Conditionally suppress when

```
{DATA_DICTIONARY.OBJECT_TYPE}<>'SYNONYM'
```

► GH5n (Synonyms)
Contents: S_TABLE_OWNER, S_TABLE_NAME, S_DB_LINK

Section: Conditionally suppress when

```
{DATA_DICTIONARY.OBJECT_TYPE}<>'SYNONYM'
```

▶ GH5o (Sequences)
Contents: Field headers for GH5p

Section: Conditionally suppress when

`{DATA_DICTIONARY.OBJECT_TYPE}<>'SEQUENCE'`

▶ GH5p (Sequences)
Contents: Q_MIN_VALUE, Q_MAX_VALUE, Q_INCREMENT_BY,
Q_CYCLE_FLAG, Q_ORDER_FLAG, Q_CACHE_SIZE, Q_LAST_NUMBER

Section: Conditionally suppress when

`{DATA_DICTIONARY.OBJECT_TYPE}<>'SEQUENCE'`

▶ GH5q (Procedures)
Contents: P_AGGREGATE, P_PARALLEL, P_AUTHID, and field headers

Section: Conditionally suppress when

`NOT({DATA_DICTIONARY.OBJECT_TYPE} IN ['FUNCTION', 'PROCEDURE'])`

▶ GH5r (Indexes)
Contents: I_INDEX_TYPE, I_UNIQUENESS, I_COMPRESSION, and field
headers as appropriate

Section: Conditionally suppress when

`{DATA_DICTIONARY.OBJECT_TYPE}<>'INDEX'`

▶ GH5s (Referential constraints)
Contents: @Ref Constraint

GH5s	.		@Ref Constraint	┐

Section: Underlay following sections and conditionally suppress when

```
{DATA_DICTIONARY.OBJECT_TYPE}<>'CONSTRAINT'
```

▶ GH5t (Constraints)
Contents: @Constraint Type, R_SEARCH_CONDITION, R_VALIDATED

GH5t	▷ @Constraint Type	R_SEARCH_CONDITION	R_VALIDATED

Section: Conditionally suppress when

```
{DATA_DICTIONARY.OBJECT_TYPE}<>'CONSTRAINT'
```

▶ GH5u (Detail headers)
Contents: Field headers for section D, including @Detail Column Header over the NULLABLE field

GH5u	▷	Column Name	Data Type	Length	Precision	Scale	tail Column Head

Section: Conditionally suppress when

```
{DATA_DICTIONARY.OBJECT_TYPE} IN ['DB_LINK','SEQUENCE','SYNONYM']
OR
 ({DATA_DICTIONARY.OBJECT_TYPE}='CONSTRAINT'
 AND
 {DATA_DICTIONARY.R_CONSTRAINT_TYPE} in ['C','R','O','V'])
OR
 ({DATA_DICTIONARY.OBJECT_TYPE}='ATTRIBUTE'
 AND
 {DATA_DICTIONARY.Y_TYPECODE}='COLLECTION')
```

▶ D (Column level detail)
Contents: COLUMN_ID, COLUMN_NAME, DATA_TYPE, DATA_LENGTH, DATA_PRECISION, DATA_SCALE, NULLABLE (should already be populated from earlier steps)

D	▷ MN_ID	COLUMN_NAME	DATA_TYPE	LENGTH	PRECISION	SCALE	NULLABLE

Section: Conditionally suppress when

```
{DATA_DICTIONARY.OBJECT_TYPE} IN ['DB_LINK','SEQUENCE','SYNONYM']
OR
 ({DATA_DICTIONARY.OBJECT_TYPE}='CONSTRAINT'
 AND
 {DATA_DICTIONARY.R_CONSTRAINT_TYPE} in ['C','R','O','V'])
OR
 ({DATA_DICTIONARY.OBJECT_TYPE}='ATTRIBUTE'
 AND
 {DATA_DICTIONARY.Y_TYPECODE}='COLLECTION')
```

▶ GF5, GF4, GF3, GF2, GF1
   Section: Suppress

▶ RF
   Contents: The SQL statistics, execution plan, and/or session statistics
   subreports can be placed in the report footer if so desired. All three are
   included in the 9*i* example report.

▶ PF
   Contents: Print date, page number

The report is now complete. The 9*i* version is included with the download files as
Chapter 10\Data Dictionary.rpt. The 8*i* version is Chapter 10\Data Dictionary 8i.rpt.
Figure 10-6 shows the SUPPLIER_RPTS.SUPPLIER_REPORT as it is displayed in
the report.

XTREME

PACKAGE

SUPPLIER_RPTS   **Continued**

PROCEDURE

SUPPLIER_REPORT   *VALID*

	Aggregate:NO	Parallel:NO	AUTHID: DEFINER		
Column Name	Data Type	Length	Precision	Scale	In/Out
1 SUPP_RPT_CUR	REF CURSOR				OUT
2 SUPPLIER_PAR	NUMBER	22	10		IN
	PL/SQL RECORD				OUT
SUPPLIER_ID	NUMBER	22	10		OUT
SUPPLIER_NAME	VARCHAR2	50			OUT
COUNTRY	VARCHAR2	50			OUT
PHONE	VARCHAR2	20			OUT
AUSID	NUMBER	22			OUT

Figure 10-6   *SUPPLIER_RPTS.SUPPLIER_REPORT*

You now have a report that you can use to document any schema in your database. You can add to the query any other data dictionary information that you require and modify the report accordingly keeping to the general structures outlined in this chapter. You should find the report performance to be quite speedy even though a large amount of data is returned.

The next chapter will discuss creating and using a Crystal repository in Oracle. In addition, security will be added to the repository to make its use feasible in a multiuser environment.

The Crystal Repository

The Crystal object repository is a powerful new feature in Crystal Reports 9. The object repository is aptly named: it is a storage place for Crystal objects that can be shared among many developers and reports, including semiautomatic updating of changed objects. The object types that can be stored in the repository include text, graphics, custom formulas, and custom database queries or commands.

In this chapter, you will create the repository in an Oracle database, set up privileges, practice using the repository, and create a repository report. Oracle 9*i* will be used in the illustrations, with any differences for Oracle 8*i* noted. Oracle Virtual Private Database features will also be used to create a security scheme for the repository.

Creating the Repository

Crystal documentation states that you must create an ODBC DSN (Data Source Name) for the target database, set the configuration file to point to the DSN, and then Crystal Reports will create the database tables for you. Although this process does work for Oracle databases, you should be aware that only two tables are created initially, with the others created as they are required. In addition, no tables are populated with sample data. Therefore, the tables initially created will not be equivalent to the sample Access repository, in either the number of tables created or their content.

Creating the Oracle Schema

The following instructions assume that the user is familiar with Oracle database administration topics, that all configuration necessary to connect to the Oracle instance and issue commands has been completed, and that the user has DBA privileges. If not, these instructions should be passed on to the DBA for execution.

The first step is to create an Oracle user/schema to contain the repository objects. The sample code will use a schema named COR (Crystal Object Repository), a password of COR, and default tablespace assignments. Any desired schema name can be substituted and, of course, in a real-world situation the password should be something other than the user ID. Create the COR user with whatever tablespace defaults and other settings which are appropriate to your database. Log in to your database as an administrator and execute the following statement from your Oracle tool of choice, such as SQL*Plus:

```
CREATE USER COR PROFILE DEFAULT
    IDENTIFIED BY COR
    DEFAULT TABLESPACE USERS
    TEMPORARY TABLESPACE TEMP;
```

Then grant COR the CONNECT and RESOURCE roles.

```
GRANT CONNECT, RESOURCE TO COR;
```

Creating the Repository Tables

The repository consists of six tables. The sample tables can be observed in the Microsoft Access sample repository, which is created during a standard Crystal Reports 9 installation at C:\Program Files\Common Files\Crystal Decisions\2.0\Bin\ Repository_en.mdb. The tables are OR_OBJECTS, which is a master table holding the object IDs of every repository object; OR_TYPE_SCHEMA, which is a lookup table containing one record for each of the object types that can be stored in the repository, plus a "FOLDER" record; and four type-specific tables, one for each object type. The type-specific tables are OR_OBJECTDETAILS_30, which contains the detail about graphic objects; OR_OBJECTDETAILS_31, which contains the detail about text objects; OR_OBJECTDETAILS_32, which contains the detail about custom function objects; and OR_OBJECTDETAILS_33, which contains the detail about query definitions. Presumably, if new objects are added in the future, each new type will have a corresponding table.

After the creation of the repository user ID, you could create the ODBC DSN, modify the configuration file, run Crystal Reports, log in to the repository, and the repository tables would be created. However, because not all of the tables are created initially and you will be making some changes to their structure, instructions for creating the tables via Oracle commands will be given. The repository structure that would be created by default by Crystal Reports is shown in Figure 11-1.

You will make some noninvasive changes to the original structure. First, you will add a primary key on the fields OBJECT_ID and VERSION to the OR_OBJECTDETAILS_nn tables. This is the logical primary key and will facilitate backend processing. You will also change the data type for OR_OBJECTS .OWNER_ID. The reasons for this change will be explained later.

To create the repository tables, execute the following Oracle commands logged in as COR. Add any specific storage options appropriate to your database. The scripts for creating the repository objects are available as Repository.sql and Repository 8i.sql in the download files for this chapter. VARCHAR2 instead of NVARCHAR2 is used for the Oracle 8i tables.

OR_TYPE_SCHEMA		
PK	**TYPE**	**NUMBER**
	TYPE_NAME	NVARCHAR2(255)
	TABLE_NAME	NVARCHAR2(255)
	META_INFO	NVARCHAR2(255)

OR_OBJECTS		
PK	**OBJECT_ID**	**NVARCHAR2(50)**
	OBJECT_NAME	NVARCHAR2(255)
	PARENT_ID	NVARCHAR2(50)
	OWNER_ID	NUMBER
	TYPE	NUMBER

OR_OBJECTDETAILS_30		
I1	OBJECT_ID	NVARCHAR2(50)
	VERSION	NUMBER
	CREATING_TIME	NVARCHAR2(50)
	MODIFIED_TIME	NVARCHAR2(50)
	MODIFIER_NAME	NVARCHAR2(50)
	CONTENTS	BLOB
	DELETED	NUMBER
	SIGNATURE	VARCHAR2(32)
	ATTRIBUTES	BLOB
	LOCALE	NVARCHAR2(255)

OR_OBJECTDETAILS_31		
I1	OBJECT_ID	NVARCHAR2(50)
	VERSION	NUMBER
	CREATING_TIME	NVARCHAR2(50)
	MODIFIED_TIME	NVARCHAR2(50)
	MODIFIER_NAME	NVARCHAR2(50)
	CONTENTS	BLOB
	DELETED	NUMBER
	SIGNATURE	VARCHAR2(32)
	ATTRIBUTES	NVARCHAR2(50)
	LOCALE	NVARCHAR2(255)

OR_OBJECTDETAILS_32		
I1	OBJECT_ID	NVARCHAR2(50)
	VERSION	NUMBER
	CREATING_TIME	NVARCHAR2(50)
	MODIFIED_TIME	NVARCHAR2(50)
	MODIFIER_NAME	NVARCHAR2(50)
	CONTENTS	BLOB
	DELETED	NUMBER
	SIGNATURE	VARCHAR2(32)
	ATTRIBUTES	BLOB
	LOCALE	NVARCHAR2(255)

OR_OBJECTDETAILS_33		
I1	OBJECT_ID	NVARCHAR2(50)
	VERSION	NUMBER
	CREATING_TIME	NVARCHAR2(50)
	MODIFIED_TIME	NVARCHAR2(50)
	MODIFIER_NAME	NVARCHAR2(50)
	CONTENTS	BLOB
	DELETED	NUMBER
	SIGNATURE	VARCHAR2(32)
	ATTRIBUTES	BLOB
	LOCALE	NVARCHAR2(255)

Figure 11-1   *Crystal Reports, Oracle object repository*

OR_OBJECTS

```
CREATE TABLE OR_OBJECTS
  (OBJECT_ID NVARCHAR2(50) NOT NULL,
   OBJECT_NAME NVARCHAR2(255),
   PARENT_ID NVARCHAR2(50),
   OWNER_ID NVARCHAR2(50) DEFAULT USER,
   TYPE NUMBER,
   CONSTRAINT OR_OBJECTS_PK PRIMARY KEY(OBJECT_ID));
```

The type for the OWNER_ID field is Number in the original Access database. It has been changed to a character type for reasons that will be explained later.

OR_TYPE_SCHEMA

```
CREATE TABLE OR_TYPE_SCHEMA
  (TYPE NUMBER NOT NULL,
   TYPE_NAME NVARCHAR2(255),
   TABLE_NAME NVARCHAR2(255),
   META_INFO NVARCHAR2(255),
   CONSTRAINT OR_TYPE_SCHEMA_PK PRIMARY KEY(TYPE));
```

OR_OBJECTDETAILS_30

```
CREATE TABLE OR_OBJECTDETAILS_30
  (OBJECT_ID NVARCHAR2(50) NOT NULL,
   VERSION NUMBER NOT NULL,
   CREATING_TIME NVARCHAR2(50) NOT NULL,
   MODIFIED_TIME NVARCHAR2(50),
   MODIFIER_NAME NVARCHAR2(50),
   CONTENTS BLOB DEFAULT EMPTY_BLOB(),
   DELETED NUMBER,
   SIGNATURE NVARCHAR2(32),
   ATTRIBUTES BLOB DEFAULT EMPTY_BLOB(),
   LOCALE NVARCHAR2(255),
   CONSTRAINT OR_OBDETAILS_30_PK
      PRIMARY KEY(OBJECT_ID, VERSION));
```

OR_OBJECTDETAILS_31

```
CREATE TABLE OR_OBJECTDETAILS_31
  (OBJECT_ID NVARCHAR2(50) NOT NULL,
   VERSION NUMBER NOT NULL,
   CREATING_TIME NVARCHAR2(50) NOT NULL,
   MODIFIED_TIME NVARCHAR2(50),
   MODIFIER_NAME NVARCHAR2(50),
   CONTENTS BLOB DEFAULT EMPTY_BLOB(),
   DELETED NUMBER,
   SIGNATURE NVARCHAR2(32),
   ATTRIBUTES BLOB DEFAULT EMPTY_BLOB(),
   LOCALE NVARCHAR2(255),
   CONSTRAINT OR_OBDETAILS_31_PK
      PRIMARY KEY(OBJECT_ID, VERSION));
```

OR_OBJECTDETAILS_32

```
CREATE TABLE OR_OBJECTDETAILS_32
  (OBJECT_ID NVARCHAR2(50) NOT NULL,
   VERSION NUMBER NOT NULL,
   CREATING_TIME NVARCHAR2(50) NOT NULL,
   MODIFIED_TIME NVARCHAR2(50),
   MODIFIER_NAME NVARCHAR2(50),
   CONTENTS BLOB DEFAULT EMPTY_BLOB(),
   DELETED NUMBER,
   SIGNATURE NVARCHAR2(32),
   ATTRIBUTES BLOB DEFAULT EMPTY_BLOB(),
   LOCALE NVARCHAR2(255),
   CONSTRAINT OR_OBDETAILS_32_PK
      PRIMARY KEY(OBJECT_ID, VERSION));
```

OR_OBJECTDETAILS_33

```
CREATE TABLE OR_OBJECTDETAILS_33
  (OBJECT_ID NVARCHAR2(50) NOT NULL,
   VERSION NUMBER NOT NULL,
   CREATING_TIME NVARCHAR2(50) NOT NULL,
   MODIFIED_TIME NVARCHAR2(50),
   MODIFIER_NAME NVARCHAR2(50),
   CONTENTS BLOB DEFAULT EMPTY_BLOB(),
   DELETED NUMBER,
   SIGNATURE NVARCHAR2(32),
   ATTRIBUTES BLOB DEFAULT EMPTY_BLOB(),
   LOCALE NVARCHAR2(255),
   CONSTRAINT OR_OBDETAILS_33_PK
      PRIMARY KEY(OBJECT_ID, VERSION));
```

After you complete these commands, the new, empty repository tables will exist in the Oracle database.

Creating an ODBC DSN

Use of the repository requires an ODBC DSN because "native" connectivity to the repository is not possible. Although an Oracle ODBC or Microsoft Oracle ODBC driver may have been installed during the Oracle client or Microsoft Data Access

Components (MDAC) installations to your system, Crystal Decisions recommends using the CR Oracle ODBC Driver 4.10 for repository access. The DataDirect Technologies driver must be installed with Crystal Reports, and you will need to know your Oracle TNS service name to complete the configuration.

Open the ODBC Data Source Administrator. The ODBC Data Source Administrator can usually be found in the Control Panel or Control Panel | Administrative Tools, depending on your version of Windows. Choose Add. Select the CR Oracle ODBC Driver 4.10 and click Finish. Populate the dialog as shown in Figure 11-2, using any Data Source Name and Description you want. The example uses CR_REPOS as the DSN. Enter your TNS Service Name in the Server Name field.

All other parameters can be left at their default values. Click Test Connect; use COR as the User ID for now. Do not continue until the connection is successful.

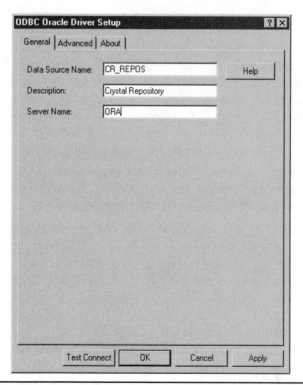

Figure 11-2   *ODBC DSN setup for the Crystal repository*

Populating Repository Sample Data

If you wish to populate the repository tables with sample objects, you can use any
method available to move the data from the sample Access Crystal Repository database
at C:\Program Files\Common Files\Crystal Decisions\2.0\Bin\Repository_en.mdb
(for a standard installation) into the corresponding Oracle tables. Data loading
insert statements are not supplied with this book because of the large size of the
CONTENTS fields.

One simple method to populate the tables with sample data is to create database
links in the sample Access database to the Oracle tables and then create append queries
to move the data. To use this method, you must have an ODBC DSN for your Oracle
database where the repository resides that does *not* use the Crystal-supplied ODBC
driver. The Crystal-supplied drivers are not licensed to function outside of Crystal
Reports. For this example, you will use the Oracle-ODBC-ORA DSN that was set
up in Chapter 1, which uses the Oracle-supplied ODBC driver. Open the sample
Crystal Repository at C:\Program Files\Common Files\Crystal Decisions\2.0\Bin\
Repository_en.mdb. Choose File | Get External Data | Link Tables. In the drop-down
box for Files of Type, choose ODBC Databases and pick the Oracle-ODBC-ORA
data source name. Log in to the database as COR. A list of tables will be displayed.
Select the six repository tables and click OK. Links to the six Oracle tables will
be created.

Now go to the Queries tab in Access, double-click Create Query in Design
View, and close the Show Tables dialog box. Choose View | SQL View and enter
the following statement, replacing any existing text. A text file containing the load
statements can be found at Chapter 11\Load sample data.sql.

```
INSERT INTO COR_OR_OBJECTS
  (OBJECT_ID, OBJECT_NAME, PARENT_ID, OWNER_ID, TYPE)
  SELECT OR_OBJECTS.Object_id, OR_OBJECTS.Object_name,
       OR_OBJECTS.Parent_id, OR_OBJECTS.Owner_id, OR_OBJECTS.Type
    FROM OR_OBJECTS;
```

Run the query to populate the Oracle OR_OBJECTS table.

Repeat the preceding process for each remaining table using the following five
queries. Name and save the queries, if desired.

Note that OR_OBJECTDETAILS_33 has duplicate records and some records will
fail to load.

OR_TYPE_SCHEMA

```
INSERT INTO COR_OR_TYPE_SCHEMA
  (TYPE, TYPE_NAME, TABLE_NAME, META_INFO)
```

```
SELECT OR_TYPE_SCHEMA.Type, OR_TYPE_SCHEMA.Type_name,
       OR_TYPE_SCHEMA.Table_name, OR_TYPE_SCHEMA.Meta_info
  FROM OR_TYPE_SCHEMA;
```

OR_OBJECTDETAILS_30

```
INSERT INTO COR_OR_OBJECTDETAILS_30
  (OBJECT_ID, VERSION, CREATING_TIME, MODIFIED_TIME,
  MODIFIER_NAME, CONTENTS, DELETED, SIGNATURE, ATTRIBUTES, LOCALE )
  SELECT OR_OBJECTDETAILS_30.Object_id, OR_OBJECTDETAILS_30.Version,
       OR_OBJECTDETAILS_30.Creating_time,
       OR_OBJECTDETAILS_30.Modified_time,
       OR_OBJECTDETAILS_30.Modifier_name,
       OR_OBJECTDETAILS_30.Contents,
       OR_OBJECTDETAILS_30.Deleted,
       OR_OBJECTDETAILS_30.Signature,
       OR_OBJECTDETAILS_30.Attributes, OR_OBJECTDETAILS_30.Locale
    FROM OR_OBJECTDETAILS_30;
```

OR_OBJECTDETAILS_31

```
INSERT INTO COR_OR_OBJECTDETAILS_31
  (OBJECT_ID, VERSION, CREATING_TIME, MODIFIED_TIME,
  MODIFIER_NAME, CONTENTS, DELETED, SIGNATURE,
  ATTRIBUTES, LOCALE )
  SELECT OR_OBJECTDETAILS_31.Object_id,
       OR_OBJECTDETAILS_31.Version,
       OR_OBJECTDETAILS_31.Creating_time,
       OR_OBJECTDETAILS_31.Modified_time,
       OR_OBJECTDETAILS_31.Modifier_name,
       OR_OBJECTDETAILS_31.Contents,
       OR_OBJECTDETAILS_31.Deleted,
       OR_OBJECTDETAILS_31.Signature,
       OR_OBJECTDETAILS_31.Attributes,
       OR_OBJECTDETAILS_31.Locale
    FROM OR_OBJECTDETAILS_31;
```

OR_OBJECTDETAILS_32

```
INSERT INTO COR_OR_OBJECTDETAILS_32
  (OBJECT_ID, VERSION, CREATING_TIME, MODIFIED_TIME,
  MODIFIER_NAME, CONTENTS, DELETED, SIGNATURE, ATTRIBUTES, LOCALE )
  SELECT OR_OBJECTDETAILS_32.Object_id, OR_OBJECTDETAILS_32.Version,
       OR_OBJECTDETAILS_32.Creating_time,
       OR_OBJECTDETAILS_32.Modified_time,
```

```
            OR_OBJECTDETAILS_32.Modifier_name,
            OR_OBJECTDETAILS_32.Contents, OR_OBJECTDETAILS_32.Deleted,
            OR_OBJECTDETAILS_32.Signature,
            OR_OBJECTDETAILS_32.Attributes, OR_OBJECTDETAILS_32.Locale
     FROM OR_OBJECTDETAILS_32;
```

OR_OBJECTDETAILS_33

```
INSERT INTO COR_OR_OBJECTDETAILS_33
  (OBJECT_ID, VERSION, CREATING_TIME, MODIFIED_TIME,
   MODIFIER_NAME, CONTENTS, DELETED, SIGNATURE, ATTRIBUTES, LOCALE )
  SELECT OR_OBJECTDETAILS_33.Object_id, OR_OBJECTDETAILS_33.Version,
            OR_OBJECTDETAILS_33.Creating_time,
            OR_OBJECTDETAILS_33.Modified_time,
            OR_OBJECTDETAILS_33.Modifier_name,
            OR_OBJECTDETAILS_33.Contents, OR_OBJECTDETAILS_33.Deleted,
            OR_OBJECTDETAILS_33.Signature,
            OR_OBJECTDETAILS_33.Attributes, OR_OBJECTDETAILS_33.Locale
     FROM OR_OBJECTDETAILS_33;
```

Verify that the data has been moved to Oracle.

Configuring Crystal to Use the New Repository

At this point, you must modify the Crystal Reports configuration file to point to the new repository tables. Open C:\Program Files\Common Files\Crystal Decisions\2.0\ Bin\orMap.ini with Notepad. Modify the following line:

```
Crystal Repository=Crystal Repository
```

to the following, where CR_REPOS is the name you gave the new Oracle ODBC data source:

```
Crystal Repository=CR_REPOS
```

Close and save the file.

Test the New Repository Tables

Open an existing report in Crystal Reports. If the Repository Explorer is not open, open it. When prompted to log on to the repository, use the COR user ID and password, and the repository explorer will open. Explore the repository and try moving objects from the repository to your report and from your report to the repository. See Crystal Documentation for detailed information on how to use the repository.

Configuring Security for the Repository

Because all of the report writers in your group will use the repository, assigning appropriate database privileges is necessary to prevent users from overwriting each other's objects, as well as for general sharing of standard objects. The sample Access repository database has no security restrictions—all users can see and modify all objects. The default Oracle repository, because it is created in a particular schema, can be seen and used only by the schema owner and other users with broad scope privileges. It cannot be used by other report writers unless they are granted specific privileges for it.

Understanding the Repository Data Model

In order to decide on a proper security scheme for the Crystal Repository in Oracle, it is necessary to understand the data model and how the repository is maintained via Crystal Reports and to decide which levels of security suit your particular purposes.

Refer to the repository data model in Figure 11-1. Note that there are no relationships shown in the diagram. The original repository database has no built-in referential integrity and no primary keys on the OR_OBJECTDETAILS_nn tables, although there is an index on OBJECT_ID for those tables.

Understanding the way Crystal Reports uses the repository tables is vital to creating a viable security scheme.

OR_OBJECTS contains one record for each active (not deleted) object stored in the repository and one record for each active folder in the repository; it has five fields:

► OBJECT_ID is a generated key.

► OBJECT_NAME is the user-defined name of the object or folder and need not be unique. However, Crystal Reports will not allow duplicate OBJECT_NAMEs in the same folder and will assume that the user wants to update the existing object if an object of the same name is added to that folder.

► PARENT_ID is the OBJECT_ID of the folder that contains the object or subfolder.

▶ OWNER_ID does not appear to be used currently and is always populated with zero.

▶ TYPE is one of the types defined in OR_TYPE_SCHEMA.

When an object is deleted from the repository, its OR_OBJECTS record is deleted.

The OR_TYPE_SCHEMA table is a lookup table containing one record for the FOLDER type and one record for each of the currently defined object types. Users should never have to modify the data in this table. It has three fields:

▶ TYPE_NAME is a longer name for the type, though it is not necessarily made up of recognizable words. Objects defined as FOLDER types are used to create the folders in the Repository Explorer tree.

▶ The TABLE_NAME field has an entry for each of the other four object types, text objects, graphics, custom functions, and commands. This TABLE_NAME is used to determine which of the OR_OBJECTDETAILS_nn tables contains the detail for that type of object. For example, the text object type is related to the OR_OBJECTDETAILS_31 table.

▶ The META_INFO field appears to be unused.

The four OR_OBJECTDETAILS_nn tables contain the actual object descriptions and each correspond to an object type. There will be one OR_OBJECTDETAILS record for each version of any object that has been created; note that no OR_OBJECTDETAILS records are ever really deleted or updated. When an object is modified, a new version is created—that is, a new record is inserted with a new version number. When an object is deleted, all versions of that object's DELETED field are set to 1, though the corresponding OBJECT_ID *is* deleted from the OR_OBJECTS table.

The OR_OBJECTDETAILS has nine fields:

▶ OBJECT_ID is the same as the object's ID in the OR_OBJECTS table.

▶ VERSION is a number showing which version of the object the record is for.

▶ CREATING_TIME is a string containing the timestamp of when the object was created and is the same for every version of the object (that is, for every record with the same OBJECT_ID).

▶ MODIFIED_TIME is the timestamp when the new object version was inserted.

▶ MODIFIER_NAME is the database user ID of the user who inserted the record.

▶ SIGNATURE does not appear to be populated.

▶ LOCALE does not appear to be populated, though Crystal Reports does query it.

▶ ATTRIBUTES contains descriptive information about the object.

▶ CONTENTS contains the actual object definition.

Manipulation of the repository follows these steps:

1. Folder objects are read from OR_OBJECTS to create the tree.
2. Objects belonging to each folder are read from OR_OBJECTS.
3. For each object, the appropriate OR_OBJECTDETAILS_nn table is queried in descending order by version number for all versions of the object.
4. Data for only the first record returned, which is the most recent version, is actually retrieved.

Folders do not have any related OR_OBJECTDETAILS_nn records, so their processing is straightforward: new folder records are inserted and folder names can be updated. Note that folder records can be deleted, but folders cannot be moved.

Objects other than folders are more complex. When a new object is created, a record is inserted into OR_OBJECTS and the appropriate OR_OBJECTDETAILS_nn table simultaneously. If an object is moved, its PARENT_ID in OR_OBJECTS is modified. If an object is updated, a new version record is inserted into OR_OBJECTDETAILS_nn. If an object is deleted, it is deleted from OR_OBJECTS, and the DELETED property in OR_OBJECTDETAILS_nn is set to 1 for all versions, leaving a situation where an OBJECT_ID exists in an OR_OBJECTDETAILS_nn table, but there is no corresponding OBJECT_ID in OR_OBJECTS.

Determining Security Levels

Crystal Decisions recommends using the underlying database's security features to add security to the repository. However, the actual security scheme is up to the individual user and should reflect their unique situation. As an example, let's say you want each developer to be able to store and modify their own objects, but there are also certain objects that are considered standard and need to be shared across the development team. You also do not want any developer to be able to modify another developer's objects. Moreover, you need an administrator who can manipulate the standard objects and upgrade regular developer objects to standard status. This is the example security scheme that will be demonstrated. In no way should it be considered the only possible or desirable scheme. A much simpler scheme might be sufficient for some users, or a more complex scheme might be required for others.

The example security scheme requires users to have different rights, depending on which objects they own in the repository. It would also be desirable to restrict users so that they see only the folders that they own, plus the standard folders. However, because of the processes that Crystal Reports uses to create the repository tree and populate it with objects, that restriction is difficult to implement. Therefore, in this example, all folders will be accessible to all users.

You will create one database role, COR_User, for basic repository users. In the example, the user ID COR will be the administrator and objects owned by COR will be the standard objects. You want to grant privileges to the COR_User role as shown in Table 11-1: you want members of the COR_User role to be able to insert new objects, see and use their own objects, see and use COR's objects, modify or delete their own objects, and be restricted from modifying or deleting anyone else's objects.

The UPDATE privilege on the OR_OBJECTS table allows the PARENT_ID to be updated when an object is moved between folders. Selection and update of the

		COR_User Role			
		Objects Owned By			
		Connected User		**COR**	**Other Users**
Object Type		**New Objects**	**Existing Objects**	**Existing Objects**	**Existing Objects**
OR_OBJECTS	Select	N/A	√	√	×
	Insert	√	N/A	N/A	N/A
	Update	N/A	√	×	×
	Delete	N/A	√	×	×
OR_OBJECTDETAILS_nn	Select (latest version only)	N/A	√	√	×
	Insert (first version)	√	N/A	N/A	N/A
	Insert (next version)	N/A	Allow only if connected user owns current version	N/A	N/A
	Update (latest version only)	N/A	√	×	×

Table 11-1   *COR_User Role Desired Privileges*

OR_OBJECTDETAILS_nn records is restricted to the most recent version by native Crystal Reports processing, but you need to keep that constraint in mind when developing your restrictions by user because the constraint to the most current version must be the first level of filtering, independent of the owner of the versions. Older versions might be kept for auditing purposes only. For deleting objects, the UPDATE privilege is required on OR_OBJECTDETAILS_nn records to allow the DELETED field to be set to 1. Because new versions are added rather than existing versions updated, it's possible for a user to disconnect a standard object (an object owned by COR) from the repository and then store an updated version, in effect replacing the standard version. The distinction in Table 11-1 between inserting new records and inserting updates is made to account for this possibility. No deletions are ever made from the OR_OBJECTDETAILS_nn tables.

Desired privileges for the COR user (the administrator) are shown in Table 11-2.

COR is allowed to insert next versions even when the current version is owned by another user; this is how COR can take ownership of another user's object and turn it into a standard object. COR must also have update privileges for records that it does not own so that the triggers that maintain the deleted field and the current owner field will function when COR takes ownership of another user's object.

		Administrator (COR)		
		Objects Owned By		
		COR	COR	Other Users
Object Type		**New Objects**	**Existing Objects**	**Existing Objects**
OR_OBJECTS	Select	N/A	√	√
	Insert	√	N/A	N/A
	Update	N/A	√	√
	Delete	N/A	√	√
OR_OBJECTDETAILS_nn	Select (latest version only)	N/A	√	√
	Insert (first version)	√	N/A	N/A
	Insert (next version)	N/A	√	N/A
	Update (latest version only)	N/A	√	√

Table 11-2   *COR User Desired Privileges*

Implementing Repository Security

Implementing your security scheme will require two steps. First, you will add triggers to the repository tables that will simplify the addition of the security policies, and then you will add the security policies.

Configuring Tables

The somewhat awkward repository data model, along with the versioning process, makes creating the desired security model difficult. It would simplify the security implementation if you could tell, via a simple query, which OR_OBJECTDETAILS_nn record was the current version for each object. Because you know that only the most recent version of an object is used by the repository (and therefore ever read by Crystal Reports), you can safely tag the older version records in some way. The DELETED field is set to 1 for all versions when an object is deleted. It seems reasonable to use the DELETED field and set it to 1 immediately for the old version when a new version is created. If all old versions are set to 1, you know that any record whose version is 0 is a current version record. You can implement this via triggers on the OR_OBJECTDETAILS_nn tables.

You also need to take steps to simplify security constraints for the OR_OBJECTS table. To do that, you need to track the current owner of each object and use the already existing OWNER_ID column and triggers to keep it updated. It would be more desirable to create a new column for this purpose since you do not know what future use Crystal Decisions might have in mind for the OWNER_ID column. However, if you add a column, the insert commands, which are of the form "Insert into OR_OBJECTS Values ( )" (with no list of column names), will fail. Because there is no list of column names, Oracle expects a value for every column in the appropriate order, and if you add a column, Crystal Reports will not know to supply a value for it and the insert would fail. You could still add a column and then create a view named OR_OBJECTS containing only the original columns, but then you would have to write INSTEAD OF triggers for the view, and all processing would be more complex.

Instead, you should set the previous version of the OR_OBJECTDETAILS_nn deleted field to 1 when the new version is added. This requires you to update a record in the same table that contains the record that is being inserted, so you cannot use a straightforward trigger because mutating table problems would result. Instead, save the OBJECT_ID and VERSION of the old record into a temporary table in a row-level trigger and have a second statement level trigger apply the updates.

For OR_OBJECTS, update the OWNER_ID when changes are made to the detail tables so that the OR_OBJECTS.OWNER_ID is always equal to the modifier name of the current detail record.

Because you will be using COR as the administrator, set COR as the owner of all existing objects using the following commands. These commands are available in Chapter 11\Set COR as owner.sql.

```
UPDATE OR_OBJECTS
   SET owner_id='COR'
 WHERE owner_id IS NULL
    OR owner_id='0';
UPDATE OR_OBJECTDETAILS_30
   SET Modifier_Name='COR'
 WHERE Modifier_Name IS NULL;
UPDATE OR_OBJECTDETAILS_31
   SET Modifier_Name='COR'
 WHERE Modifier_Name IS NULL;
UPDATE OR_OBJECTDETAILS_32
   SET Modifier_Name='COR'
 WHERE Modifier_Name IS NULL;
UPDATE OR_OBJECTDETAILS_33
   SET Modifier_Name='COR'
 WHERE Modifier_Name IS NULL;
```

Create the temporary table and triggers as follows, logged in as COR. These commands are available in Chapter 11\Repository triggers.sql and Repository triggers 8i.sql.

```
CREATE GLOBAL TEMPORARY TABLE OLD_VERSIONS
   (OBJECT_ID NVARCHAR2(50) NOT NULL,
    VERSION NUMBER NOT NULL,
    PRIMARY KEY(OBJECT_ID, VERSION))
   ON COMMIT DELETE ROWS;
```

This creates a temporary table for storage of the old version's primary key fields. The contents of the temporary table will be deleted after the actions are completed.

```
CREATE OR REPLACE TRIGGER TRIGGER_30_ROW
 BEFORE INSERT ON COR.OR_OBJECTDETAILS_30 FOR EACH ROW
BEGIN
   :NEW.Modifier_Name:=UPPER(:NEW.Modifier_Name);
```

```
UPDATE COR.OR_OBJECTS
   SET Owner_ID=:NEW.Modifier_Name
 WHERE Object_ID=:NEW.Object_ID;

INSERT INTO COR.OLD_VERSIONS
 VALUES (:NEW.OBJECT_ID, :NEW.VERSION-1);
END;
```

This is the row-level trigger on the detail table. It converts the new Modifier_Name to uppercase because Crystal Reports sends the user name that the user types into the logon dialog, which may be in lowercase or mixed case, then it updates the OWNER_ID in the OR_OBJECTS table to match the MODIFIER_NAME of the most recent version of the object in the detail table. It also inserts the OBJECT_ID and old version number into the temporary table for use by the statement level trigger. It is executed before the insert.

This update trigger is required to keep the Modifier_Name in uppercase because Crystal Reports applies an update after the initial insert into the OR_OBJECTDETAILS tables.

```
CREATE OR REPLACE TRIGGER TRIGGER_30_UPDATE
 BEFORE UPDATE ON COR.OR_OBJECTDETAILS_30 FOR EACH ROW
BEGIN
   :NEW.Modifier_Name:=UPPER(:NEW.Modifier_Name);
END;
```

This is the statement level trigger that reads the temporary table and sets the DELETED field to 1 for the old version of the object in the detail table. It is executed after the insert.

```
CREATE OR REPLACE TRIGGER TRIGGER_30_STATEMENT
 AFTER INSERT ON COR.OR_OBJECTDETAILS_30
BEGIN
  FOR UPD IN (SELECT OBJECT_ID, VERSION FROM COR.OLD_VERSIONS) LOOP
    UPDATE COR.OR_OBJECTDETAILS_30
       SET Deleted=1
     WHERE OBJECT_ID=UPD.OBJECT_ID
       AND VERSION=UPD.VERSION;
  END LOOP;
END;
```

Similar triggers for the other object detail tables must be created.

```
CREATE OR REPLACE TRIGGER TRIGGER_31_ROW
 BEFORE INSERT ON COR.OR_OBJECTDETAILS_31 FOR EACH ROW
```

```
BEGIN
  :NEW.Modifier_Name:=UPPER(:NEW.Modifier_Name);

  UPDATE COR.OR_OBJECTS
     SET Owner_ID=:NEW.Modifier_Name
   WHERE Object_ID=:NEW.Object_ID;

  INSERT INTO COR.Old_Versions
   VALUES (:NEW.OBJECT_ID, :NEW.VERSION-1);
END;
/
CREATE OR REPLACE TRIGGER TRIGGER_31_UPDATE
 BEFORE UPDATE ON COR.OR_OBJECTDETAILS_31 FOR EACH ROW
BEGIN
  :NEW.Modifier_Name:=UPPER(:NEW.Modifier_Name);
END;
/
CREATE OR REPLACE TRIGGER TRIGGER_31_STATEMENT
 AFTER INSERT ON COR.OR_OBJECTDETAILS_31
BEGIN
  FOR UPD IN (SELECT OBJECT_ID, VERSION FROM COR.OLD_VERSIONS) LOOP
    UPDATE COR.OR_OBJECTDETAILS_31
       SET Deleted=1
     WHERE OBJECT_ID=UPD.OBJECT_ID
       AND VERSION=UPD.VERSION;
  END LOOP;
END;
/
CREATE OR REPLACE TRIGGER TRIGGER_32_ROW
 BEFORE INSERT ON COR.OR_OBJECTDETAILS_32 FOR EACH ROW
BEGIN
  :NEW.Modifier_Name:=UPPER(:NEW.Modifier_Name);

  UPDATE COR.OR_OBJECTS
     SET Owner_ID=:NEW.Modifier_Name
   WHERE Object_ID=:NEW.Object_ID;

  INSERT INTO COR.Old_Versions
   VALUES (:NEW.OBJECT_ID, :NEW.VERSION-1);
END;
/
CREATE OR REPLACE TRIGGER TRIGGER_32_UPDATE
 BEFORE UPDATE ON COR.OR_OBJECTDETAILS_32 FOR EACH ROW
BEGIN
```

```
    :NEW.Modifier_Name:=UPPER(:NEW.Modifier_Name);
END;
/
CREATE OR REPLACE TRIGGER TRIGGER_32_STATEMENT
 AFTER INSERT ON COR.OR_OBJECTDETAILS_32
BEGIN
  FOR UPD IN (SELECT OBJECT_ID, VERSION FROM COR.OLD_VERSIONS) LOOP
    UPDATE COR.OR_OBJECTDETAILS_32
       SET Deleted=1
     WHERE OBJECT_ID=UPD.OBJECT_ID
       AND VERSION=UPD.VERSION;
  END LOOP;
END;
/
CREATE OR REPLACE TRIGGER TRIGGER_33_ROW
 BEFORE INSERT ON COR.OR_OBJECTDETAILS_33 FOR EACH ROW
BEGIN
  :NEW.Modifier_Name:=UPPER(:NEW.Modifier_Name);

  UPDATE COR.OR_OBJECTS
     SET Owner_ID=:NEW.Modifier_Name
   WHERE Object_ID=:NEW.Object_ID;

  INSERT INTO COR.Old_Versions
   VALUES (:NEW.OBJECT_ID, :NEW.VERSION-1);
END;
/
CREATE OR REPLACE TRIGGER TRIGGER_33_UPDATE
 BEFORE UPDATE ON COR.OR_OBJECTDETAILS_33 FOR EACH ROW
BEGIN
  :NEW.Modifier_Name:=UPPER(:NEW.Modifier_Name);
END;
/
CREATE OR REPLACE TRIGGER TRIGGER_33_STATEMENT
 AFTER INSERT ON COR.OR_OBJECTDETAILS_33
BEGIN
  FOR UPD IN (SELECT OBJECT_ID, VERSION FROM COR.OLD_VERSIONS) LOOP
    UPDATE COR.OR_OBJECTDETAILS_33
       SET Deleted=1
     WHERE OBJECT_ID=UPD.OBJECT_ID
       AND VERSION=UPD.VERSION;
  END LOOP;
END;
```

Because Crystal Reports tries to populate the OWNER_ID with the number 0, you also need to reset it to the real user ID when an object is inserted:

```
CREATE OR REPLACE TRIGGER OR_OBJECTS_TRIGGER
 BEFORE INSERT ON COR.OR_OBJECTS FOR EACH ROW
BEGIN
  :NEW.OWNER_ID:=UPPER(USER);
END;
```

To initialize the existing records, run the following commands. This will set the current owner and deleted fields properly for any already existing repository objects. These commands are available in Chapter 11\Initialize Repository.sql.

The UPDATE commands for the OR_OBJECTDETAILS_nn tables set the deleted field to 1 for every version of an object except the most recent version. The most recent version is the record with the highest version number as returned by the inline view called b.

```
UPDATE OR_OBJECTDETAILS_30
   SET deleted=1
 WHERE ROWID IN
       (SELECT a.rowid
          FROM OR_OBJECTDETAILS_30 a,
               (SELECT object_id, MAX(version) version
                  FROM OR_OBJECTDETAILS_30
                 GROUP BY object_id) b
         WHERE a.object_id=b.object_id
           AND a.version<>b.version);
/
UPDATE OR_OBJECTDETAILS_31
   SET deleted=1
 WHERE ROWID IN
       (SELECT a.rowid
          FROM OR_OBJECTDETAILS_31 a,
               (SELECT object_id, MAX(version) version
                  FROM OR_OBJECTDETAILS_31
                 GROUP BY object_id) b
         WHERE a.object_id=b.object_id
           AND a.version<>b.version);
/
UPDATE OR_OBJECTDETAILS_32
   SET deleted=1
 WHERE ROWID IN
```

```
        (SELECT a.rowid
           FROM OR_OBJECTDETAILS_32 a,
                (SELECT object_id, MAX(version) version
                   FROM OR_OBJECTDETAILS_32
                  GROUP BY object_id) b
          WHERE a.object_id=b.object_id
            AND a.version<>b.version);
/
UPDATE OR_OBJECTDETAILS_33
   SET deleted=1
 WHERE ROWID IN
        (SELECT a.rowid
           FROM OR_OBJECTDETAILS_33 a,
                (SELECT object_id, MAX(version) version
                   FROM OR_OBJECTDETAILS_33
                  GROUP BY object_id) b
          WHERE a.object_id=b.object_id
            AND a.version<>b.version);
```

The UPDATE statements that follow for the OR_OBJECTS table set the Owner_ID to equal the Modifier_Name of the most recent version of an object as found in the OR_OBJECTDETAILS_nn tables. There are four update statements, one for each object type:

```
UPDATE OR_OBJECTS a
   SET Owner_Id=
     (SELECT Modifier_Name
        FROM OR_OBJECTDETAILS_30 b
       WHERE b.object_id=a.object_id
         AND b.deleted=0)
  WHERE Object_ID IN
     (Select Object_ID
        from OR_OBJECTDETAILS_30);
/
UPDATE OR_OBJECTS a
   SET Owner_Id =
     (SELECT Modifier_Name
        FROM OR_OBJECTDETAILS_31 b
       WHERE b.object_id=a.object_id
         AND b.deleted=0)
  WHERE Object_ID IN
     (Select Object_ID
        from OR_OBJECTDETAILS_31);
/
```

```
UPDATE OR_OBJECTS a
   SET Owner_Id =
     (SELECT Modifier_Name
        FROM OR_OBJECTDETAILS_32 b
       WHERE b.object_id=a.object_id
         AND b.deleted=0)
  WHERE Object_ID IN
     (Select Object_ID
        from OR_OBJECTDETAILS_32);
/
UPDATE OR_OBJECTS a
   SET Owner_Id =
     (SELECT Modifier_Name
        FROM OR_OBJECTDETAILS_33 b
       WHERE b.object_id=a.object_id
         AND b.deleted=0)
  WHERE Object_ID IN
     (Select Object_ID
        from OR_OBJECTDETAILS_33);
```

Crystal Reports will check to see if tables of the appropriate names are available to the logged in user. If they are not available, it will create tables in the logged in user's schema. To avoid this, create public synonyms for the COR tables. Chapter 11\Create Synonyms.sql contains the following commands. For the COR user to be able to create these public synonyms, the COR user must be granted the CREATE PUBLIC SYNONYM privilege. Alternatively, a DBA can create the synonyms.

```
CREATE PUBLIC SYNONYM OR_OBJECTS FOR COR.OR_OBJECTS;
CREATE PUBLIC SYNONYM OR_TYPE_SCHEMA FOR COR.OR_TYPE_SCHEMA;
CREATE PUBLIC SYNONYM OR_OBJECTDETAILS_30
      FOR COR.OR_OBJECTDETAILS_30;
CREATE PUBLIC SYNONYM OR_OBJECTDETAILS_31
      FOR COR.OR_OBJECTDETAILS_31;
CREATE PUBLIC SYNONYM OR_OBJECTDETAILS_32
      FOR COR.OR_OBJECTDETAILS_32;
CREATE PUBLIC SYNONYM OR_OBJECTDETAILS_33
      FOR COR.OR_OBJECTDETAILS_33;
```

Implementing Security Policies

Beginning with version 8*i,* Oracle contains a feature called Virtual Private Database (VPD) or fine-grained access control. Traditional access control mechanisms can restrict access at the table or column level. VPD allows access restrictions at the row level without requiring the creation of views. Before VPD, if restrictions were required at the row level, views were created that returned only the rows that a certain user or group of users had access to, and privileges were granted to the views instead of the underlying tables. With VPD, the creation of views is not necessary. VPD works by appending a WHERE clause, transparently, to every query executed against the table in question. Functions are created that return a string containing the filtering clause, and then functions are applied to tables via new security policy procedures.

You can implement your security model using Oracle's Virtual Private Database or fine-grained access control features. You will create three functions to implement the security scheme: one for inserts, one for selects, and one for updates and deletes. However, you must first create the COR_USER role and grant privileges on the repository objects to that role, which will give members of the COR_USER role table level privileges to the COR objects. The VPD functions will then add row level restrictions to those privileges.

A user with DBA privileges must create the COR_USER role as shown:

```
CREATE ROLE COR_USER NOT IDENTIFIED;
```

Then the user COR can grant the appropriate privileges. These grant statements can be found in Chapter 11\COR_USER.sql.

```
GRANT SELECT, INSERT, UPDATE, DELETE
      ON   COR.OR_OBJECTS            TO COR_USER;
GRANT SELECT
      ON   COR.OR_TYPE_SCHEMA        TO COR_USER:
GRANT SELECT, INSERT, UPDATE
      ON   COR.OR_OBJECTDETAILS_30   TO COR_USER;
GRANT SELECT, INSERT, UPDATE
      ON   COR.OR_OBJECTDETAILS_31   TO COR_USER;
GRANT SELECT, INSERT, UPDATE
      ON   COR.OR_OBJECTDETAILS_32   TO COR_USER;
GRANT SELECT, INSERT, UPDATE
      ON   COR.OR_OBJECTDETAILS_33   TO COR_USER;
GRANT SELECT, INSERT
      ON   COR.OLD_VERSIONS          TO COR_USER;
```

The insert function must create a string that is usable as a WHERE clause, adds no restrictions on inserts for the user COR who is allowed to insert into OR_OBJECTS, and inserts both first versions and subsequent versions into the OR_OBJECTDETAILS. For other users, the clause must add no restrictions for the OR_OBJECTS table and, for the OR_OBJECTDETAILS tables, it must restrict the session user to inserting new versions or inserting subsequent versions only when they own the current version.

```
CREATE OR REPLACE  FUNCTION OR_INSERT_FUNCTION
  (Schema_Name IN VARCHAR2, Table_Name IN VARCHAR2)
    RETURN VARCHAR2
AS
  Clause VARCHAR2(2000);
BEGIN
 Clause:='';
 IF Table_Name LIKE 'OR_OBJECTDETAILS___' THEN
   IF USER<>'COR' THEN
     Clause:='Version=1
              OR
              UPPER(NVL(USER,''COR''))=
                (SELECT UPPER(NVL(Owner_ID,''COR''))
                   FROM COR.OR_OBJECTS
                  WHERE COR.'||Table_name||'.Object_ID
                        =COR.OR_OBJECTS.Object_ID)';
   END IF;
 END IF;
 RETURN Clause;
END;
```

For the OR_OBJECTS table, the select function must allow COR to select any objects (with no restrictions) and allow other users to select only folders or objects that they own or objects that are owned by COR. For the OR_OBJECTDETAILS tables, the select function must allow COR to select only the most recent version of objects and allow other users to select only the most recent version of objects that they own or that are owned by COR.

```
CREATE OR REPLACE  FUNCTION OR_SELECT_FUNCTION
   (Schema_Name IN VARCHAR2, Table_Name IN VARCHAR2)
    RETURN VARCHAR2
AS
  Clause VARCHAR2(2000);
BEGIN
 Clause:='';
 IF Table_Name='OR_OBJECTS' THEN
   IF USER<>'COR' THEN
     Clause:='TYPE=0
              OR
```

```
                    (UPPER(NVL(Owner_ID,''COR''))=UPPER(USER)
                    OR
                    UPPER(NVL(Owner_ID,''COR''))=''COR'')';
        END IF;
    END IF;
    IF Table_Name LIKE 'OR_OBJECTDETAILS___' THEN
        IF USER='COR' THEN
            Clause:='Deleted=0';
        ELSE
            Clause:='Deleted=0
                    AND
                    (UPPER(NVL(Modifier_Name,''COR''))=UPPER(USER)
                    OR
                    UPPER(NVL(Modifier_Name,''COR''))=''COR'')';
        END IF;
    END IF;
    RETURN Clause;
END;
```

For the OR_OBJECTS table, the function used for updates and deletes must restrict users other than COR from updating any object they do not own. For the OR_OBJECTDETAILS tables, the function must restrict updates for users other than COR to the current version only for objects owned by the session user. For COR, the function must restrict updates to the current version. COR must be allowed to update any records in both of these tables in order to be able to take ownership of objects and have those objects treated as standard objects in the future.

```
CREATE OR REPLACE FUNCTION OR_UPDATE_OR_DELETE_FUNCTION
    (Schema_Name IN VARCHAR2, Table_Name IN VARCHAR2)
    RETURN VARCHAR2
AS
    Clause VARCHAR2(2000);
BEGIN
    Clause:='';
    IF Table_Name='OR_OBJECTS' THEN
        IF USER<>'COR' THEN
            Clause:='UPPER(NVL(Owner_ID,''COR''))=UPPER(USER)';
        END IF;
    END IF;
    IF Table_Name LIKE 'OR_OBJECTDETAILS___' THEN
        IF USER='COR' THEN
            Clause:='Deleted=0';
        ELSE
```

```
    Clause:='Deleted=0
            AND
            UPPER(NVL(Modifier_Name,''COR''))=UPPER(USER)';
  END IF;
 END IF;
 RETURN Clause;
END;
```

The security functions are implemented with the following commands. To successfully execute these commands the COR user must be granted the EXECUTE privilege on the DBMS_RLS package by a DBA.

```
GRANT EXECUTE ON DBMS_RLS TO COR;
```

The security policy creation statements follow and can also be found in Chapter 11\ Policy Creation.sql:

```
EXECUTE DBMS_RLS.ADD_POLICY('COR','OR_OBJECTS',
        'OR_SELECT_POLICY','COR', 'OR_SELECT_FUNCTION','SELECT');
EXECUTE DBMS_RLS.ADD_POLICY ('COR','OR_OBJECTDETAILS_30',
        'OR_SELECT_POLICY', 'COR','OR_SELECT_FUNCTION','SELECT');
EXECUTE DBMS_RLS.ADD_POLICY ('COR','OR_OBJECTDETAILS_31',
        'OR_SELECT_POLICY', 'COR','OR_SELECT_FUNCTION','SELECT');
EXECUTE DBMS_RLS.ADD_POLICY ('COR','OR_OBJECTDETAILS_32',
        'OR_SELECT_POLICY', 'COR','OR_SELECT_FUNCTION','SELECT');
EXECUTE DBMS_RLS.ADD_POLICY ('COR','OR_OBJECTDETAILS_33',
        'OR_SELECT_POLICY', 'COR','OR_SELECT_FUNCTION','SELECT');
EXECUTE DBMS_RLS.ADD_POLICY ('COR','OR_OBJECTS',
        'OR_INSERT_POLICY','COR', 'OR_INSERT_FUNCTION','INSERT');
EXECUTE DBMS_RLS.ADD_POLICY ('COR','OR_OBJECTDETAILS_30',
      'OR_INSERT_POLICY', 'COR','OR_INSERT_FUNCTION','INSERT',TRUE);
EXECUTE DBMS_RLS.ADD_POLICY ('COR','OR_OBJECTDETAILS_31',
      'OR_INSERT_POLICY', 'COR','OR_INSERT_FUNCTION','INSERT',TRUE);
EXECUTE DBMS_RLS.ADD_POLICY ('COR','OR_OBJECTDETAILS_32',
      'OR_INSERT_POLICY', 'COR','OR_INSERT_FUNCTION','INSERT',TRUE);
EXECUTE DBMS_RLS.ADD_POLICY ('COR','OR_OBJECTDETAILS_33',
      'OR_INSERT_POLICY', 'COR','OR_INSERT_FUNCTION','INSERT',TRUE);
EXECUTE DBMS_RLS.ADD_POLICY 'COR','OR_OBJECTS',
      'OR_UPDATE_OR_DELETE_POLICY', 'COR',
      'OR_UPDATE_OR_DELETE_FUNCTION','UPDATE,DELETE');
EXECUTE DBMS_RLS.ADD_POLICY ('COR','OR_OBJECTDETAILS_30',
      'OR_UPDATE_OR_DELETE_POLICY','COR',
      'OR_UPDATE_OR_DELETE_FUNCTION', 'UPDATE,DELETE');
```

```
EXECUTE DBMS_RLS.ADD_POLICY ('COR','OR_OBJECTDETAILS_31',
      'OR_UPDATE_OR_DELETE_POLICY','COR',
      'OR_UPDATE_OR_DELETE_FUNCTION', 'UPDATE,DELETE');
EXECUTE DBMS_RLS.ADD_POLICY ('COR','OR_OBJECTDETAILS_32',
      'OR_UPDATE_OR_DELETE_POLICY','COR',
      'OR_UPDATE_OR_DELETE_FUNCTION', 'UPDATE,DELETE');
EXECUTE DBMS_RLS.ADD_POLICY ('COR','OR_OBJECTDETAILS_33',
      'OR_UPDATE_OR_DELETE_POLICY','COR',
      'OR_UPDATE_OR_DELETE_FUNCTION','UPDATE,DELETE');
```

Now your security policy is implemented. Create new user IDs, assign the COR_User role to them, and test that their privileges are as expected. You should also grant the COR_User role to Xtreme:

```
GRANT COR_USER TO XTREME;
```

Using this security scheme, it is recommended that you create separate folders for standard objects and move any user objects into those folders when COR takes ownership of those objects. Otherwise, users may see standard objects showing up in other user's folders and be confused. Crystal Reports has no knowledge of the security policies that have been implemented. If you attempt a repository action that will not be allowed due to the security policies, you may receive a generic error message stating that the action could not be completed or no error message at all. You should also note that the user logged in to the repository is completely independent of the database connections for the report. You may be logged in to the repository as one user and to the report datasources as a different user.

Using the Repository

Storing objects in the repository allows you to share them with other report developers. It also allows you to modify an object in the repository and then update reports that contain that object so that those reports will use the new version. This is a great addition to efficiency and standards maintenance.

As mentioned previously, there are four types of objects that can be stored in the repository: SQL Commands, custom functions, graphics, and text objects. For SQL Commands against Oracle databases and custom functions written to be used only against Oracle databases, I recommend creating Oracle views and PL/SQL functions instead of depending on the repository. You will get the same benefits of sharable code, with truly automatic version updating, plus speed and security enhancements. If you need to report off non-Oracle databases, or cannot create views and functions, then the repository is the second best solution.

There is no Oracle substitute for storing graphic and text objects in the repository. These objects are used for formatting and there is no database equivalent. (You could create a table for these objects and join them into your report, but that would be awkward and nonintuitive.) You should take advantage of the repository for objects of these types.

Refer to Crystal Reports or other third-party documentation for details concerning the use of the repository. How to use the repository is not specific to the database being used to house it, so there are no specific Oracle topics to cover, other than those related to the backend security scheme described in the previous section.

A Repository Report

Because the repository has been moved into an Oracle database, you can create a Crystal Report to list the repository objects. Most repository-related information is readily available from the Repository Explorer, but a paper report might be desirable documentation, especially for determining the owner of various objects, since the owner is not displayed in the Repository Explorer.

For the report, you will want information from the OR_OBJECTS table and from the OR_OBJECTDETAILS tables. Because all of the OR_OBJECTDETAILS tables have the same columns defined and are joined to OR_OBJECTS on the same field, it will simplify the report if you union the detail tables together. Here is a view definition that implements the union and converts the datetime string fields into Oracle date fields. This statement is available as Chapter 11\OR_OBJECTDETAILS_VIEW.sql. Create the view logged in as the COR user.

```
CREATE OR REPLACE VIEW OR_OBJECTDETAILS_VIEW
AS
SELECT  TO_DATE(CREATING_TIME,'YYYY-MM-DD HH24:MI:SS    ') CREATING_TIME,
        TO_DATE(MODIFIED_TIME,'YYYY-MM-DD HH24:MI:SS    ') MODIFIED_TIME,
        OBJECT_ID, VERSION
  FROM COR.OR_OBJECTDETAILS_30
  UNION ALL
```

```
SELECT  TO_DATE(CREATING_TIME,'YYYY-MM-DD HH24:MI:SS    '),
        TO_DATE(MODIFIED_TIME,'YYYY-MM-DD HH24:MI:SS    '),
        OBJECT_ID, VERSION
  FROM  COR.OR_OBJECTDETAILS_31
 UNION ALL
SELECT  TO_DATE(CREATING_TIME,'YYYY-MM-DD HH24:MI:SS    '),
        TO_DATE(MODIFIED_TIME,'YYYY-MM-DD HH24:MI:SS    '),
        OBJECT_ID, VERSION
  FROM  COR.OR_OBJECTDETAILS_32
 UNION ALL
SELECT  TO_DATE(CREATING_TIME,'YYYY-MM-DD HH24:MI:SS    '),
        TO_DATE(MODIFIED_TIME,'YYYY-MM-DD HH24:MI:SS    '),
        OBJECT_ID, VERSION
  FROM  COR.OR_OBJECTDETAILS_33
WITH READ ONLY;
```

Note that the contents or attributes fields are not included. They are BLOB fields that contain XML-like information, and Crystal Reports cannot interpret them correctly.

Once the view is created, SELECT privileges for it should be granted to the COR_User role as shown here:

```
GRANT SELECT ON OR_OBJECTDETAILS_VIEW TO COR_USER;
```

Note that even though the OR_OBJECTDETAILS tables contain multiple versions of objects, you will never see more than one version. The security policy will restrict the SELECT to returning the current version. Likewise, the security policies that were implemented for using the repository apply equally to the report. You will only be able to report on repository objects that you have privileges to see via the security policies, so you do not need to implement separate security for the report.

Open Chapter 11\Repository.rpt. You will receive an error stating that a repository object has been deleted because the report contains two objects that are linked to my repository and do not exist in your repository. The report will run anyway because local copies of the objects are kept in the report file. Run the report logging in as any user who has the COR_User role. You will see something similar to Figure 11-3.

The report uses the OR_OBJECTS table and the OR_OBJECTDETAILS_VIEW view and will return any rows that pass the security policy conditions for the logged in user. It is grouped hierarchically to show the folder locations of the objects. You may substitute your own graphic and contact text for that which is included in the sample report.

Sage Link, LLC

Repository

	Object Type	Owner	Version	Last Modified	Created
My Company	Folder	COR			
My Company Contact	Text	COR	2	23-Jul-2003 3:15:31 pm	23-Jul-2003
My Company Logo	Graphic	COR	2	23-Jul-2003 3:09:55 pm	23-Jul-2003
Commands	Folder	COR			
CustomerOrdersShipped	Command	COR	1	10-Apr-2002 1:24:00 pm	10-Apr-2002
EmployeeInfo	Command	COR	1	10-Apr-2002 1:24:37 pm	10-Apr-2002
Text Objects	Folder	COR			
Copyright	Text	COR	1	10-Apr-2002 1:20:02 pm	10-Apr-2002
Crystal Care	Text	COR	1	10-Apr-2002 1:19:47 pm	10-Apr-2002
Feedback Email	Text	COR	1	10-Apr-2002 1:20:16 pm	10-Apr-2002

Figure 11-3   *Repository report*

Whether you use an Access database or an Oracle database to contain the repository objects, the repository features can be useful to you. This chapter introduced an example that can be used to implement multiuser security for a repository in an Oracle database, and many other security options are possible as well.

Common Issues

T his chapter covers issues that commonly occur when using Crystal Reports with Oracle. Problems arising in the Crystal development environment will be described, specific Oracle errors will be listed, the proper use of date literals will be explained, and methods to report on user private data will be explored. Other common problems will also be described, along with solutions to those problems.

The list of issues given in this chapter is not exhaustive, of course. If you have a problem that is not covered here, you should browse the Crystal Decisions website or other third-party websites such as tek-tips.com for possible solutions.

Crystal Problems

This section lists problems that might occur inside the Crystal Reports environment but which are not native Oracle errors or ODBC errors.

Oracle Server Not Listed in the Database Explorer

This problem will occur if the Oracle option is not chosen during the installation of Crystal Reports. See Chapter 1 for installation instructions.

This problem may also occur if the Oracle client DLLs are not properly installed. Of particular concern is the OCIW32.DLL, which should exist in the system's environment path statement. However, there should not be multiple versions of this DLL on the system.

Selection Formulas Containing String Comparisons to Parameter Values Not Functioning as Expected

If you have a selection formula that contains a string comparison to a parameter and your results are not as you expect, the problem may be related to the parameter value case compared to the database field value's case. If you want the condition to match regardless of case, you must wrap the UPPER function around both the parameter (because you do not want to force the user to enter uppercase) and the database field in the selection formula as shown here:

```
UPPERCASE({database field}) = UPPERCASE({?parameter})
```

Query Engine Error: An Invalid Join Type Has Been Encountered

This error is displayed if you attempt to change a database link to full outer join. To use an Oracle full outer join, you must use a SQL Command.

Oracle Errors

Oracle errors can occur at a couple of different points in the reporting process. First, there may be errors in connecting to Oracle, and second, there may be some problem executing the query sent by Crystal Reports to Oracle.

ORA-00904: <field name> invalid identifier

This error means that a SELECT statement contains a field name that Oracle does not recognize. Other than the obvious problem of entering an incorrect field name, there is possibly a more subtle problem. Oracle field names are usually defined entirely in uppercase. If an Oracle field name is created as uppercase, then queries against it may use any case. For example, if the field name is FIELD_NAME, then you can query it as FIELD_NAME, Field_Name, or field_name, and each query will succeed. However, if the field name was defined in mixed case, it must be referenced exactly as it was defined and it must be surrounded by double quotes; for example, if the field name was created as Field_Name, you may only reference it as "Field_Name."

This is never a problem when choosing fields using the Database Explorer because Crystal Reports will use the proper syntax. However, you may see this problem when using SQL Commands where the field name is not properly formed. This error is also more likely to occur when the database has been created by converting from some other database type where the use of mixed case is more common.

ORA-00942: Table or view does not exist

This error usually occurs when the logged in user does not have the SELECT privilege on the report objects. Granting the logged in user the proper privileges should resolve the problem. You may also receive this error even if your report is based on a stored procedure if you do not have the EXECUTE privilege on the stored procedure.

This error can also occur when mixed case table names exist. As with field names, if a table name is defined with mixed case, it must be referenced exactly as it was defined and surrounded by double quotes.

ORA-04068: Existing state of packages has been discarded

This error will occur when the package containing a stored procedure is invalid. A package may become invalid because a database object used in the package has changed. If this is the case, recompiling the package should solve the problem. (A second call to the package procedure will usually succeed because Oracle will automatically try to recompile the package.) If the package fails to compile, you must troubleshoot the code to discover the root of the error.

ORA-06575: Package or function <> is in an invalid state

This error will occur if an Oracle function being called from a SQL Expression field is invalid. Recompile the function to correct the problem. If the function will not compile, you will need to resolve the error condition that is causing the compile to fail.

ORA-01722: Invalid number

This error occurs when a conversion from a string to a number fails because the string is not of the proper form; for example, it may contain alphabetic characters or punctuation or in some other manner be non-numeric. This error usually arises during an implicit conversion where you may not be expecting a conversion to take place. Review the SQL query and determine where the conversion is happening.

This error will also occur if you attempt to use (+) as a concatenation operator in a SQL Expression. If you use (+) Oracle will assume that you want to do addition and attempt to convert the operands into numbers. If you need to concatenate, use the double pipes concatenation operator (||).

ORA-01841: (Full) year must be between -4713 and +9999 and not be 0

This error occurs if a date literal is used in a SQL Expression or SQL Command and is improperly formed; specifically, if a month or day number is where Oracle expects the year to be. One solution is to fix the format of the date literal, but a better solution is to avoid the use of date literals entirely and use the TO_DATE function instead.

ORA-01858: A non-numeric character was found where a numeric was expected

This error occurs if a date literal is used in a SQL Expression or SQL Command and is improperly formed; specifically if a month abbreviation is found where a year or day is expected. One solution is to fix the format of the date literal, but a better solution is to avoid the use of date literals entirely and use the TO_DATE function instead.

ORA-12154 TNS: Could not resolve service name

This error indicates that the Oracle client is not properly installed or configured; see your DBA for resolution. Most commonly, the service name does not exist in the TNSnames.ORA file. The proper TNS name must exist in this file before it can be used for Crystal Reports connections. For a native connection, this is used as the service name and is entered in the Crystal environment. For ODBC connections, the TNS name is entered in the ODBC DSN configuration. For a CR ODBC connection, the TNS name is used as the server name. For a Wire Protocol connection, it is used as the SID. For an Oracle ODBC connection, it is used as the TNS service name. See Chapter 1 for step-by-step setup instructions.

Other conditions that might cause this error include the TNSnames.ORA file being in the wrong location or not existing, a syntax error in the TNSnames.ORA file, the client not being properly installed, or the name in the Crystal connection not matching the name in the TNSnames.ORA file.

If your Oracle environment does not use local TNSnames files, see your DBA for assistance.

ORA-24338: Statement handle not executed

This error will result when using a REF CURSOR stored procedure as a data source if the REF CURSOR is not in an open state when the end of the procedure is reached. Verify that the REF CURSOR used in the stored procedure is opened and not subsequently closed or fetched from within the stored procedure.

ORA-24372: Invalid object for describe

This error will occur if you are using a standalone stored procedure and the procedure is invalid. A procedure may become invalid because a database object used in the procedure has changed. If this is the case, recompiling the procedure should solve the problem. If the procedure fails to compile, you must troubleshoot the code to discover the root of the error.

PLS-00306: Wrong number or types of arguments in call to <procedure name>

This error occurs when using stored procedures with the Crystal-supplied ODBC drivers for Oracle, either the regular driver or the Wire Protocol driver, and the Procedure Returns Results checkbox on the Advanced tab of the ODBC Data Source Administrator is unchecked. Check the Procedure Returns Results option and the error will be resolved.

This error also occurs when attempting to use the Oracle OLE DB driver with stored procedures. Switch to a different driver to solve the problem.

This error may also occur if a procedure call attempts to use named notation but the call is improperly formed. If you need to use named notation make sure that your references are properly formed.

PLS-00363: <Parameter> cannot be used as an assignment target

This error occurs when using the Oracle ODBC driver with stored procedures. Switch to a different driver to solve the problem.

Crystal Reports Nuances

This section contains several little-known tips that are useful to report writers who are developing against Oracle databases.

Using Date Literals

You might use date literals in SQL Expressions or SQL Commands. If so, be aware that Crystal Reports sets the Oracle NLS_DATE_FORMAT for the session to 'YYYY/MM/DD HH24:MI:SS'. If you use any other date format, errors will result, with the following exceptions:

▶   The time part is optional.

▶   The month part can be MON (three character month abbreviation) as well as MM.

▶   The separator character can be – as well as /.

For example, the following WHERE clause in a SQL Command will perform as expected:

```
WHERE   "ORDERS"."ORDER_DATE">'2002/05/01 00:00:01'
```

But the following clause will not:

```
WHERE   "ORDERS"."ORDER_DATE">'01/05/2002 00:00:01'
```

It is recommended that you avoid the use of date literals and use the TO_DATE function instead.

Using Timestamp Fields

Crystal Reports does not currently support Oracle 9*i* Timestamp and Interval datatypes. You must convert these datatypes to dates and numbers respectively in order to use them with Crystal. This conversion can be done in SQL Expressions or SQL Commands, but if you have many of these fields, you should consider creating an Oracle function to do the conversion. You might also want to create views that contain the converted fields for easy use with Crystal.

See Appendix B for example functions.

Reporting on User Private Data or Moving Reports Between Schemas

Some applications are written so that each user has a copy of the application tables in their own schema. In this case, when reporting is needed, it is desirable to distribute the same report to each user, with the report defaulting to the tables in the proper schema, depending on the logged in user. In other cases, identical tables may exist in both a test schema and a production schema, and you should use the same reports for each schema.

Experienced Oracle users are often dismayed at how difficult this is to accomplish with Crystal Reports. The difficulty arises because Crystal embeds the schema name into the queries that it generates and does not supply a mechanism for easily changing it. The Crystal capability to change locations can be used to switch each data source to an identical data source in a different schema, if the developer has access to both schemas. However, that requires significant labor and results in multiple reports, one for each schema.

Solutions to this problem take advantage of how Oracle resolves table names. When an Oracle query does not include the schema name prefixed to the table names, Oracle will go through several steps to determine which schema to use. It will first look in the schema that belongs to the session user. If it does not find a table match there, it will look for private synonyms matching the table name. If the table is still not found, it will look for public synonyms matching the table name. If the table name is not found in any of these sources, an error will be returned.

In the case where each user has their own copies of the tables, if you use a SQL Command as your data source and do not append schema names to the table names, then the report will function as discussed in the preceding paragraph. Oracle will resolve the table names as described and each user will see the result of the query for their own tables. In the case where you want to point the report at different schemas, but not necessarily at the logged in user's schema, you should still use a SQL Command without embedded schema names, but you must also use either private or public synonyms to ensure that the correct schema is queried.

Left Outer Join Loses Records

If you are using a left outer join to ensure that all records from the left-hand table are returned but you are still losing records, check the filtering conditions. In a left outer join where no matching record exists in the right-hand table, all report fields from the right-hand table will be treated as if they were null. If you have a filtering condition that uses a right-hand table field, be sure to use the Oracle function NVL to return a not null value or use the ISNULL Crystal function as needed in the selection formula to make sure that the row containing the null value is retained.

Smart Linking by Key Fails

Smart Linking by key fails in the release version of Crystal Reports 9. However, it has been fixed as of the February 2003 hot fix release.

APPENDIX

B

Functions

T his appendix contains the code listings for functions used in the book. A script containing the PL/SQL functions is available at Appendix B\ Functions.sql.

Reproducing Crystal Functions

Some Crystal Reports functions have no equivalent in Oracle. This section contains the code necessary to create those Oracle functions. Note that no exception handling is performed in these functions.

CRMOD

CRMOD is an Oracle equivalent for the Crystal MOD function. The existing Oracle MOD function does not behave identically to Crystal's version, but this version will:

```
CREATE OR REPLACE  FUNCTION CRMOD
  (XVal IN NUMBER,
   YVal IN NUMBER)
RETURN NUMBER
AS
BEGIN
    RETURN MOD(ROUND(XVal),ROUND(YVal));
END;
```

INT_DIV

INT_DIV can be used instead of the Crystal integer division operator (\):

```
CREATE OR REPLACE  FUNCTION INT_DIV
  (Numerator IN NUMBER,
   Denominator IN NUMBER)
RETURN NUMBER
AS
BEGIN
 RETURN FLOOR(ROUND(Numerator)/ROUND(Denominator));
END;
```

PERCENT

The PL/SQL function PERCENT is a replacement for the Crystal (%) operator:

```
CREATE OR REPLACE  FUNCTION PERCENT
 (Numerator IN NUMBER,
  Denominator IN NUMBER)
RETURN NUMBER
AS
BEGIN
 RETURN 100*(Numerator/Denominator);
END;
```

Other Functions

Several conversion functions are beneficial when using Crystal Reports with Oracle. In the future, they may become obsolete as Crystal incorporates native support for Oracle 9*i*'s new datatypes.

TIMESTAMP_TO_DATE

TIMESTAMP_TO_DATE converts a timestamp to a date:

```
CREATE OR REPLACE  FUNCTION TIMESTAMP_TO_DATE
 (TimestampVar IN TIMESTAMP)
RETURN DATE
AS
BEGIN
 RETURN TO_DATE(TO_CHAR(TimestampVar,'DD-MON-YYYY HH24:MI:SS'),
               'DD-MON-YYYY HH24:MI:SS');
END;
```

INTERVAL_TO_YEARS

INTERVAL_TO_YEARS converts a YEAR TO MONTH interval variable to a number of years, including the number of months as a fractional portion of a year:

```
CREATE OR REPLACE  FUNCTION INTERVAL_TO_YEARS
 (IntervalVar IN INTERVAL YEAR TO MONTH)
RETURN NUMBER
AS
BEGIN
 RETURN EXTRACT(YEAR FROM IntervalVar)
        +EXTRACT(MONTH FROM IntervalVar)/12;
END;
```

INTERVAL_TO_MONTHS

INTERVAL_TO_MONTHS converts a YEAR TO MONTH interval variable to a number of months:

```
CREATE OR REPLACE  FUNCTION INTERVAL_TO_MONTHS
  (IntervalVar IN INTERVAL YEAR TO MONTH)
RETURN NUMBER
AS
BEGIN
 RETURN EXTRACT(YEAR FROM IntervalVar)*12
        +EXTRACT(MONTH FROM IntervalVar);
END;
```

INTERVAL_TO_DAYS

INTERVAL_TO_DAYS converts a DAY TO SECOND interval to a number of days including hours, minutes, and seconds as a fractional portion of a day:

```
CREATE OR REPLACE  FUNCTION INTERVAL_TO_DAYS
  (IntervalVar IN INTERVAL DAY TO SECOND)
RETURN NUMBER
AS
BEGIN
 RETURN EXTRACT(DAY FROM IntervalVar)
      +EXTRACT(HOUR FROM IntervalVar)/24
      +EXTRACT(MINUTE FROM IntervalVar)/(24*60)
      +EXTRACT(SECOND FROM IntervalVar)/(24*60*60);
END;
```

INTERVAL_TO_HOURS

INTERVAL_TO_HOURS converts a DAY TO SECOND interval to a number of hours, which may be more than 24 and includes minutes and seconds as a fractional portion of an hour:

```
CREATE OR REPLACE  FUNCTION INTERVAL_TO_HOURS
  (IntervalVar IN INTERVAL DAY TO SECOND)
RETURN NUMBER
AS
BEGIN
```

```
    RETURN EXTRACT(DAY FROM IntervalVar)*24
        +EXTRACT(HOUR FROM IntervalVar)
        +EXTRACT(MINUTE FROM IntervalVar)/60
        +EXTRACT(SECOND FROM IntervalVar)/(60*60);
END;
```

INTERVAL_TO_MINUTES

INTERVAL_TO_MINUTES converts a DAY TO SECOND interval to a number of minutes, which may be more than 60 and includes seconds as a fractional portion of a minute:

```
CREATE OR REPLACE  FUNCTION INTERVAL_TO_MINUTES
  (IntervalVar IN INTERVAL DAY TO SECOND)
RETURN NUMBER
AS
BEGIN
  RETURN EXTRACT(DAY FROM IntervalVar)*24*60
        +EXTRACT(HOUR FROM IntervalVar)*60
        +EXTRACT(MINUTE FROM IntervalVar)
        +EXTRACT(SECOND FROM IntervalVar)/60;
END;
```

INTERVAL_TO_SECONDS

INTERVAL_TO_SECONDS converts a DAY TO SECOND interval to a number of seconds:

```
CREATE OR REPLACE  FUNCTION INTERVAL_TO_SECONDS
  (IntervalVar IN INTERVAL DAY TO SECOND)
RETURN NUMBER
AS
BEGIN
  RETURN EXTRACT(DAY FROM IntervalVar)*60*60*24
        +EXTRACT(HOUR FROM IntervalVar)*60*60
        +EXTRACT(MINUTE FROM IntervalVar)*60
        +EXTRACT(SECOND FROM IntervalVar);
END;
```

Index

About the Source Code: All report files, SQL scripts, and other files referenced in this book are available for download from www.osborne.com. (*See* page xvi.)

INTERNATIONAL CONTACT INFORMATION

AUSTRALIA
McGraw-Hill Book Company
Australia Pty. Ltd.
TEL +61-2-9900-1800
FAX +61-2-9878-8881
http://www.mcgraw-hill.com.au
books-it_sydney@mcgraw-hill.com

CANADA
McGraw-Hill Ryerson Ltd.
TEL +905-430-5000
FAX +905-430-5020
http://www.mcgraw-hill.ca

**GREECE, MIDDLE EAST, & AFRICA
(Excluding South Africa)**
McGraw-Hill Hellas
TEL +30-210-6560-990
TEL +30-210-6560-993
TEL +30-210-6560-994
FAX +30-210-6545-525

MEXICO (Also serving Latin America)
McGraw-Hill Interamericana Editores
S.A. de C.V.
TEL +525-1500-5108
FAX +525-117-1589
http://www.mcgraw-hill.com.mx
carlos_ruiz@mcgraw-hill.com

SINGAPORE (Serving Asia)
McGraw-Hill Book Company
TEL +65-6863-1580
FAX +65-6862-3354
http://www.mcgraw-hill.com.sg
mghasia@mcgraw-hill.com

SOUTH AFRICA
McGraw-Hill South Africa
TEL +27-11-622-7512
FAX +27-11-622-9045
robyn_swanepoel@mcgraw-hill.com

SPAIN
McGraw-Hill/
Interamericana de España, S.A.U.
TEL +34-91-180-3000
FAX +34-91-372-8513
http://www.mcgraw-hill.es
professional@mcgraw-hill.es

**UNITED KINGDOM, NORTHERN,
EASTERN, & CENTRAL EUROPE**
McGraw-Hill Education Europe
TEL +44-1-628-502500
FAX +44-1-628-770224
http://www.mcgraw-hill.co.uk
emea_queries@mcgraw-hill.com

ALL OTHER INQUIRIES Contact:
McGraw-Hill/Osborne
TEL +1-510-420-7700
FAX +1-510-420-7703
http://www.osborne.com
omg_international@mcgraw-hill.com

Sound Off!

Visit us at **www.osborne.com/bookregistration** and let us know what you thought of this book. While you're online you'll have the opportunity to register for newsletters and special offers from McGraw-Hill/Osborne.

We want to hear from you!

Sneak Peek

Visit us today at **www.betabooks.com** and see what's coming from McGraw-Hill/Osborne tomorrow!

Based on the successful software paradigm, Bet@Books™ allows computing professionals to view partial and sometimes complete text versions of selected titles online. Bet@Books™ viewing is free, invites comments and feedback, and allows you to "test drive" books in progress on the subjects that interest you the most.